Data Science on the Google Cloud Platform

Implementing End-to-End Real-Time Data Pipelines: From Ingest to Machine Learning

Valliappa Lakshmanan

Beijing · Boston · Farnham · Sebastopol · Tokyo   **O'REILLY®**

Data Science on the Google Cloud Platform

by Valliappa Lakshmanan

Copyright © 2018 Google Inc. All rights reserved.

Printed in the United States of America.

Published by O'Reilly Media, Inc., 1005 Gravenstein Highway North, Sebastopol, CA 95472.

O'Reilly books may be purchased for educational, business, or sales promotional use. Online editions are also available for most titles (*http://oreilly.com/safari*). For more information, contact our corporate/institutional sales department: 800-998-9938 or *corporate@oreilly.com*.

Editor: Tim McGovern	**Indexer:** Judith McConville
Production Editor: Kristen Brown	**Interior Designer:** David Futato
Copyeditor: Octal Publishing, Inc.	**Cover Designer:** Karen Montgomery
Proofreader: Rachel Monaghan	**Illustrator:** Rebecca Demarest

January 2018:   First Edition

Revision History for the First Edition

2017-12-12:   First Release

See *http://oreilly.com/catalog/errata.csp?isbn=9781491974568* for release details.

978-1-491-97456-8

[LSI]

Table of Contents

Preface

In my current role at Google, I get to work alongside data scientists and data engineers in a variety of industries as they move their data processing and analysis methods to the public cloud. Some try to do the same things they do on-premises, the same way they do them, just on rented computing resources. The visionary users, though, rethink their systems, transform how they work with data, and thereby are able to innovate faster.

As early as 2011, an article in Harvard Business Review (*http://bit.ly/2AfaBCl*) recognized that some of cloud computing's greatest successes come from allowing groups and communities to work together in ways that were not previously possible. This is now much more widely recognized—an MIT survey in 2017 (*http://bit.ly/2jlabQj*) found that more respondents (45%) cited increased agility rather than cost savings (34%) as the reason to move to the public cloud.

In this book, we walk through an example of this new transformative, more collaborative way of doing data science. You will learn how to implement an end-to-end data pipeline—we will begin with ingesting the data in a serverless way and work our way through data exploration, dashboards, relational databases, and streaming data all the way to training and making operational a machine learning model. I cover all these aspects of data-based services because data engineers will be involved in designing the services, developing the statistical and machine learning models and implementing them in large-scale production and in real time.

Who This Book Is For

If you use computers to work with data, this book is for you. You might go by the title of data analyst, database administrator, data engineer, data scientist, or systems programmer today. Although your role might be narrower today (perhaps you do only data analysis, or only model building, or only DevOps), you want to stretch your wings a bit—you want to learn how to create data science models as well as how to implement them at scale in production systems.

Google Cloud Platform is designed to make you forget about infrastructure. The marquee data services—Google BigQuery, Cloud Dataflow, Cloud Pub/Sub, and Cloud ML Engine—are all serverless and autoscaling. When you submit a query to BigQuery, it is run on thousands of nodes, and you get your result back; you don't spin up a cluster or install any software. Similarly, in Cloud Dataflow, when you submit a data pipeline, and in Cloud Machine Learning Engine, when you submit a machine learning job, you can process data at scale and train models at scale without worrying about cluster management or failure recovery. Cloud Pub/Sub is a global messaging service that autoscales to the throughput and number of subscribers and publishers without any work on your part. Even when you're running open source software like Apache Spark that's designed to operate on a cluster, Google Cloud Platform makes it easy. Leave your data on Google Cloud Storage, not in HDFS, and spin up a job-specific cluster to run the Spark job. After the job completes, you can safely delete the cluster. Because of this job-specific infrastructure, there's no need to fear overprovisioning hardware or running out of capacity to run a job when you need it. Plus, data is encrypted, both at rest and in transit, and kept secure. As a data scientist, not having to manage infrastructure is incredibly liberating.

The reason that you can afford to forget about virtual machines and clusters when running on Google Cloud Platform comes down to networking. The network bisection bandwidth within a Google Cloud Platform datacenter is 1 PBps, and so sustained reads off Cloud Storage are extremely fast. What this means is that you don't need to shard your data as you would with traditional MapReduce jobs. Instead, Google Cloud Platform can autoscale your compute jobs by shuffling the data onto new compute nodes as needed. Hence, you're liberated from cluster management when doing data science on Google Cloud Platform.

These autoscaled, fully managed services make it easier to implement data science models at scale—which is why data scientists no longer need to hand off their models to data engineers. Instead, they can write a data science workload, submit it to the cloud, and have that workload executed automatically in an autoscaled manner. At the same time, data science packages are becoming simpler and simpler. So, it has become extremely easy for an engineer to slurp in data and use a canned model to get an initial (and often very good) model up and running. With well-designed packages and easy-to-consume APIs, you don't need to know the esoteric details of data science algorithms—only what each algorithm does, and how to link algorithms together to solve realistic problems. This convergence between data science and data engineering is why you can stretch your wings beyond your current role.

Rather than simply read this book cover-to-cover, I strongly encourage you to follow along with me by also trying out the code. The full source code for the end-to-end pipeline I build in this book is on GitHub (*https://github.com/GoogleCloudPlatform/ data-science-on-gcp*). Create a Google Cloud Platform project (*https://*

cloud.google.com/) and after reading each chapter, try to repeat what I did by referring to the code and to the *README.md*[1] file in each folder of the GitHub repository.

Conventions Used in This Book

The following typographical conventions are used in this book:

Italic
: Indicates new terms, URLs, email addresses, filenames, and file extensions.

`Constant width`
: Used for program listings, as well as within paragraphs to refer to program elements such as variable or function names, databases, data types, environment variables, statements, and keywords.

`Constant width bold`
: Shows commands or other text that should be typed literally by the user.

`Constant width italic`
: Shows text that should be replaced with user-supplied values or by values determined by context.

 This element signifies a tip or suggestion.

 This element signifies a general note.

 This element indicates a warning or caution.

---

1 For example, see *https://github.com/GoogleCloudPlatform/data-science-on-gcp/blob/master/06_dataproc/ README.md*.

Using Code Examples

Supplemental material (code examples, exercises, etc.) is available for download at *https://github.com/GoogleCloudPlatform/data-science-on-gcp*.

This book is here to help you get your job done. In general, if example code is offered with this book, you may use it in your programs and documentation. You do not need to contact us for permission unless you're reproducing a significant portion of the code. For example, writing a program that uses several chunks of code from this book does not require permission. Selling or distributing a CD-ROM of examples from O'Reilly books does require permission. Answering a question by citing this book and quoting example code does not require permission. Incorporating a significant amount of example code from this book into your product's documentation does require permission.

We appreciate, but do not require, attribution. An attribution usually includes the title, author, publisher, and ISBN. For example: "*Data Science on the Google Cloud Platform* by Valliappa Lakshmanan (O'Reilly). Copyright 2018 Google Inc., 978-1-491-97456-8."

If you feel your use of code examples falls outside fair use or the permission given above, feel free to contact us at *permissions@oreilly.com*.

O'Reilly Safari

Safari (formerly Safari Books Online) is a membership-based training and reference platform for enterprise, government, educators, and individuals.

Members have access to thousands of books, training videos, Learning Paths, interactive tutorials, and curated playlists from over 250 publishers, including O'Reilly Media, Harvard Business Review, Prentice Hall Professional, Addison-Wesley Professional, Microsoft Press, Sams, Que, Peachpit Press, Adobe, Focal Press, Cisco Press, John Wiley & Sons, Syngress, Morgan Kaufmann, IBM Redbooks, Packt, Adobe Press, FT Press, Apress, Manning, New Riders, McGraw-Hill, Jones & Bartlett, and Course Technology, among others.

For more information, please visit *http://oreilly.com/safari*.

How to Contact Us

Please address comments and questions concerning this book to the publisher:

O'Reilly Media, Inc.
1005 Gravenstein Highway North
Sebastopol, CA 95472
800-998-9938 (in the United States or Canada)
707-829-0515 (international or local)
707-829-0104 (fax)

We have a web page for this book, where we list errata, examples, and any additional information. You can access this page at *http://bit.ly/datasci_GCP*.

To comment or ask technical questions about this book, send email to *bookquestions@oreilly.com*.

For more information about our books, courses, conferences, and news, see our website at *http://www.oreilly.com*.

Find us on Facebook: *http://facebook.com/oreilly*

Follow us on Twitter: *http://twitter.com/oreillymedia*

Watch us on YouTube: *http://www.youtube.com/oreillymedia*

Acknowledgments

When I took the job at Google about a year ago, I had used the public cloud simply as a way to rent infrastructure—so I was spinning up virtual machines, installing the software I needed on those machines, and then running my data processing jobs using my usual workflow. Fortunately, I realized that Google's big data stack was different, and so I set out to learn how to take full advantage of all the data and machine learning tools on Google Cloud Platform.

The way I learn best is to write code, and so that's what I did. When a Python meetup group asked me to talk about Google Cloud Platform, I did a show-and-tell of the code that I had written. It turned out that a walk-through of the code to build an end-to-end system while contrasting different approaches to a data science problem was quite educational for the attendees. I wrote up the essence of my talk as a book proposal and sent it to O'Reilly Media.

A book, of course, needs to have a lot more depth than a 60-minute code walk-through. Imagine that you come to work one day to find an email from a new employee at your company, someone who's been at the company less than six months.

Somehow, he's decided he's going to write a book on the pretty sophisticated platform that you've had a hand in building and is asking for your help. He is not part of your team, helping him is not part of your job, and he is not even located in the same office as you. What is your response? Would you volunteer?

What makes Google such a great place to work is the people who work here. It is a testament to the company's culture that so many people—engineers, technical leads, product managers, solutions architects, data scientists, legal counsel, directors—across so many different teams happily gave of their expertise to someone they had never met (in fact, I still haven't met many of these people in person). This book, thus, is immeasurably better because of (in alphabetical order) William Brockman, Mike Dahlin, Tony Diloreto, Bob Evans, Roland Hess, Brett Hesterberg, Dennis Huo, Chad Jennings, Puneith Kaul, Dinesh Kulkarni, Manish Kurse, Reuven Lax, Jonathan Liu, James Malone, Dave Oleson, Mosha Pasumansky, Kevin Peterson, Olivia Puerta, Reza Rokni, Karn Seth, Sergei Sokolenko, and Amy Unruh. In particular, thanks to Mike Dahlin, Manish Kurse, and Olivia Puerta for reviewing every single chapter. When the book was in early access, I received valuable error reports from Anthonios Partheniou and David Schwantner. Needless to say, I am responsible for any errors that remain.

A few times during the writing of the book, I found myself completely stuck. Sometimes, the problems were technical. Thanks to (in alphabetical order) Ahmet Altay, Eli Bixby, Ben Chambers, Slava Chernyak, Marian Dvorsky, Robbie Haertel, Felipe Hoffa, Amir Hormati, Qi-ming (Bradley) Jiang, Kenneth Knowles, Nikhil Kothari, and Chris Meyers for showing me the way forward. At other times, the problems were related to figuring out company policy or getting access to the right team, document, or statistic. This book would have been a lot poorer had these colleagues not unblocked me at critical points (again in alphabetical order): Louise Byrne, Apurva Desai, Rochana Golani, Fausto Ibarra, Jason Martin, Neal Mueller, Philippe Poutonnet, Brad Svee, Jordan Tigani, William Vampenebe, and Miles Ward. Thank you all for your help and encouragement.

Thanks also to the O'Reilly team—Marie Beaugureau, Kristen Brown, Ben Lorica, Tim McGovern, Rachel Roumeliotis, and Heather Scherer for believing in me and making the process of moving from draft to published book painless.

Finally, and most important, thanks to Abirami, Sidharth, and Sarada for your understanding and patience even as I became engrossed in writing and coding. You make it all worthwhile.

## CHAPTER 1

Making Better Decisions Based on Data

The primary purpose of data analysis is to make better decisions. There is rarely any need for us to spend time analyzing data if we aren't under pressure to make a decision based on the results of that analysis. When you are purchasing a car, you might ask the seller what year the car was manufactured and the odometer reading. Knowing the age of the car allows you to estimate the potential value of the car. Dividing the odometer reading by the age of the car allows you to discern how hard the car has been driven, and whether it is likely to last the five years you plan to keep it. Had you not cared about purchasing the car, there would have been no need for you to do this data analysis.

In fact, we can go further—the purpose of collecting data is, in many cases, only so that you can later perform data analysis and make decisions based on that analysis. When you asked the seller the age of the car and its mileage, you were collecting data to carry out your data analysis. But it goes beyond your data collection. The car has an odometer in the first place because many people, not just potential buyers, will need to make decisions based on the mileage of the car. The odometer reading needs to support many decisions—should the manufacturer pay for a failed transmission? Is it time for an oil change? The analysis for each of these decisions is different, but they all rely on the fact that the mileage data has been collected.

Collecting data in a form that enables decisions to be made often places requirements on the collecting infrastructure and the security of such infrastructure. How does the insurance company that receives an accident claim and needs to pay its customer the car's value know that the odometer reading is accurate? How are odometers calibrated? What kinds of safeguards are in place to ensure that the odometer has not been tampered with? What happens if the tampering is inadvertent, such as installing tires whose size is different from what was used to calibrate the odometer? The auditability of data is important whenever there are multiple parties involved, and ownership and use of the data are separate. When data is unverifiable, markets fail, optimal decisions cannot be made, and the parties involved need to resort to signaling and screening.[1]

Not all data is as expensive to collect and secure as the odometer reading of a car.[2] The cost of sensors has dropped dramatically in recent decades, and many of our daily processes throw off so much data that we find ourselves in possession of data that we had no intention of explicitly collecting. As the hardware to collect, ingest, and store the data has become cheaper, we default to retaining the data indefinitely, keeping it around for no discernable reason. However, we still need a purpose to perform analysis on all of this data that we somehow managed to collect and store. Labor remains expensive.

The purpose that triggers data analysis is a decision that needs to be made. To move into a market or not? To pay a commission or not? How high to bid up the price? How many bags to purchase? Whether to buy now or wait a week? The decisions keep multiplying, and because data is so ubiquitous now, we no longer need to make those decisions based on heuristic rules of thumb. We can now make those decisions in a data-driven manner.

Of course, we don't need to make every data-driven decision ourselves. The use case of estimating the value of a car that has been driven a certain distance is common enough that there are several companies that provide this as a service—they will verify that an odometer is accurate, confirm that the car hasn't been in an accident, and compare the asking price against the typical selling price of cars in your market. The real value, therefore, comes not in making a data-driven decision once, but in being able to do it systematically and provide it as a service. This also allows companies to specialize, and continuously improve the accuracy of the decisions that can be made.

Many Similar Decisions

Because of the lower costs associated with sensors and storage, there are many more industries and use cases that now have the potential to support data-driven decision making. If you are working in such an industry, or you want to start a company that will address such a use case, the possibilities for supporting data-driven decision

---

1 The classic paper on this is George Akerlof's 1970 paper titled "The Market for Lemons." Akerlof, Michael Spence (who explained signaling), and Joseph Stiglitz (who explained screening) jointly received the 2001 Nobel Prize in Economics for describing this problem.

2 The odometer itself might not be all that expensive, but collecting that information and ensuring that it is correct has considerable costs. The last time I sold a car, I had to sign a statement that I had not tampered with the odometer, and that statement had to be notarized by a bank employee with a financial guarantee. This was required by the company that was loaning the purchase amount on the car to the buyer. Every auto mechanic is supposed to report odometer tampering, and there is a state government agency that enforces this rule. All of these costs are significant.

making have just become wider. In some cases, you will need to collect the data. In others, you will have access to data that was already collected, and, in many cases, you will need to supplement the data you have with other datasets that you will need to hunt down for which you'll need to create proxies. In all these cases, being able to carry out data analysis to support decision making systematically on behalf of users is a good skill to possess.

In this book, I will take a decision that needs to be made and apply different statistical and machine learning methods to gain insight into making that decision. However, we don't want to make that decision just once, even though we might occasionally pose it that way. Instead, we will look at how to make the decision in a systematic manner. Our ultimate goal will be to provide this decision-making capability as a service to our customers—they will tell us the things they reasonably can be expected to know, and we will either know or infer the rest (because we have been systematically collecting data).

When we are collecting the data, we will need to look at how to make the data secure. This will include how to ensure not only that the data has not been tampered with, but also that users' private information is not compromised—for example, if we are systematically collecting odometer mileage and know the precise mileage of the car at any point in time, this knowledge becomes extremely sensitive information. Given enough other information about the customer (such as the home address and traffic patterns in the city in which the customer lives), the mileage is enough to be able to infer that person's location at all times. So, the privacy implications of hosting something as seemingly innocuous as the mileage of a car can become enormous. Security implies that we need to control access to the data, and we need to maintain immutable audit logs on who has viewed or changed the data.

It is not enough to simply collect the data or use it as is. We must understand the data. Just as we needed to know the kinds of problems associated with odometer tampering to understand the factors that go into estimating a vehicle's value based on mileage, our analysis methods will need to consider how the data was collected in real time, and the kinds of errors that could be associated with that data. Intimate knowledge of the data and its quirks is invaluable when it comes to doing data science—often the difference between a data-science startup idea that works and one that doesn't is whether the appropriate nuances have all been thoroughly evaluated and taken into account.

When it comes to providing the decision-support capability as a service, it is not enough to simply have a way to do it in some offline system somewhere. Enabling it as a service implies a whole host of other concerns. The first set of concerns is about the quality of the decision itself—how accurate is it typically? What are the typical sources of errors? In what situations should this system not be used? The next set of concerns, however, is about the quality of service. How reliable is it? How many queries per second can it support? What is the latency between some piece of data being available, and it being incorporated into the model that is used to provide systematic decision making? In short, we will use this single use case as a way to explore many different facets of practical data science.

The Role of Data Engineers

"Wait a second," I imagine you saying, "I never signed up for queries-per-second of a web service. We have people who do that kind of stuff. My job is to write SQL queries and create reports. I don't recognize this thing you are talking about. It's not what I do at all." Or perhaps the first part of the discussion was what has you puzzled. "Decision making? That's for the business people. Me? What I do is to design data processing systems. I can provision infrastructure, tell you what our systems are doing right now, and keep it all secure. Data science sure sounds fancy, but I do engineering. When you said *Data Science on the Google Cloud Platform*, I was thinking that you were going to talk about how to keep the systems humming and how to offload bursts of activity to the cloud." A third set of people are wondering, "How is any of this data science? Where's the discussion of different types of models and of how to make statistical inferences and evaluate them? Where's the math? Why are you talking to data analysts and engineers? Talk to me, I've got a PhD." This is a fair point—I seem to be mixing up the jobs done by different sets of people in your organization.

In other words, you might agree with the following:

- Data analysis is there to support decision making
- Decision making in a data-driven manner can be superior to heuristics
- The accuracy of the decision models depends on your choice of the right statistical or machine learning approach
- Nuances in the data can completely invalidate your modeling, so understanding the data and its quirks is crucial
- There are large market opportunities in supporting decision making systematically and providing it as a service
- Such services require ongoing data collection and model updates
- Ongoing data collection implies robust security and auditing
- Customers of the service require reliability, accuracy, and latency assurances

What you might not agree with is whether these aspects are all things that you, personally and professionally, need to be concerned about.

At Google,[3] we look on the role a little more expansively. Just as we refer to all our technical staff as engineers, we look at data engineers as an inclusive term for anyone who can "shape business outcomes by performing data analysis" (*http://bit.ly/2AUAcA3*). To perform data analysis, you begin by building statistical models that support smart (not heuristic) decision making in a data-driven way. It is not enough to simply count and sum and graph the results using SQL queries and charting software—you must understand the statistical framework within which you are interpreting the results, and go beyond simple graphs to deriving the insight toward answering the original problem. Thus, we are talking about two domains: (a) the statistical setting in which a particular aggregate you are computing makes sense, and (b) understanding how the analysis can lead to the business outcome we are shooting for. This ability to carry out statistically valid data analysis to solve specific business problems is of paramount importance—the queries, the reports, the graphs are not the end goal. A verifiably accurate decision is.

Of course, it is not enough to do one-off data analysis. That data analysis needs to scale. In other words, the accurate decision-making process must be repeatable and be capable of being carried out by many users, not just you. The way to scale up one-off data analysis is to make it automated. After a data engineer has devised the algorithm, she should be able to make it systematic and repeatable. Just as it is a lot easier when the folks in charge of systems reliability can make code changes themselves, it is considerably easier when people who understand statistics and machine learning can code those models themselves. A data engineer, Google believes, should be able to go from building statistical and machine learning models to automating them. They can do this only if they are capable of designing, building, and troubleshooting data processing systems that are secure, reliable, fault-tolerant, scalable, and efficient.

This desire to have engineers who know data science and data scientists who can code is not Google's alone—it's across the industry. Jake Stein, founder of startup Stitch, concludes after looking at job ads that data engineers are the most in-demand skill in the world of big data (*http://bit.ly/2B7cmkL*). Carrying out analysis similar to Stein's on Indeed job data in San Francisco and accounting for jobs that listed multiple roles, I found that the number of data engineer listings was higher than those for data analysts and data scientists combined, as illustrated in Figure 1-1.

---

3 In general, you should consider everything I say in this book as things said by someone who happens to work at Google and not as official Google policy. In this case, though, Google has announced (*http://bit.ly/2AUAcA3*) a data engineer certification (*https://cloud.google.com/certification/data-engineer*) that addresses a mix of roles today performed by data analysts, IT professionals, and data scientists. In this book, when I talk about official Google statements, I'll footnote the official Google source. But even when I talk about official Google documents, the interpretation of the documents remains mine (and could be mistaken)—you should look at the linked material for what the official position is.

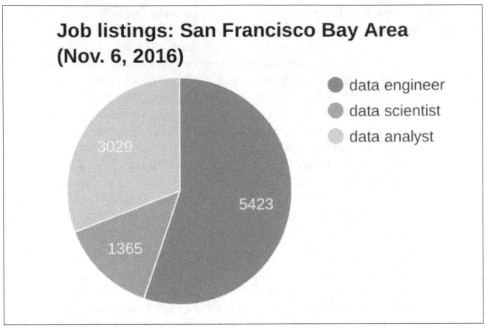

Figure 1-1. Analysis of Indeed job data in San Francisco shows that data engineers are the most in-demand skill in the world of big data

Even if you don't live in San Francisco and do not work in high-tech, this is the direction that all data-focused industries in other cities are headed. The trend is accentuated by the increasing need to make repeatable, scalable decisions on the basis of data. When companies look for data engineers, what they are looking for is a person who can combine all three roles.

How realistic is it for companies to expect a Renaissance man, a virtuoso in different fields? Can they reasonably expect to hire data engineers? How likely is it that they will find someone who can design a database schema, write SQL queries, train machine learning models, code up a data processing pipeline, and figure out how to scale it all up? Surprisingly, this is a very reasonable expectation, because the amount of knowledge you need in order to do these jobs has become a lot less than what you needed a few years ago.

The Cloud Makes Data Engineers Possible

Because of the ongoing movement to the cloud, data engineers can do the job that used to be done by four people with four different sets of skills. With the advent of autoscaling, serverless, managed infrastructure that is easy to program, there are more and more people who can build scalable systems. Therefore, it is now reasonable to expect to be able to hire data engineers who are capable of creating holistic data-driven solutions to your thorniest problems. You don't need to be a polymath to be a data engineer—you simply need to learn how to do data science on the cloud.

Saying that the cloud is what makes data engineers possible seems like a very tall claim. This hinges on what I mean by "cloud"—I don't mean simply migrating workloads that run on-premises to infrastructure that is owned by a public cloud vendor. I'm talking, instead, about truly autoscaling, managed services that automate a lot of the infrastructure provisioning, monitoring, and management—services such as Google BigQuery, Cloud Dataflow, and Cloud Machine Learning Engine on Google Cloud Platform. When you consider that the scaling and fault-tolerance of many data analysis and processing workloads can be effectively automated, provided the right set of tools is being used, it is clear that the amount of IT support that a data scientist needs dramatically reduces with a migration to the cloud.

At the same time, data science tools are becoming simpler and simpler to use. The wide availability of frameworks like Spark, scikit-learn, and Pandas has made data science and data science tools extremely accessible to the average developer—no longer do you need to be a specialist in data science to create a statistical model or train a random forest. This has opened up the field of data science to people in more traditional IT roles.

Similarly, data analysts and database administrators today can have completely different backgrounds and skillsets because data analysis has usually involved serious SQL wizardry, and database administration has typically involved deep knowledge of database indices and tuning. With the introduction of tools like BigQuery, in which tables are denormalized and the administration overhead is minimal, the role of a database administrator is considerably diminished. The growing availability of turnkey visualization tools like Tableau that connect to all the data stores within an enterprise makes it possible for a wider range of people to directly interact with enterprise warehouses and pull together compelling reports and insights.

The reason that all these data-related roles are merging together, then, is because the infrastructure problem is becoming less intense and the data analysis and modeling domain is becoming more democratized.

If you think of yourself today as a data scientist, or a data analyst, or a database administrator, or a systems programmer, this is either totally exhilarating or totally unrealistic. It is exhilarating if you can't wait to do all the other tasks that you've considered beyond your ken if the barriers to entry have fallen as low as I claim they have. If you are excited and raring to learn the things you will need to know in this new world of data, welcome! This book is for you.

If my vision of a blend of roles strikes you as an unlikely dystopian future, hear me out. The vision of autoscaling services that require very little in the form of infrastructure management might be completely alien to your experience if you are in an enterprise environment that is notoriously slow moving—there is no way, you might think, that data roles are going to change as dramatically as all that by the time you retire.

Well, maybe. I don't know where you work, and how open to change your organization is. What I believe, though, is that more and more organizations and more and more industries are going be like the tech industry in San Francisco. There will be increasingly more data engineer openings than openings for data analysts and data scientists, and data engineers will be as sought after as data scientists are today. This is because data engineers will be people who can do data science and know enough about infrastructure so as to be able to run their data science workloads on the public cloud. It will be worthwhile for you to learn data science terminology and data science frameworks, and make yourself more valuable for the next decade.

Growing automation and ease-of-use leading to widespread use is well trodden in technology. It used to be the case that if you wanted vehicular transport, you needed a horse-drawn carriage. This required people to drive you around and people to tend to your horses because driving carriages and tending to horses were such difficult things to do. But then automobiles came along, and feeding automobiles got to be as simple as pumping gas into a tank. Just as stable boys were no longer needed to take care of horses, the role of carriage drivers also became obsolete. The kind of person who didn't have a stablehand would also not be willing to employ a dedicated driver. So, democratizing the use of cars required cars to be simple enough to operate that you could do it yourself. You might look at this and bemoan the loss of all those chauffeur jobs. The better way to look at it is that there are a lot more cars on the road because you don't need to be able to afford a driver in order to own a car, and so all the would-be chauffeurs now drive their own cars. Even the exceptions prove the rule— this growing democratization of car ownership is only true if driving is easy and not a time sink. In developing countries where traffic is notoriously congested and labor is cheap, even the middle class might have chauffeurs. In developed countries, the time sink associated with driving and the high cost of labor has prompted a lot of research into self-driving cars.

The trend from chauffeured horse-driven carriages to self-driving cars is essentially the trend that we see in data science—as infrastructure becomes easier and easier, and involves less and less manual management, more and more data science workloads become feasible because they require a lot less scaffolding work. This means that more people can now do data science. At Google, for example, nearly 80% of employees use Dremel (Dremel is the internal counterpart to Google Cloud's BigQuery) every month.[4] Some use data in more sophisticated ways than others, but everyone touches data on a regular basis to inform their decisions. Ask someone a question,

---

4 Source: Jordan Tigani, GCP Next 2016. See *http://bit.ly/2j0lEbd*.

and you are likely to receive a link to a BigQuery view or query rather than to the actual answer: "Run this query every time you want to know the most up-to-date answer," goes the thinking. BigQuery in the latter scenario has gone from being the no-ops database replacement to being the self-serve data analytics solution.

As another example of change in the workplace, think back to how correspondence used to be created. Companies had rows and rows of low-wage workers whose job was to take down dictation and then type it up. The reason that companies employed typists is that typing documents was quite time-consuming and had low value (and by this, I mean that the direct impact of the role of a typist to a company's core mission was low). It became easier to move the responsibility for typing correspondences to low-paid workers so that higher-paid employees had the time to make sales calls, invent products, and drink martinis at lunch. But this was an inefficient way for those high-wage workers to communicate. Computerization took hold, and word processing made document creation easier and typing documents became self-serve. These days, all but the seniormost executives at a firm type their own correspondence. At the same time, the volume of correspondence has greatly exploded. That is essentially the trend you will see with data science workloads—they are going to become easier to test and deploy. So, many of the IT jobs involved with these will morph into that of writing those data science workloads because the writing of data science workloads is also becoming simplified. And as a result, data science and the ability to work with data will spread throughout an enterprise rather than being restricted to a small set of roles.

The target audience for this book is people who do computing with data. If you are a data analyst, database administrator, data engineer, data scientist, or systems programmer today, this book is for you. I foresee that your role will soon require both creating data science models and implementing them at scale in a production-ready system that has reliability and security considerations.

The current separation of responsibility between data analysts, database administrators, data scientists, and systems programmers came about in an era when each of these roles required a lot more specialized knowledge than they will in the near future. A practicing data engineer will no longer need to delegate that job to someone else. Complexity was the key reason that there came to be this separation of responsibility between the people who wrote models and the people who productionized those models. As that complexity is reduced by the advent of autoscaled, fully managed services, and simpler and simpler data science packages, it has become extremely easy for an engineer to write a data science workload, submit it to the cloud, and have that workload be executed automatically in an autoscaled manner. That's one end of the equation—as a data scientist, you do not need a specialized army of IT specialists to make your code ready for production.

On the other side, data science itself has become a lot less complex and esoteric. With well-designed packages and easy-to-consume APIs, you do not need to implement all of the data science algorithms yourself—you need to know only what each algorithm does and be able to connect them together to solve realistic problems. Because designing a data science workload has become easier to do, it has come to be a lot more democratized. So, if you are an IT person whose job role so far has been to manage processes but you know some programming—particularly Python—and you understand your business domain well, it is quite possible for you to begin designing data processing pipelines and to begin addressing business problems with those programming skills.

In this book, therefore, we'll talk about all these aspects of data-based services because data engineers will be involved from the designing of those services, to the development of the statistical and machine learning models, to the scalable production of those services in real time.

The Cloud Turbocharges Data Science

Before I joined Google, I was a research scientist working on machine learning algorithms for weather diagnosis and prediction. The machine learning models involved multiple weather sensors, but were highly dependent on weather radar data. A few years ago, when we undertook a project to reanalyze historical weather radar data using the latest algorithms, it took us four years to do. However, more recently, my team was able to build rainfall estimates off the same dataset, but were able to traverse the dataset in about two weeks. You can imagine the pace of innovation that results when you take something that used to take four years and make it doable in two weeks.

Four years to two weeks. The reason was that much of the work as recently as five years ago involved moving data around. We'd retrieve data from tape drives, stage it to disk, process it, and move it off to make way for the next set of data. Finding out what jobs had failed was time consuming, and retrying failed jobs involved multiple steps including a human in the loop. We were running it on a cluster of machines that had a fixed size. The combination of all these things meant that it took incredibly long periods of time to process the historical archive. After we began doing everything on the public cloud, we found that we could store all of the radar data on cloud storage, and as long as we were accessing it from virtual machines (VMs) in the same region, data transfer speeds were fast enough. We still had to stage the data to disks, carry out the computation, and bring down the VMs, but this was a lot more manageable. Simply lowering the amount of data migration and running the processes on many more machines enabled us to carry out processing much faster.

Was it more expensive to run the jobs on 10 times more machines than we did when we did the processing on-premises? No, because the economics are in favor of renting rather than buying processing power. Whether you run 10 machines for 10 hours or 100 machines for 1 hour, the cost remains the same. Why not, then, get your answers in an hour rather than 10 hours?

As it turns out, though, we were still not taking full advantage of what the cloud has to offer. We could have completely foregone the process of spinning up VMs, installing software on them, and looking for failed jobs—what we should have done was to use an autoscaling data processing pipeline such as Cloud Dataflow. Had we done that, we could have run our jobs on thousands of machines and brought our processing time from two weeks to a few hours. Not having to manage any infrastructure is itself a huge benefit when it comes to trawling through terabytes of data. Having the data processing, analysis, and machine learning autoscale to thousands of machines is a bonus.

The key benefit of performing data engineering in the cloud is the amount of time that it saves you. You shouldn't need to wait days or months—instead, because many jobs are embarrassingly parallel, you can get your results in minutes to hours by having them run on thousands of machines. You might not be able to afford permanently owning so many machines, but it is definitely possible to rent them for minutes at a time. These time savings make autoscaled services on a public cloud the logical choice to carry out data processing.

Running data jobs on thousands of machines for minutes at a time requires fully managed services. Storing the data locally on the compute nodes or persistent disks as with the Hadoop Distributed File System (HDFS) doesn't scale unless you know precisely what jobs are going to be run, when, and where. You will not be able to downsize the cluster of machines if you don't have automatic retries for failed jobs. The uptime of the machines will be subject to the time taken by the most overloaded worker unless you have dynamic task shifting among the nodes in the cluster. All of these point to the need for autoscaling services that dynamically resize the cluster, move jobs between compute nodes, and can rely on highly efficient networks to move data to the nodes that are doing the processing.

On Google Cloud Platform, the key autoscaling, fully managed, "serverless" services are BigQuery (for SQL analytics), Cloud Dataflow (for data processing pipelines), Google Cloud Pub/Sub (for message-driven systems), Google Cloud Bigtable (for high-throughput ingest), Google App Engine (for web applications), and Cloud Machine Learning Engine (for machine learning). Using autoscaled services like these makes it possible for a data engineer to begin tackling more complex business problems because they have been freed up from the world of managing their own machines and software installations whether in the form of bare hardware, virtual machines, or containers. Given the choice between a product that requires you to first configure a container, server, or cluster, and another product that frees you from those considerations, choose the serverless one. You will have more time to solve the problems that actually matter to your business.

Case Studies Get at the Stubborn Facts

This entire book consists of an extended case study. Why write a book about data science, not as a reference text, but as a case study? There is a reason why case studies are so popular in fields like medicine and law—case studies can help keep discussion, in the words of Paul Lawrence, "grounded in upon some of the stubborn facts that must be faced in real-life situations."[5] A case study, Lawrence continued, is "the record of complex situations that must be literally pulled apart and pulled together again for the expression of attitudes or ways of thinking brought into the classroom."

Solving a real-world, practical problem will help cut through all the hype that surrounds big data, machine learning, cloud computing, and so on. Pulling a case study apart and putting it together in multiple ways can help illuminate the capabilities and shortcomings of the various big data and machine learning tools that are available to you. A case study can help you identify the kinds of data-driven decisions that you can make in your business and illuminate the considerations behind the data you need to collect and curate, and the kinds of statistical and machine learning models you can use.

Case studies are unfortunately too rare in the field of data analysis and machine learning—books and tutorials are full of toy problems with neat, pat solutions that fall apart in the real world. Witten and Frank, in the preface to their (excellent) book on data mining,[6] captured the academic's disdain of the practical, saying that their book aimed to "gulf [the gap] between the intensely practical approach taken by trade books that provide case studies on data mining and the more theoretical, principle-driven exposition found in current textbooks on machine learning."[7] In this book, I try to change that: it is possible to be both practical and principled. I do not, however, concern myself too much with theory. Instead, my aim will be to provide broad strokes that explain the intuition that underlies a particular approach and then dive into addressing the case study question using that approach.

---

5 Paul Lawrence, 1953. "The Preparation of Case Material," *The Case Method of Teaching Human Relations and Administration*. Kenneth R. Andrews, ed. Harvard University Press.

6 The field of study that broadly examines the use of computers to derive insight from data has gone through more name changes than a KGB agent—statistical inference, pattern recognition, artificial intelligence, data mining, data analytics/visualization, predictive analysis, knowledge discovery, machine learning, and learning theory are some that come to mind. My recommendation would be to forget what the fad du jour calls it, and focus on the key principles and techniques that, surprisingly, haven't changed all that much in three decades.

7 Ian Witten and Eibe Frank, 2005. *Data Mining: Practical Machine Learning Tools and Techniques*. 2nd ed. Elsevier.

You'll get to see data science done, warts and all, on a real-world problem. One of the ways that this book will mirror practice is that I will use a real-world dataset to solve a realistic problem and address problems as they come up. So, I will begin with a decision that needs to be made and apply different statistical and machine learning methods to gain insight into making that decision in a data-driven manner. This will give you the ability to explore other problems and the confidence to solve them from first principles. As with most things, I will begin with simple solutions and work my way to more complex ones. Starting with a complex solution will only obscure details about the problem that are better understood when solving it in simpler ways. Of course, the simpler solutions will have drawbacks, and these will help to motivate the need for additional complexity.

One thing that I do not do, however, is to go back and retrofit earlier solutions based on knowledge that I gain in the process of carrying out more sophisticated approaches. In your practical work, however, I strongly recommend that you maintain the software associated with early attempts at a problem, and that you go back and continuously enhance those early attempts with what you learn along the way. Parallel experimentation is the name of the game. Due to the linear nature of a book, I don't do it, but I heartily recommend that you continue to actively maintain several models. Given the choice of two models with similar accuracy measures, you can then choose the simpler one—it makes no sense to use more complex models if a simpler approach can work with some modifications. This is an important enough difference between what I would recommend in a real-world project and what I do in this book that I will make a note of situations in which I would normally circle back and make changes to a prior approach.

A Probabilistic Decision

Imagine that you are about to take a flight and just before the flight takes off from the runway (and you are asked to switch off your phone), you have the opportunity to send one last text message. It is past the published departure time and you are a bit anxious. Figure 1-2 presents a graphic view of the scenario.

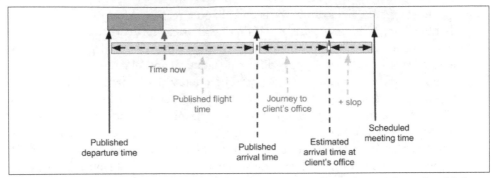

Figure 1-2. A graphic illustration of the case study: if the flight departs late, should the road warrior cancel the meeting?

The reason for your anxiety is that you have scheduled an important meeting with a client at its offices. As befits a rational data scientist,[8] you scheduled things rather precisely. You have taken the airline at its word with respect to when the flight would arrive, accounted for the time to hail a taxi, and used an online mapping tool to estimate the time to the client's office. Then, you added some leeway (say 30 minutes) and told the client what time you'd meet her. And now, it turns out that the flight is departing late. So, should you send a text informing your client that you will not be able to make the meeting because your flight will be late or should you not?

This decision could be made in many ways, including by gut instinct and using heuristics. Being very rational people, we (you and I) will make this decision informed by data. Also, we see that this is a decision made by many of the road warriors in our company day in and day out. It would be a good thing if we could do it in a systematic way and have a corporate server send out an alert to travelers about anticipated delays if we see events on their calendar that they are likely to miss. Let's build a data framework to solve this problem.

Even if we decide to make the decision in a data-driven way, there are several approaches we could take. Should we cancel the meeting if there is greater than a 30% chance that you will miss it? Or should we assign a cost to postponing the meeting (the client might go with our competition before we get a chance to demonstrate our great product) versus not making it to a scheduled meeting (the client might never take our calls again) and minimize our expected loss in revenue? The probabilistic

---

8 Perhaps I'm simply rationalizing my own behavior—if I'm not getting to the departure gate with less than 15 minutes to spare at least once in about five flights, I decide that I must be getting to the airport too early and adjust accordingly. Fifteen minutes and 20% tend to capture my risk aversion. Yours might be different, but it shouldn't be two hours and 1%—the time you waste at the airport could be used a lot more productively by doing more of whatever it is that you traveled to do. If you are wondering why my risk aversion threshold is not simply 15 minutes but includes an associated probabilistic threshold, read on.

approach translates to risk, and many practical decisions hinge on risk. In addition, the probabilistic approach is more general because if we know the probability and the monetary loss associated with missing the meeting, it is possible to compute the expected value of any decision that we make. For example, suppose the chance of missing the meeting is 20% and we decide to not cancel the meeting (because 20% is less than our decision threshold of 30%). But there is only a 25% chance that the client will sign the big deal (worth a cool million bucks) for which you are meeting her. Because there is an 80% chance that we will make the meeting, the expected upside value of not canceling the meeting is 0.8 * 0.25 * 1 million, or $200,000. The downside value is that we do miss the meeting. Assuming that the client is 90% likely to blow us off if we miss a meeting with her, the downside value is 0.2 * 0.9 * 0.25 * 1 million, or $45,000. This yields an expected value of $155,000 in favor of not canceling the meeting. We can adjust these numbers to come up with an appropriate probabilistic decision threshold.

Another advantage of a probabilistic approach is that we can directly take into account human psychology. You might feel frazzled if you arrive at a meeting only two minutes before it starts and, as a result, might not be able to perform at your best. It could be that arriving only two minutes early to a very important meeting doesn't feel like being on time. This obviously varies from person to person, but let's say that this time interval that you need to settle down is 15 minutes. You want to cancel a meeting for which you cannot arrive 15 minutes early. You could also treat this time interval as your personal risk aversion threshold, a final bit of headroom if you will. Thus, you want to arrive at the client's site 15 minutes before the meeting and you want to cancel the meeting if there is a less than 70% of chance of doing that. This, then, is our decision criterion:

Cancel the client meeting if the likelihood of arriving 15 minutes early is 70% or less.

I've explained the 15 minutes, but I haven't explained the 70%. Surely, you can use the aforementioned model diagram (in which we modeled our journey from the airport to the client's office), plug in the actual departure delay, and figure out what time you will arrive at the client's offices. If that is less than 15 minutes before the meeting starts, you should cancel! Where does the 70% come from?

It is important to realize that the model diagram of times is not exact. The probabilistic decision framework gives you a way to treat this in a principled way. For example, although the airline company says that the flight is 127 minutes long and publishes an arrival time, not all flights are exactly 127 minutes long. If the plane happens to take off with the wind, catch a tail wind, and land against the wind, the flight might take only 90 minutes. Flights for which the winds are all precisely wrong might take 127 minutes (i.e., the airline might be publishing worst-case scenarios for the route). Google Maps is publishing predicted journey times based on historical data (*http://bit.ly/2AXZrBp*), and the actual journeys by taxi might be centered around those times. Your estimate of how long it takes to walk from the airport gate to the taxi stand might be predicated on landing at a specific gate, and actual times may vary. So, even though the model depicts a certain time between airline departure and your arrival at the client site, this is not an exact number. The actual time between departure and arrival might have a distribution that looks that shown in Figure 1-3.

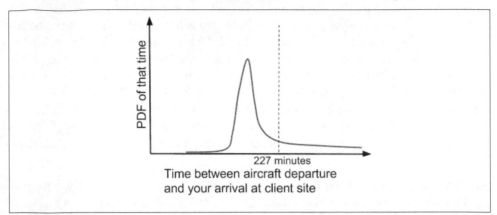

Figure 1-3. There are many possible time differences between aircraft departure and your arrival at a client site, and the distribution of those differences is called the probability distribution function

Intuitively, you might think that the way to read this graph is that given a time on the x-axis, you can look up the probability of that time difference on the y-axis. Given a large enough dataset (i.e., provided we made enough journeys to this client site on this airline), we can estimate the probability of a specific time difference (e.g., 227 minutes) by computing the fraction of flights for which the time difference is 227. Because the time is a continuous variable, though, the probability of any exact time is exactly zero—the probability of the entire journey taking exactly 227 minutes (and not a nanosecond more) is zero—there are infinitely many possible times, so the probability of any specific time is exactly zero.

What we would need to calculate is the probability that the time lies between $227 - \varepsilon$ and $227 + \varepsilon$, where the epsilon is suitably small. Figure 1-4 depicts this graphically.

In real-world datasets, you won't have continuous variables—floating-point values tend to be rounded off to perhaps six digits. Therefore, the probability of exactly 227 minutes will not be zero, given that we might have some 227-minute data in our dataset. In spite of this, it is important to realize the general principle that the probability of a time difference of 227.000000 minutes is meaningless.

Instead, you should compute the probability that the value lies between two values (such as 226.9 and 227.1, with the lefthand limit being inclusive of 226.9 and the righthand limit exclusive of 227.1). You can calculate this by adding up the number of times that 226.90, 226.91, 226.92, and so on appear in the dataset. You can calculate the desired probability by adding up the occurrences. Addition of the counts of the discrete occurrences is equivalent to integrating the continuous values. Incidentally, this is what you are doing when you use a histogram to approximate a probability—a histogram implies that you will have discretized the x-axis values into a specific number of bins.

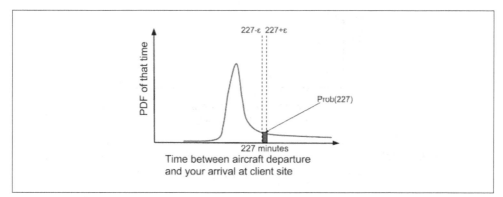

Figure 1-4. The probability of any exact time difference (such as 227 minutes) is zero. Therefore, we usually think of the probability that the time difference is within, say 30 seconds of 227 minutes.

The fact that you need to integrate the curve to get a probability implies that the y-axis value is not really the probability. Rather, it is the density of the probability and referred to as the probability density function (abbreviated as the PDF). It is a density because if you multiply it by the x-axis value, you get the area of the blue box, and that area is the probability. In other words, the y-axis is the probability divided by the x-axis value. In fact, the PDF can be (and often is) greater than one.

Integrating probability density functions to obtain probabilities is needed often enough and PDFs are unintuitive enough (it took me four paragraphs to explain the probability distribution function, and even that involved a fair amount of hand-waving) that it is helpful to look around for an alternative. The cumulative probability distribution function of a value x is the probability that the observed value X is less than the threshold x. For example, you can get the Cumulative Distribution Function (CDF) for 227 minutes by finding the fraction of flights for which the time difference is less than 227 minutes, as demonstrated in Figure 1-5.

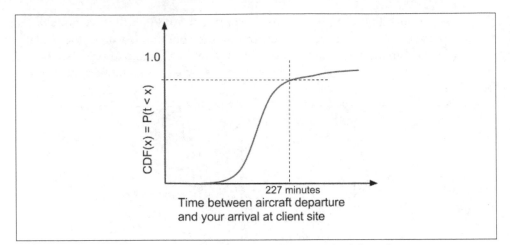

Figure 1-5. The CDF is easier to understand and keep track of than the PDF. In particular, it is bounded between 0 and 1, whereas the PDF could be greater than 1.

Let's interpret the graph in Figure 1-5. What does a CDF(227 minutes) = 0.8 mean? It means that 80% of flights will arrive such that we will make it to the client's site in less than 227 minutes—this includes both the situation in which we can make it in 100 minutes and the situation in which it takes us 226 minutes. The CDF, unlike the PDF, is bounded between 0 and 1. The y-axis value is a probability, just not the probability of an exact value. It is, instead, the probability of observing all values less than that value.

Because the time to get from the arrival airport to the client's office is unaffected by the flight's departure delay,[9] we can ignore it in our modeling. We can similarly ignore the time to walk through the airport, hail the taxi, and get ready for the meeting. So, we need only to find the likelihood of the arrival delay being more than 15 minutes. If that likelihood is 0.3 or more, we will need to cancel the meeting. In terms of the CDF, that means that the probability of arrival delays of less than 15 minutes has to be at least 0.7, as presented in Figure 1-6.

Thus, our decision criteria translate to the following:

Cancel the client meeting if the CDF of an arrival delay of 15 minutes is less than 70%.

---

9 This is not strictly true. If the flight is late due to bad weather at the destination airport, it is likely that taxi lines will be longer and ground transportation snarled as well. However, we don't want to become bogged down in multiple sets of probability analysis, so for the purposes of this book, we'll use the simplifying assumption of independence.

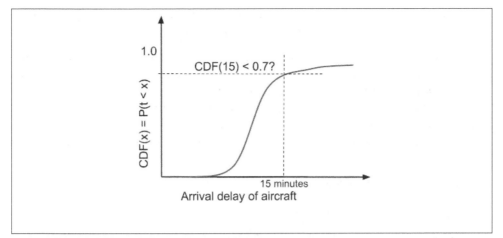

Figure 1-6. Our decision criterion is to cancel the meeting if the CDF of an arrival delay of 15 minutes is less than 70%. Loosely speaking, we want to be 70% sure of the aircraft arriving no more than 15 minutes late.

The rest of this book is going to be about building data pipelines that enable us to compute the CDF of arrival delays using statistical and machine learning models. From the computed CDF of arrival delays, we can look up the CDF of a 15-minute arrival delay and check whether it is less than 70%.

Data and Tools

What data do we need to predict the likelihood of a specific flight delay? What tools shall we use? Should we use Hadoop? BigQuery? Should we do it on my laptop or should we do it in the public cloud? The question about data is easily answered—we will use historical flight arrival data published by the US Bureau of Transportation Statistics, analyze it, and use it to inform our decision. Often, a data scientist would choose the best tool based on his experience and just use that one tool to help make the decision, but here, I will take you on a tour of several ways that we could carry out the analysis. This will also allow us to model best practice in the sense of picking the simplest tool and analysis that suffices.

On a cursory examination of the data, we discover that there were more than 5.8 million flights in 2015 alone. We can easily envision going back and making our dataset more robust by using data from previous years also. My laptop, nice as it is, is not going to cut it. We will do the data analysis on the public cloud. Which cloud? We will use the Google Cloud Platform (GCP). Although some of the tools we use in this book (notably MySQL, Hadoop, Spark, etc.) are available on other cloud platforms, other tools (BigQuery, Cloud Dataflow, etc.) are specific to the GCP. Even in the case of MySQL, Hadoop, and Spark, using GCP will allow me to avoid fiddling around with virtual machines and machine configuration and focus solely on the data analysis. Also, I do work at Google, so this is the platform I know best.

This book is not an exhaustive look at data science—there are other books (often based on university courses) that do that. Instead, the information it contains allows you to look over my shoulder as I solve one particular data science problem using a variety of methods and tools. I promise to be quite chatty and tell you what I am thinking and why I am doing what I am doing. Instead of presenting you with fully formed solutions and code, I will show you intermediate steps as I build up to a solution.

This learning material is presented to you in two forms:

- This book that you are reading
- The code that is referenced throughout the book is on GitHub at *https://github.com/GoogleCloudPlatform/data-science-on-gcp/*.

Rather than simply read this book cover to cover, I strongly encourage you to follow along with me by also taking advantage of the code. After reading each chapter, try to repeat what I did, referring to the code if something's not clear.

Getting Started with the Code

To begin working with the code, create a project and single-region[10] bucket on *https://cloud.google.com/* if necessary, open up a CloudShell window (*https://cloud.google.com/shell/docs/quickstart*), `git clone` the repository and follow along with me through the rest of this book. Here are more detailed steps:

1. If you do not already have an account, create one by going to *https://cloud.google.com/*.
2. Click the Go To Console button and you will be taken to your existing GCP project.
3. Create a regional bucket to store data and intermediate outputs. On the Google Cloud Platform Console, navigate to Google Cloud Storage and create a bucket. Bucket names must be globally unique, and one way to create a memorable and potentially unique string is to use your Project ID (which is also globally unique; you can find it by going to Home on the Cloud Platform Console).
4. Open CloudShell, your terminal access to GCP. Even though the Cloud Platform Console is very nice, I typically prefer to script things rather than go through a graphical user interface (GUI). To me, web GUIs are great for occasional and/or

---

10 Single-region is explained in Chapter 2. In short, it's because we don't need global access.

first-time use, but for repeatable tasks, nothing beats the terminal. To open CloudShell, on the menu bar, click the Activate CloudShell icon, as shown here:

This actually starts a micro-VM that is alive for the duration of the browser window and gives you terminal access to the micro-VM. Close the browser window, and the micro-VM goes away. The CloudShell VM is free and comes loaded with many of the tools that developers on Google Cloud Platform will need. For example, it has Python, Git, the Google Cloud SDK and Orion (*https://orionhub.org/*) (a web-based code editor) installed on it.

5. In the CloudShell window, `git clone` my repository by typing the following:

```
git clone \
   https://github.com/GoogleCloudPlatform/data-science-on-gcp
cd data-science-on-gcp
```

Although the CloudShell VM is ephemeral, it is attached to a persistent disk that is tied to your user account. Files that you store in that filesystem are saved across different CloudShell sessions. Hence, this Git repository and the code in it will be present in any CloudShell VM that you launch.

If you prefer to do development on your local machine (rather than in CloudShell), install the Cloud SDK and `git clone` the repository locally:

1. Install `gcloud` on your local machine using the directions in *https://cloud.google.com/sdk/downloads* (gcloud is already installed in CloudShell and other Google Compute Engine VMs—so this step and the next are needed only if you want to do development on your own machine).

2. If necessary, install Git for your platform[11] by following the instructions at *https://git-scm.com/book/en/v2/Getting-Started-Installing-Git*. Then, open up a terminal window and `git clone` my repository by typing the following:

```
git clone \
   https://github.com/GoogleCloudPlatform/data-science-on-gcp
cd data-science-on-gcp
```

That's it. You are now ready to follow along with me. As you do, remember that you need to change my project ID (`cloud-training-demos`) to the ID of your project (you can find this on the dashboard of the Cloud Platform Console) and bucket-

---

11 Software identified in this book are suggestions only. You are responsible for evaluating whether to use any particular software and accept its license terms.

name (`gs://cloud-training-demos-ml/`) to your bucket on Cloud Storage (you create this Chapter 2). In Chapter 2, we look at ingesting the data we need into the Cloud.

Summary

A key goal of data analysis is to be able to provide data-driven guidance toward making accurate decisions systematically. Ideally, this guidance can be provided as a service, and providing as a service gives rise to questions of service quality—both in terms of the accuracy of the guidance and the reliability, latency, and security of the implementation.

A data engineer needs to be able to go from designing data-based services and building statistical and machine learning models to implementing them as reliable, high-quality services. This has become easier with the advent of cloud services that provide an autoscaling, serverless, managed infrastructure. Also, the wide availability of data science tools has made it so that you don't need to be a specialist in data science to create a statistical or machine learning model. As a result, the ability to work with data will spread throughout an enterprise—no longer will it be a restricted skill.

Our case study involves a traveler who needs to decide whether to cancel a meeting depending on whether the flight she is on will arrive late. The decision criterion is that the meeting should be canceled if the CDF of an arrival delay of 15 minutes is less than 70%. To estimate the likelihood this arrival delay, we will use historical data from the US Bureau of Transportation Statistics.

To follow along with me, create a project on Google Cloud Platform and a clone of the GitHub repository of the source code listings in this book. The folder for each of the chapters in GitHub contains a *README.md* file that lists the steps to be able to replicate what I do in the chapters. So, if you get stuck, refer to those README files.

## CHAPTER 2

Ingesting Data into the Cloud

In Chapter 1, we explored the idea of making a data-driven decision as to whether to cancel a meeting and decided on a probabilistic decision criterion. We decided that we would cancel the meeting with a client if the likelihood of the flight arriving within 15 minutes of the scheduled arrival time was less than 70%. To model the arrival delay given a variety of attributes about the flight, we need historical data that covers a large number of flights. Historical data that includes this information from 1987 onward is available from the US Bureau of Transportation Statistics (*http:// www.transtats.bts.gov/*) (BTS). One of the reasons that the government captures this data is to monitor the fraction of flights by a carrier that are on-time (defined as flights that arrive less than 15 minutes late), so as to be able to hold airlines accountable.[1] Because the key use case is to compute on-time performance, the dataset that captures flight delays is called *Airline On-time Performance Data*. That's the dataset we will use in this book.

Airline On-Time Performance Data

For the past 30 years, all major US air carriers[2] have been required to file statistics about each of their domestic flights with the BTS. The data they are required to file includes the *scheduled* departure and arrival times as well as the *actual* departure and arrival times. From the scheduled and actual arrival times, the arrival delay associated

---

1 See, for example, *https://www.congress.gov/congressional-report/107th-congress/senate-report/13/1*. The bill referenced in the report was not enacted into law, but it illustrates Congress's monitoring function based on the statistics collected by the Department of Transportation.

2 "Major" here is defined as any air carrier whose total revenue would put it at 1% or more of the revenue associated with transporting all domestic scheduled passengers.

with each flight can be calculated. Therefore, this dataset can give us the true value or "label" for building a model to predict arrival delay.

The actual departure and arrival times are defined rather precisely, based on when the parking brake of the aircraft is released and when it is later reactivated at the destination. The rules even go as far as to define what happens if the pilot forgets to engage the parking brake—the time that the passenger door is closed or opened is used instead. In the case of aircraft that have a "Docking Guidance System," the departure time is defined as 15 seconds before the first 15-second interval in which the aircraft moves a meter or more. Because of the precise nature of the rules, and the fact that they are enforced, we can treat arrival and departure times from all carriers uniformly. Had this not been the case, we would have to dig deeper into the quirks of how each carrier defines "departure" and "arrival," and do the appropriate translations.[3] Good data science begins with such standardized, repeatable, trustable data collection rules; you should use the BTS's very well-defined data collection rules as a model when creating standards for your own data collection, whether it is log files, web impressions, or sensor data that you are collecting. The airlines report this particular data monthly, and it is collated by the BTS across all carriers and published as a free dataset on the web.

In addition to the scheduled and actual departure and arrival times, the data includes information such as the origin and destination airports, flight numbers, and nonstop distance between the two airports. It is unclear from the documentation whether this distance is the distance taken by the flight in question or whether it is simply a computed distance—if the flight needs to go around a thunderstorm, is the distance in the dataset the actual distance traveled by the flight or the *great-circle*[4] distance between the airports? This is something that we will need to examine—it should be easy to ascertain whether the distance between a pair of airports remains the same or changes. In addition, a flight is broken into three parts (Figure 2-1)—taxi-out time, air time, and taxi-in time—and all three time intervals are reported.

---

3 For example, weather radar data from before 2000 had timestamps assigned by a radar engineer. Essentially, the engineers would look at their wristwatches and enter a time into the radar products generator. Naturally, this was subject to all kinds of human errors—dates could be many hours off. The underlying problem was fixed by the introduction of network clocks to ensure consistent times between all the radars on the US weather radar network. When using historical weather data, though, time correction is an important preprocessing step.

4 The shortest path between two points on the globe.

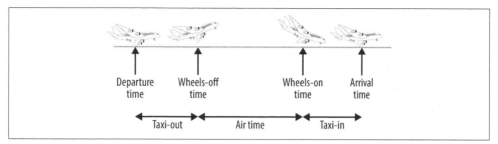

Figure 2-1. A flight is broken into three parts: taxi-out time, air time, and taxi-in time

Knowability

Before we get started with ingesting data, we need to decide what it is that we have to ingest into our model. There are two potential traps—causality and training-serving skew (I'll define them shortly). We should take care to avoid these problems during the ingest phase, in order to save us a lot of heartburn later.

Some of these attributes in the historical dataset could form the inputs to our model to help us predict the arrival delay as a function of these variables. Some, but not all. Why? It should be clear that we cannot use taxi-in time or actual flight distance because at the time the aircraft is taking off and we need to make our decision on whether to cancel the meeting, we will not know either of these things. The in-air flight time between two airports is not known *a priori* given that pilots have the ability to speed up or slow down (*http://n.pr/2AAcCFT*). Thus, even though we have these fields in our historical dataset, we should not use them in our prediction model. This is called a *causality constraint*.

The causality constraint is one instance of a more general principle. Before using any field as input, we should consider whether the data could be knowable at the time we make the decision. It is not always a matter of a logic as with the taxi-in time. Sometimes, practical considerations such as security (is the decision maker allowed to know this data?), the latency between the time the data is collected and the time it is available to the model, and cost of obtaining the information also play a part in making some data unusable. At the same time, it is possible that approximations might be available for fields that we cannot use because of causality—even though, for example, we cannot use the actual flight distance, we should be able to use the great-circle distance between the airports in our model.

Similarly, we might be able to use the data itself to create approximations for fields that are obviated by the causality constraint. Even though we cannot use the actual taxi-in time, we can use the mean taxi-in time of this flight at this airport on previous days, or the mean taxi-in time of all flights at this airport over the past hour to approximate what the taxi-in time might be. Over the historical data, this could be a simple batch operation after grouping the data by airport and hour. When predicting in real time, though, this will need to be a moving average on streaming data. Indeed, approximations to unknowable data will be an important part of our models.

Training–Serving Skew

A training–serving skew is the condition in which you use a variable that's computed differently in your training dataset than in the production model. For example, suppose that you train a model with the distance between cities in miles, but when you predict, the distance that you receive as input is actually in kilometers. That is obviously a bad thing and will result in a bad result from the model because the model will be providing predictions based on the distances being 1.6 times their actual value. Although it is obvious in clear-cut cases such as unit mismatches, the same principle (that the training dataset has to reflect what is done to inputs at prediction time) applies to more subtle scenarios as well.

For example, it is important to realize that even though we have the actual taxi-in time in the data, we cannot use that taxi-in time in our modeling. Instead, we must approximate the taxi-in time using time aggregates and use those time aggregates in our training; otherwise, it will result in a training–serving skew. If our model uses taxi-in time as an input, and that input in real-time prediction is going be computed as an average of taxi-in times over the previous hour, we will need to ensure that we also compute the average in the same way during training. We cannot use the recorded taxi-in as it exists in the historical dataset. If we did that, our model will be treating our time averages (which will tend to have the extrema averaged out) as the actual value of taxi-in time (which in the historical data contained extreme values). If the model, in our training, learns that such extreme values of taxi-in time are significant, the training–serving skew caused by computing the taxi-in time in different ways could be as bad as treating kilometers as miles.

As our models become increasingly sophisticated—and more and more of a black box—it will become extremely difficult to troubleshoot errors that are caused by a training–serving skew. This is especially true if the code bases for computing inputs for training and during prediction are different and begin to diverge over time. We will always attempt to design our systems in such a way that the possibilities of a training–serving skew are minimized. In particular, we will gravitate toward solutions in which we can use the same code in training (building a model) as in prediction.

The dataset includes codes for the airports (such as ATL for Atlanta) from which and to which the flight is scheduled to depart and land. Planes might land at an airport other than the one they are scheduled to land at if there are in-flight emergencies or if weather conditions cause a deviation. In addition, the flight might be canceled. It is important for us to ascertain how these circumstances are reflected in the dataset— although they are relatively rare occurrences, our analysis could be adversely affected if we don't deal with them in a reasonable way. The way we deal with these out-of-the-ordinary situations also must be consistent between training and prediction.

The dataset also includes airline codes (such as AA for American Airlines), but it should be noted that airline codes can change over time (for example, United Airlines and Continental Airlines merged and the combined entity began reporting as United Airlines in 2012). If we use airline codes in our prediction, we will need to cope with these changes in a consistent way, too.

Download Procedure

As of November 2016, there were nearly 171 million records in the on-time performance dataset, with records starting in 1987. The last available data was September 2016, indicating that there is more than a month's delay in updating the dataset.

In this book, our model will use attributes mostly from this dataset, but where feasible and necessary, we will include other datasets such as airport locations and weather. We can download the on-time performance data from the BTS website as comma-separated value (CSV) files. The web interface requires you to select which fields you want from the dataset (*http://www.transtats.bts.gov/DL_SelectFields.asp? Table_ID=236*) and requires you to specify a geography and time period, as illustrated in Figure 2-2.

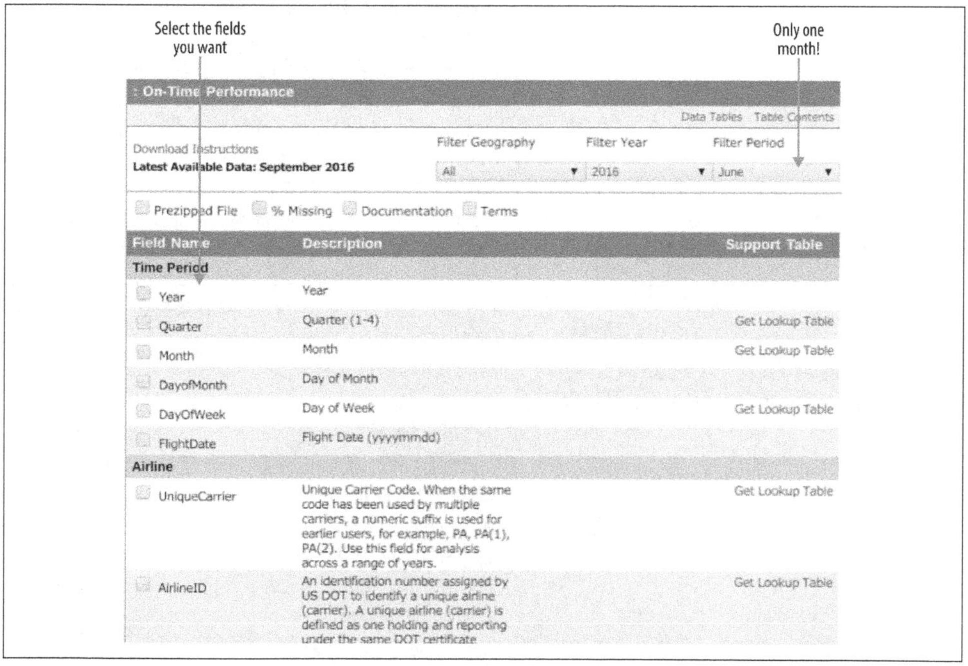

Figure 2-2. The BTS web interface to download the flights on-time arrival dataset

This is not the most helpful way to provide data for download. For one thing, the data can be downloaded only one month at a time. For another, you must select the fields that you want. Imagine that you want to download all of the data for 2015. In that scenario, you'd painstakingly select the fields you want for January 2015, submit the form, and then have to repeat the process for February 2015. If you forgot to select a field in February, that field would be missing, and you wouldn't know until you began analyzing the data! Obviously, we need to script this download to make it less tiresome and ensure consistency.

Dataset Attributes

After reading through the descriptions of the 100-plus fields in the dataset, I selected a set of 27 fields that might be relevant to the problem of training, predicting, or evaluating flight arrival delay. Table 2-1 presents these fields.

Table 2-1. Selected fields from the airline on-time performance dataset downloaded from the BTS (there is a separate table for each month)

Column	Field	Field name	Description (copied from BTS website)
1	FlightDate	FL_DATE	Flight Date (yyyymmdd).
2	UniqueCarrier	UNIQUE_CARRIER	Unique Carrier Code. When the same code has been used by multiple carriers, a numeric suffix is used for earlier users; for example, PA, PA(1), PA(2). Use this field for analysis across a range of years.
3	AirlineID	AIRLINE_ID	An identification number assigned by the US Department of Transportation (DOT) to identify a unique airline (carrier). A unique airline (carrier) is defined as one holding and reporting under the same DOT certificate regardless of its Code, Name, or holding company/corporation.
4	Carrier Code	CARRIER	Assigned by International Air Transport Association (IATA) and commonly used to identify a carrier. Because the same code might have been assigned to different carriers over time, the code is not always unique. For analysis, use the Unique Carrier Code.
5	FlightNum	FL_NUM	Flight Number.
6	OriginAirportID	ORIGIN_AIRPORT_ID	Origin Airport, Airport ID. An identification number assigned by the DOT to identify a unique airport. Use this field for airport analysis across a range of years because an airport can change its airport code and airport codes can be reused.
7	OriginAirportSeqID	ORIGIN_AIRPORT_SEQ_ID	Origin Airport, Airport Sequence ID. An identification number assigned by the DOT to identify a unique airport at a given point of time. Airport attributes, such as airport name or coordinates, can change over time.
8	OriginCityMarketID	ORIGIN_CITY_MARKET_ID	Origin Airport, City Market ID. City Market ID is an identification number assigned by the DOT to identify a city market. Use this field to consolidate airports serving the same city market.

Column	Field	Field name	Description (copied from BTS website)
9	Origin	ORIGIN	Origin Airport.
10	DestAirportID	DEST_AIRPORT_ID	Destination Airport, Airport ID. An identification number assigned by the DOT to identify a unique airport. Use this field for airport analysis across a range of years because an airport can change its airport code and airport codes can be reused.
11	DestAirportSeqID	DEST_AIRPORT_SEQ_ID	Destination Airport, Airport Sequence ID. An identification number assigned by US DOT to identify a unique airport at a given point of time. Airport attributes, such as airport name or coordinates, can change over time.
12	DestCityMarketID	DEST_CITY_MARKET_ID	Destination Airport, City Market ID. City Market ID is an identification number assigned by the DOT to identify a city market. Use this field to consolidate airports serving the same city market.
13	Dest	DEST	Destination Airport.
14	CRSDepTime	CRS_DEP_TIME	Computerized Reservation System (CRS) Departure Time (local time: hhmm).
15	DepTime	DEP_TIME	Actual Departure Time (local time: hhmm).
16	DepDelay	DEP_DELAY	Difference in minutes between scheduled and actual departure time. Early departures show negative numbers.
17	TaxiOut	TAXI_OUT	Taxi-Out time, in minutes.
18	WheelsOff	WHEELS_OFF	Wheels-Off time (local time: hhmm).
19	WheelsOn	WHEELS_ON	Wheels-On Time (local time: hhmm).
20	TaxiIn	TAXI_IN	Taxi-In time, in minutes.
21	CRSArrTime	CRS_ARR_TIME	CRS Arrival Time (local time: hhmm).
22	ArrTime	ARR_TIME	Actual Arrival Time (local time: hhmm).
23	ArrDelay	ARR_DELAY	Difference in minutes between scheduled and actual arrival time. Early arrivals show negative numbers.
24	Cancelled	CANCELLED	Cancelled flight indicator (1 = Yes).
25	CancellationCode	CANCELLATION_CODE	Specifies the reason for cancellation.
26	Diverted	DIVERTED	Diverted flight indicator (1 = Yes).
27	Distance	DISTANCE	Distance between airports (miles).

As far as the rest of this book is concerned, these are the fields in our "raw" dataset. Let's begin by downloading one year of data (2015, the last complete year available as I was writing this book) and exploring it.

Why Not Store the Data in Situ?

But before we begin to script the download, let's step back a bit and consider why we are downloading the data in the first place. Our discussion here will help illuminate the choices we have when working with large datasets. The way you do data processing is influenced by the type of infrastructure that you have available to you, and this section (even as it forays into networking and disk speeds and datacenter design) will help explain how to make the appropriate trade-offs. The Google Cloud Platform is different from the infrastructure with which you might have firsthand experience. Therefore, understanding the concepts discussed here will help you design your data processing systems in such a way that they take full advantage of what Google Cloud Platform provides.

Even if you are used to downloading data to your laptop for data analysis and development, you should realize that this is a suboptimal solution. In some ways, the data as stored on BTS is available in small enough chunks (monthly) that it could conceivably be far better if we were able to directly ingest them into our data analysis programs without having to go through a step of downloading it. Having a single source of truth has many advantages, ranging from security (providing and denying access) to error correction (no need to worry about stale copies of the data lying around). It would be best to store the data in place and have it served on demand. So, why not keep the data in situ?

Not only might it be better to leave the data in place, but we are about to do something rather strange. We are about to download the data, but we are going to turn around and upload it back to the public cloud (Google Cloud Storage). The data will continue to reside on a network computer, just not one associated with the BTS, but with Google Cloud Platform. What's the purpose of doing this?

To understand why we are downloading the data to a local drive instead of keeping the data on the BTS's computers and accessing it on demand, it helps to consider two factors: cost and speed. Leaving the data on BTS's computers involves no permanent storage on our part (so the cost is zero), but we are at the mercy of the public internet when it comes to the speed of the connection. Public internet speeds in the US can range from 8 Mbps at your local coffee house (1 MBps since 8 bits make a byte) to 1,000 Mbps ("Gigabit ethernet" is 125 MBps) in particularly well-connected cities.[5] According to Akamai's State of the Internet Q3 2015 Report (*http://bit.ly/2AdSoF5*), South Korea, with an average internet speed of 27 Mbps (a little over 3 MBps), has the fastest public internet in the world. Based on this range of speeds, let's grant that the public internet typically has speeds of 3 to 10 MBps. If you are carrying out analysis on your laptop, accessing data via the internet every time you need it will become a serious bottleneck.

---

[5] For example, Kansas City, Missouri (*https://fiber.google.com/cities/kansascity/plans/*) and Chattanooga, Tennessee (*http://money.cnn.com/2014/05/20/technology/innovation/chattanooga-internet/*).

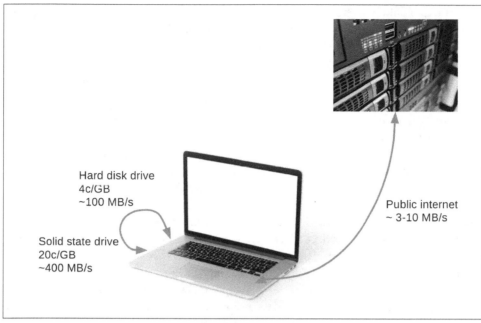

Figure 2-3. Comparison of data access speeds if data is accessed over the public internet versus from a disk drive

If you were to download the data to your drive, you'd incur storage costs but gain much higher data access speeds. A hard-disk drive (HDD; i.e., a spinning drive) costs about 4¢ per gigabyte[6] and typically provides file access speeds of about 100 MBps. A solid-state drive (SSD) costs about five times as much and provides about four times the file access speed. Either type of drive is an order of magnitude faster than trying to access the data over the public internet. It is no wonder that we typically download the data to our local drive to carry out data analysis.

For small datasets and short, quick computation, it's perfectly acceptable to download data to your laptop and do the work there. This doesn't scale, though. What if our data analysis is very complex or the data is so large that a single laptop is no longer enough? We have two options: scale up or scale out.

Scaling Up

One option to deal with larger datasets or more difficult computation jobs is to use a larger, more powerful machine with many CPUs, lots of RAM, and many terabytes of drive space. This is called *scaling up*, and it is a perfectly valid solution. However, such

---

6 All prices are estimates, in US dollars, and are current as of the writing of this book.

a computer is likely to be quite expensive. Because we are unlikely to be using it 24 hours a day, we might choose to rent an appropriately large computer from a public cloud provider. If we do that, though, storing data on drives attached to the rented compute instance is not a good choice—we'll lose our data when we release the compute instance. Instead, we could download the data once from BTS onto a persistent drive which is attached to our compute instance.

Persistent drives in Google Cloud Platform can either be HDDs or SSDs, so we have similar cost/speed trade-offs to the laptop situation. SSDs that are physically attached to your instance on the cloud do offer higher throughput and lower latency, but because many data analysis tasks need sustained throughput as we traverse the entire dataset, the difference in performance between local SSDs and solid-state persistent drives is about 2 times, not 10 times.[7] Besides the cost-effectiveness gained by not paying for a Compute Engine instance in Google Cloud Platform when not using it, persistent drives also offer durable storage—data stored on persistent drives on Google Cloud Platform is replicated to guard against data loss (*https://cloud.google.com/persistent-disk/*). In addition, you can share data on persistent drives (in read-only mode) between multiple instances. In short, then, if you want to do your analysis on one large machine but keep your data permanently in the cloud, a good solution would be to marry a powerful, high-memory Compute Engine instance with a persistent drive, download the data from the external datacenter (BTS's computer in our case) onto the persistent drive, and start up compute instances on demand, as depicted in Figure 2-4 (cloud prices in Figure 2-4 are estimated monthly charges; actual costs may be higher or lower than the estimate).

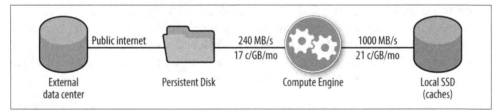

Figure 2-4. One solution to cost-effective and fast data analysis is to store data on a persistent disk that is attached to an ephemeral, high-memory Compute Engine instance

---

7 See *https://cloud.google.com/compute/docs/disks/performance* to see the difference in performance for sustained throughput.

When you are done with the analysis, you can delete the Compute Engine instance.[8] Provision the smallest persistent drive that adequately holds your data—temporary storage (or caches) during analysis can be made to an attached SSD that is deleted along with the instance, and persistent drives can always be resized if your initial size proves too small. This gives you all the benefits of doing local analysis but with the ability to use a much more powerful machine at a lower cost. I will note here that this recommendation assumes several things: the ability to rent powerful machines by the minute, to attach resizeable persistent drives to compute instances, and to achieve good-enough performance by using solid-state persistent drives. These are true of Google Cloud, but if you are using some other platform, you should find out if these assumptions hold.

Scaling Out

The solution of using a high-memory Compute Engine instance along with persistent drives and caches might be reasonable for jobs that can be done on a single machine, but it doesn't work for jobs that are bigger than that. Configuring a job into smaller parts so that processing can be carried out on multiple machines is called *scaling out*. One way to scale out a data processing job is to shard[9] the data and store the pieces on the drives attached to multiple compute instances or persistent drives that will be attached to multiple instances. Then, each compute instance can carry out analysis on a small chunk of data at high speeds—these operations are called the *map* operations. The results of the analysis on the small chunks can be combined, after some suitable collation, on a different set of compute nodes—these combination operations are called the *reduce* operations. Together, this model is known as *MapReduce*. This approach also requires an initial download of the data from the external datacenter to the cloud. In addition, we also need to split the data onto preassigned drives or nodes.

Whenever we need to carry out analysis, we will need to spin up the entire cluster of nodes, reattach the persistent drives and carry out the computation. Fortunately, we don't need to build the infrastructure to do the sharding or cluster creation ourselves. We could store the data on the Hadoop Distributed File System (HDFS), which will do the sharding for us, spin up a Cloud Dataproc cluster (which has Hadoop, Pig,

---

8 You could also just stop (and not delete) the Google Cloud Platform Compute Engine instance. Stopping the instance stops the bill associated with the compute machine, but you will continue to pay for storage. In particular, you will continue to pay for the SSD associated with the Compute Engine instance. The key advantage of a stopped instance is that you get to resume exactly where you left off, but this might not be important if you always start from a clean (known) state each time.

9 To shard a large database is to partition it into smaller, more easily managed parts. Whereas normalization of a database table places the columns of a database into different tables, sharding splits the rows of the database and uses different database server instances to handle each part. For more information, go to *https://en.wikipedia.org/wiki/Shard_(database_architecture)*.

Spark, etc. preinstalled on a cluster of Compute Engine VMs), and run our analysis job on that cluster. Figure 2-5 presents an overview of this approach.

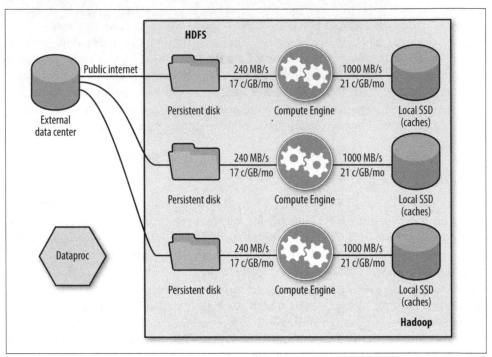

Figure 2-5. For larger datasets, one potential solution is to store data on the HDFS and use an ephemeral Dataproc cluster to carry out the analysis

A MapReduce framework like the Hadoop ecosystem requires data to be presharded. Because the presharded data must be stored on drives that are attached to compute instances, the scheme can be highly wasteful unless all the data happens to get used all the time by those compute instances. In essence, whenever you need to run a job, you ship the code to whichever nodes happen to be storing the data. What you should be doing is to trying to find a machine that has free capacity. Shipping the analysis code to run on storage nodes regardless of their computational load leads to poor efficiency because it is likely that there are long periods during which a node might have nothing to do, and other periods when it is subject to resource contention.

In summary, we have two options to work with large datasets: keep the data as is and scale up by using a large-enough computer, or scale out by sharding the data and shipping code to the nodes that store the data. Both of these options have some drawbacks. Scaling up is subject to the limitations of whatever the most powerful machine available to you can do. Scaling out is subject to inefficiencies of resource allocation. Is there a way to keep data in situ and scale out?

Data in Situ with Colossus and Jupiter

Recall that much of the economics of our case for downloading the data onto nodes on which we can do the compute relied on the slowness of an internet connection as compared to drive speeds—it is because the public internet operates at only 3 to 10 MBps, whereas drives offer two orders of magnitude faster access, that we moved the data to a large Compute Engine instance (scaling up) or sharded it onto persistent drives attached to Compute Engine instances (scaling out).

What if, though, you are operating in an environment in which networking speeds are higher, and files are available to all compute instances at those high speeds? For example, what if you had a job that uses 100,000 servers and those servers could communicate with one another at 1 GBps? This is seriously fast—it is twice the speed of SSD, 10 times the speed of a local hard drive, and 100 times faster than the public internet. What if, in addition, you have a cluster-level filesystem (not node-by-node[10]) whose metadata is sharded across the datacenter and replicated on-write for durability? Because the total bisection bandwidth of the Jupiter networks in Google's datacenters is 125,000 GBps[11] and because Google's next-generation Colossus filesystem operates at the cluster level, this is the scenario that operates if your data is available in a bucket on Google Cloud Storage and your jobs are running on Compute Engine instances in the same region as the bucket. At that point, it becomes worthwhile to treat the entire datacenter as a single computer. The speed of the network and the design of the storage make both compute and data fungible resources that can be allocated to whichever part of the datacenter is most free. Scheduling a set of jobs over a single large domain provides much higher utilization than scheduling the same set of jobs over many smaller domains. This resource allocation can be automatic—there is no need to preshard the data, and if we use an appropriate computation framework (such as BigQuery, Cloud Dataflow, or Cloud ML Engine), we don't even need to instantiate a Compute Engine instance ourselves. Figure 2-6 presents this framework.

I should point out that most datacenters are not optimized for total bisection bandwidth. Instead of being optimized to maximize the network bandwidth between nodes on the backend ("East-West communications" in networking parlance), they are optimized to minimize the network time with an outside client sending, for example, a web request ("North-South communications"). You would design a data-

---

10 In other words, rather than a filesystem that is local to a single machine, it is common to the entire cluster of machines that form the datacenter.

11 The blog on Google's networking infrastructure (*https://research.googleblog.com/2015/08/pulling-back-curtain-on-googles-network.html*) is worth a read. One petabit is 1 million gigabits, so the 1 Pbps quoted in the article works out to 125,000 GBps.

center for East-West networking only if the amount of network calls you do on the backend in response to a user request is several times the traffic of the request itself.

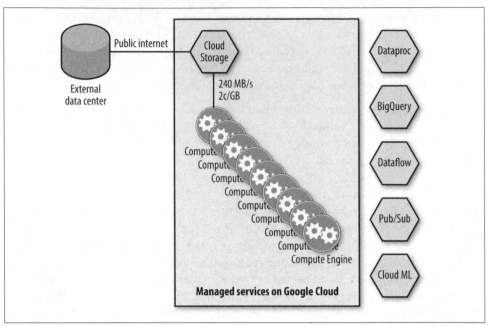

Figure 2-6. On the Google Cloud Platform, the speed of the networking within a datacenter allows us to store the data persistently and cheaply on Cloud Storage and access it as needed from a variety of ephemeral managed services

That is the case for most of Google's own jobs—a search query, for example, can result in hundreds of "fan-out" requests to microservices. Because of this, it was important for Google to avoid having to make early decisions on where to locate data and servers. The problem of resource stranding, in which there is leftover CPU in one part of the datacenter and leftover memory in another, can be minimized by dynamic resource allocation. Because the network supports tens of thousands of servers with flat bandwidth, individual applications can scale to those tens of thousands of compute instances quite easily. It is also possible to build federated services that collaborate on larger problems. Finally, this design also allows for better failure recovery because any compute instance in the datacenter can be brought to bear on the problem.

The Google File System (or GFS, on which the Hadoop Distributed File System, or HDFS, is based) was built for batch operations, whereas Colossus was designed for real-time updates. Although GFS/HDFS suffice for batch processing operations that happen over a few days, Colossus is required to update Google's search index in real time—this is why Google's search can now reflect current events. There are several other innovations that were necessary to get to this data processing architecture in which data does not need to be presharded. For example, when performing large fan-out operations, you must be tolerant of latency and design around it. This involves slicing up requests to reduce head-of-line blocking,[12] creating hundreds of partitions per machine to make it easy to move partitions elsewhere, making replicas of heavily used data chunks, using backup requests, and canceling other requests as soon as one is completed, among other strategies. To build a cluster-wide filesystem with high throughput speeds to any compute instance within the datacenter, it is necessary to minimize the number of network hops within the datacenter. Software-Defined Networking (SDN) is, therefore, extremely important. Within the Google Cloud Platform, any two machines in the same zone are only one network hop away.

The innovation in networking, compute, and storage at Google and elsewhere is by no means over. Even though the Jupiter network provides bisection bandwidths of 125,000 GBps, engineers estimate that 600,000 GBps is what's required even today. Moreover, jobs are not being sliced finely enough—because I/O devices have response times on the order of microseconds, decisions should be scheduled even more finely than the current milliseconds. Next-generation flash storage is still largely untapped within the datacenter. Colossus addresses the issue of building a cluster-level filesystem, but there are applications that need global consistency not just consistency within a single-region cluster. The challenge of building a globally distributed database is being addressed by Cloud Spanner (*http://bit.ly/2AyfRQf*). The ongoing innovations in computational infrastructure promise exciting times ahead.

All of this is in the way of noting (again!) that your mileage will vary if you do your data processing on other infrastructure—there is a reason why the title of this book includes the words "on Google Cloud Platform." The hardware optimizations if you implement your data pipelines on-premises or in a different cloud provider will typically target different things.[13] Therefore, choose between scaling up, scaling out with data sharding, or scaling out with data in situ depending on the infrastructure you have (see Table 2-2). The APIs might look the same, and in many cases, you can run the same software as I do, but the performance characteristics will be different. Google TensorFlow, Apache Beam, and others are open source and portable to on-premises infrastructure and across different cloud providers, but the execution frameworks that make Cloud ML Engine and Cloud Dataflow so powerful may not translate well to infrastructure that is not built the same way as Google Cloud Platform.

---

12 A condition in which network packets need to be delivered in order; thus, a slow packet holds up delivery of later packets.

13 Microsoft's working prototype, described in *https://www.microsoft.com/en-us/research/publication/vl2-a-scalable-and-flexible-data-center-network/*, seems to involve a centralized host layer, for example. You'd design your software for such infrastructure differently.

Table 2-2. How to choose between scaling up, scaling out with data sharding, or scaling out with data in situ

Option	Performance and cost	What you need	How to implement on Google Cloud Platform
Scaling up	Expensive on both compute and storage; fast, but limited to capability of most powerful machine	Very powerful machines; ability to rent machines by the minute; attachable persistent SSDs	Compute Engine with persistent SSDs
Scaling out	High storage costs; inexpensive compute; add machines to achieve desired speed, but limited to ability to preshard the data on a cluster of desired size	Data local to the compute nodes; attachable persistent SSDs	Cloud Dataproc (with Spark) and HDFS
Data in situ	Inexpensive storage, compute; add machines to achieve desired speed	Extremely fast networking, cluster-wide filesystem	Cloud Dataproc + Spark on Cloud Storage, BigQuery, Cloud Dataflow, Cloud ML Engine, etc.

Ingesting Data

To carry out our data analysis on the on-time performance dataset, we will need to download the monthly data from the BTS website and then upload it to Google Cloud Storage. Doing this manually will be tedious and error-prone, so let's script this operation.

How do you script filling out a web form?[14] First, learn the web calls the form makes and repeat those web calls in a script. To find out what the form does, let's use the Chrome browser and do a request manually. Visit the BTS download website (*http://bit.ly/2AXgpQk*), fill out a few fields, and then click on the Download button; a zip file download begins, as illustrated in Figure 2-7.

312822343_T_ONTIME.zip
downloaded

1,452 KB from tsdata.bts.gov

Figure 2-7. A ZIP file download, shown in the Chrome browser

It is not clear what the number in the downloaded filename corresponds to. Perhaps it's the request number. Because I selected January 2015, I'd probably want to rename it to *201501.zip*.

---

14 Before proceeding, verify that the website's terms of use do not bar you from automated downloads.

Reverse Engineering a Web Form

To script this workflow, we need to find out the HTTP request(s) that the form makes. The BTS web form is a simple HTML form with no dynamic behavior. This type of form collects all the user selections into a single POST request. If we can create that same POST request from a script, we will be able to obtain the data without going through the web form.

We can find out the exact HTTP command sent by the browser after we make our selections on the BTS website. To do this, while on the BTS website, in the Chrome web browser,[15] in the upper-right menu bar, navigate to the Developer Tools menu, as shown in Figure 2-8.

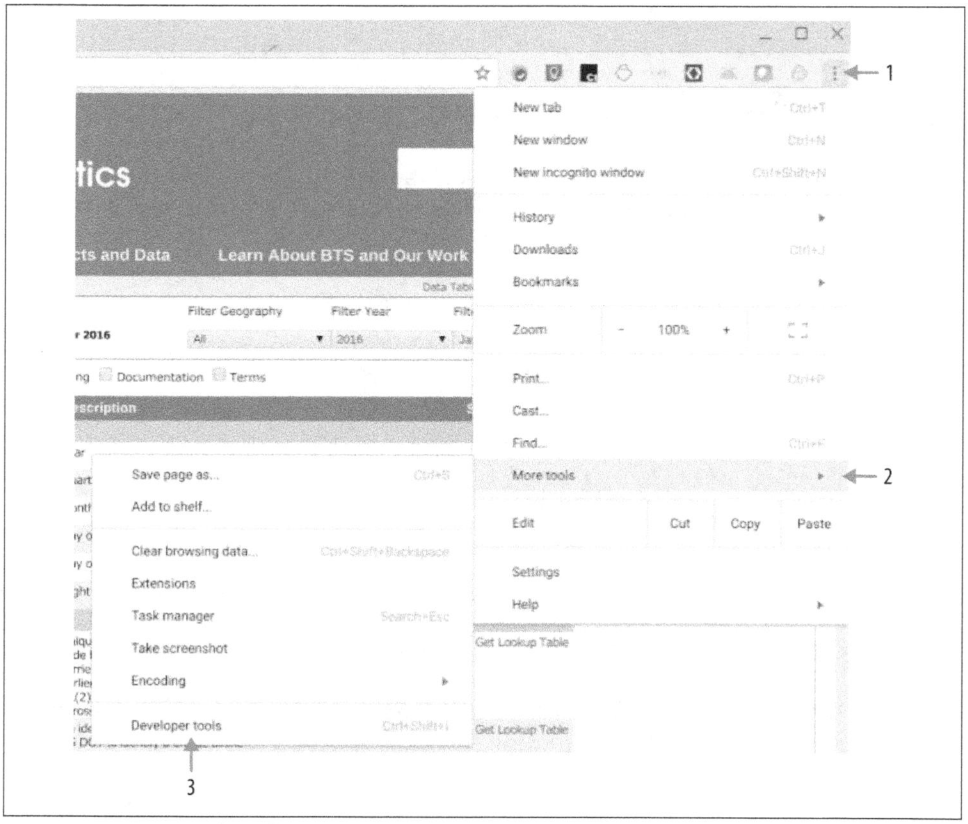

Figure 2-8. Navigating to the Developer Tools menu in Chrome

---

15 Or any other web development tool or browser that supports looking at the web traffic.

In the Network section of Developer Tools, click Preserve Log (Figure 2-9) so that we know all the network calls being made.

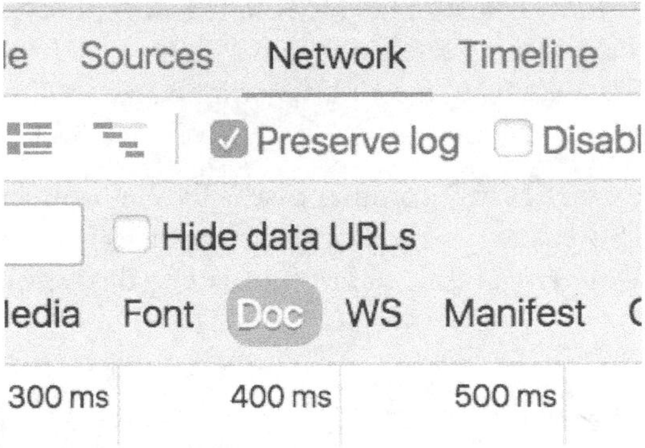

Figure 2-9. The Preserve Log section of the Developer Tools menu

Now, repeat the download, taking care to select the 27 fields that we identified earlier, and switch over to the All view. You will be able to see the HTTP request sent to the BTS server, as demonstrated in Figure 2-10.

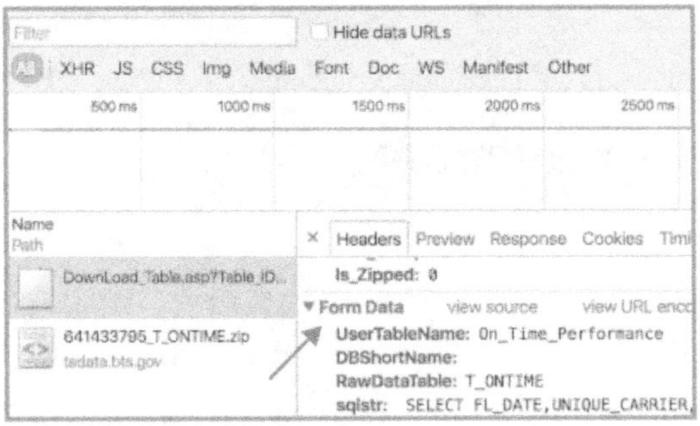

Figure 2-10. The HTTP request sent to the BTS server

It appears that the *Download_Table.asp* page POSTs some data and gets a redirect to a ZIP file in return. Scroll down to the Form Data and you can see the data being submitted.

On the Form Data tab, switch to "view source" to see the complete request, as depicted in Figure 2-11.

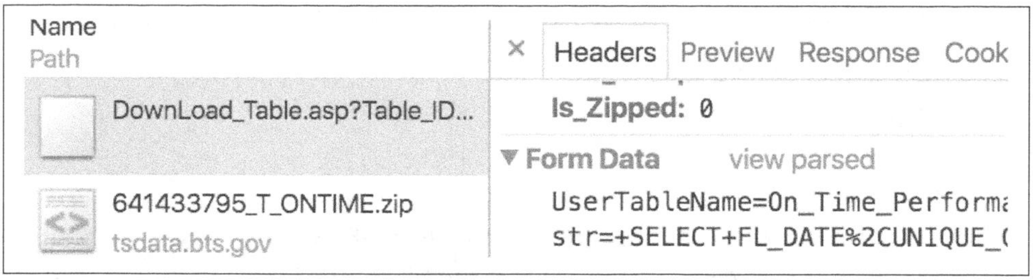

Figure 2-11. You can see the complete request from the Form Data tab

In Linux, you can make the web request by using the `curl` command-line tool, passing in the parameters that you copy and paste into the command line from the request shown in Figure 2-11. No web browser is needed, and no clicking, either:

```
curl -X POST --data "copy-paste-stuff-from-window"
http://www.transtats.bts.gov/DownLoad_Table.asp?Table_ID=236&Has_Group=3&Is_
Zipped=0
```

Unfortunately, the response turns out to be a redirect to the ZIP file and not the contents of the ZIP file itself. So, we'll need to issue another `curl` request to get the actual data or ask `curl` to follow redirects.

Dataset Download

In the data exploration phase, I'll do most of my processing interactively with Linux command-line tools. If your local computer runs Linux, Mac, or cygwin (on Windows), you could follow along on your local machine as long as the Cloud SDK is installed. Because I tend to use a Chromebook when traveling, I used CloudShell. From this point on, in the interest of not overloading this book with a painful amount of details for other systems, I will assume that this is what you are using as well. Adapt the commands as necessary if you are working locally in some other environment (e.g., where I ask you to do a `sudo apt-get install`, you might use the appropriate install command for your Linux-like environment). When we have settled on the processing to be done, we'll look at how to make this more automated.

For now, my script to download 12 months of data from the BTS website is called *download.sh*[16] and the key lines are as follows:

```
YEAR=2015
for MONTH=`seq -w 1 12`; do
PARAMS="UserTableName...
RESPONSE=$(curl -X POST --data "$PARAMS"
```

---

16 All of the code snippets in this book are extracts from the GitHub repository at *https://github.com/Google CloudPlatform/data-science-on-gcp/*, and are subject to the Apache License, Version 2.0. For the full license text, go to *https://github.com/GoogleCloudPlatform/data-science-on-gcp/blob/master/LICENSE*.

```
http://www.transtats.bts.gov/DownLoad_Table.asp?Table_ID=236&Has_Group=3&Is_
Zipped=0)
echo "Received $RESPONSE"
ZIPFILE=$(echo $RESPONSE | tr '\"' '\n' | grep zip)
echo $ZIPFILE
curl -o $YEAR$MONTH.zip $ZIPFILE
done
```

The line marked PARAMS= consists of the entire block of text in the Form Data tab of Chrome—i.e., the form data that the browser submits to the BTS website. I looked for the month and year and replaced those in the query with ${MONTH} and ${YEAR}, respectively. Because the response to that query is a redirect, I tried adding -L to the curl path—this is supposed to follow redirects, but it doesn't seem to pass along the content-length, which the BTS web server needed. So I just pull the URL of the ZIP file from the redirect response and download it, naming the file appropriately.

The complete download script is on GitHub at *https://github.com/GoogleCloudPlatform/data-science-on-gcp/tree/master/02_ingest*—if you want to follow along with me, perform these steps:

1. Go to *https://console.cloud.google.com/*.

2. On the top strip, activate CloudShell using the button shown in Figure 2-12.

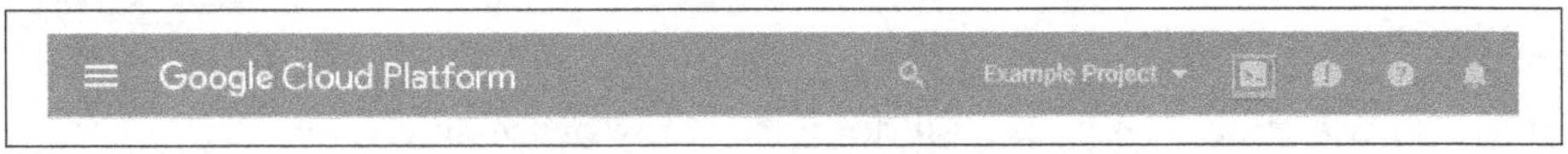

Figure 2-12. The CloudShell button on the Google Cloud Platform web console

3. In CloudShell, type the following:

   ```
   git clone \
       https://github.com/GoogleCloudPlatform/data-science-on-gcp/
   ```

   This downloads the GitHub code to your CloudShell home directory.

4. Navigate into the flights folder:

   ```
   cd data-science-on-gcp
   ```

5. Make a new directory to hold the data, and then change into that directory:

   ```
   mkdir data
   cd data
   ```

6. Run the code to download the files from the BTS website:

   ```
   bash ../02_ingest/download.sh
   ```

7. When the script completes, look at the downloaded ZIP files, shown in Figure 2-13:

   ```
   ls -lrt
   ```

```
vlakshmanan@cloud-training-demos:~/training-data-analyst/flights-data-analysis/data$ ls -lrt
total 176112
-rw-r--r-- 1 vlakshmanan vlakshmanan 14522505 Jun  6 21:57 201501.zip
-rw-r--r-- 1 vlakshmanan vlakshmanan 13197362 Jun  6 21:57 201502.zip
-rw-r--r-- 1 vlakshmanan vlakshmanan 15560327 Jun  6 21:57 201503.zip
-rw-r--r-- 1 vlakshmanan vlakshmanan 14999778 Jun  6 21:57 201504.zip
-rw-r--r-- 1 vlakshmanan vlakshmanan 15390279 Jun  6 21:58 201505.zip
-rw-r--r-- 1 vlakshmanan vlakshmanan 15743756 Jun  6 21:58 201506.zip
-rw-r--r-- 1 vlakshmanan vlakshmanan 16226840 Jun  6 21:58 201507.zip
-rw-r--r-- 1 vlakshmanan vlakshmanan 15905194 Jun  6 21:58 201508.zip
-rw-r--r-- 1 vlakshmanan vlakshmanan 14359781 Jun  6 21:58 201509.zip
-rw-r--r-- 1 vlakshmanan vlakshmanan 15034742 Jun  6 21:59 201510.zip
-rw-r--r-- 1 vlakshmanan vlakshmanan 14498350 Jun  6 21:59 201511.zip
-rw-r--r-- 1 vlakshmanan vlakshmanan 14874348 Jun  6 21:59 201512.zip
```

Figure 2-13. Details of downloaded files as seen in CloudShell

This looks quite reasonable—all the files have different sizes and the sizes are robust enough that one would assume they are not just error messages.

Exploration and Cleanup

A bit of Bash scripting allows me to unzip all the files and name them appropriately:

```
for month in `seq -w 1 12`; do
   unzip 2015$month.zip
   mv *ONTIME.csv 2015$month.csv
   rm 2015$month.zip
done
```

I can run this command directly from the terminal, but I prefer to save the script as *02_ingest/zip_to_csv.sh* and run it that way.

At this point, I have 12 CSV files. Let's look at the first few lines of one of them to ensure the data matches what we think it ought to be:

```
head 201503.csv
```

There is a header in each CSV file, and the second line of data looks like this:

```
2015-03-01,"EV",20366,"EV","4457",12945,1294503,32945,"LEX",12266,1226603,31453,
"IAH","1720","1715",-5.00,10.00,"1725","1851",17.00,"1902","1908",6.00,0.00,"",
0.00,828.00,
```

The strings all seem to be quoted (perhaps in case the strings themselves have commas), and there seems to be a pesky extra comma at the end.

We expect to see 27 fields. Are there 27? We can check:

```
head -2 201503.csv  | tail -1 | sed 's/,/ /g' | wc -w
```

Indeed, the number of words is 27. Here's how: the command gets the first two lines of the data file (with head -2), and the last line of that (with tail -1) so that we are looking at the second line of *201503.csv*. Then, we replace all the commas by spaces and count the number of words with wc -w.

How much data is there? A quick shell command (wc for wordcount, with an -l [lowercase letter L] to display only the line count) informs us that there are between 43,000 and 52,000 flights per month:

```
$ wc -l *.csv
  469969 201501.csv
  429192 201502.csv
  504313 201503.csv
  485152 201504.csv
  496994 201505.csv
  503898 201506.csv
  520719 201507.csv
  510537 201508.csv
  464947 201509.csv
  486166 201510.csv
  467973 201511.csv
  479231 201512.csv
 5819091 total
```

This adds up to nearly six million flights in 2015!

If the quotes and commas cause problems in downstream analysis, we'll need to come back and clean up the data files. Because this is a tour through so many different tools, the likelihood of this happening is quite high. Conversely, we do know that the fields we have selected (e.g., airport IDs) will never have commas in them and that the extra comma at the end serves no purpose. So, for the purposes of this book, we can avoid the potential problem by removing the quotes and extra comma now before we begin doing any analysis on the dataset. In general, though, you want to keep the ingested data in as raw a form as possible because mistakes at this stage are often irreversible. The removal of quotes, in particular, could potentially break later processing, especially if we later incorporate fields that do have commas in them.

We can remove quotes and commas by using Bash scripting, as well:

```
for month in `seq -w 1 12`; do
    sed 's/,$//g' 2015$month.csv | sed 's/"//g' > tmp
    mv tmp 2015$month.csv
done
```

The first sed command replaces the comma at the end of any line (/,$/) with an empty space (//) and the second sed replaces all quotes with an empty space. It's possible to combine two string replacements with a single one using a logical OR, but this is clearer. In any case, these scripts are going to be thrown away, because I will formalize the ingest program shortly in the form of a single script. If necessary, I can improve the code at that time.

After running the preceding Bash command, we can examine the first few lines of the data file using the following:

```
head 201503.csv
```

We see that the header in each CSV file is cleaner, and the first line of data looks like this:

```
2015-03-01,UA,19977,UA,1025,14771,1477101,32457,SFO,11618,1161802,31703,EWR,
0637,0644,7.00,15.00,0659,1428,12.00,1450,1440,-10.00,0.00,,0.00,2565.00
```

As you might have realized by now, knowing a little Unix scripting can come in very handy at this initial stage of data analysis.

Uploading Data to Google Cloud Storage

For durability of this raw dataset, let's upload it to Google Cloud Storage. To do that, you first need to create a *bucket,* essentially a namespace for Binary Large Objects (blobs) stored in Cloud Storage that you typically want to treat similarly from a permissions perspective. You can create a bucket from the Google Cloud Platform Console (*http://console.cloud.google.com/storage*). For reasons that we will talk about shortly, make the bucket a single-region bucket.

Bucket names must be globally unique (i.e., unique not just within your project or organization, but across Google Cloud Platform). This means that bucket names are globally knowable even if the contents of the bucket are not accessible. This can be problematic. For example, if you created a bucket named `acme_gizmo`, a competitor might later try to create a bucket also named `acme_gizmo`, but fail because the name already exits. This failure can alert your competitor to the possibility that Acme Corp. is developing a new Gizmo. It might seem like it would take Sherlock Holmes–like powers of deduction to arrive at this conclusion, but it's simply best for you want to avoid revealing sensitive information in bucket names. A common pattern to create unique bucket names is to use suffixes on the project ID. Project IDs are globally unique,[17] and thus a bucket name such as `<projectid>-ds32` will also tend to be unique. In my case, my project ID is `cloud-training-demos` and my bucket name is `cloud-training-demos-ml`.

Cloud Storage will also serve as the staging ground to many of the GCP tools and enable collaborative sharing of the data with our colleagues. In my case, to upload the files to Cloud Storage, I type the following:

```
gsutil -m cp *.csv gs://cloud-training-demos-ml/flights/raw/
```

This uploads the files to Cloud Storage to my bucket `cloud-training-demos-ml` in a multithreaded manner (`-m`) and makes me the owner. If you are working locally,

---

[17] You can get your unique project ID from the Cloud Platform Console dashboard; it could be different from the common name that you assigned to your project. By default, Google Cloud Platform tries to give you a project ID that is the same as your project name, but if that name is already taken, you will get an autogenerated, unique project ID. Because of this default, you should be similarly careful about giving projects sensitive names.

another way to upload the files would be to use the Cloud Platform Console (*http:// console.cloud.google.com/storage*).

It is better to keep these as separate files instead of concatenating them into a single large file because Cloud Storage is a blob store (*https://en.wikipedia.org/wiki/ Binary_large_object*), and not a regular filesystem. In particular, it is not possible to append to a file on Cloud Storage; you can only replace it. Therefore, although concatenating all 12 files into a single file containing the entire year of data will work for this batch dataset, it won't work as well if we want to later add to the dataset one month at a time, as new data become available. Secondly, because Cloud Storage is blob storage, storing the files separately will permit us to more easily process parts of the entire archive (for example, only the summer months) without having to build in slicing into our data processing pipeline. Thirdly, it is generally a good idea to keep ingested data in as raw a form as possible.

It is preferable that this bucket to which we upload the data is a single-region bucket. For the most part, we will create Compute Engine instances in the same region as the bucket and access it only from this one region. In a sense, a multiregion bucket is overkill because we don't need global availability. Also, a single-region bucket is less expensive than a multiregion one. However, the difference in cost is not material enough to affect our behavior, so shouldn't we use a multiregion bucket just in case? As of this writing, single-region buckets in Google Cloud Platform offer strong consistency, but multiregion buckets do not. That difference is significant enough for me to prefer to use single-region buckets for data analysis and machine learning.

What exactly is strong versus eventual consistency, and why does it matter for our purposes? Suppose that a worker in a distributed application updates a piece of data and another worker views that piece of data immediately afterward. Does the second worker always see the updated value? Then, what you have is *strong consistency*. If, on the other hand, there could be a potential lag between an update and availability (i.e., if different viewers can see potentially different values of the data at the same instant in time), what you have is *eventual consistency*. Eventually, all viewers of the data will see the updated value, but that lag will be different for different viewers. Strong consistency is an implicit assumption that is made in a number of programming paradigms. However, to achieve strong consistency, we have to make compromises on scalability and performance (this is called *Brewer's theorem*). For example, we might need to lock readers out of the data while it is being updated so that that simultaneous readers always see a consistent and correct value.

Brewer's theorem, also called the CAP theorem, states that no computer system can simultaneously guarantee consistency, availability, and partition resilience. Consistency is the guarantee that every reader sees the latest written information. Availability is the guarantee that a response is sent to every request (regardless of whether it is the most current information or not). Partition resilience is the guarantee that the system continues to operate even if the network connecting readers, writers, and storage drops an arbitrary number of messages. Since network failures are a fact of life in distributed systems, the CAP theorem essentially says that you need to choose between consistency and availability. Cloud Spanner, which was released into beta during the writing of this book, doesn't change this: it essentially makes choices during partitioning—Cloud Spanner is always consistent and achieves five-9s (but not perfect) availability despite operating over a wide area. For more details, see *http://bit.ly/2Abs7D8*.

For scalability and performance reasons, it might be advantageous to design with eventual consistency instead. For example, internet Domain Name System (DNS) servers cache values and have their values replicated across many DNS servers all over the internet. If a DNS value is updated, it takes some time for this modified value to become replicated at every DNS server. Eventually, this does happen, though. Having a centralized DNS server that is locked whenever any DNS value is modified would have led to an extremely brittle system. Because the DNS system is based on eventual consistency, it is highly available and extremely scalable, enabling name lookups for/to millions of internet-capable devices. Multiregion objects on Google Cloud Storage must be replicated across regions, and to preserve scalability and performance, multiregion buckets today support only eventual consistency (this is a design/implementation decision and not implicit to the problem of having buckets across multiple regions, and so could be changed in the future[18]). To avoid the problems inherent in writing data and not having it be immediately available to readers of the data, we will use a single-region bucket.

This being public data, I will ensure that my colleagues can use this data without having to wait on me:

```
gsutil acl ch -R -g google.com:R \
    gs://cloud-training-demos-ml/flights/raw/
```

That changes the access control list (`acl`) recursively (`-R`), applying to the group google.com read permission (`:R`) on everything starting from the Cloud Storage URL supplied. Had there been sensitive information in the dataset, I would have to be

---

18 Indeed, by the time this book went to print, this had changed. Multiregion buckets on Cloud Storage today support strong consistency.

more careful, of course. We'll discuss fine-grained security, by providing views with different columns to different roles in my organization, when we talk about putting the data in BigQuery. We'll also discuss information leakage when information about the flights that people take can leak from the predictions we make on their behalf and how to guard against this when we talk about machine learning predictions.

Scheduling Monthly Downloads

Now that we have some historical flight data in our Cloud Storage bucket, it is natural to wonder how to keep the bucket current. After all, airlines didn't stop flying in 2015, and the BTS continues to refresh its website on a monthly basis. It would be good if we could schedule monthly downloads to keep ourselves synchronized with the BTS.

There are two scenarios to consider here. The BTS could let us know when it has new data, and we could then proceed to ingest the data. The other option is that we periodically monitor the BTS website and ingest new data as it becomes available. The BTS doesn't offer a mechanism by which we can be notified about data updates, so we will need to resort to polling. We can, of course, be smart about how we do the polling. For example, if the BTS tends to update its website around the 5th of every month, we could poll at that time.

Where should this ingest program be executed? Realizing that this is a program that will be invoked only once a month (more often if retries are needed if an ingest fails), we realize that this is not a long-running job, but is instead something that should be scheduled to run periodically. The traditional way to do this is to schedule a *cron*[19] job in Unix/Linux. To schedule a cron job, you add a line to a *crontab*[20] file and then register it with a Unix daemon that takes care of the scheduling. For example, adding this line

```
1 2 10 * * /etc/bin/ingest_flights.py
```

to `crontab` will cause the Python program */etc/bin/ingest_flights.py* (that would carry out the same steps to ingest the flights data that we did on the command line in the previous section) to be run by the system at 02:01 on the 10th of every month.

---

19 A shortened form of a misspelling of chronos, Greek for time, `cron` is the name of the Unix daemon process that executes scheduled jobs at specific times.

20 Shortened form of cron table.

Although cron jobs are a straightforward solution, there are several problems that all come down to resilience and repeatability:

- The cron job is scheduled on a particular server. If that server happens to be rebooted around 2 AM on April 10, the ingest might never take place that month.

- The environment that cron executes in is very restricted. Our task will need to download data from BTS, uncompress it, clean it up, and upload it to the cloud. These impose a variety of requirements in terms of memory, space, and permissions and it can be difficult to configure cron appropriately. In practice, system administrators configure cron jobs on particular machines, and find it difficult to port them to other machines that do not have the same system paths.

- If the ingest job fails (if, for example, the network is down), there is no way to retry it. Retries and other such failure-recovery efforts will have to be explicitly coded in our Python program.

- Remote monitoring and one-time, ad hoc executions are not part of the cron interface. If you need to monitor, troubleshoot, and restart the ingest from a mobile device, good luck.

This litany of drawbacks is not unique to cron. They are implicit in any solution that is tied to specific servers. So, how would you do it on the cloud? What you should not do is to create a Compute Engine VM and schedule a cron job on it—that will be subject to some of the same problems!

For resilience and reliability, we need a serverless way to schedule ingest jobs. Obviously, the ingest job will need to be run on some machine somewhere. However, we shouldn't need to manage that machine at all. This is a job that needs perhaps two minutes of compute resources a month. We should be looking for a way to write the ingest code and let the cloud infrastructure take care of provisioning resources, making retries, and providing for remote monitoring and ad hoc execution.

On Google Cloud Platform, Google App Engine provides a service called Cron service to schedule periodic jobs in a serverless manner. Figure 2-14 presents our architecture for the monthly ingest job.

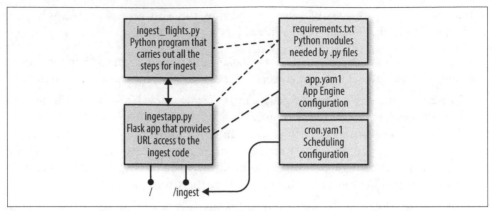

Figure 2-14. The architecture of the monthly ingest job in App Engine

First, we will write a standalone *ingest_flights.py* application that is capable of downloading the data for a specific year/month and uploading the data to Cloud Storage. Because downloading data involves access to the filesystem, we will need to use the "Flex" version of App Engine that runs our code in a Docker container[21] on Compute Engine VMs. It is a little slower than the Standard version, which runs in a sandbox and can autoscale much faster. However, speed of deployment and autoscaling are not primary motivations for our monthly ingest job—our app is not redeployed often, and will need to service only one user (the Cron service).

The way scheduling works in App Engine is that we must specify a URL that will be invoked. Whereas in the previous Linux cron example we specified a script on the server that was running the cron daemon, on Google Cloud Platform, the Cron service endpoint will be a URL. App Engine will visit the URL according to the schedule that we specify (this can be any URL; it doesn't need to be a service that we write). Because our ingest code is a standalone Python program, we will wrap that ingest code into a Flask web application (*ingestapp.py*) so that we can invoke it by using a URL.

The Flex version of App Engine requires us to specify our dependencies so that it can create an appropriate Dockerfile; we do this in *requirements.txt*. The App Engine configuration (URL mapping, security, etc.) goes in *app.yaml*. The schedule itself goes in *cron.yaml*. The entire package is deployed into App Engine, which publishes the application online and then manages everything.

---

21 Docker containers (*http://www.docker.com/*) are lightweight wrappers around a piece of software (here, the Flask application *ingestapp.py*) that contain everything needed to run that software—code (e.g., *ingest_flights.py*), runtime (Flask, Python dependencies, etc.), configuration files (e.g., *app.yaml*) and system libraries (here, a specific Linux distribution). Unlike a virtual machine, different containers running on the same machine can share layers of operating system dependencies.

Ingesting in Python

While exploring the data, we carried out the ingest on the command line in Bash. We saved our commands as we went along in the form of Bash scripts. We could create our ingest program by simply making a Bash script that invokes those intermediate steps:

```
#!/bin/bash
bash download.sh
bash zip_to_csv.sh
bash quotes_comma.sh
bash upload.sh
```

This is the sort of decision that leads to spaghetti-like code that is difficult to unravel and to maintain. There are many assumptions made by this set of Bash scripts in terms of what to download, where the temporary storage resides, and where to upload it. Changing any of these will involve changing multiple scripts. Using Bash to quickly get a handle on the data is a good idea, as is the idea of saving these scripts so as to continue the exploration. But when it comes to making the ingest more systematic and routine, you do not want to use a shell scripting language; a more formal programming language is better.

In this book, we will use Python wherever we can because of its ability to span a wide range of computing tasks, from systems programming to statistics and machine learning. Python is currently the best choice if you need to pick a single language in which to do most of your work. Java is typesafe and performant. Its object-orientation and packaging architecture are suitable for large, multideveloper programs, but it makes the code too verbose. Moreover, the lack of a Read-Evaluate-Process-Loop (REPL) interpreter makes Java unwieldy for quick experimentation. C++ is numerically very efficient but standard libraries for non-numerical computing are often nonexistent. Given the choice of a data package available in Python, Scala, R, and Java, significant majorities choose Python and Scala over R and Java.[22] Scala combines the benefits of Python (easy scriptability, conciseness) with the benefits of Java (type-safety, speed), but as of this writing, the tooling for Scala (such as for statistics and visualization) is not as pervasive as it is for Python. Several tools I will use in this book have no officially supported Scala API.[23] Today, therefore, the best choice of

---

22 In 2016, Databricks found that 65% of survey respondents used Spark in Scala versus 62% in Python, 44% in SQL, 29% in Java and 20% in R. See the infographic and survey linked from *https://databricks.com/blog/2016/09/27/spark-survey-2016-released.html*.

23 App Engine Flex, for example, supports Java, Python, Node.js, Go, and Ruby. Cloud Dataflow, to take another example, is supported in Java and Python only. Because Scala runs on the Java virtual machine, it is possible to invoke a Java library from Scala, and vice versa. Thus, there are open source ports that enable Scala code to work on App Engine (*https://github.com/sbt/sbt-appengine*) and Cloud Dataflow (*https://github.com/spotify/scio*). But there is a price paid for the unofficial nature of these tools: as of this writing, the Spotify Dataflow API targets one major version behind the official Java service available on Google Cloud Platform.

programming language is Python. For certain use cases for which speed is important and Python is not performant enough, it might be necessary to use Java.

The ingest program in Python goes through the same four steps as before when we did it manually on the command line:

1. Download data from the BTS website to a local file.

2. Unzip the downloaded ZIP file and extract the CSV file it contains.

3. Remove quotes and the trailing comma from the CSV file.

4. Upload the CSV file to Google Cloud Storage.

Whereas our download Bash script got all 12 months of a hardcoded year (2015), our download subroutine in Python will take as input the year and month:

```
def download(YEAR, MONTH, destdir):
   '''
    Downloads on-time performance data and returns local filename
    YEAR e.g.'2015'
    MONTH e.g. '01' for January
   '''
   PARAMS="...".format(YEAR, MONTH)
   url='http://www.transtats.bts.gov/DownLoad_Table.asp?...'
   filename = os.path.join(destdir, "{}{}.zip".format(YEAR, MONTH))
   with open(filename, "wb") as fp:
     response = urlopen(url, PARAMS)
     fp.write(response.read())
   return filename
```

Another thing to note is that our Bash script simply downloaded the ZIP file from BTS to the current working directory of the user. However, since our Python script is meant to be executed on demand by the Cron service, we cannot make assumptions about the directory in which the script will be run. In particular, we don't know whether that directory will be writeable and have enough space. Hence, we ask the caller of the function to provide an appropriate destination directory in which to store the downloaded ZIP file. urlopen in Python, unlike curl, does follow redirects, so we are able to simply write out the response rather than issue a second HTTP request. Unfortunately, urlopen is one of those commands in Python that changed its behavior and location from Python 2.7 to Python 3. In Python 2.7, this command is part of the module urllib2, and the second parameter to urlopen can be a string. In Python 3, this command is part of the module urllib, and the second parameter has to be an array of bytes. Hence, by writing the preceding code, we are assuming that we will be using Python 2.7 (I chose Python 2.7 because it is currently the default for App Engine Flex).

Here's how to unzip the file and extract the CSV contents:

```
def zip_to_csv(filename, destdir):
    zip_ref = zipfile.ZipFile(filename, 'r')
    cwd = os.getcwd()
    os.chdir(destdir)
    zip_ref.extractall()
    os.chdir(cwd)
    csvfile = os.path.join(destdir, zip_ref.namelist()[0])
    zip_ref.close()
    return csvfile
```

Annoyingly, the `zipfile` module in Python doesn't provide a way to extract contents to a specific directory—it insists on extracting the contents in the current working directory. So, we make sure to change to the destination directory before doing the extraction. Then, we change back.

Here's how to remove quotes and the trailing comma:

```
def remove_quotes_comma(csvfile, year, month):
  try:
    outfile = os.path.join(os.path.dirname(csvfile),
                          '{}{}.csv'.format(year, month))
    with open(csvfile, 'r') as infp:
      with open(outfile, 'w') as outfp:
        for line in infp:
            outline = line.rstrip().rstrip(',').translate(None, '"')
            outfp.write(outline)
            outfp.write('\n')
  finally:
    print ("... removing {}".format(csvfile))
    os.remove(csvfile)
```

You can remove the quotes and the trailing comma by using a single line of code:

```
outline = line.rstrip().rstrip(',').translate(None, '"')
```

The rest is simply scaffolding to ensure that opened files are closed properly.

Before uploading the data to Cloud Storage, though, we should add some fault tolerance and defensive programming. When we ask the BTS web application for data it doesn't have (perhaps for data corresponding to a future year), it returns a ZIP file that has a CSV file that contains only the header. In terms of defensive programming, one of the most common errors that can happen in ingest is for the data provider to add columns or change the schema of the input in some way—as we increasingly automate everything about our systems, we should ensure that potentially breaking changes cause loud failures. Consequently, we will add two checks on the downloaded data: (1) that it has more than one line, and (2) that the CSV file has the exact header we expect:

```
class DataUnavailable(Exception):
    def __init__(self, message):
        self.message = message
```

```python
class UnexpectedFormat(Exception):
    def __init__(self, message):
        self.message = message


def verify_ingest(outfile):
    expected_header =
'FL_DATE,UNIQUE_CARRIER,AIRLINE_ID,CARRIER,FL_NUM,ORIGIN_AIRPORT_ID,'+
'ORIGIN_AIRPORT_SEQ_ID,ORIGIN_CITY_MARKET_ID,ORIGIN,DEST_AIRPORT_ID,'+
'DEST_AIRPORT_SEQ_ID,DEST_CITY_MARKET_ID,DEST,CRS_DEP_TIME,DEP_TIME,'+
'DEP_DELAY,TAXI_OUT,WHEELS_OFF,WHEELS_ON,TAXI_IN,CRS_ARR_TIME,ARR_TIME,'+
'ARR_DELAY,CANCELLED,CANCELLATION_CODE,DIVERTED,DISTANCE'

    with open(outfile, 'r') as outfp:
        firstline = outfp.readline().strip()
        if (firstline != expected_header):
            os.remove(outfile)
            msg = 'Got header={}, but expected={}'.format(
                                firstline, expected_header)
            logging.error(msg)
            raise UnexpectedFormat(msg)

        if next(outfp, None) == None:
            os.remove(outfile)
            msg = ('Received file from BTS with only header and no content')
            raise DataUnavailable(msg)
```

Raising an exception instead of returning an error code greatly simplifies the code that calls this function. We can leave exception handling to the outermost code, which in our case will be the command-line main() (in the case of standalone execution) or the Flask app (in the case of the Cron service). However, because we are expecting upstream callers to do something intelligent, we need to ensure that we throw different exceptions for the two cases.

Here's the code to upload the CSV file for a given month to Cloud Storage:

```python
def upload(csvfile, bucketname, blobname):
    client = storage.Client()
    bucket = client.get_bucket(bucketname)
    blob = Blob(blobname, bucket)
    blob.upload_from_filename(csvfile)
    gcslocation = 'gs://{}/{}'.format(bucketname, blobname)
    print ('Uploaded {} ...'.format(gcslocation))
    return gcslocation
```

The code asks for the bucketname (the single-region bucket that was created during our exploration) and a blobname (e.g., *flights/201501.csv*) and carries out the upload using the Cloud Storage Python library. Although it can be tempting to simply use the subprocess module in Python to invoke gsutil operations, it is better not to do so. If you go the subprocess route, you will then need to ensure that the Cloud SDK (that `gsutil` comes with) is installed on whichever machine this is going to run on. In App Engine Flex, it depends on which Docker image you choose to use as your base. It is preferable to use pure Python modules when possible and add those modules to *requirements.txt*, as follows:

```
Flask==0.11.1
gunicorn==19.6.0
google-cloud-storage==0.21.0
```

The first two requirements are for the Flask web application and Google Cloud Storage to invoke the `get_bucket()` and `upload_from_filename()` operations.

We can now write an `ingest()` method that calls the four major steps, plus the verification, in order:

```
def ingest(year, month, bucket):
    '''
    ingest flights data from BTS website to Google Cloud Storage
    return cloud-storage-blob-name on success.
    raises DataUnavailable if this data is not on BTS website
    '''
    tempdir = tempfile.mkdtemp(prefix='ingest_flights')
    try:
        zipfile = download(year, month, tempdir)
        bts_csv = zip_to_csv(zipfile, tempdir)
        csvfile = remove_quotes_comma(bts_csv, year, month)
        verify_ingest(csvfile) # throws exceptions
        gcsloc = 'flights/raw/{}'.format(os.path.basename(csvfile))
        return upload(csvfile, bucket, gcsloc)
    finally:
        print ('Cleaning up by removing {}'.format(tempdir))
        shutil.rmtree(tempdir)
```

The destination directory that we use to stage the downloaded data before uploading to Cloud Storage is obtained using the `tempfile` package in Python. This ensures that if, for whatever reason, there are two instances of this program running at the same time, they will not cause contention issues.

We can try out the code by writing a `main()` that is executed if this program[24] is run on the command line:

```
if __name__ == '__main__':
    import argparse
    parser = argparse.ArgumentParser(
     description='ingest flights data from BTS website to GCS')
    parser.add_argument('--bucket', help='GCS bucket to upload data to',
                        required=True)
    parser.add_argument('--year', help='Example: 2015.', required=True)
```

---

24 The full program is available as *ingest_flights.py* on GitHub at *http://bit.ly/2BPhya4*—try it out.

```
    parser.add_argument('--month', help='01 for Jan.', required=True)

    try:
        args = parser.parse_args()
        gcsfile = ingest(args.year, args.month, args.bucket)
        print ('Success ... ingested to {}'.format(gcsfile))
    except DataUnavailable as e:
        print ('Try again later: {}'.format(e.message))
```

Trying to download a month that is not yet available results in an error message:

```
$ ./ingest_flights.py  --bucket cloud-training-demos-ml \
                 --year 2018 --month 01
...
Try again later: Received a file from BTS with only header and no content
```

while specifying a valid month ends with a new (or replaced) file on Cloud Storage:

```
$ ./ingest_flights.py  --bucket cloud-training-demos-ml \
                 --year 2015 --month 01
...
Success ... ingested to gs://cloud-training-demos-ml/flights/201501.csv
```

Specifying a nonexistent bucket, on the other hand, results in an uncaught exception:

```
$ ./ingest_flights.py --bucket cant-write-to-bucket \
                 --year 2015 --month 01
...
Traceback (most recent call last):
  File "./ingest_flights.py", line 144, in <module>
    gcsfile = ingest(year, month, args.bucket)
  ...
google.cloud.exceptions.NotFound: 404 Not Found (GET
https://www.googleapis.com/storage/v1/b/cant-write-to-bucket?projection=noAcl)
```

On the Cron service, this will result in the call failing and being retried subject to a maximum number of retries. Retries will also happen if the BTS web server cannot be reached.

At this point, we have the equivalent of our exploratory Bash scripts, but with some additional resilience, repeatability, and fault tolerance built in. Our Python program expects us to provide a year, month, and bucket. However, if we are doing monthly ingests, we already know which year and month we need to ingest. No, not the current month—recall that there is a time lag between the flight events and the data being reported by the carriers to the BTS. Instead, it is simply the month after whatever files we already have on Cloud Storage! So, we can automate this, too:

```
def next_month(bucketname):
    '''
        Finds which months are on GCS, and returns next year,month to download
    '''
    client = storage.Client()
    bucket = client.get_bucket(bucketname)
```

```
blobs   = list(bucket.list_blobs(prefix='flights/raw/'))
files = [blob.name for blob in blobs if 'csv' in blob.name] # csv files only
lastfile = os.path.basename(files[-1]) # e.g. 201503.csv
year = lastfile[:4]
month = lastfile[4:6]
dt = datetime.datetime(int(year), int(month), 15) # 15th of month
dt = dt + datetime.timedelta(30) # will always go to next month
return '{}'.format(dt.year), '{:02d}'.format(dt.month)
```

To get the next month given that there is a file, say *201503.csv*, on Cloud Storage, we add 30 days to the Ides of March—this gets around the fact that there can be anywhere from 28 days to 31 days in a month, and that `timedelta` requires a precise number of days to add to a date.

By changing the year and month to be optional parameters, we can try out the ingest program's ability to find the next month and ingest it to Cloud Storage. We simply add:

```
if args.year is None or args.month is None:
    year, month = next_month(args.bucket)
else:
    year = args.year
    month = args.month
gcsfile = ingest(year, month, args.bucket)
```

Now that we have an ingest program that is capable of updating our Cloud Storage bucket one month at a time, we can move on to building the scaffolding to have it be executed in a serverless way.

Flask Web App

Flask (*http://flask.pocoo.org/*) is a microframework for writing web applications in Python. Because we want an extremely lightweight and intuitive framework to write a Cron-invokable web application in Python, Flask fits the bill perfectly. In our web application, we'll have two URLs. The first is a welcome page that simply returns a page with a link to the second URL:

```
@app.route('/')
def welcome():
        return '<html><a href="ingest">' +
                'ingest next month</a> flight data</html>'
```

We could have replaced the welcome page by a static page outside of Flask, but then I'd be tempted to make it pretty. This way, we get to focus on what really matters—the ingest itself:

```
@app.route('/ingest')
def ingest_next_month():
    try:
        # next month
        bucket = CLOUD_STORAGE_BUCKET
```

```
    year, month = ingest_flights.next_month(bucket)
    logging.info('Ingesting year={} month={}'.format(year, month))

    # ingest
    gcsfile = ingest_flights.ingest(year, month, bucket)

    # return page, and log
    status = 'Successfully ingested {}'.format(gcsfile)
except ingest_flights.DataUnavailable:
    status = 'File for {}-{} not available yet ...'.format(
                    year, month)
logging.info(status)
return status
```

The ingest code simply calls out to our standalone ingest program (the module
`ingest_flights`) for the necessary functionality and returns plain text to display on
the website.

Running on App Engine

To run on App Engine, we will write a configuration file called *app.yaml* that informs
App Engine that we have a Flask application that needs to be invoked whenever
someone visits *http://flights.cloud-training-demos.appspot.com/* (cloud-training-
demos is my Project ID; you can find yours from the Dashboard on *https://
console.cloud.google.com/*):

```
runtime: python
env: flex
entrypoint: gunicorn -b :$PORT ingestapp:app
service: flights

#[START env]
env_variables:
    CLOUD_STORAGE_BUCKET: cloud-training-demos-ml
#[END env]

handlers:
- url: /.*
  script: ingestapp.app
```

When you are trying this out, change the environment variable to reflect the name of
your bucket. You can then deploy this to App Engine by typing on the command line
(in CloudShell):

```
gcloud app deploy
```

This deploys the application to App Engine and makes the URLs available.

In a web browser, visit *flights.<YOUR-PROJECT-ID>.appspot.com* and click the link
to ingest the next available month of data. That's all it takes to make a Python program executable via a web link! Realize that the Python program will be autoscaled if

---

necessary and we have no infrastructure to manage. The Dashboard on *console.cloud.google.com* will show you the number of requests and the resource usage of your App Engine services.

Securing the URL

There is one tiny problem, though. Our configuration is not secure—anyone can visit this website and cause your bucket to be updated. Even though updating the bucket is not harmful per se, repeated invocation of the link can cause you to run up networking and computing bills. We need to add a layer of security through authentication or authorization. Fortunately, though, we don't plan on the ingest link being invoked manually—it is going to be invoked from the App Engine Cron service—and limiting access to our ingest task to only the Cron service is much simpler.

The Cron service adds a custom header to the HTTP request that it makes. App Engine will strip off such a header if it is received by an outside party. So, we can add a check to our */ingest* handler:

```
    try:
        # verify that this is a cron job request
        is_cron = flask.request.headers['X-Appengine-Cron']
        logging.info('Received cron request {}'.format(is_cron))

        # as before
    except KeyError as e:
        logging.info('Rejected non-Cron request')
```

Python throws a KeyError if X-Appengine-Cron is not present in the request headers. If that exception is thrown, we reject the request.

An additional consideration is that we don't really need more than one instance of our application, because the only client is the Cron service. We can specify this in *app.yaml*:

```
    manual_scaling:
      instances: 1
```

Scheduling a Cron Task

Now that we have a URL that when invoked from Cron will launch a monthly ingest task, we can schedule the Cron service to visit the page periodically. To do that, we will create a file called *cron.yaml* and specify the periodicity:

```
    cron:
    - description : ingest monthly flight data
      url : /ingest
      schedule: 8 of month 10:00
      timezone: US/Eastern
      target: flights
```

This specifies that on the 8th of every month at 10:00 Eastern Time in the US, the flight service should be invoked with the URL *ingest*; that is, the Cron service will visit *flights.<YOUR-PROJECT-ID>.appspot.com* every month. Besides calendar-based repetition such as the one we are using, you can also specify periodicity ("every 5 minutes"[25] or "every day at 10:00"). The default time zone is UTC. If we have multiple tasks to schedule, we will have multiple sections in the `cron` specification, each with its own `description`, `url`, `schedule`, and `target`.

By default, App Engine will keep trying until the request succeeds, but gradually back off the time between retries to about once an hour. You can explicitly specify repetition criteria for fault tolerance:

```
retry_parameters:
    min_backoff_seconds: 600
    max_backoff_seconds: 3600
    max_doublings: 20
```

The preceding parameters would make the first retry happen after 10 minutes, the second 20 minutes after that, the third 40 minutes after the second. The fourth and subsequent retries happen an hour apart indefinitely. We can use the `max_doublings` parameter to limit the exponential backoff. For example, if we had specified it as 0, the retry intervals would increase linearly—10, 20, 30, and so on. If we specify it as 2, the first two interval changes would be doublings, and all subsequent interval changes would be linear (10, 20, 40, 80, 120, …). You can also fail the task permanently if it fails a certain number of times within a defined time period:

```
retry_parameters:
    task_retry_limit: 7
    task_age_limit: 1d
```

Both limits must be passed for the task to fail.

You can upload a new *cron.yaml* file or replace an existing one by using `gcloud` (you can do this without stopping the service):

```
gcloud app deploy cron.yaml
```

More often, you'll update an application that contains both an *app.yaml* and a *cron.yaml* file:

```
gcloud app deploy --quiet app.yaml cron.yaml
```

The `--quiet` option instructs `gcloud` to not make us confirm the deploy. The `gcloud app` command also allows you to view the logs from your application:

```
gcloud app logs read -s flights
```

---

25 Assuming that you are not reading this on the 8th of the month, specify "every 5 minutes" in your *cron.yaml* file so that you can verify that things are working as intended.

In this example, `flights` is the name of your service. Existing cron jobs are shown in the "Task Queues" section of the App Engine Cloud Platform Console (*https://console.cloud.google.com/appengine/*). From that section, you can view the last time it was run, see its status, and execute the task on an ad hoc basis.

The monthly update mechanism works if you have the previous month's data on Cloud Storage. If you start out with only 2015 data, updating it monthly means that you will inevitably be many months behind. So, you will need to run it ad hoc until your data is up to date and then let the Cron service take care of things after that. Alternately, you can take advantage of the fact that the ingest task is cheap and nonintrusive when there is no new data. Because the lack of new data is not a failure of the task (no exception is thrown), such requests will not be retried. So, you can change the schedule to be every day instead of every month. A better solution is to change the ingest task so that if it is successful in ingesting a new month of data, it immediately tries to ingest the next month. This way, your program will crawl month-by-month to the latest available month and then keep itself always up-to-date.

At this point, it is worth reflecting a bit on what we have accomplished. We are able to ingest data and keep it up-to-date by doing just these steps:

1. Write some Python code.
2. Deploy that Python code to the Google Cloud Platform.

We did not need to manage any infrastructure in order to do this. We didn't install any OS, manage accounts on those machines, keep them up to date with security patches, maintain failover systems, and so on—a serverless solution that consists simply of deploying code to the cloud is incredibly liberating. Not only is our ingest convenient, it is also very inexpensive. As of this writing, network ingest into Google Cloud is free. Compute in the Flex environment costs about 6¢/hour and we'll use no more than 10 minutes a month, so that's less than a penny. Storage in a single-region bucket costs about 1¢/GB/month and that accumulates over time. Assuming that we work up to a storage of about 5 GB for this dataset, our total cost is perhaps 6¢/month —your actual costs will vary, of course, and could be higher or lower.

Summary

The US BTS collects, and makes publicly available, a dataset of flight information. It includes nearly a hundred fields, including scheduled and actual departure and arrival times, origin and destination airports, and flight numbers of every domestic flight scheduled by every major carrier. We will use this dataset to estimate the likelihood of an arrival delay of more than 15 minutes of the specific flight whose outcome needs to be known in order for us to decide whether to cancel the meeting.

To choose the variables in the dataset that we can use in our prediction problem, we need to consider whether the variable is related to the problem at hand and whether it will violate causality constraints or incur a training–serving skew. Based on these considerations, we selected 27 fields to download.

There are three possible data processing architectures on the cloud for large datasets: scaling up, scaling out, and data in situ. Scaling up is very efficient, but is limited by the size of the largest machine you can get a hold of. Scaling out is very popular but requires that you preshard your data by splitting it among compute nodes, which leads to maintaining expensive clusters unless you can hit sustained high utilization. Keeping data in situ is possible only if your datacenter supports petabits per second of bisectional bandwidth so that any file can be moved to any compute node in the datacenter on demand. Because Google Cloud Platform has this capability, we will upload our data to Google Cloud Storage, a blob storage that is not presharded.

To automate the ingest of the files, we reverse engineered the BTS's web form and obtained the format of the POST request that we need to make. With that request in hand, we were able to write a Bash script to pull down 12 months of data, uncompress the ZIP file, and carry out some minor cleanup.

We discussed the difference between strong consistency and eventual consistency and how to make the appropriate trade-off imposed by Brewer's CAP theorem. In this case, we wanted strong consistency and do not need global availability. Hence, we chose to use a single-region bucket. We then uploaded the downloaded, unzipped, and cleaned CSV files to Google Cloud Storage.

To schedule monthly downloads of the BTS dataset, we made our download and cleanup Python program and made it callable from a web service using Flask. We were able to wrap the Flask web application into App Engine Flex so that it was completely serverless. Finally, we scheduled the Cron service to periodically request the Flask web application to download BTS data, unzip it, clean it up, and upload it to Cloud Storage.

Code Break

This is the point at which you should put this book off to the side and attempt to repeat all the things I've talked about. If you haven't already done so, follow the directions at the end of Chapter 1 to create a project, set up a bucket, and `git clone` the book's code repository. Then, step through the expository commands in this chapter. All the code snippets in this book have corresponding code in the GitHub repository.

I strongly encourage you to play around with the code in *02_ingest* with the goal of understanding why it is organized that way and being able to write similar code yourself. At minimum, though, you should do the following:

1. Go to the *02_ingest* folder of the repository.

2. Change the BUCKET variable in *upload.sh*.

3. Run `./ingest_2015.sh`.

4. Run `monthlyupdate/ingest_flights.py`, specifying your bucket name, a year of 2016, and a month of 01. Type **`monthlyupdate/ingest_flights.py --help`** to get usage help.

This will initialize your bucket with the input files corresponding to 2015 and January 2016. You need these files to carry out the steps that come later in this book.

To try out the Cron service (this is optional), do the following:

1. Go to the *02_ingest/monthlyupdate* folder in the repo.

2. Initialize a default App Engine application in your project by running `./init_appengine.sh`.

3. Open the file *app.yaml* and change the CLOUD_STORAGE_BUCKET to reflect the name of your bucket.

4. Run `./deploy.sh` to deploy the Cron service app. This will take 5 to 10 minutes.

5. Visit the Google Cloud Platform web console and navigate to the App Engine section. You should see two services: one the default (which is just a Hello World application) and the other is the flights service.

6. Click the flights service, follow the link to ingest the data, and you'll find that your access is forbidden—the ingest capability is available only to the Cron service (or from the Google Cloud Platform web console by clicking the "Run now" button in the task queues section of App Engine). If you click "Run now," a few minutes later, you'll see the next month's data show up in the storage bucket.

7. Stop the flights application—you won't need it any further.

8. Because software changes, an up-to-date list of the preceding steps is available in the course repository in *02_ingest/README.md*. This is true for all the following chapters.

## CHAPTER 3

Creating Compelling Dashboards

In Chapter 2, we ingested On-time Performance Data from the US Bureau of Transportation Statistics (BTS) so as to be able to model the arrival delay given various attributes of an airline flight—the purpose of the analysis is to cancel a meeting if the likelihood of the flight arriving within 15 minutes of the scheduled arrival time is less than 70%.

Before we delve into building statistical and machine learning models, it is important to explore the dataset and gain an intuitive understanding of the data—this is called *exploratory data analysis*, and it's covered in more detail in Chapter 5. You should always carry out exploratory data analysis for any dataset that will be used as the basis for decision making. In this chapter, though, I talk about a different aspect of depicting data—of depicting data to end users and decision makers so that they can understand the recommendation that you are making. The audience of these visual representations, called *dashboards*, that we talk about in this chapter are not other data scientists, but are instead the end users. Keep the audience in mind as we go through this chapter, especially if you come from a data science background—the purpose of a dashboard is to explain an existing model, not to develop it. A dashboard is an end-user report that is interactive, tailored to end users, and continually refreshed with new data. See Table 3-1.

Table 3-1. A dashboard is different from exploratory data analysis

Aspect	Dashboard	Exploratory data analysis
Audience	End users, decision makers	Data scientists
Kinds of depictions	Current status, pie charts, trendlines	Model fits with error bars, kernel density estimates
What does it explain?	Model recommendations and confidence	Input data, feature importance, model performance, etc.
Data represented	Subset of dataset, tailored to user's context	Aggregate of historical data

Aspect	Dashboard	Exploratory data analysis
Typical tools	Data Studio, Tableau, Qlik, Looker, etc.	Cloud Datalab, Jupyter, matplotlib, seaborn, R, S-plus, Matlab, etc.
Mode of interaction	GUI-driven	Code-driven
Update	Real time	Not real time
Covered in	Chapter 3, Chapter 4	Chapter 5
Example		

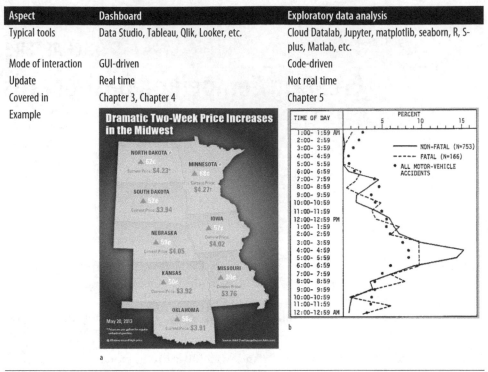

ᵃ From AAA fuel-gauge report (*http://newsroom.aaa.com/2013/05/gas-prices-aaas-fuel-gauge-report-may-20-2013/*)
ᵇ From AAA safety and educational foundation (*http://www.truewheelers.org/research/studies/aaa/04desc.htm*)

Very often, this step of creating end-user visual depictions goes by the anodyne name of "visualization," as in visualizing data. However, I have purposefully chosen not to call it by that name, because there is more to this than throwing together a few bar graphs and charts. Dashboards are highly visual, interactive reports that have been designed to depict data and explain models.

Explain Your Model with Dashboards

The purpose of this step in the modeling process is not simply to depict the data, but to improve your users' understanding of why the model is the way it is. Whenever you are designing the display of a dataset, evaluate the design in terms of three aspects:

- Does it accurately and honestly depict the data? This is important when the raw data itself can be a basis for decision making.

- How well does it help envision not just the raw data, but the information content embodied in the data? This is crucial for the cases when you are relying on human pattern recognition and interaction to help reveal insights about the environment in which the data was collected.

- Is it constructed in such a way that it explains the model being used to provide recommendations?

What you want to do is to build displays that are always accurate and honest. At the same time, they need to be interactive so as to give viewers the ability to gain insights. Insights that users have gained should be part of the display of that information going forward in such a way that those insights can be used to explain the data.

The last point, that of explanatory power, is very important. The idea is to disseminate data understanding throughout your company. A statistical or machine learning model that you build for your users will be considered a black box, and while you might get feedback on when it works well and when it doesn't, you will rarely get pointed suggestions on how to actually improve that model in the field. In many cases, your users will use your model at a much more fine-grained level than you ever will, because they will use your model to make a single decision, whereas in both training and evaluation, you would have been looking at model performance as a whole.

Although this holistic overview is useful for statistical rigor, you need people taking a close look at individual cases, too. Because users are making decisions one at a time, they are analyzing the data one scenario at a time. If you provide your users not just with your recommendation, but with an explanation of why you are recommending it, they will begin to develop insights into your model. However, your users will be able to develop such insights into the problem and your recommendations only if you give them ways to observe the data that went into your model. Give enough users ways to view and interact with your data, and you will have unleashed a never-ending wave of innovation.

Your users have other activities that require their attention. Why would they spend their time looking at the raw data? One of the ways to entice them to do that is by making the depiction of the information compelling. In my experience,[1] the most compelling displays are displays of real-time information in context. You can show

---

1 When I worked on developing machine learning algorithms for weather prediction, nearly every one of the suggestions and feature requests that I received emanated when the person in question was looking at the real-time radar feed. There would be a storm, my colleague would watch it go up on radar, observe that the tracking of the storm was patchy, and let me know what aspect of the storm made it difficult to track. Or, someone would wake up, look at the radar image, and discover that birds leaving to forage from their roost had been wrongly tagged a mesocyclone. It was all about the real-time data. No matter how many times I asked, I never ever got anyone to look at how the algorithms performed on historical data. It was also often about Oklahoma (where our office was) because that's what my colleagues would concentrate on. Forecasters from around the country would derisively refer to algorithms that had been hypertuned to Oklahoma supercells.

people the average airline delay at JFK on January 12, 2012, and no one will care. But show a traveler in Chicago the average airline delay at *ORD*, *right now* and you will have their interest—the difference is that the data is in context (O'Hare Airport, or ORD, for a traveler in Chicago) and that it is real time.

In this chapter, therefore, we will look at building dashboards that combine accurate depictions with explanatory power and interactivity in a compelling package. This seems to be a strange time to be talking about building dashboards—shouldn't the building of a dashboard wait until after we have built the best possible predictive model?

Why Build a Dashboard First?

Building a dashboard when building a machine learning model is akin to building a form or survey tool to help you build the machine learning model. To build powerful machine learning models, you need to understand the dataset and devise features that help with prediction. By building a dashboard, you get to rope in the eventual users of the predictive model to take a close look at your data. Their fine-grained look at the data (remember that everyone is looking at the data corresponding to their context) will complement your more overarching look at it. As they look at the data and keep sending suggestions and insights about the data to your team, you will be able to incorporate them into the machine learning model that you actually build.

In addition, when presented with a dataset, you should be careful that the data is the way you imagine it to be. There is no substitute for exploring the data to ensure that. Doing such exploratory data analysis with an immediately attainable milestone—building a dashboard from your dataset—is a fine way to do something real with the data and develop awareness of the subtleties of your data. Just as you often understand a concept best when you explain it to someone, building an explanatory display for your data is one of the best ways to develop your understanding of a dataset. The fact that you have to visualize the data in order to do basic preprocessing such as outlier detection makes it clear that building visual representations is work you will be doing anyway. If you are going to be doing it, you might as well do it well, with an eye toward its eventual use in production.

Eventual use in production is the third reason why you should develop the dashboard first instead of leaving it as an afterthought. Building explanatory power should be constantly on your mind as you develop the machine learning model. Giving users just the machine learning model will often go down poorly—they have no insight into why the system is recommending whatever it does. Adding explanations to the recommendations will help assuage their initial reluctance. For example, if you accompany your model prediction with five of the most salient features presented in an explanatory way, it will help make the final score the system assigns more believable and trustworthy.

Even for cases for which the system performs poorly, you will receive feedback along the lines of "the prediction was wrong, but it is because Feature #3 was fishy. I think maybe you should also look at Factor Y." In other words, shipping your machine learning model along with an explanation of its behavior gets you more satisfied users, and users whose criticism will be a lot more constructive. It can be tempting to ship the machine learning model as soon as it is ready, but if there is a dashboard already available (because you were building it in parallel), it is easier to counsel that product designers consider the machine learning model and its explanatory dashboard as the complete product.

Where should these dashboards be implemented? Find out the environment that gets the largest audience of experts and eventual users and build your dashboard to target that environment.

Your users might already have a visualization interface with which they are familiar. Especially when it comes to real-time data, your users might spend their entire workday facing a visualization program that is targeted toward power users—this is true of weather forecasts, air traffic controllers, and options traders. If that is the case, look for ways to embed your visualizations into that interface. In other cases, your users might prefer that your visualizations be available from the convenience of their web browser. If this is the case, look for a visualization tool that lets you share the report as an interactive, commentable document (not just a static web page). In many cases, you might have to build multiple dashboards for different sets of users (don't shoehorn everything into the same dashboard).

Accuracy, Honesty, and Good Design

Because the explanatory power of a good dashboard is why we are building visualizations, it is important to ensure that our explanations are not misleading. In this regard, it is best not to do anything too surprising. Although modern-day visualization programs are chock-full of types of graphs and palettes, it is best to pair any graphic with the idiom for which it is appropriate. For example, some types of graphics are better suited to relational data than others, and some graphics are better suited to categorical data than to numerical data.

Broadly, there are four fundamental types of graphics: relational (illustrating the relationship between pairs of variables), time–series (illustrating the change of a variable over time), geographical maps (illustrating the variation of a variable by location), and narratives (to support an argument). Narrative graphics are the ones in magazine spreads, which win major design awards. The other three are more worker-like.

You have likely seen enough graphical representations to realize intuitively that the graph is somehow wrong when you violate an accuracy, honesty, or aesthetic principle,[2] but this section of the book lists a few of the canonical ones. For example, it is advisable to choose line graphs or scatter plots for relational graphics, and to ensure that autoscaling of the axes doesn't portray a misleading story about your data. A good design principle is that your time–series graphs should be more horizontal than vertical, and that it is the data lines and not the graph's accoutrements (grid lines, labels, etc.) that ought to dominate your graphics. Maximizing the ratio of data to space and ink is a principle that will stand you in good stead when it comes to geographical data—ensure that the domain is clipped to the region of interest, and go easy on place names and other text labels.

Just as you probably learned to write well by reading good writers, one of the best ways to develop a feel for accurate and compelling graphics is to increase your exposure to good exemplars. The *Economist* newspaper[3] has a Graphic Detail blog (*http://www.economist.com/blogs/graphicdetail/*) that is worth following—they publish a chart, map, or infographic every weekday, and these run the gamut of the fundamental graphics types. Figure 3-1 shows the latest graphic from the blog as I was writing this section of the book.[4]

The graphic depicts the increase in the number of coauthors on scientific papers over the past two decades. The graphic itself illustrates several principles of good design. It is a time–series, and as you'd expect of this type of graphic, the time is on the x-axis and the time-varying quantity (number of authors per article or the number of articles per author) is on the y-axis. The y-axis values start out at zero, so that the height of the graphs is an accurate indicator of magnitude. Note how minimal the chart junk is—the axes labels and gridlines are very subtle and the title doesn't draw attention to itself. The data lines, on the other hand, are what pop out. Note also the effective use of repetition—instead of all the different disciplines (Economics, Engineering, etc.) being on the same graph, each discipline is displayed on its own panel. This serves to reduce clutter and makes the graphs easy to interpret. Each panel has two graphs, one for authors per article and the other for articles per author. The colors remain consistent across the panels for easy comparison, and the placement of the panels also encourages such comparisons. We see, for example, that the increase in number of authors per article is not accompanied by an increase in articles per author in any of the disciplines, except for Physics & Astronomy. Perhaps the physicists and astronomers are gaming the system?

2 If you are not familiar with design principles, I recommend *The Visual Display of Quantitative Information* (*https://www.edwardtufte.com/tufte/books_vdqi*) by Edward Tufte.

3 The *Economist* is published weekly as an 80-page booklet stapled in the center, and each page is about the size of a letter paper. However, for historical reasons, the company refers to itself as a newspaper rather than a magazine.

4 *http://www.economist.com/blogs/graphicdetail/2016/11/daily-chart-18*, published on Nov. 25, 2016.

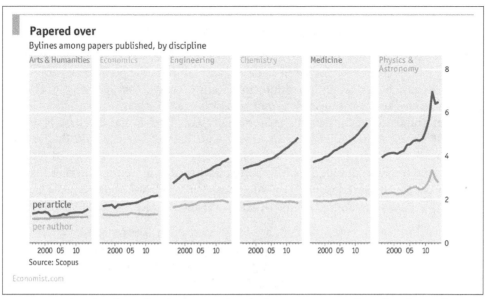

Figure 3-1. Graphic from the Economist showing increase in number of authors of papers in various academic disciplines over time

The graphic does, however, subtly mislead viewers who are in a hurry. Take a moment and try to critique the graphic—figure out how a viewer might have been misled. It has to do with the arrangement of the panels. It appears that the creator of the graphic has arranged the panels to provide a pleasing upward trend between the panels, but this upward trend is misleading because there is no relationship between the number of authors per article in Economics in 2016 and the same quantity in Engineering in 1996. This misdirection is concerning because the graph is supposed to support the narrative of an increasing number of authors, but the increase is not from one author to six authors over two decades—the actual increase is much less dramatic (for example, from four to six in medicine). However, a viewer who only glances at the data might wrongly believe that the increase in number of authors is depicted by the whole graph, and is therefore much more than it really is.

Loading Data into Google Cloud SQL

To create dashboards to allow interactive analysis of the data, we will need to store the data in a manner that permits fast random access and aggregations. Because our flights data is tabular, SQL is a natural choice, and if we are going to be using SQL, we should consider whether a relational database meets our needs. Relational databases are a mature technology and remain the tool of choice for many business problems. Relational database technology is well known and comes with a rich ecosystem of interoperable tools. The problem of standardized access to relational databases from high-level programming languages is pretty much solved.

Relational databases are particularly well suited to smallish datasets on which we wish to do ad hoc queries. Even for larger datasets, you can tune the performance of a relational database by indexing the columns of interest. Further, because relational databases typically support transactions and guarantee strong consistency, they are an excellent choice for data that will be updated often. A relational database is a poor choice if your data is primarily read-only, if your dataset sizes go into the terabyte range, or if your data streams in at high rates—in such cases, a more targeted solution might be preferable. Although we will spend considerably more time on these aspects in later chapters, don't lose sight of the idea that a relational database is a great general-purpose solution for fast and distributed random access to data.

MySQL (*https://www.mysql.com/*) is a widely used open source relational database whose use cases run the gamut from embedded applications that require a small code base and high-volume websites that require high query performance, all the way to transaction processing systems that require high speeds, row-level locking, and data integrity. In addition to its high performance, MySQL is easy to program against—it supports ANSI-SQL, client libraries in a variety of programming languages, and standard connector technologies such as Open Database Connectivity (ODBC) and Java Database Connectivity (JDBC). Because of these factors, MySQL is a popular choice of relational database.

Create a Google Cloud SQL Instance

Google Cloud SQL offers a managed MySQL service (*https://cloud.google.com/sql/*). Cloud SQL manages backups, patches, updates, and even replication while providing for global availability, automatic failover, and high uptime. For best performance, choose a machine whose RAM is large enough to hold your largest table in memory —as of this writing, available machine types range from a single CPU with less than 4 GB of memory all the way to a 16 CPU machine with more than 100 GB of memory. Balance this desire for speed with the monthly cost of a machine, of course.

Let's configure a Cloud SQL instance, create a database table in it, and load the table with the data we ingested into Cloud Storage. You can do all these things on the command line using gcloud, but let's begin by using the Cloud Platform Console at *https://console.cloud.google.com/*. On the left side of the window that opens, scroll to and click the SQL button, and then, in the pane on the right, click Create Instance, as depicted in Figure 3-2.

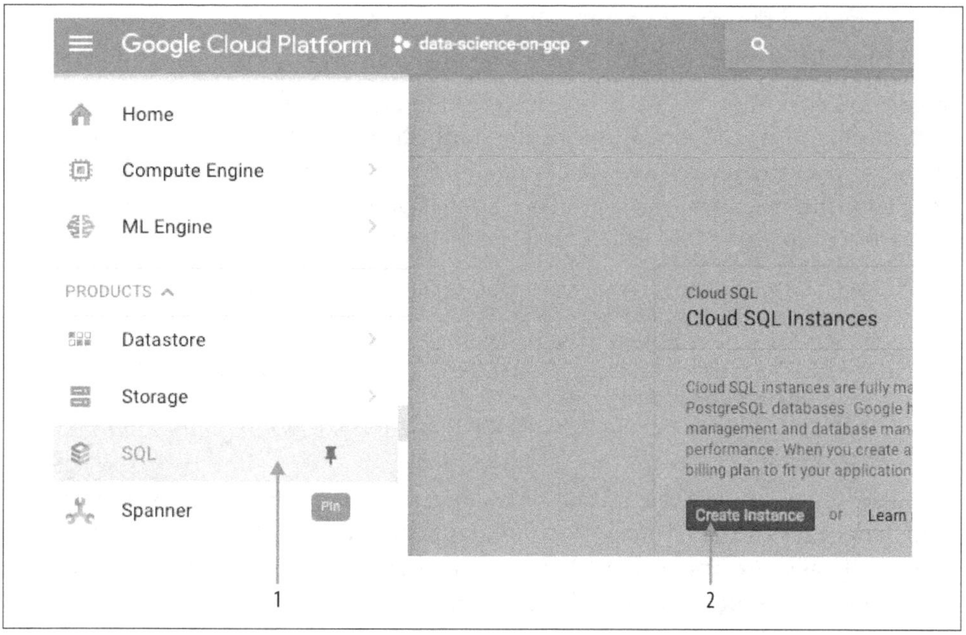

Figure 3-2. Creating a Cloud SQL instance from the Google Cloud Platform web console

If prompted, choose the second-generation instance; you should be in a dialog box that asks you for parameters to create an instance. For the Instance ID, type **flights**, change the region if necessary, accept all other defaults, and then click Create.

Interacting with Google Cloud Platform

Instead of filling out the dialog box by hand, we could have used the command-line tool gcloud from CloudShell (or any other machine that has gcloud installed); here's how to do that:

```
gcloud sql instances create flights \
    --tier=db-n1-standard-1 --activation-policy=ALWAYS
```

In the rest of the book, I will show you just the gcloud commands, but you don't need to memorize them. You can use --help at any time on gcloud to get a list of options. For example,

```
gcloud sql instances create --help
```

will give you all the options available to create Cloud SQL instances (the tier of machine, its region, its zone, etc.), whereas

```
gcloud sql instances --help
```

will give you all the ways in which you can work with Cloud SQL instances (`create`, `delete`, `restart`, `export`, etc.).

In general, everything you can do on the command line is doable using the Cloud Platform Console, and vice versa. In fact, both the Cloud Platform Console and the `gcloud` command invoke REST API actions. You can invoke the same REST APIs from your programs (the APIs are documented on the Google Cloud Platform website). Here is the REST API call to create an instance from Bash:

```
ACCESS_TOKEN="$(gcloud auth application-default print-access-token)"
curl --header "Authorization: Bearer ${ACCESS_TOKEN}" \
    --header 'Content-Type: application/json' \
    --data '{"name":"flights", "settings": {"tier":"db-n1-standard-1", "activa \
    tionPolicy":"ALWAYS"}}' \
    https://www.googleapis.com/sql/v1beta4/projects/[PROJECT-ID]/instances \
    -X POST
```

Alternately, you can use the `gcloud` client library (available for a variety of programming languages (*https://cloud.google.com/apis/docs/cloud-client-libraries*)) to issue the REST API calls. We saw this in Chapter 2 when we used the `google.cloud.storage` Python package to interact with Cloud Storage.

In summary, there are four ways to interact with Google Cloud Platform:

- The Cloud Platform Console
- `gcloud` command from the command line in CloudShell or a machine that has the `gcloud` SDK installed
- Directly invoke the REST API
- Google Cloud Client library (available as of this writing for Go, Java, Node.js, Python, Ruby, PHP, and C#)

In this book, I use primarily option 2 (from the shell) and option 4 (from Python programs).

Controlling Access to MySQL

You do not want to leave MySQL with its default password, so the first thing to do after creating the instance is to set its root password. If you are on a single-user machine, use the `gcloud` command to set the password from the command line:

```
gcloud sql instances set-root-password flights --password <PASSWD>
```

If you are on a multiuser machine, specifying the password in plain text on the command line as just shown is not secure. Anyone who is able to look at a history of processes or running jobs will be able to see the password. You can create a password file and pass it into the `gcloud` command (this takes advantage of Unix security to ensure that your password file is not readable by anyone else), but a simpler approach would be to set the password from the Cloud Platform Console. Navigate to your Cloud SQL instance on the website, and then, on the "Instance details" page, click the Access Control tab. Next, click the Users subtab. There. You can change the root password, as demonstrated in Figure 3-3.

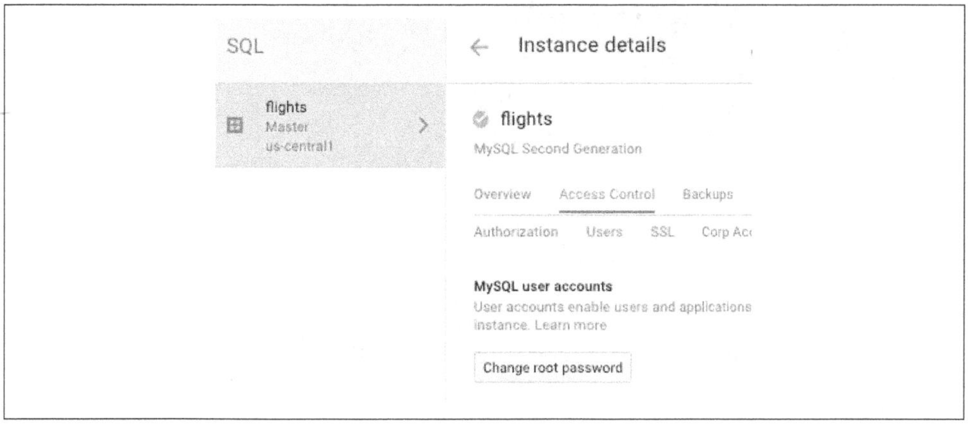

Figure 3-3. The Access Control section of the Cloud SQL configuration page

Whenever you need to connect to a MySQL database, you will need to authorize the machine that you will be connecting from—MySQL rejects mysql, JDBC, and other connections from anywhere other than authorized hosts. So, authorize CloudShell by patching the list of authorized networks:

```
gcloud sql instances patch flights \
    --authorized-networks $(wget -qO - http://ipecho.net/plain)
```

The wget sends a request to an internet website (ipecho.net) that returns the IP address of the caller.[5] This is the IP address that MySQL will also see when we talk to it. Because CloudShell is an ephemeral VM, you might need to repeat this step if your CloudShell VM is recycled.

Create Tables

To create a table, write a *.sql* file[6] containing the schema of that table's columns:

---

5 Public IP addresses are like a party where people walk around with a picture stuck to their foreheads. They don't know what picture they have on their forehead—they need to ask someone who will then tell them. To find out the IP address of CloudShell, we need to make an internet request and find out what IP address is seen by the website to which we're talking.

6 This snippet appears in *03_sqlstudio/create_table.sql* in the GitHub repository for this book. All the snippets of code that appear in this chapter are in the *03_sqlstudio* directory.

```
create database if not exists bts;
use bts;
drop table if exists flights;
create table flights (
  FL_DATE date,
  UNIQUE_CARRIER varchar(16),
  AIRLINE_ID varchar(16),
  CARRIER varchar(16),
  FL_NUM integer,
  ORIGIN_AIRPORT_ID varchar(16),
  ORIGIN_SEQ_ID varchar(16),
  ORIGIN_CITY_MARKET_ID varchar(16),
  ORIGIN varchar(16),
  DEST_AIRPORT_ID varchar(16),
  DEST_AIRPORT_SEQ_ID varchar(16),
  DEST_CITY_MARKET_ID varchar(16),
  DEST varchar(16),
  CRS_DEP_TIME integer,
  DEP_TIME integer,
  DEP_DELAY float,
  TAXI_OUT float,
  WHEELS_OFF integer,
  WHEELS_ON integer,
  TAXI_IN float,
  CRS_ARR_TIME integer,
  ARR_TIME integer,
  ARR_DELAY float,
  CANCELLED float,
  CANCELLATION_CODE varchar(16),
  DIVERTED float,
  DISTANCE float,
  INDEX (FL_DATE), INDEX (ORIGIN_AIRPORT_ID),
  INDEX(ARR_DELAY), INDEX(DEP_TIME), INDEX(DEP_DELAY)
);
```

In the last few lines of the CREATE TABLE command, notice that I create four indexes on columns against which I expect to filter quite often. Indexes increase the write time and the storage, but can greatly speed up SELECT queries that involve these columns.

You can import a *.sql* file into the MySQL database using the command-line tool mysql that comes with MySQL. This command-line tool is already present in Cloud-Shell, but you might need to download and install it if you are working elsewhere. Alternatively, of course, use the import button on the Cloud Platform Console and point at the file (you will need to upload it to Cloud Storage first).

You inform mysql as to which MySQL machine you want to connect to by specifying the IP address of that MySQL instance. We have a name (flights), but not an IP address. Find it using gcloud as follows:

```
gcloud sql instances describe \
    flights --format="value(ipAddresses.ipAddress)"
```

The describe command provides a lot of information about the Cloud SQL instance; we use the --format option to print out only the specific value that we are interested in. Leave out the --format option to see the entire JSON output and see whether you can parse some other value from it—it's quite intuitive.

Knowing the IP address of the MySQL host, we can run mysql from CloudShell[7] to import the table definition:

```
MYSQLIP=$(gcloud sql instances describe \
    flights --format="value(ipAddresses.ipAddress)")
mysql --host=$MYSQLIP --user=root \
    --password --verbose < create_table.sql
```

You can verify that the import succeeded using the mysql command-line client:

```
mysql --host=$MYSQLIP --user=root  --password
```

At the prompt, type your password, and at the interactive prompt, type the following:

```
mysql> use bts;
mysql> describe flights;
```

You should see a description of the various columns in the table. The table is empty, which you can verify by typing the following:

```
mysql> select DISTINCT(FL_DATE) from flights;
```

Next, let's import the data from Cloud Storage to populate the table.

Populating Tables

To populate the tables in MySQL, we can use the command-line tool mysqlimport that comes with the MySQL database (and is installed by default on the CloudShell VM). Because mysqlimport cannot read directly from Cloud Storage, we'll need to copy the file to the local directory, and because mysqlimport will use the basename of the comma-separated value (CSV) file to infer the table into which to import, we must rename the copied file to have the base name flights:

```
counter=0
for FILE in 201501.csv 201507.csv; do
   gsutil cp gs://cloud-training-demos-ml/flights/raw/$FILE \
           flights.csv-${counter}
```

---

7 If you haven't authorized CloudShell (or if your CloudShell VM has been refreshed since the time you authorized it), you need to authorize CloudShell by using gcloud sql instances patch flights \ --authorized-networks $(wget -qO - http://ipecho.net/plain).

```
        counter=$((counter+1))
    done
```

I am copying only two files: the one for January 2015 and the one for July 2015. We could import everything, but because we picked a relatively small-sized machine to experiment on, we're probably better off limiting ourselves to about a million rows.

We then can run `mysqlimport` to read these CSV files from the local disk (`--local`), connect to the MySQL host with a username of root (`--user=root`), and ask `mysqlimport` to prompt for the password:

```
mysqlimport --local --host=$MYSQLIP --user=root --password \
    --ignore-lines=1 --fields-terminated-by=',' \
    bts flights.csv-*
```

Our CSV files have a one-line header that should be ignored (`--ignore-lines=1`) and have fields separated by commas. The database to import into is called `bts` and the files to import are given by the wildcard match. The base name of the files (`flights`, in this case) is used to infer the name of the table into which to import.

After importing, we can repeat the query from the previous section:

```
mysql --host=$MYSQLIP --user=root  --password
```

At the prompt, type your password, and at the interactive prompt, type the following:

```
mysql> use bts;
mysql> describe flights;
```

You should see a description of the various columns in the table. Check that the table is no longer empty by typing this:

```
mysql> select DISTINCT(FL_DATE) from flights;
```

Rather instantaneously (this is an indexed column, after all), you should get back a set of dates in two months. The dataset is small enough, though, that retrieving a nonindexed column also performs quite well:

```
mysql> select DISTINCT(CARRIER) from flights;
```

Now that we have our data in a place and can quickly query it, let's build our first model.

Building Our First Model

Intuitively, we feel that if the flight is delayed by 15 minutes, it will also tend to arrive 15 minutes late. So, our model could be that we cancel the meeting if the departure delay of the flight is 15 minutes or more. Of course, there is nothing here about the probability (recall that we wanted to cancel if the probability of an arrival delay of 15 minutes was greater than 30%). Still, it will be a quick start and give us something that we can ship now and iterate upon.

Contingency Table

Suppose that we need to know how often we will be making the right decision if our decision rule is the following:

> If DEP_DELAY ≥ 15, cancel the meeting; otherwise, go ahead.

There are four possibilities called the *contingency table* or the *confusion matrix*, which you can see in Table 3-2.

Table 3-2. Confusion matrix for the decision to cancel the meeting

	Arrival delay < 15 minutes	Arrival delay ≥ 15 minutes
We did not cancel meeting	Correct (true negative)	False negative
We cancel meeting	False positive	Correct (true positive)

If we don't cancel the meeting and it turns out that the flight arrived more than 15 minutes late, it is clear that we made a wrong decision. It is arbitrary whether we refer to it as a false negative (treating the decision to cancel the meeting as a positive event) or as a false positive (treating the decision to cancel the meeting as a negative event). The common approach is to term the rarer event, or the event we are looking for, as the positive. Here, delayed flights are (hopefully) rarer, and we are deciding whether to cancel the meeting. Thus, we term "cancel" the positive decision and "don't cancel" the negative decision.

How do we find out how often the decision rule of thresholding the departure delay at 15 minutes will tend to be correct? We can evaluate the efficacy of the decision rule on the dataset that is stored in Cloud SQL. Essentially, we have to carry out four queries:

```
select count(dest) from flights where arr_delay < 15 and dep_delay < 15;
select count(dest) from flights where arr_delay >= 15 and dep_delay < 15;
select count(dest) from flights where arr_delay < 15 and dep_delay >= 15;
select count(dest) from flights where arr_delay >= 15 and dep_delay >= 15;
```

Filling in the table, based on the query results on the two months of data we have in our database table, we get Table 3-3.

Table 3-3. Confusion matrix on two months of data

	Arrival delay < 15 minutes	Arrival delay ≥ 15 minutes
We did not cancel meeting (`dep_delay < 15`)	747,099 (Correct: true negative)	42,725 (False negative)
We cancel meeting (`dep_delay >= 15`)	40,009 (False positive)	160,853 (Correct: true positive)

Recall that our goal (see Chapter 1) is to cancel the client meeting if the likelihood of arriving 15 minutes early is 70% or less. How close did we get?

Threshold Optimization

When we don't cancel the client meeting (Table 3-3, top row), we arrive early 747,099 out of (747,099 + 42,725) times or about 95%. Meanwhile, when we do cancel the client meeting (bottom row), we arrive late 160,853 out of (160,853 + 40,009) times or about 80% of the time. Overall, we are making the correct decision (747,099 + 160,853) / (747,099 + 42,725 + 40,009 + 160,853) or 91.6% of the time. There seems to be a lot of daylight between these numbers and our target of 70%. Our decision certainly appears suboptimal. But suboptimal in what direction? Are we canceling too many meetings, or too few? Think about it a bit, and see if your reasoning matches what happens when we change the departure delay threshold to 10 minutes and to 20 minutes.

First, let's try to lower the decision threshold on departure delay to 10 minutes and repeat the analysis. Obviously, we don't want to type in all the queries again, so let's script it, changing the queries to look like this:

```
select count(dest) from flights where
arr_delay < ARR_DELAY_THRESH and dep_delay < DEP_DELAY_THRESH;
```

We then put them into a file, replacing the values before we call `mysql` (Table 3-4 shows the results):

```
cat contingency.sql | sed 's/DEP_DELAY_THRESH/10/g' |
sed 's/ARR_DELAY_THRESH/15/g' |
mysql --host=$MYSQLIP --user=root --password --verbose
Running this results in this table:
```

Table 3-4. Confusion matrix for a decision threshold of 10 minutes

	Arrival delay < 15 minutes	Arrival delay ≥ 15 minutes
We did not cancel meeting (dep_delay < 10)	713545 (Correct: true negative)	33823 (False negative)
We cancel meeting (dep_delay >= 10)	73563 (False positive)	169755 (Correct: true positive)

This time we make the correct decision 95% of the time when don't cancel the meeting and 70% of the time when we cancel the meeting. Overall, we are correct 89.2% of the time.

Changing the departure delay threshold to 20 minutes, we get Table 3-5.

Table 3-5. Confusion matrix for a departure delay threshold of 20 minutes

	Arrival delay < 15 minutes	Arrival delay ≥ 15 minutes
We did not cancel meeting (dep_delay < 20)	767041 (Correct: True negative)	53973 (False negative)
We cancel meeting (dep_delay >= 20)	20067 (False positive)	149605 (Correct: True positive)

Now, when we don't cancel, we are correct 93% of the time. When we cancel, we are correct 88% of the time. Overall, we are correct 92.5% of the time. So, it appears that 20 minutes is overall a better threshold than 15. We can try out every possible value of departure delay and pick the one that gives us the maximum overall accuracy.

Is the maximum overall accuracy what we want, though? Recall that we started out by saying that what we want is to make the correct decision to *cancel* 70% of the time. In that case, among 10, 15, and 20, we'd pick a threshold of 10 minutes even though it means canceling the most number of meetings because it provides the precision (TP/(FP+TP)) that is closest to our target.

Machine Learning

What we did here—trying different thresholds—is at the heart of machine learning. Our model is a simple rule that has a single parameter (the departure delay threshold) and we can tune it to maximize some objective measure (here, the desired precision). We can (and will) use more complex models, and we can definitely make our search through the parameter space a lot more systematic, but this process of devising a model and tuning it is the gist of machine learning. We haven't evaluated the model (we can't take the 70% we got on these two months of data and claim that to be our model performance—we need an independent dataset to do that), and that is a key step in machine learning. However, we can plausibly claim that we have built a simple machine learning model to provide guidance on whether to cancel a meeting based on historical flight data.

Building a Dashboard

Even this simple model is enough for us to begin getting feedback from end users. Recall that my gut instinct at the beginning of the previous section was that I needed to use a 15-minute threshold on the departure delay. Analysis of the contingency table, however, indicated that the right threshold to use was 10 minutes. I'm satisfied with this model as a first step, but will our end users be? Let's go about building a dashboard that explains the model recommendations to end users. Doing so will also help clarify what I mean by explaining a model to end users.

There is a large number of business intelligence and visualization tools available, and many of them connect with data sources like BigQuery and Cloud SQL on Google Cloud Platform. In this chapter, we build dashboards using Data Studio, which is part of Google Cloud Platform, but you should be able to do similar things with Tableau, QlikView, Looker, and so on.

For those of you with a data science background, I'd like to set expectations here—a dashboard is a way for end users to quickly come to terms with the current state of a system and is not a full-blown, completely customizable, statistical visualization package. Think about the difference between what's rendered in the dashboard of a car versus what would be rendered in an engineering visualization of the aerodynamics of the car in a wind tunnel—that's the difference between what we will do in Data Studio versus what we will use Cloud Datalab for in later chapters. Here, the emphasis is on providing information effectively to end users—thus, the key aspects are interactivity and collaboration. With Data Studio, you can share reports similarly to GSuite documents; that is, you can give different colleagues viewing or editing rights, and colleagues with whom you have shared a visualization can refresh the charts to view the most current data.

Getting Started with Data Studio

To work with Data Studio, navigate to *http://datastudio.google.com/*. There are two key concepts in Data Studio—reports and data sources. A report is a set of charts and commentary that you create and share with others. The charts in the report are built from data that is retrieved from a data source. The first step, therefore, is to set up a data source. Because our data is in a Cloud SQL database, the data source we need to set up is for Data Studio to connect to Cloud SQL.

On the Data Studio home page, in the pane on the left, click the Data Sources menu item, and then, in the lower right, click the blue plus sign (+), as illustrated in Figure 3-4.[8]

---

8 Graphical user interfaces are often the fastest-changing parts of any software. So, if the user interface has changed from these screenshots by the time this book gets into your hands, please hunt around a bit. There will be some way to add a new data source.

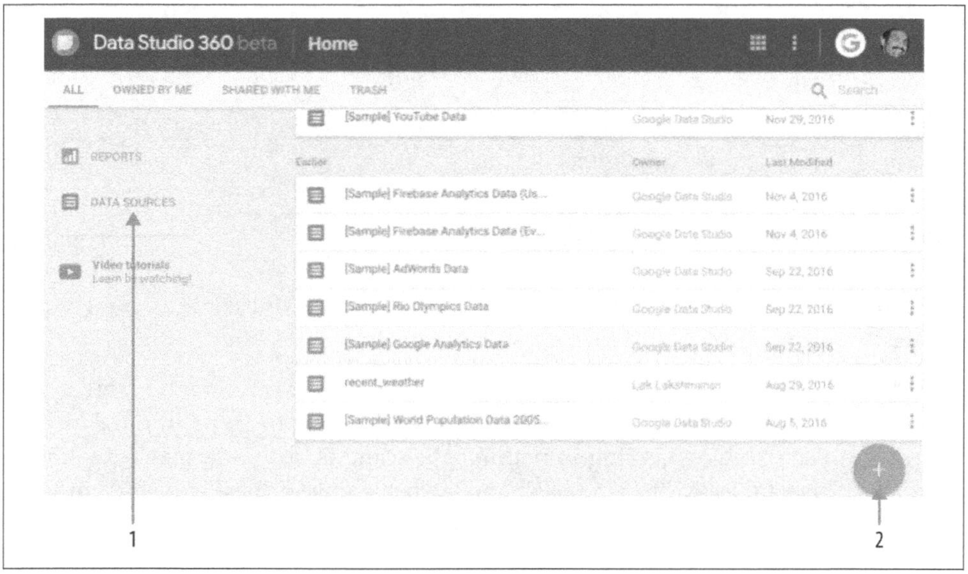

Figure 3-4. Data Sources menu item in Data Studio

This brings up a list of supported types of Data Sources (Figure 3-5). Because our data is in a Cloud SQL database, that's the one we want.

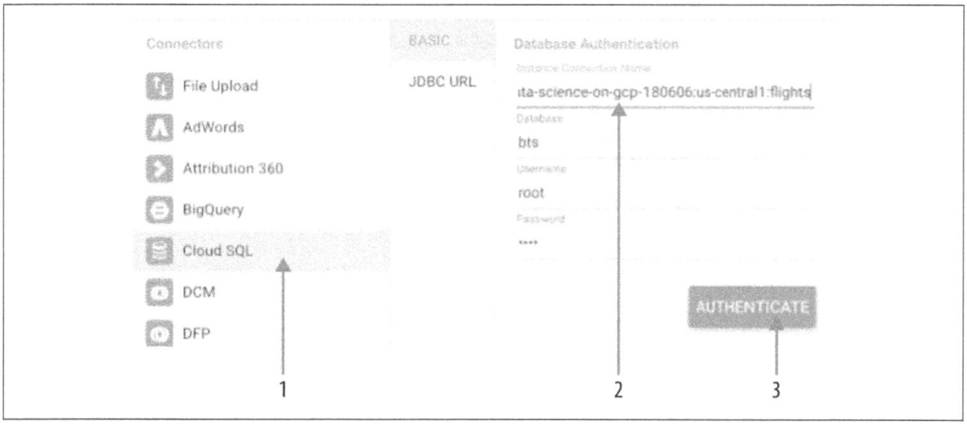

Figure 3-5. Selecting Cloud SQL as the data source for the report

The instance connection name for my Cloud SQL instance will be of the form *project-id*:*region*:flights. You can copy and paste it from the Google Cloud Platform web console in the Cloud SQL section, as shown in Figure 3-6.

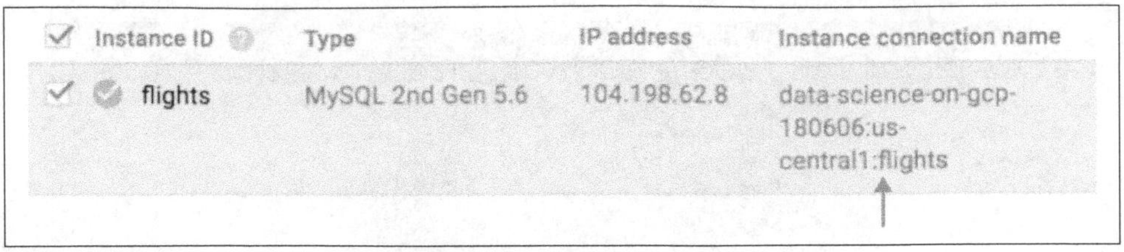

Instance ID	Type	IP address	Instance connection name
flights	MySQL 2nd Gen 5.6	104.198.62.8	data-science-on-gcp-180606:us-central1:flights

Figure 3-6. Setting up the Cloud SQL connection

The name of the database that we set up is "bts." Specify the username as **root**, supply the password you created, and then click Authenticate.

You should see a list of tables in the database. Here, we have only one table, called "flights," so select that and click the Connect button. A list of fields in the table displays, with Data Studio inferring something about the fields based on a sampling of the data in that table. We'll come back and correct some of these, but for now, just click Create Report, accepting all the prompts.

Creating Charts

On the top ribbon, select the scatter chart icon (see Figure 3-7) and draw a rectangle somewhere in the main window; Data Studio will draw a chart. The data that is rendered is pulled from some rather arbitrary columns.

Ignoring the Date Range Dimension for now, there are three columns being used: the Dimension is the quantity being plotted; Metric X is along the x-axis; and Metric Y is along the y-axis. Change Metric X to DEP_DELAY, Metric Y to ARR_DELAY, and Dimension to UNIQUE_CARRIER. Ostensibly, this should give us the average departure delay and arrival delay of different carriers. Click the Style tab and add in a linear trendline and show the data labels. Figure 3-8 depicts the resulting chart.

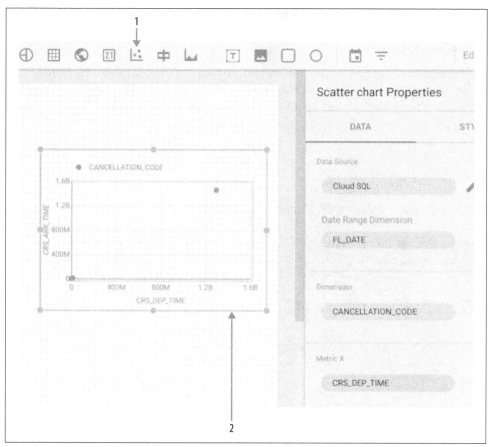

Figure 3-7. Initial chart rendered by Data Studio

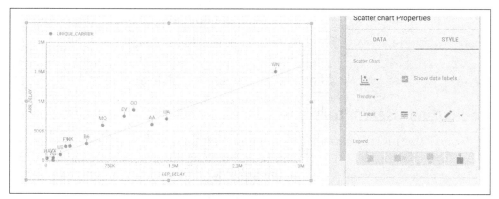

Figure 3-8. Chart after changing metric and dimension

What we have now is the *total* arrival and departure delays for each carrier. That would explain why the x- and y-axes are in millions of minutes. Why did we get the sum of all the delays?

This is because of the automatic inferring of column types of the fields by Data Studio when we added the data source. We can fix it by clicking the X metric again, but selecting Create New Metric.[9] Notice that the aggregates of the two delay fields had defaulted to being Sum, as demonstrated in Figure 3-9.

| 11 | DEP_DELAY | ⋮ | 123 | Number | ▼ | Sum | ▼ |
| 12 | ARR_DELAY | | 123 | Number | ▼ | Sum | ▼ |

Figure 3-9. The two delay fields default to being Sum

Change both of those to Average, then remove and re-add one of the metrics (so that the chart recalculates). We end up with the chart shown in Figure 3-10.

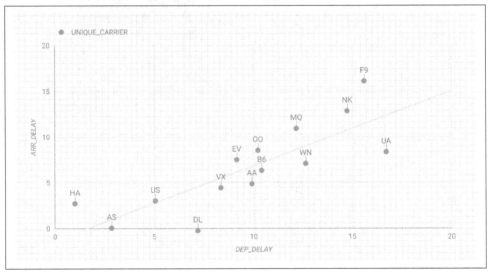

Figure 3-10. Chart after the delay fields are changed from Sum to Average

Adding End-User Controls

So far, our chart is static—there is nothing for end users to interact with. They get to see a pretty picture, but do not get to change anything about our graph. To permit the end user to change something about the graph, we should add *controls* to our graph.

---

9 By the time this book is in print, you might be able to access this by clicking the pencil icon next to the data source, or directly in the property panel.

Let's give our end users the ability to set a date range. On the top icon ribbon, click the "Date range" button, as illustrated in Figure 3-11.

Figure 3-11. The Date Range button on the top icon ribbon

On your chart, draw a rectangle where you'd like the control to appear. You'll see something like that shown in Figure 3-12.

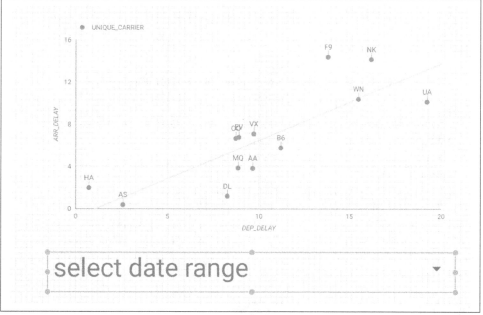

Figure 3-12. The Date Range control

In the upper-right corner, change the toggle to switch to the View mode (Figure 3-13). This is the mode in which users interact with your report.

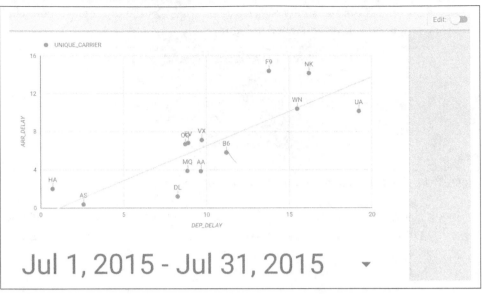

Figure 3-13. Chart with a date range

You should be able to select a date range on the control and see the graphs update (our instructions had you load only two months—January and July of 2015—into the database).

Pause a bit here and ask yourself what kind of a model the chart in Figure 3-13 would explain. Because there is a line, it strongly hints at a linear model. If we were to recommend meeting cancellations based on this chart, we'd be suggesting, based on the linear trend of arrival delay with departure delay, that departure delays of more than 20 minutes lead to arrival delays of more than 15 minutes. That, of course, was not our model—we did not do linear regression, and certainly not airline by airline. Instead, we picked a departure threshold based on a contingency table over the entire dataset. So, we should not use the graph above in our dashboard—it would be a misleading description of our actual model.

Showing Proportions with a Pie Chart

How would you explain our contingency table–based thresholds to end users in a dashboard? Recall that the choice comes down to the proportion of flights that arrive more than 15 minutes after their scheduled time. That is what our dashboard needs to show.

One of the best ways to show a proportion is to use a pie chart.[10] On the top ribbon, click the "pie chart" button, and then, on your report, draw a square where you'd like the pie chart to appear (it is probably best to delete the earlier scatter plot from it). As we did earlier, we need to edit the dimensions and metrics to fit what it is that we want to display. Perhaps things will be clearer if you see what the end product ought to look like. Figure 3-14 gives you a glimpse.

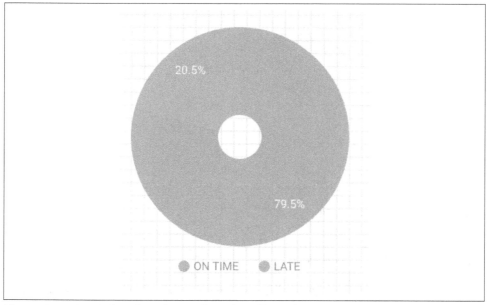

Figure 3-14. Desired end result is a chart that shows the proportion of flights that are late versus on time

In this chart, we are displaying the proportion of flights that arrived late versus those that arrived on time. The labeled field ON TIME versus LATE is the Dimension. The number of flights is the metric that will be apportioned between the labels. So, how do you get these values from the Cloud SQL table?

It is clear that there is no column in the database that indicates the total number of flights. Instead, the total number of flights is an aggregate of all the rows, which you can obtain as the Count of any field in the dataset that doesn't have null values. So, we could use the FL_NUM field as the metric (Figure 3-15), after making sure to change the aggregate from the default Sum to Count.

---

10 An alternative way to show proportions, especially of a time-varying whole, is a stacked column plot. See, for example, *https://developers.google.com/chart/interactive/docs/gallery/columnchart#stacked-column-charts*.

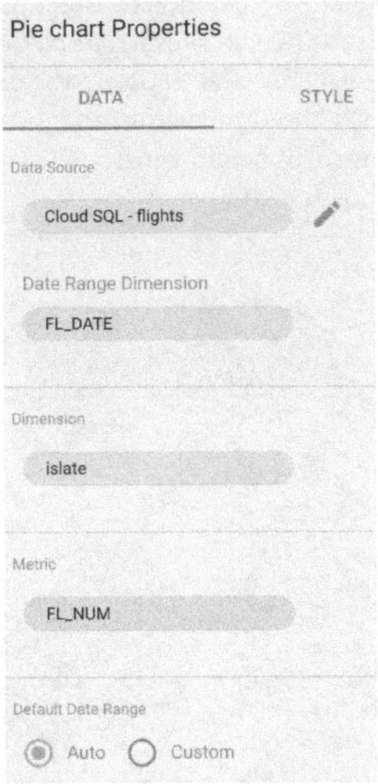

Figure 3-15. Pie chart properties

The "islate" value, though, will have to be computed as a formula. Conceptually, we need to add a new calculated field (*https://support.google.com/360suite/datastudio/answer/7020724*) to the data that looks like this:

```
CASE WHEN
(ARR_DELAY < 15)
THEN
"ON TIME"
ELSE
"LATE"
END
```

Unfortunately, though, we are already using ARR_DELAY as an Average metric. So, we will not be able to get the individual values that will allow this CASE statement to work. So, before we can create a new Dimension with the "islate" field, we must duplicate the ARR_DELAY field (in the table definition, right-click the field, and you'll see an option to duplicate it). Change the aggregation on the duplicated field to None, and then set up the "islate" definition to look like Figure 3-16.

islate		ID calc_SNO852		Formula ⑦ CASE WHEN (ARR_DELAY_copy < 15) THEN "ON TIME" ELSE "LATE" END

Figure 3-16. How to set up the islate definition

The pie chart is now complete and reflects the proportion of flights that are late versus those that are on time. You can switch over to the Style tab if you'd like to change the appearance of the pie chart to be similar to mine.

Because the proportion of flights that end up being delayed is the quantity on which we are trying to make decisions, the pie chart translates quite directly to our use case. However, it doesn't tell the user what the typical delay would be. To do that, let's create a bar chart that looks like the one shown in Figure 3-17 (the All Flights to the side of my bar chart is simply a text label).

Figure 3-17. Typical delay for each carrier

Here, the labeled quantity (or Dimension) is the Carrier. There are two metrics being displayed: the DEP_DELAY and ARR_DELAY, both of which are aggregated to their averages over the dataset. Figure 3-18 shows the specifications.

Note the Sort column at the end—it is important to have a reliable sort order in dashboards so that users become accustomed to finding the information they want in a known place.

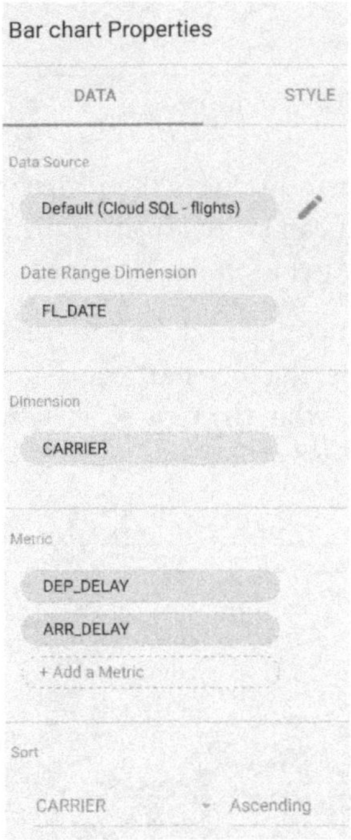

Figure 3-18. How to set the bar chart properties to generate the desired chart

Finally, Data Studio defaults to 10 bars. On the Style tab (Figure 3-19), change this to reflect that we expect to have up to 20 unique carriers.

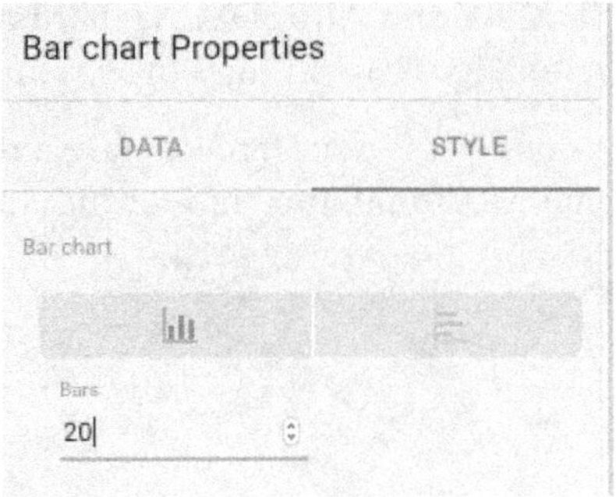

Figure 3-19. Change the default number of carriers from 10 to 20

Of course, we can now add in a date control, as demonstrated in Figure 3-20.

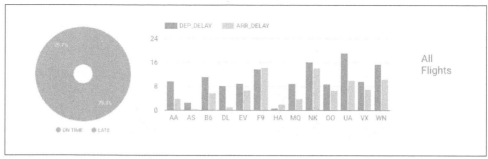

Figure 3-20. Resulting dashboard consisting of a pie chart and bar chart

It appears that, on average, about 80% of flights are on time and that the typical arrival delay varies between airlines but lies in a range of 0 to 15 minutes.

Explaining a Contingency Table

Even though the dashboard we just created shows users the decision-making criterion (proportion of flights that will be late) and some characteristics of that decision (the typical arrival delay), it doesn't actually show our model. Recall that our model involved a threshold on the departure delay. We need to show that. Figure 3-21 shows what we want the dashboard to look like.

In other words, we want to show the same two charts, but for the decision thresholds that we considered—departure delays of 10, 15, and 20 minutes or more.

To get there, we need to change our data source. No longer can we populate the chart from the entire table. Instead, we should populate it from a query that pulls only those flights whose departure delay is greater than the relevant threshold. In Cloud SQL, we can create the views we need[11] and use those views as data sources. Here's how:

```
CREATE VIEW delayed_10 AS SELECT * FROM flights WHERE dep_delay > 10;
CREATE VIEW delayed_15 AS SELECT * FROM flights WHERE dep_delay > 15;
CREATE VIEW delayed_20 AS SELECT * FROM flights WHERE dep_delay > 20;
```

---

11 As of this writing, Data Studio supports a BigQuery query as a data source, but Cloud SQL supports only a table (or view) as a data source. However, even if the connector supports reading from a query, it is preferable to read from a view because views are more reusable.

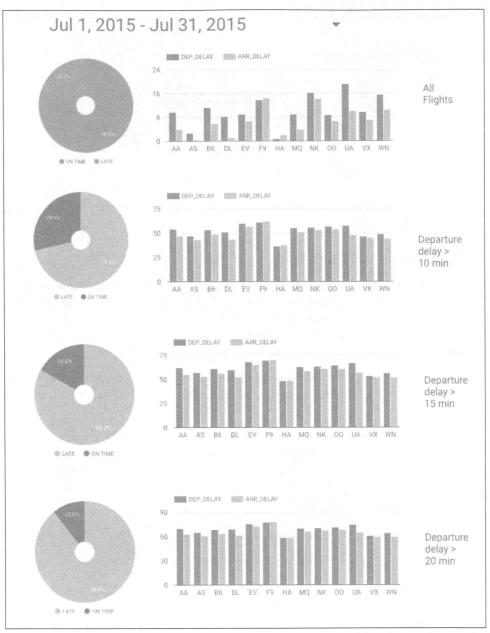

Figure 3-21. Dashboard consisting of three pairs of pie charts and bar charts along with a date control

Looking at the resulting pie chart for a 10 minute-threshold (Figure 3-22), we see that it comes quite close to our target of 30% on-time arrivals. The bar chart for the

10-minute delay explains why the threshold is important. Hint: it is not about the 10 minutes. It is about what the 10-minute delay is indicative of. Can you decipher what is going on?

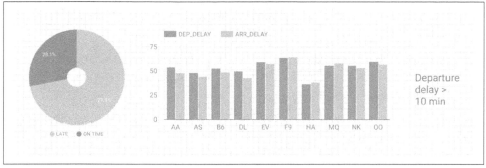

Figure 3-22. Dashboard for a 10-minute threshold on departure delay

Although the typical departure delay of a flight is only about 5 minutes (see the chart corresponding to all flights that we created earlier), flights that are delayed by more than 10 minutes fall into a separate statistical regime. The typical departure delay of an aircraft that departs more than 10 minutes late is around 50 minutes! A likely explanation is that a flight that is delayed by 10 minutes or more typically has a serious issue that will not be resolved quickly. If you are sitting in an airplane and it is more than 10 minutes late in departing, you might as well cancel your meeting—you are going to be sitting at the gate for a while.[12]

At this point, we have created a very simple model and created dashboards to explain the model to our end users. Our end users have a visual, intuitive way to see how often our model is correct and how often is wrong. The model might be quite simple, but the explanation of why the model works is a satisfying one.

There is one teeny, tiny thing missing, though. Context. The dashboard that we have built so far is all about historical data, whereas real dashboards need to be timely. Our dashboard shows aggregates of flights all over the country, but our users will probably care only about the airport from which they are departing and the airport to which they are going. We have a wonderfully informative dashboard, but without such time and location context, few users would care. In Chapter 4, we look at how to build real-time, location-aware dashboards—unfortunately, however, there is a problem with our dataset that prevents us from doing so immediately.

---

12 Road warriors know this well. Ten minutes in, and they whip out their phones to try to get on a different flight.

Summary

In this chapter, we discussed the importance of bringing the insights of our end users into our data modeling efforts as early as possible. Bringing their insights is possible only if you make it a point to explain your models to themes in context from the get-go.

We populated our dashboard from Cloud SQL, a transactional, relational database whose management is simplified by virtue of it running on the cloud and being managed by Google Cloud Platform.

The model that we built was to suggest that our road warriors cancel their immediately scheduled meeting if the departure delay of the flight was more than 10 minutes. This would enable them to make 70% of their meetings with 15 minutes to spare.

We then built a dashboard in Data Studio to explain the contingency table model. Because our choice of threshold was driven by the proportion of flights that arrived late given a particular threshold, we illustrated the proportion using a pie chart for two different thresholds. We also depicted the average arrival delay given some departure delay—this gives users an intuitive understanding of why we recommend a 10-minute threshold.

## CHAPTER 4

Streaming Data: Publication and Ingest

In Chapter 3, we developed a dashboard to explain a contingency table–based model of suggesting whether to cancel a meeting. However, the dashboard that we built lacked immediacy because it was not tied to users' context. Because users need to be able to view a dashboard and see the information that is relevant to them at that point, we need to build a real-time dashboard with location cues.

How would we add context to our dashboard? We'd have to show maps of delays in real time. To do that, we'll need locations of the airports, and we'll need real-time data. Airport locations can be obtained from the US Bureau of Transportation Statistics (BTS; the same US government agency from which we obtained our historical flight data). Real-time flight data, however, is a commercial product. If we were to build a business out of predicting flight arrivals, we'd purchase that data feed. For the purposes of this book, however, let's just simulate it.

Simulating the creation of a real-time feed from historical data has the advantage of allowing us to see both sides of a streaming pipeline (production as well as consumption). In the following section, we look at how we could stream the ingest of data into the database if we were to receive it in real time.

Designing the Event Feed

To create a real-time stream of flight information, we begin by using historical data that is appropriately transformed from what we downloaded from the BTS. What kinds of transformations are needed?

The historical data has this structure:

```
FL_DATE,UNIQUE_CARRIER,AIRLINE_ID,CARRIER,FL_NUM,ORIGIN_AIRPORT_ID,
ORIGIN_AIRPORT_SEQ_ID,ORIGIN_CITY_MARKET_ID,ORIGIN,DEST_AIRPORT_ID,
DEST_AIRPORT_SEQ_ID,DEST_CITY_MARKET_ID,DEST,CRS_DEP_TIME,DEP_TIME,
```

```
DEP_DELAY,TAXI_OUT,WHEELS_OFF,WHEELS_ON,TAXI_IN,CRS_ARR_TIME,
ARR_TIME,ARR_DELAY,CANCELLED,CANCELLATION_CODE,DIVERTED,DISTANCE
```

An example row of the historical data in the comma-separated value (CSV) file looks like this:

```
2015-01-01,AA,19805,AA,1,12478,1247802,31703,JFK,12892,1289203,32575,LAX,0900,
0855,-5.00,17.00,0912,1230,7.00,1230,1237,7.00,0.00,,0.00,2475.00
```

To simulate real-time behavior, we need to key off the timestamps in the historical data. The departure time is present in the BTS flights dataset in the form of two columns: FL_DATE and DEP_TIME (bolded in the example). The FL_DATE is of the form 2015-07-03 for July 3, 2015, and DEP_DATE is of the form 1406 for 2:06 PM local time. This is unfortunate. I'm not worried about the separation of date and time into two columns—we can remedy that. What's unfortunate is that there is no time zone offset associated with the departure time. Thus, in this dataset, a departure time of 1406 in different rows can be different times depending on the time zone of the origin airport.

The time zone offsets (there are two, one for the origin airport and another for the destination) are not present in the data. Because the offset depends on the airport location, we need to find a dataset that contains the timezone offset of each airport and then mash this data with that dataset.[1] To simplify downstream analysis, we will then put all the times in the data in a common time zone—Coordinated Universal Time (UTC) is the traditional choice of common time zone for datasets. We cannot however, get rid of the local time—we will need the local time in order to carry out analysis, such as the typical delay associated with morning flights versus evening flights. So, although we will convert the local times to UTC, we will also store the time zone offset (e.g., –3,600 minutes) to retrieve the local time if necessary.

Therefore, we are going to carry out two transformations to the original dataset. First, we will convert all the time fields in the raw dataset to UTC. Secondly, in addition to the fields present in the raw data, we will add three fields to the dataset for the origin airport and the same three fields for the destination airport: the latitude, longitude, and time zone offset. These fields will be named:

DEP_AIRPORT_LAT, DEP_AIRPORT_LON, DEP_AIRPORT_TZOFFSET

ARR_AIRPORT_LAT, ARR_AIRPORT_LON, ARR_AIRPORT_TZOFFSET

---

1 Note that this is a common situation. It is only as you start to explore a dataset that you discover you need ancillary datasets. Had I known beforehand, I would ingested both datasets. But you are following my work-flow, and as of this point, I knew that I needed a dataset of timezone offsets but hadn't yet searched for it!

Another aspect that we must take into account when simulating a real-time feed is that if we wait until the aircraft has arrived to send out a single event containing all the row data, it is too late. If we do this at the time the aircraft departs, our models will be violating causality constraints. Instead, we will need to send out events corresponding to each state the flight is in. Let's choose to send out five events for each flight: when the flight is first scheduled, when the flight departs the gate, when the flight lifts off, when the flight lands, and when the flight arrives. These five events cannot have all the same data associated with them because the knowability of the columns changes during the flight. For example, when sending out an event at the departure time, we will not know the arrival time. For simplicity, we can notify the same structure, but we will need to ensure that unknowable data is marked by a null and not with the actual data value.

The third transformation that we will need to carry out is that for every row in the historical dataset, we will need to publish five events. Table 4-1 lists when those events can be sent out and the fields that will be included in each event.

Table 4-1. Fields that will be included in each of the five events that will be published

Event	Sent at (UTC)	Fields included in event message
Scheduled	CRS_DEP_TIME minus 7 days	FL_DATE,UNIQUE_CARRIER,AIRLINE_ID,CARRIER,FL_NUM,ORIGIN_AIRPORT_ID, ORIGIN_AIRPORT_SEQ_ID,ORIGIN_CITY_MARKET_ID,ORIGIN,DEST_AIRPORT_ID, DEST_AIRPORT_SEQ_ID,DEST_CITY_MARKET_ID,DEST,CRS_DEP_TIME, [nulls],CRS_ARR_TIME,[nulls],DISTANCE,[nulls]
Departed	DEP_TIME	All fields available in scheduled message, plus: DEP_TIME,DEP_DELAY CANCELLED,CANCELLATION_CODE DEP_AIRPORT_LAT,DEP_AIRPORT_LON,DEP_AIRPORT_TZOFFSET
Wheelsoff	WHEELS_OFF	All fields available in departed message, plus: TAXI_OUT,WHEELS_OFF
Wheelson	WHEELS_ON	All fields available in wheelsoff message, plus: WHEELS_ON DIVERTED ARR_AIRPORT_LAT,ARR_AIRPORT_LON,ARR_AIRPORT_TZOFFSET
Arrived	ARR_TIME	All fields available in wheelson message, plus: ARR_TIME,ARR_DELAY

We will carry out the transformations needed and then store the transformed data in a database so that it is ready for the event simulation code to use. Figure 4-1 shows the steps we are about to carry out in our Extract-Transform-Load (ETL) pipeline.

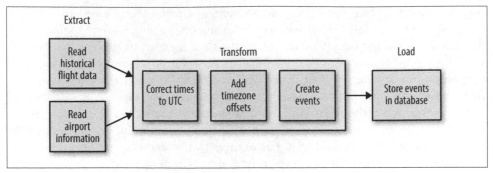

Figure 4-1. Steps in our ETL pipeline

Time Correction

Correcting times reported in local time to UTC is not a simple endeavor. There are several steps:

1. Local time depends on, well, the location. The flight data that we have records only the name of the airport (ALB for Albany). We, therefore, need to obtain the latitude and longitude given an airport code. The BTS has a dataset (*http://bit.ly/ 2AzeLUf*) that contains this information, which we can use to do the lookup.

2. Given a latitude/longitude pair, we need to look up the time zone from a map of global time zones (*http://bit.ly/2k34YMG*). For example, given the latitude and longitude of the airport in Albany, we would need to get back America/New_York. There are several web services that do this, but the Python package timezone finder (*https://pypi.python.org/pypi/timezonefinder*) is a more efficient option because it works completely offline. The drawback is that this package does not handle oceanic areas and some historical time zone changes,[2] but that's a trade-off that we can make for now.

3. The time zone offset at a location changes during the year due to daylight savings corrections. In New York, for example, it is six hours in summer and five hours in winter. Given the time zone (America/New_York), therefore, we also need the local departure date and time (say Jan 13, 2015 2:08 PM) in order to find the corresponding time zone offset. The Python package pytz provides this capability by using the underlying operating system.

The problem of ambiguous times still remains—every instant between 01:00 and 02:00 local time occurs twice on the day that the clock switches from daylight savings

---

2 For example, the time zone of Sevastopol changed in 2014 from Eastern European Time (UTC+2) to Moscow Time (UTC+4) after the annexation of Crimea by the Russian Federation.

time (summer time) to standard time (winter time). So, if our dataset has a flight arriving at 01:30, we need to make a choice of what time that represents. In a real-world situation, you would look at the typical duration of the flight and choose the one that is more likely. For the purposes of this book, I'll always assume the winter time (i.e., is_dst is False) on the dubious grounds that it is the standard time zone for that location.

The complexity of these steps should, I hope, convince you to follow best practices when storing time. Always try to store two things in your data: (1) the timestamp in UTC so that you can merge data from across the world if necessary and (2) the currently active time zone offset so that you can carry out analysis that requires the local time.[3]

Apache Beam/Cloud Dataflow

The canonical way to build data pipelines on Google Cloud Platform is to use Cloud Dataflow. Cloud Dataflow is an externalization of technologies called Flume (*http://research.google.com/pubs/pub35650.html*) and Millwheel (*http://research.google.com/pubs/pub41378.html*) that have been in widespread use at Google for several years. It employs a programming model that handles both batch and streaming data in a uniform manner, thus providing the ability to use the same code base both for batch and continuous stream processing. The code itself is written in Apache Beam (*http://beam.apache.org/*), either in Java or Python,[4] and is portable in the sense that it can be executed on multiple execution environments including Apache Flink[5] and Apache Spark (*https://github.com/apache/incubator-beam/tree/master/runners/spark*). On Google Cloud Platform, Cloud Dataflow provides a fully managed (serverless) service that is capable of executing Beam pipelines. Resources are allocated on-demand and they autoscale so as to achieve both minimal latency and high resource utilization.

Beam programming involves building a pipeline (a series of data transformations) that is submitted to a runner. The runner will build a graph and then stream data through it. Each input dataset comes from a source and each output dataset is sent to a sink. Figure 4-2 illustrates the Beam pipeline that we are about to build.

Compare the steps in Figure 4-2 with the block diagram of the ETL pipeline at the beginning of this section in Figure 4-1. Let's build the data pipeline piece by piece.

---

3 For example, is there a spike associated with traffic between 5 PM and 6 PM local time?

4 As this book was going to print, the Python API for streaming had just become available in beta.

5 See *http://data-artisans.com/why-apache-beam/* and *https://github.com/apache/incubator-beam/tree/master/runners/flink*.

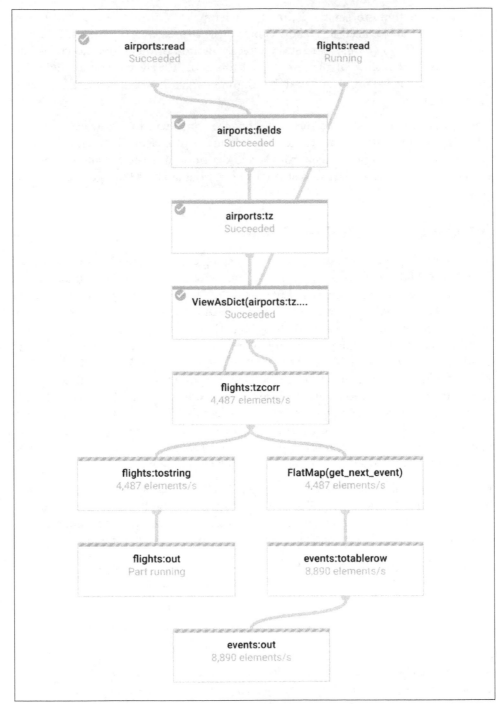

Figure 4-2. The Dataflow pipeline that we are about to build

Parsing Airports Data

You can download information about the location of airports (*http://bit.ly/2AzeLUf*) from the BTS website. I selected all of the fields, downloaded it to my local hard drive, extracted the CSV file, and compressed it with gzip. The gzipped airports file is available in the GitHub repository for this book (*https://github.com/GoogleCloudPlatform/data-science-on-gcp/blob/master/04_streaming/simulate/airports.csv.gz*).

The Read transform in the Beam pipeline that follows reads in the airports file line by line.[6]

```
pipeline = beam.Pipeline('DirectPipelineRunner')
airports = (pipeline
   | beam.Read(beam.io.TextFileSource('airports.csv.gz'))
   | beam.Map(lambda line: next(csv.reader([line])))
   | beam.Map(lambda fields: (fields[0], (fields[21], fields[26]))))
)
```

For example, suppose that one of the input lines read out of the text file source is the following:

```
1000401,10004,"04A","Lik Mining Camp","Lik, AK",101,1,"United
States","US","Alaska","AK","02",3000401,30004,"Lik,
AK",101,1,68,"N",5,0,68.08333333,163,"W",10,0,-163.16666667,"",2007-07-01,,0,1,
```

The first Map takes this line and passes it to a CSV reader that parses it (taking into account fields like "Lik, AK" that have commas in them) and pulls out the fields as a list of strings. These fields are then passed to the next transform. The second Map takes the fields as input and outputs a tuple of the form (the extracted fields are shown in bold in the previous example):

```
(1000401, (68.08333333,-163.16666667))
```

The first number is the unique airport code (we use this, rather than the airport's three-letter code, because airport locations can change over time) and the next two numbers are the latitude/longitude pair for the airport's location. The variable air ports, which is the result of these three transformations, is not a simple in-memory list of these tuples. Instead, it is an immutable collection, termed a PCollection, that you can take out-of-memory and distribute.

We can write the contents of the PCollection to a text file to verify that the pipeline is behaving correctly:

```
airports | beam.Map(lambda (airport, data):
                     '{},{}'.format(airport, ','.join(data)) )
         | beam.io.textio.WriteToText('extracted_airports')
```

---

6 This code is in *04_streaming/simulate/df01.py* of the GitHub repository of this book.

Try this out: the code, in *04_streaming/simulate/df01.py*, is just a Python program that you can run from the command line. First, install the Cloud Dataflow package (Cloud Dataflow is an execution environment for Apache Beam) and then run the program *df01.py* while you are in the directory containing the GitHub repository of this book:

```
cd 04_streaming/simulate
./install_packages.sh
python ./df01.py
```

This runs the code in *df01.py* on the Google Cloud Platform using the Cloud Dataflow service. In other words, simply running the Python program launches the data pipeline on multiple workers in the cloud. As with many distributed systems, the output of Cloud Dataflow is potentially sharded to one or more files. You will get a file whose name begins with "extracted_airports" (mine was *extracted_airports-00000-of-00014*), the first few lines of which might look something like this:

```
1000101,58.10944444,-152.90666667
1000301,65.54805556,-161.07166667
```

The columns are `AIRPORT_SEQ_ID,LATITUDE,LONGITUDE`—the order of the rows you get depends on which of the parallel workers finished first, and so could be different.

Adding Time Zone Information

Let's now change the code to determine the time zone corresponding to a latitude/longitude pair. In our pipeline, rather than simply emitting the latitude/longitude pair, we emit a list of three items: latitude, longitude, and time zone:

```
airports = (pipeline
    | beam.Read(beam.io.TextFileSource('airports.csv.gz'))
    | beam.Map(lambda line: next(csv.reader([line])))
    | beam.Map(lambda fields: (fields[0], addtimezone(fields[21], fields[26])))
)
```

The `lambda` keyword in Python sets up an anonymous function. In the case of the first use of `lambda` in the above snippet, that method takes one parameter (`line`) and returns the stuff following the colon. We can determine the time zone by using the `timezonefinder` package:[7]

```
def addtimezone(lat, lon):
    try:
        import timezonefinder
        tf = timezonefinder.TimezoneFinder()
        tz = tf.timezone_at(lng=float(lon), lat=float(lat)) # throws ValueError
        if tz is None:
```

---

[7] This code is in *04_streaming/simulate/df02.py* of the GitHub repository of this book.

```
        tz = 'UTC'
    return (lat, lon, tz)
except ValueError:
    return (lat, lon, 'TIMEZONE') # header
```

The location of the import statement in the preceding example might look strange (most Python imports tend to be at the top of the file), but is recommended by Cloud Dataflow[8] so that pickling of the main session when we finally do submit it to the cloud doesn't end up pickling imported packages, also.

For now, though, we are going to run this (*df02.py*) locally. This will take a while[9] because the time zone computation involves a large number of polygon intersection checks. The extracted information now looks like this:

```
1000101,58.10944444,-152.90666667,America/Anchorage
1000301,65.54805556,-161.07166667,America/Anchorage
1000401,68.08333333,-163.16666667,America/Nome
```

The last column now has the time zone, which was determined from the latitude and longitude of each airport.

Converting Times to UTC

Now that we have the time zone for each airport, we are ready to tackle converting the times in the flights data to UTC. While we are developing the program, we'd prefer not to process all the months we have in Cloud Storage. Instead, we will create a small sample of the flights data against which to try our code:

```
gsutil cat gs://cloud-training-demos-ml/flights/raw/201501.csv \
                      | head -1000 > 201501_part.csv
```

The *201501_part.csv* file contains 1,000 lines, which is enough to test the pipeline against locally.

Reading the flights data starts out similar to reading the airports data:[10]

```
flights = (pipeline
  | 'flights:read' >> beam.Read(beam.io.TextFileSource('201501_part.csv'))
```

This is the same code as when we read the *airports.csv.gz* file, except that I am also giving a name (`flights:read`) to this transform step.

The next step, though, is different because it involves two PCollections. We need to join the flights data with the airports data to find the time zone corresponding to each

---

8 See the answer to the question "How do I handle NameErrors?" at *https://cloud.google.com/dataflow/faq*.

9 If you are running this in CloudShell, find the button on the top right that allows you to "boost" the virtual machine. You will have to reinstall the packages using the *install_packages.sh* script.

10 This code is in *04_streaming/simulate/df03.py* of the GitHub repository of this book.

flight. To do that, we make the airports PCollection a "side input." Side inputs in Beam are like views into the original PCollection, and are either lists or dicts. In this case, we will create a dict that maps airport ID to information about the airports:

```
flights = (pipeline
 |'flights:read' >> beam.Read(beam.io.TextFileSource('201501_part.csv'))
 |'flights:tzcorr' >> beam.FlatMap(tz_correct, beam.pvalue.AsDict(airports))
   )
```

The FlatMap() method calls out to a method tz_correct(), which takes a line from *201501_part.csv* (containing a single flight's information) and a Python dictionary (containing all the airports' time zone information):

```
def tz_correct(line, airport_timezones):
    fields = line.split(',')
    if fields[0] != 'FL_DATE' and len(fields) == 27:
        # convert all times to UTC
        dep_airport_id = fields[6]
        arr_airport_id = fields[10]
        dep_timezone = airport_timezones[dep_airport_id][2]
        arr_timezone = airport_timezones[arr_airport_id][2]

        for f in [13, 14, 17]: #crsdeptime, deptime, wheelsoff
            fields[f] = as_utc(fields[0], fields[f], dep_timezone)
        for f in [18, 20, 21]: #wheelson, crsarrtime, arrtime
            fields[f] = as_utc(fields[0], fields[f], arr_timezone)

        yield ','.join(fields)
```

Why FlatMap() instead of Map to call tz_correct()? A Map is a 1-to-1 relation between input and output, whereas a FlatMap() can return 0–*N* outputs per input. The way it does this is with a Python generator function (i.e., the yield keyword— think of the yield as a return that returns one item at a time until there is no more data to return).

The tz_correct() code gets the departure airport ID from the flight's data and then looks up the time zone for that airport ID from the airport's data. After it has the time zone, it calls out to the method as_utc() to convert each of the date–times reported in that airport's time zone to UTC:

```
def as_utc(date, hhmm, tzone):
    try:
        if len(hhmm) > 0 and tzone is not None:
            import datetime, pytz
            loc_tz = pytz.timezone(tzone)
            loc_dt = loc_tz.localize(datetime.datetime.strptime(date,'%Y-%m-%d'),
                                     is_dst=False)
            loc_dt += datetime.timedelta(hours=int(hhmm[:2]),
                                         minutes=int(hhmm[2:]))
            utc_dt = loc_dt.astimezone(pytz.utc)
            return utc_dt.strftime('%Y-%m-%d %H:%M:%S')
```

```
        else:
            return '' # empty string corresponds to canceled flights
    except ValueError as e:
        print '{} {} {}'.format(date, hhmm, tzone)
        raise e
```

As before, you can run this locally. To do that, run df03.py. A line that originally (in the raw data) looked like

```
2015-01-01,AA,19805,AA,8,12173,1217302,32134,HNL,11298,1129803,30194,DFW,1745,
1933,108.00,15.00,1948,0648,11.00,0510,0659,109.00,0.00,,0.00,3784.00
```

now becomes:

```
2015-01-01,AA,19805,AA,8,12173,1217302,32134,HNL,11298,1129803,30194,DFW,2015-01-
02 03:45:00,2015-01-02 05:33:00,108.00,15.00,2015-01-02 05:48:00,
2015-01-01 12:48:00,11.00,2015-01-01 11:10:00,2015-01-01
12:59:00,109.00,0.00,,0.00,3784.00
```

All the times have been converted to UTC. For example, the 0648 time of arrival in Dallas has been converted to UTC to become 12:48:00.

Correcting Dates

Look carefully at the previous line involving a flight from Honolulu (HNL) to Dallas–Fort Worth (DFW). Do you notice anything odd?

Carefully take a look at the departure time in Honolulu and the arrival time in Dallas:

```
2015-01-01,AA,19805,AA,8,12173,1217302,32134,HNL,11298,1129803,30194,DFW,
2015-01-02 03:45:00,2015-01-02 05:33:00,108.00,15.00,
2015-01-02 05:48:00,2015-01-01 12:48:00,11.00,2015-01-01 11:10:00,
2015-01-01 12:59:00,109.00,0.00,,0.00,3784.00
```

The flight is arriving the day before it departed! That's because the flight date (2015-01-01) is the date of departure in local time. Add in a time difference between airports, and it is quite possible that it is not the date of arrival. We'll look for these situations and add 24 hours if necessary. This is, of course, quite a hack (have I already mentioned that times ought to be stored in UTC?!):

```
def add_24h_if_before(arrtime, deptime):
    import datetime
    if len(arrtime) > 0 and len(deptime) > 0 and arrtime < deptime:
        adt = datetime.datetime.strptime(arrtime, '%Y-%m-%d %H:%M:%S')
        adt += datetime.timedelta(hours=24)
        return adt.strftime('%Y-%m-%d %H:%M:%S')
    else:
        return arrtime
```

The 24-hour hack is called just before the yield in `tz_correct`.[11] Now that we have new data about the airports, it is probably wise to add it to our dataset. Also, as remarked earlier, we want to keep track of the time zone offset from UTC because some types of analysis might require knowledge of the local time. Thus, the new `tz_correct` code becomes the following:

```
def tz_correct(line, airport_timezones):
    fields = line.split(',')
    if fields[0] != 'FL_DATE' and len(fields) == 27:
        # convert all times to UTC
        dep_airport_id = fields[6]
        arr_airport_id = fields[10]
        dep_timezone = airport_timezones[dep_airport_id][2]
        arr_timezone = airport_timezones[arr_airport_id][2]

        for f in [13, 14, 17]: #crsdeptime, deptime, wheelsoff
            fields[f], deptz = as_utc(fields[0], fields[f], dep_timezone)
        for f in [18, 20, 21]: #wheelson, crsarrtime, arrtime
            fields[f], arrtz = as_utc(fields[0], fields[f], arr_timezone)

        for f in [17, 18, 20, 21]:
            fields[f] = add_24h_if_before(fields[f], fields[14])

        fields.extend(airport_timezones[dep_airport_id])
        fields[-1] = str(deptz)
        fields.extend(airport_timezones[arr_airport_id])
        fields[-1] = str(arrtz)

        yield ','.join(fields)
```

Creating Events

After we have our time-corrected data, we can move on to creating events. We'll limit ourselves for now to just the `departed` and `arrived` messages—we can rerun the pipeline to create the additional events if and when our modeling efforts begin to use other events:

```
def get_next_event(fields):
    if len(fields[14]) > 0:
        event = list(fields) # copy
        event.extend(['departed', fields[14]])
        for f in [16,17,18,19,21,22,25]:
            event[f] = ''  # not knowable at departure time
        yield event
    if len(fields[21]) > 0:
        event = list(fields)
```

---

11 This code is in *04_streaming/simulate/df04.py* of the GitHub repository of this book.

```
        event.extend(['arrived', fields[21]])
        yield event
```

Essentially, we pick up the departure time and create a departed event at that time after making sure to null out the fields we cannot know at the departure time. Similarly, we use the arrival time to create an arrived event. In the pipeline, this is called on the flights PCollection after the conversion to UTC has happened:

```
flights = (pipeline
|'flights:read' >> beam.Read(beam.io.TextFileSource('201501_part.csv'))
|'flights:tzcorr' >> beam.FlatMap(tz_correct, beam.pvalue.AsDict(airports))
    )
events = flights | beam.FlatMap(get_next_event)
```

If we now run the pipeline,[12] we will see two events for each flight:

```
2015-01-01,AA,19805,AA,1,12478,1247802,31703,JFK,12892,1289203,32575,LAX,2015-01-
01T14:00:00,2015-01-01T13:55:00,-5.00,,,,,2015-01-01T20:30:00,,,0.00,,,
2475.00,40.63972222,-73.77888889,-18000.0,33.94250000,-118.40805556,
-28800.0,departed,2015-01-01T13:55:00
2015-01-01,AA,19805,AA,1,12478,1247802,31703,JFK,12892,1289203,32575,LAX,2015-01-
01T14:00:00,2015-01-01T13:55:00,-5.00,17.00,2015-01-01T14:12:00,2015-01-01
T20:30:00,7.00,2015-01-01T20:30:00,2015-01-01T20:37:00,7.00,0.00,,0.00,
2475.00,40.63972222,-73.77888889,-18000.0,33.94250000,-118.40805556,
-28800.0,arrived,2015-01-01T20:37:00
```

The first event is a departed event and is to be published at the departure time, while the second is an arrived event and is to be published at the arrival time. The depar ted event has a number of empty fields corresponding to data that is not known at that time.

Running the Pipeline in the Cloud

That last run took a few minutes on the local virtual machine (VM), and we were processing only a thousand lines! We need to distribute the work, and to do that, we will change the runner from DirectPipelineRunner (which runs locally) to Dataflow PipelineRunner (which lobs the job off to the cloud and scales it out).[13] We'll change the input data to be in Cloud Storage (as discussed in Chapter 2, the data is in situ; i.e., we don't need to preshard the data):

```
argv = [
        '--project={0}'.format(project),
        '--job_name=ch03timecorr',
        '--save_main_session',
        '--staging_location=gs://{0}/flights/staging/'.format(bucket),
        '--temp_location=gs://{0}/flights/temp/'.format(bucket),
```

---

12 This code is in *04_streaming/simulate/df05.py* of the GitHub repository of this book.

13 Code for this section is in *04_streaming/simulate/df06.py* of the GitHub repository of this book.

```
    '--setup_file=./setup.py',
    '--max_num_workers=10',
    '--autoscaling_algorithm=THROUGHPUT_BASED',
    '--runner=DataflowPipelineRunner'
]
airports_filename =
    'gs://{}/flights/airports/airports.csv.gz'.format(bucket)
flights_raw_files = 'gs://{}/flights/raw/*.csv'.format(bucket)
flights_output = 'gs://{}/flights/tzcorr/all_flights'.format(bucket)
events_output = '{}:flights.simevents'.format(project)

pipeline = beam.Pipeline(argv=argv)
```

The file *setup.py* should list the Python packages that we needed to install (`timezone finder` and `pytz`) as we went along—Cloud Dataflow will need to install these packages on the Compute Engine instances that it launches behind the scenes:

```
REQUIRED_PACKAGES = [
    'timezonefinder',
    'pytz'
    ]
```

As a final touch, we store the time-corrected flight data as CSV files in Cloud Storage but store the events in BigQuery. BigQuery is Google Cloud Platform's data warehouse that supports SQL queries and makes it easier if you want to pull out a subset of events to simulate.

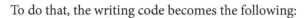 We look at BigQuery in more detail in Chapter 5.

To do that, the writing code becomes the following:

```
schema = 'FL_DATE:date,UNIQUE_CARRIER:string,...'
(events
 | 'events:totablerow' >> beam.Map(lambda fields: create_row(fields))
 | 'events:out' >> beam.io.Write(beam.io.BigQuerySink(
                            events_output, schema=schema,
write_disposition=beam.io.BigQueryDisposition.WRITE_TRUNCATE,
create_disposition=beam.io.BigQueryDisposition.CREATE_IF_NEEDED))
    )
```

The `create_row()` method simply creates a dictionary of the fields to be written:

```
def create_row(fields):
    header = 'FL_DATE,UNIQUE_CARRIER,...'.split(',')
    featdict = {}
    for name, value in zip(header, fields):
        featdict[name] = value
    return featdict
```

Before you run this program, you need to create a dataset in BigQuery called `flights` because the `simevents` table will be created by the pipeline if necessary,[14] but not the dataset. To do that, type the following:

```
bq mk flights
```

You also need to upload the *airports.csv.gz* file from the course repository to your Cloud Storage bucket:

```
gsutil cp airports.csv.gz \
    gs://<BUCKET-NAME>/flights/airports/airports.csv.gz
```

Running the Python program with the preceding code[15] submits the job to the cloud. Cloud Dataflow autoscales each step of the pipeline based on throughput, and streams the events data into BigQuery. You can monitor the running job on the Cloud Platform Console in the Cloud Dataflow section.

Even as the events data is being written out, we can query it by browsing to the Big-Query console (*http://bigquery.cloud.google.com/*) and typing the following (change the project name as appropriate):

```
SELECT
  ORIGIN,
  DEP_TIME,
  DEP_DELAY,
  DEST,
  ARR_TIME,
  ARR_DELAY,
  NOTIFY_TIME
FROM
  flights.simevents
WHERE
  (DEP_DELAY > 15 and ORIGIN = 'SEA') or
  (ARR_DELAY > 15 and DEST = 'SEA')
ORDER BY NOTIFY_TIME ASC
LIMIT
  10
```

Figure 4-3 shows what I got when I ran this query.

---

14 It might be better to create the table outside of the pipeline if you want to partition it by date, for example.

15 The file *04_streaming/simulate/df06.py* of the GitHub repository of this book.

Row	ORIGIN	DEP_TIME	DEP_DELAY	DEST	ARR_TIME	ARR_DELAY	NOTIFY_TIME
1	SEA	2015-01-01 08:21:00 UTC	43.0	IAD	null	null	2015-01-01 08:21:00 UTC
2	SEA	2015-01-01 08:21:00 UTC	43.0	IAD	2015-01-01 12:48:00 UTC	22.0	2015-01-01 12:48:00 UTC
3	KOA	2015-01-01 10:11:00 UTC	66.0	SEA	2015-01-01 15:45:00 UTC	40.0	2015-01-01 15:45:00 UTC
4	SEA	2015-01-01 16:43:00 UTC	38.0	PSP	null	null	2015-01-01 16:43:00 UTC
5	SEA	2015-01-01 16:57:00 UTC	17.0	FLL	null	null	2015-01-01 16:57:00 UTC
6	SEA	2015-01-01 17:01:00 UTC	16.0	HNL	null	null	2015-01-01 17:01:00 UTC
7	SEA	2015-01-01 17:33:00 UTC	48.0	PHL	null	null	2015-01-01 17:33:00 UTC

Figure 4-3. Result of query as events data were being written out

As expected, we see two events for the SEA-IAD flight, one at departure and the other at arrival.

BigQuery is a columnar database, so a query that selects all fields

```
SELECT
  *
FROM
  `cloud-training-demos.flights.simevents`
ORDER BY NOTIFY_TIME ASC
```

will be very inefficient. However, we do need all of the event data in order to send out event notifications. Therefore, we trade off storage for speed by adding an extra column called EVENT_DATA to our BigQuery table and then populate it in our pipeline as follows (we also have to modify the BigQuery schema appropriately):

```
def create_row(fields):
    header = 'FL_DATE,UNIQUE_CARRIER,...,NOTIFY_TIME'.split(',')

    featdict = {}
    for name, value in zip(header, fields):
        featdict[name] = value
    featdict['EVENT_DATA'] = ','.join(fields)
    return featdict
```

Then, our query to pull the events could simply be as follows:

```
SELECT
  EVENT,
  NOTIFY_TIME,
  EVENT_DATA
FROM
  `cloud-training-demos.flights.simevents`
WHERE
  NOTIFY_TIME >= TIMESTAMP('2015-05-01 00:00:00 UTC')
  AND NOTIFY_TIME < TIMESTAMP('2015-05-03 00:00:00 UTC')
ORDER BY
  NOTIFY_TIME ASC
LIMIT
  10
```

Figure 4-4 depicts the query results.

Row	EVENT	NOTIFY_TIME	
1	departed	2015-05-01 00:00:00 UTC	2015-04-30,AA,19805,AA,141
2	departed	2015-05-01 00:00:00 UTC	2015-04-30,DL,19790,DL,233
3	arrived	2015-05-01 00:00:00 UTC	2015-04-30,AA,19805,AA,136
4	arrived	2015-05-01 00:00:00 UTC	2015-04-30,EV,20366,EV,434
5	departed	2015-05-01 00:00:00 UTC	2015-04-30,WN,19393,WN,33
6	arrived	2015-05-01 00:00:00 UTC	2015-04-30,UA,19977,UA,754

Figure 4-4. Query result with the additional EVENT_DATA field

This table will serve as the source of our events; it is from such a query that we will simulate streaming flight data.

Publishing an Event Stream to Cloud Pub/Sub

Now that we have the source events from the raw flight data, we are ready to simulate the stream. Streaming data in Google Cloud Platform is typically published to Cloud Pub/Sub, a serverless real-time messaging service. Cloud Pub/Sub provides reliable delivery and can scale to more than a million messages per second. It stores copies of messages in multiple zones to provide "at least once" guaranteed delivery to subscribers, and there can be many simultaneous subscribers.

Our simulator will read from the events table in BigQuery (populated in the previous section) and publish messages to Cloud Pub/Sub based on a mapping between the event notification time (arrival or departure time based on event) and the current system time, as illustrated in Figure 4-5.

Essentially, we will walk through the flight event records, getting the notification time from each.

It is inefficient to always simulate the flights events at real-time speeds. Instead, we might want to run through a day of flight data in an hour (as long as the code that processes these events can handle the increased data rate). At other times, we may be running our event-processing code in a debugging environment that is slower and so we might want to slow down the simulation. I will refer to this ratio between the actual time and simulation time as the *speed-up factor*—the speed-up factor will be greater than 1 if we want the simulation to be faster than real time, and less than 1 if we want it to be slower than real time.

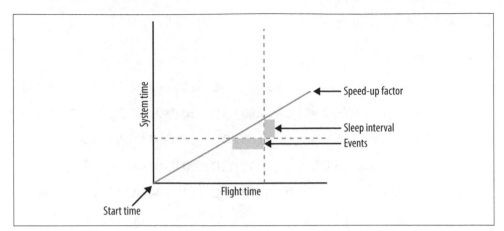

Figure 4-5. The simulator publishes messages based on a mapping between event time and system time

Based on the speed-up factor, we'll have to do a linear transformation of the event time to system time. If the speed-up factor is 1, a 60-minute difference between the start of the simulation in event time and the current record's timestamp should be encountered 60 minutes after the start of the simulation. If the speed-up factor is 60, a 60-minute difference in event time translates to a 1-minute difference in system time, and so the record should be published a minute later. If the event time clock is ahead of the system clock, we sleep for the necessary amount of time so as to allow the simulation to catch up.

The simulation consists of four steps (see also Figure 4-6).[16]

1. Run the query to get the set of flight event records to publish.
2. Page through the query.
3. Accumulate events to publish as a batch.
4. Publish accumulated events and sleep as necessary.

Even though this is an ETL pipeline, the need to process records in strict sequential order and sleep in between makes this ETL pipeline a poor fit for Cloud Dataflow. Instead, we'll implement this as a pure Python program. The problem with this choice is that the simulation code is not fault tolerant—if the simulation fails, it will not automatically restart and definitely will not start from the last successfully notified event.

---

16 The code for this is in *simulate.py* in *04_streaming/simulate* in the GitHub repository for this book.

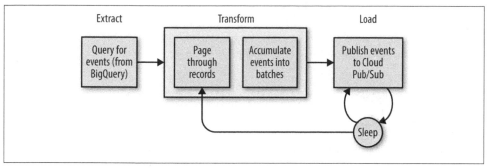

Figure 4-6. The four steps of simulation

The simulation code that we are writing is only for quick experimentation with streaming data. Hence, I will not take the extra effort needed to make it fault-tolerant. If we had to do so, we could make the simulation fault-tolerant by starting from a BigQuery query that is bounded in terms of a time range with the start of that time range automatically inferred from the last-notified record in Cloud Pub/Sub. Because Cloud Pub/Sub subscriptions are not retroactive, we need to maintain a subscriber (perhaps on App Engine) that simply returns the last-notified record whenever asked. Then, we could launch the simulation script from a Docker container and use Google Container Engine (which runs Kubernetes) to automatically restart the simulation if the simulation code fails. All this, though, strikes me as gilding the lily—for quick experimentation, it is unclear whether the code needs to be fault-tolerant. For now, therefore, let's note that the simulation code as written will not automatically restart, and even if manually restarted, it will not resume where it last left off.[17] If we need to make the simulator enterprise-grade, we can revisit this.

Get Records to Publish

The BigQuery query is parameterized by the start and end time of the simulation and can be invoked through the Google Cloud API for Python:

```
bqclient = bq.Client()
dataset = bqclient.dataset('flights')
if not dataset.exists():
    logging.error('Did not find a dataset named <flights> in your project')
    exit(-1)

# run the query to pull simulated events
querystr = """\
SELECT
  EVENT,
```

---

17 Also, when the script runs out of records to process, it will essentially just time out with an error. If that happens, restart the script.

```
    NOTIFY_TIME,
    EVENT_DATA
  FROM
    `cloud-training-demos.flights.simevents`
  WHERE
    NOTIFY_TIME >= TIMESTAMP('{}')
    AND NOTIFY_TIME < TIMESTAMP('{}')
  ORDER BY
    NOTIFY_TIME ASC
  """
      query = bqclient.run_sync_query(querystr.format(args.startTime,
                                                      args.endTime))
      query.use_legacy_sql = False # standard SQL
      query.timeout_ms = 2000
      query.max_results = 1000  # at a time
      query.run()
```

There are three possibilities as far as the BigQuery result is concerned: (1) the query
might have completed, (2) the query might have timed out, or (3) the query might
have more than 1,000 results. We can handle all three cases by using the following
code:

```
    # wait for query to complete and fetch first page of data
  if query.complete:
      rows = query.rows
      token = query.page_token
  else:
      logging.error('Query timed out ... retrying ...')
      job = query.job
      job.reload()
      retry_count = 0
      while retry_count < 5 and job.state != u'DONE':
          time.sleep(1.5**retry_count)
          retry_count += 1
          logging.error('... retrying {}'.format(retry_count))
          job.reload()
      if job.state != u'DONE':
          logging.error('Job failed')
          logging.error(query.errors)
          exit(-1)
      rows, total_count, token = query.fetch_data()
```

Paging Through Records

As we page through the query results, we need to publish to Cloud Pub/Sub. There is
a separate topic per event type (i.e., an arrived topic and a departed topic), so we
create two topics:

```
psclient = pubsub.Client()
topics = {}
for event_type in ['departed', 'arrived']:
    topics[event_type] = psclient.topic(event_type)
```

```
    if not topics[event_type].exists():
        topics[event_type].create()
```

After creating the topics, we can page through the query results by repeatedly calling `query.fetch_data()` until token is None. For each batch of records retrieved, we call the `notify()` method:

```
# notify about each row in the dataset
programStartTime = datetime.datetime.utcnow()
simStartTime = ... FORMAT) \
            .replace(tzinfo=pytz.UTC)
while True:
    notify(topics, rows, simStartTime, programStartTime, args.speedFactor)
    if token is None:
        break
    rows, total_count, token = query.fetch_data(page_token=token)
```

Building a Batch of Events

The `notify()` method consists of accumulating the rows into batches and publishing them when it is time to sleep:

```
def notify(topics, rows, simStartTime, programStart, speedFactor):
    # sleep computation
    def compute_sleep_secs(notify_time):
        time_elapsed = (datetime.datetime.utcnow() - programStart).seconds
        sim_time_elapsed = (notify_time - simStartTime).seconds / speedFactor
        to_sleep_secs = sim_time_elapsed - time_elapsed
        return to_sleep_secs

    tonotify = {}
    for key in topics:
      tonotify[key] = list()

    for row in rows:
        event, notify_time, event_data = row

        # how much time should we sleep?
        if compute_sleep_secs(notify_time) > 1:
            # notify the accumulated tonotify
            publish(topics, tonotify)
            for key in topics:
                tonotify[key] = list()

            # recompute sleep, since notification takes a while
            to_sleep_secs = compute_sleep_secs(notify_time)
            if to_sleep_secs > 0:
                logging.info('Sleeping {} seconds'.format(to_sleep_secs))
                time.sleep(to_sleep_secs)

        tonotify[event].append(event_data)
```

```
# left-over records; notify again
publish(topics, tonotify)
```

There are a few points to be made here. First is that we work completely in UTC so that the time difference computations make sense. We also notify to Cloud Pub/Sub in batches. This is important because notifying to Cloud Pub/Sub involves a network call and is subject to latency—we should minimize that if we can. Otherwise, we'll be limited in what speed-up factors we can support. Thirdly, we always compute whether to sleep by looking at the time difference since the start of the simulation. If we simply keep moving a pointer forward, errors in time will accumulate. Finally, note that we check whether the sleep time is more than a second the first time, so as to give records time to accumulate. If, when you run the program, you do not see any sleep, your speed-up factor is too high for the capability of the machine running the simulation code and the network between that machine and Google Cloud Platform. Slow down the simulation, get a larger machine, or run it behind the Google firewall (such as on a Compute Engine instance).

Publishing a Batch of Events

The `notify()` method that we saw in the previous code example has accumulated the events in between sleep calls. There is a separate batch for each topic, so the `pub` `lish()` method simply retrieves each batch and publishes it to Cloud Pub/Sub:

```
def publish(topics, allevents):
    for key in topics:  # 'departed', 'arrived', etc.
        topic = topics[key]
        events = allevents[key]
        with topic.batch() as batch:
            logging.info('Publishing {} {} events'.format(len(events), key))
            for event_data in events:
                batch.publish(event_data)
```

Another reason (besides reducing the impact of a network call) to notify in batches is that Cloud Pub/Sub does not guarantee the order in which messages will be delivered, especially if the subscriber lets a huge backlog build up. Notifying in batches helps reduces the likelihood of out-of-order messages; however, out-of-order messages will happen, and downstream subscribers will need to deal with them. Secondly, Cloud Pub/Sub guarantees "at-least once" delivery and will resend the message if the subscriber does not acknowledge a message in time. I will use Cloud Dataflow to ingest from Cloud Pub/Sub, and Cloud Dataflow deals with both these issues (out-of-order and duplication) transparently.

We can try out the simulation by typing the following:

```
python simulate.py --startTime '2015-05-01 00:00:00 UTC' \
    --endTime '2015-05-04 00:00:00 UTC' --speedFactor=60
```

This will simulate three days of flight data (the end time is exclusive) at 60 times real-time speed and stream the events into two topics on Cloud Pub/Sub. Because the simulation starts off from a BigQuery query, it is quite straightforward to limit the simulated events to just a single airport or to airports within a latitude/longitude bounding box.

In this section, we looked at how to produce an event stream and publish those events in real time. Throughout this book, we can use this simulator and these topics for experimenting with how to consume streaming data and carry out real-time analytics.

Real-Time Stream Processing

Now that we have a source of streaming data that includes location information, let's look at how to build a real-time dashboard. Figure 4-7 presents the reference architecture for many solutions on Google Cloud Platform.[18]

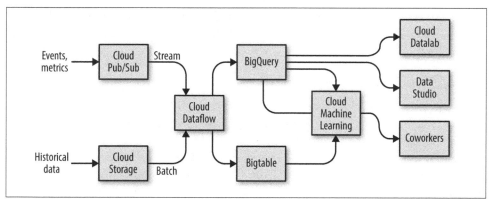

Figure 4-7. Reference architecture for data processing on Google Cloud Platform

In the previous section, we set up a real-time stream of events into Cloud Pub/Sub that we can aggregate in Cloud Dataflow and write to BigQuery. Data Studio can connect to BigQuery and provide a real-time, interactive dashboard. Let's get started.

Streaming in Java Dataflow

We used Beam/Dataflow in Python in the previous chapter because it required only batch processing. When we carried out the time correction of the raw flight data, we were working off files in Cloud Storage in batch mode, processing them in Cloud Dataflow and writing events table into BigQuery. Here, though, we need to process

---

18 For an example, go to *https://cloud.google.com/solutions/mobile/mobile-gaming-analysis-telemetry*.

events in Cloud Pub/Sub that are streaming in. As of this writing, the Python API for Apache Beam does not support streaming, so we'll have to do this in Java.[19]

We could simply receive the events from Cloud Pub/Sub and directly stream them to BigQuery using just a few lines of code:

```
String topic = "projects/" + options.getProject() + "/topics/arrived";
pipeline //
   .apply(PubsubIO.<String>read().topic(topic)) //
   .apply(ParDo.of(new DoFn<String, TableRow>() {
      @Override
      public void processElement(ProcessContext c) throws Exception {
         String[] fields = c.element().split(",");
         TableRow row = new TableRow();
         row.set("timestamp", fields[0]);
         …
         c.output(row);
   }} ) //
   .apply(BigQueryIO.Write.to(outputTable).withSchema(schema));
```

In the preceding code, we subscribe to a topic in Cloud Pub/Sub and begin reading from it. As each message streams in, we convert it to a TableRow in BigQuery and then write it out.

Windowing a pipeline

Although we could do just a straight data transfer, I'd like to do more. When I populate a real-time dashboard of flight delays, I'd like the information to be aggregated over a reasonable interval—for example, I want a moving average of flight delays and the total number of flights over the past 60 minutes at every airport. So, rather than simply take the input received from Cloud Pub/Sub and stream it out to BigQuery, I'd like to carry out time-windowed analytics on the data as I'm receiving it and write those analytics[20] to BigQuery. Cloud Dataflow can help us do this.

Because this is Java, and Java code tends to be verbose, I'll show you only the key parts of the code and keep the snippets I show conceptually relevant. For the full code, see the GitHub repository for this book.[21] You can execute it by using the

---

19 My treatment of Beam Java syntax in this section is going to be quite rapid; mostly, I focus on streaming data concepts. In Chapter 8, where Beam Java makes a reappearance, I spend more time on the syntactic details. Come back and reread this section after you read Chapter 8.

20 If you wanted to write the raw data that is received to BigQuery, you could do that, too, of course—that is what is shown in the previous code snippet. In this section, I assume that we need only the aggregate statistics over the past hour.

21 See the Java code in *04_streaming/realtime/chapter4/src* of *http://github.com/GoogleCloudPlatform/data-science-on-gcp*.

run_oncloud.sh script that is included (it relies on the Java build tool Maven (*http://maven.apache.org/*) and Java 8, so you should have both of these installed).

Creating a Java Dataflow pipeline in Java is conceptually similar to doing so in Python. We specify a project, runner, staging directory, and so on as usual on the command line and pull it into our program as command-line args. The one difference here, because we are no longer working with batch data, is that we turn on streaming mode:

```
MyOptions options = PipelineOptionsFactory.fromArgs(args).//
                    withValidation().as(MyOptions.class);
options.setStreaming(true);
Pipeline p = Pipeline.create(options);
```

The class `MyOptions` simply defines two extra command-line parameters: the averaging interval (60 minutes is what I will use in my charts in this section) and the speed-up factor. Because we are simulating real-time, aggregation of 60 minutes of data translates to an actual aggregation of over 1 minute of the incoming stream if we are simulating at 60x. The program uses the desired averaging interval and the speed-up factor to calculate this:

```
Duration averagingInterval = Duration.millis(Math.round(
    1000 * 60 * (options.getAveragingInterval() /
                options.getSpeedupFactor())));
```

While we may be averaging over 60 minutes, how often should we compute this 60-minute average? It might be advantageous, for example, to use a sliding window and compute this 60-minute average every minute. In my case, I'll use an averaging frequency that ends up computing the moving average twice[22] within the averaging interval, i.e. once every 30 minutes:

```
Duration averagingFrequency = averagingInterval.dividedBy(2);
```

Streaming aggregation

The difference between batch aggregation and streaming aggregation starts with the source of our data. Rather than read messages from Cloud Storage, we now read messages from the Cloud Pub/Sub topic. However, what does the "max" mean when the data is unbounded?

A key concept when aggregating streaming data is that of a window that becomes the scope for all aggregations. Here, we immediately apply a time-based sliding window

---

[22] Computing a moving average will end up causing loss of information, of course, but given that we are going to be computing a moving average, doing so at least twice within the window helps preserve the information whose variation can be captured by that window. This result, proved by Claude Shannon in 1948, launched information theory as a discipline.

on the pipeline. From now on, all grouping, aggregation, and so on is within that time window:

```
PCollection<Flight> flights = p //
    .apply(event + ":read", PubsubIO.<String>read().topic(topic))
    .apply(event + ":window", Window.into(SlidingWindows
        .of(averagingInterval).every(averagingFrequency)))
```

We then convert every message that we read into a `Flight` object:

```
.apply(event + ":parse", ParDo.of(new DoFn<String, Flight>() {
@Override
public void processElement(ProcessContext c) throws Exception {
    try {
        String line = c.element();
        Flight f = new Flight(line.split(","), eventType);
        c.output(f);
    } catch (NumberFormatException e) {
        // ignore errors about empty delay fields ...
    }
}
}));
```

The variable `flights` is a `PCollection` (a distributed, out-of-memory collection) that can then be passed on to new parts of the pipeline. Because no group-by has happened yet, `flights` is not yet subject to a time window.

The `Flight` object itself consists of the data corresponding to the event. For example, if the `eventType` is `arrived`, the airport information corresponds to the destination airport, whereas if the `eventType` is `departed`, the airport information corresponds to the origin airport:[23]

```
public class Flight implements Serializable {
    Airport airport;
    double delay;
    String timestamp;
}
```

The `Airport` information consists of the name of the airport and its geographic coordinates:

```
public class Airport implements Serializable {
    String name;
    double latitude;
    double longitude;
}
```

---

23 Because the `Flight` object is `Serializable`, Java serialization will be used to move the objects around. For better performance, we should consider using a protocol buffer. This pipeline is not going to be used routinely, and so I will take the simpler route of using Java serialization in this chapter. When we do real-time serialization in later chapters, we will revisit this decision.

The first statistic that we want to compute is the average delay at any airport over the past hour. We can do this very simply:

```
stats.delay = flights
    .apply(event + ":airportdelay", ParDo.of(new DoFn<Flight, KV<Airport, Double>>() {
    @Override
    public void processElement(ProcessContext c) throws Exception {
        Flight stats = c.element();
        c.output(KV.of(stats.airport, stats.delay));
    }
})))//
    .apply(event + ":avgdelay", Mean.perKey());
```

Ignoring the Java boilerplate introduced by anonymous classes and type safety, this boils down to emitting the delay value for every airport, and then computing the mean delay per airport. Cloud Dataflow takes care of windowing this computation so that the mean happens over the past 60 minutes and is computed every 30 minutes. The result, stat.delay, is also a PCollection that consists of a value for every airport. If we call the method movingAverage() that we looked at earlier, we need to calculate movingAverage() starting from the pipeline twice, once for departed events, and again for arrived events:

```
final WindowStats arr = movingAverageOf(options, p, "arrived");
final WindowStats dep = movingAverageOf(options, p, "departed");
```

We want to compute more than just the average delay, however. We want to know how many flights the airport in question handled (perhaps the number of flights at an airport is a predictor of delays) and the last timestamp of the last flight in the window. These two statistics are computed as follows (I'm omitting the boilerplate):

```
stats.timestamp = flights //
    .apply(event + ":timestamps", …
        c.output(KV.of(stats.airport, stats.timestamp));
    )//
    .apply(event + ":lastTimeStamp", Max.perKey());
for the latest timestamp and:
stats.num_flights = flights //
    .apply(event + ":numflights", ...
        c.output(KV.of(stats.airport, 1));
        )//
    .apply(event + ":total", Sum.integersPerKey());
for the total number of flights.
```

Co-join by key

At this point, we have six statistics for each airport—the mean departure delay, the mean arrival delay, the latest departure timestamp, the latest arrival timestamp, the total number of departures, and the total number of arrivals. However, they are all in separate PCollections. Because these PCollections all have a common key (the airport), we can "co-join" these to get all the statistics in one place:[24]

```
KeyedPCollectionTuple //
.of(tag0, arr_delay) // PCollection
.and(tag1, dep_delay) //
.and(tag2, arr_timestamp) //
// etc.
.apply("airport:cogroup", CoGroupByKey.<Airport> create()) //
.apply("airport:stats", ParDo.of(...
    public void processElement(ProcessContext c) throws Exception {
        KV<Airport, CoGbkResult> e = c.element();
        Airport airport = e.getKey();
        Double arrDelay = e.getValue().getOnly(tag0,
                                    new Double(-999));

        // etc.
        c.output(new AirportStats(airport, arrDelay, depDelay,
                                    timestamp, num_flights));
}})))//
```

The class AirportStats contains all the statistics that we have collected:

```
public class AirportStats implements Serializable {
    Airport airport;
    double arr_delay, dep_delay;
    String timestamp;
    int num_flights;
}
```

These can be written to BigQuery with a schema, as discussed in the section on simulating a real-time feed.

Executing the Stream Processing

To start the simulation, start the Python simulator that we developed in the previous section:

```
python simulate.py --startTime '2015-05-01 00:00:00 UTC'
--endTime '2015-05-04 00:00:00 UTC'  --speedFactor 30
```

The simulator will send events from May 1, 2015, to May 3, 2015, at 30 times real-time speed, so that an hour of data is sent to Cloud Pub/Sub in two minutes. You can do this from CloudShell or from your local laptop. (If necessary, run install_pack ages.sh to install the necessary Python packages and gcloud auth application-default login to give the application the necessary credentials to execute queries.)

---

24 The code shown here is greatly simplified. For the full code, see the GitHub repository.

Then, start the Cloud Dataflow job that will listen to the two Cloud Pub/Sub topics and stream aggregate statistics into BigQuery. You can start the Cloud Dataflow job using Apache Maven (*http://maven.apache.org/*):

```
mvn compile exec:java \
  -Dexec.mainClass=com.google.cloud.training.flights.AverageDelayPipeline
      -Dexec.args="--project=$PROJECT \
      --stagingLocation=gs://$BUCKET/staging/ \
      --averagingInterval=60 \
      --speedupFactor=30 \
      --runner=DataflowRunner"
```

If you now browse to the Cloud Platform console, to the Cloud Dataflow section, you will see that a new streaming job has started and that the pipeline looks like that shown in Figure 4-8.

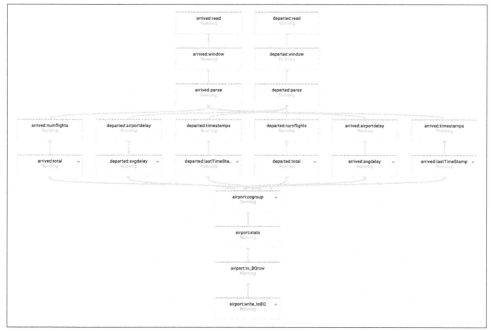

Figure 4-8. The streaming pipeline to compute three sets of statistics

From each of the topics, three sets of statistics are computed, cogrouped into a single AirportStats object and streamed into BigQuery.

Analyzing Streaming Data in BigQuery

Three minutes[25] after the launch of your program, the first set of data will make it into BigQuery. You can query for the statistics for a specific airport from the Big-Query console:

```
#standardsql
SELECT
  *
FROM
  `flights.streaming_delays`
WHERE
  airport = 'DEN'
ORDER BY
  timestamp DESC
```

Figure 4-9 presents the results that I got.

Figure 4-9. Results of the streaming pipeline shown for Denver airport

Note how the timestamps are spread about 30 minutes apart. The average delays themselves are averages over an hour. So, Denver airport in the time between 04:10 UTC and 05:10 UTC had 45 flights, and an average departure delay of 17 minutes.

The cool thing is that we can do this querying even as the data is streaming! How would we get the latest data for all airports? We could use an inner query to find the

---

25 Recall that we are computing aggregates over 60 minutes every 30 minutes. Cloud Dataflow treats the first "full" window as happening 90 minutes into the simulation. Because we are simulating at 30 times speed, this is three minutes on your clock.

---

maximum timestamp and use it in the WHERE clause to select flights within the past 30 minutes:

```
#standardsql
SELECT
  airport,
  arr_delay,
  dep_delay,
  timestamp,
  latitude,
  longitude,
  num_flights
FROM
  `flights.streaming_delays`
WHERE
  ABS(TIMESTAMP_DIFF(timestamp,
    (
    SELECT
      MAX(timestamp) latest
    FROM
      `cloud-training-demos.flights.streaming_delays` ),
    MINUTE)) < 29
  AND num_flights > 10
```

Figure 4-10 shows the results.

Row	airport	arr_delay	dep_delay	timestamp	latitude	longitude	num_flights
1	CMH	9.0	null	2015-05-01 02:20:00 UTC	39.99694444	-82.89222222	6
2	STL	12.583333333333334	13.181818181818182	2015-05-01 02:36:00 UTC	38.74861111	-90.37	23
3	PDX	-12.222222222222221	-5.0	2015-05-01 02:37:00 UTC	45.58861111	-122.59694444	14
4	RIC	-5.5	null	2015-05-01 02:37:00 UTC	37.50527778	-77.31972222	4
5	HNL	-1.8571428571428572	7.428571428571429	2015-05-01 02:35:00 UTC	21.31777778	-157.92027778	14
6	LAX	-3.4473684210526314	12.241379310344827	2015-05-01 02:37:00 UTC	33.9425	-118.40805556	67
7	PHL	2.1875	68.0	2015-05-01 02:29:00 UTC	39.87222222	-75.24083333	17
8	ATL	16.95	4.260869565217392	2015-05-01 02:36:00 UTC	33.63666667	-84.42777778	109
9	KOA	0.0	57.666666666666664	2015-05-01 02:33:00 UTC	19.73888889	-156.04555556	4

Table   JSON   First < Prev Rows 1 - 9 of 66 Next > Last

Figure 4-10. The latest results for all airports

Queries like these on streaming data will be useful when we begin to build our dashboard. For example, the first query will allow us to build a time–series chart of delays at a specific airport. The second query will allow us to build a map of average delays across the country.

Real-Time Dashboard

Now that we have streaming data in BigQuery and a way to analyze it as it is streaming in, we can create a dashboard that shows departure and arrival delays in context.

Two maps can help explain our contingency table–based model to end users: current arrival delays across the country, and current departure delays across the country.

To pull the data to populate these charts, we need to add a BigQuery data source in Data Studio. Although Data Studio supports specifying the query directly in the user interface, it is much better to create a view in BigQuery and use that view as a data source in Data Studio. BigQuery views have a few advantages over queries that you type into Data Studio: they tend to be reusable across reports and visualization tools, there is only one place to change if an error is detected, and BigQuery views map better to access privileges (Cloud Identity Access Management roles) based on the columns they need to access.

Here is the query that I used to create the view:

```
#standardSQL
SELECT
  airport,
  last[safe_OFFSET(0)].*,
  CONCAT(CAST(last[safe_OFFSET(0)].latitude AS STRING), ",",
         CAST(last[safe_OFFSET(0)].longitude AS STRING)) AS location
FROM (
  SELECT
    airport,
    ARRAY_AGG(STRUCT(arr_delay,
        dep_delay,
        timestamp,
        latitude,
        longitude,
        num_flights)
    ORDER BY
      timestamp DESC
    LIMIT
      1) last
  FROM
    `flights.streaming_delays`
  GROUP BY
    airport )
```

This is slightly different from the second query in the previous section (the one with the inner query on maximum timestamp). It retains the last received update from each airport, thus accommodating airports with very few flights and airports with which we have lost connectivity over the past hour (in practice, you'd add filtering to this query to avoid displaying data that is too old). The query also combines the latitude and longitude columns into a single text field that is separated by a comma. This is one of the geographic formats understood by Data Studio.

Figure 4-11 presents the end result.

Having saved the view in BigQuery, we can create a data source for the view in Data Studio, very similar to the way we created one for views in Cloud SQL in the previous

chapter. Make sure to change the type of the `location` column from Text to Geo →
Latitude, Longitude.

Row	airport	arr_delay	dep_delay	timestamp	latitude	longitude	num_flights	location
1	TOL	10.0	null	2015-05-01 18:33:00 UTC	41.58694444	-83.80777778	1	41.58694444,41.58694444
2	LCH	-16.0	null	2015-05-01 18:26:00 UTC	30.12611111	-93.22333333	1	30.12611111,30.12611111
3	ELM	-4.0	null	2015-05-01 18:56:00 UTC	42.15972222	-76.89194444	1	42.15972222,42.15972222
4	DHN	1.0	null	2015-05-01 18:36:00 UTC	31.32111111	-85.44944444	1	31.32111111,31.32111111
5	JLN	-14.0	null	2015-05-01 18:27:00 UTC	37.15194444	-94.49833333	1	37.15194444,37.15194444

Figure 4-11. Result of query to get latest data from all airports, along with location information

After the data source has been created, you are ready to create a geo map (using the globe icon in Data Studio). Change the zoom area to the United States, specify `dep_delay` as the metric, and change the style so that the color bar goes from green to red through white. Repeat this for the arrival delay and the total number of flights, and you'll end up with a dashboard that looks like the one shown in Figure 4-12.

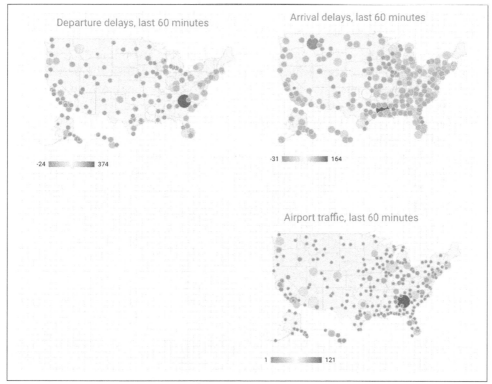

Figure 4-12. Dashboard of latest flight data from across the United States

It is worth reflecting on what we did in this section. We processed streaming data in Cloud Dataflow, creating 60-minute moving averages that we streamed into Big-Query. We then created a view in BigQuery that would show the latest data for each airport, even as it was streaming in. We connected that to a dashboard in Data Studio. Every time the dashboard is refreshed, it pulls new data from the view, which in turn dynamically reflects the latest data in BigQuery.

Summary

In this chapter, we discussed how to build a real-time analysis pipeline to carry out streaming analytics and populate real-time dashboards. In this book, we are using a dataset that is not available in real time. Therefore, we simulated the creation of a real-time feed so that I could demonstrate how to build a streaming ingest pipeline. Building the simulation also gives us a handy test tool—no longer do we need to wait for an interesting event to happen. We can simply play back a recorded event!

In the process of building out the simulation, we realized that time handling in the original dataset was problematic. Therefore, we improved the handling of time in the original data and created a new dataset with UTC timestamps and local offsets. This is the dataset that we will use going forward.

We also looked at the reference architecture for handling streaming data in Google Cloud Platform. First, receive your data in Cloud Pub/Sub so that the messages can be received asynchronously. Process the Cloud Pub/Sub messages in Cloud Dataflow, computing aggregations on the data as needed, and stream either the raw data or aggregate data (or both) to BigQuery. We worked with all three Google Cloud Platform products (Cloud Pub/Sub, Cloud Dataflow, and BigQuery) using the Google Cloud Platform client libraries in Python. However, in none of these cases did we ever need to create a virtual machine ourselves—these are all serverless and autoscaled offerings. We thus were able to concentrate on writing code, letting the platform manage the rest.

## CHAPTER 5

Interactive Data Exploration

In every major field of study, there is usually a towering figure who did much of the seminal work and blazed the trail for what that particular discipline would evolve into. Classical physics has Newton, relativity has Einstein, game theory has John Nash, and so on. When it comes to computational statistics (the field of study that develops computationally efficient methods for carrying out statistical operations), the towering figure is John W. Tukey. At Bell Labs, he collaborated with John von Neumann on early computer designs soon after World War II—famously, Tukey was responsible for coining the word *bit*. Later, at Princeton (where he founded its statistics department), Tukey collaborated with James Cooley to develop the Fast-Fourier Transform, one of the first examples of using divide-and-conquer to address a formidable computational challenge.

While Tukey was responsible for many "hard science" mathematical and engineering innovations, some of his most enduring work is about the distinctly softer side of science. Unsatisfied that most of statistics overemphasized confirmatory data analysis (i.e., statistical hypothesis testing such as paired t-tests[1]), Tukey developed a variety of approaches to do what he termed *exploratory data analysis*[2] (EDA) and many practical statistical approximations. It was Tukey who developed the box plot, jack-knifing, range test, median-median regression, and so on and gave these eminently practical methods a solid mathematical grounding by motivating them in the context of simple conceptual models that are applicable to a wide variety of datasets. In this chapter, we follow Tukey's approach of carrying out exploratory data analysis to identify impor-

---

1 See *https://en.wikipedia.org/wiki/Statistical_hypothesis_testing* for an excellent overview of statistical hypotheses testing.

2 John Tukey, 1977. *Exploratory Data Analysis*. Addison-Wesley.

tant variables, discover underlying structure, develop parsimonious models, and use that model to identify unusual patterns and values.

Exploratory Data Analysis

Ever since Tukey introduced the world to the value of EDA in 1977, the traditional first step for any data scientist has been to analyze raw data by using a variety of graphical techniques. This is not a fixed set of methods or plots; rather, it's an approach meant to develop insight into a dataset and enable the development of robust statistical models. Specifically, as a data scientist, you should create graphics that enable you to do the following:

- Test any underlying assumptions, such as that a particular value will always be present, or will always lie within a certain range. For example, as discussed in Chapter 2, the distribution of the distance between any pair of airports might help verify whether the distance is the same across the dataset or whether it reflects the actual flight distance.

- Use intuition and logic to identify important variables. Verify that these variables are, indeed, important as expected. For example, plotting the relationship between departure delay and arrival delay might validate assumptions about the recording of these variables.

- Discover underlying structure in the data (i.e., relationships between important variables and situations such as the data falling into specific statistical regimes). It might be useful to examine whether the season (summer versus winter) has an impact on how often flight delays can be made up.

- Develop a parsimonious model—a simple model with explanatory power, that you can use to hypothesize about what reasonable values in the data look like. If there is a simple relationship between departure delay and arrival delay, values of either delay that are far off the trendline might warrant further examination.

- Detect outliers, anomalies, and other inexplicable data values. This depends on having that parsimonious model. Thus, further examination of outliers from the simple trend between departure and arrival delays might lead to the discovery that such values off the trendline correspond to rerouted flights.

To carry out exploratory data analysis, it is necessary to load the data in a form that makes interactive analysis possible. In this chapter, we load data into Google Big-Query, explore the data in Cloud Datalab, carry out quality control based on what we discover about the dataset, build a new model, and evaluate the model to ensure that it is better than the model we built in Chapter 4. As we go about loading the data and exploring it and move on to building models and evaluating them, we'll discuss a variety of considerations that come up, from security to pricing.

Both exploratory data analysis and the dashboard creation discussed in Chapter 3 involve the creation of graphics. However, the steps differ in two ways—in terms of the purpose and in terms of the audience. The aim of dashboard creation is to crowd-source insight into the working of models from end users and is, therefore, primarily about presenting an explanation of the models to end users. In Chapter 3, I recommended doing it very early in your development cycle, but that advice was more about Agile development[3] and getting feedback early than about statistical rigor. The aim of EDA is for you, the data engineer, to develop insights about the data before you delve into developing sophisticated models. The audience for EDA is typically other members of your team, not end users. In some cases, especially if you uncover strange artifacts in the data, the audience could be the data engineering team that produces the dataset you are working with. For example, when we discovered the problem that the times were being reported in local time, with no UTC offsets, we could have relayed that information back to the US Bureau of Transportation Statistics (BTS).[4] In any case, the assumption is that the audience for an EDA graphic is statistically sophisticated. Although you probably would not include a violin plot[5] in a dashboard meant for end users, you would have no compunctions about using a violin plot in an EDA chart that is meant for data scientists.

Doing exploratory data analysis on large datasets poses a few challenges. To test that a particular value will always be present, for example, you would need to check every row of a tabular dataset, and if that dataset is many millions of rows, these tests can take hours. An interactive ability to quickly explore large datasets is indispensable. On Google Cloud Platform, BigQuery provides the ability to run Cloud SQL queries on unindexed datasets (i.e., your raw data) in a matter of seconds even if the datasets are in the petabyte scale. Therefore, in this chapter, we load the flights data into Big-Query.

Identifying outliers and underlying structure typically involves using univariate and bivariate plots. The graphs themselves can be created using Python plotting libraries —I use a mixture of matplotlib (*http://matplotlib.org/*) and seaborn (*http://seaborn.pydata.org/*) to do this. However, the networking overhead of moving data between storage and the graphics engine can become prohibitive if I carry out data exploration on my laptop—for exploration of large datasets to be interactive, we need to bring the analytics closer to the data. Therefore, we will want to use a cloud com-

---

3 James Shore and Shane Warden, 2007. *The Art of Agile Development*. O'Reilly Media.

4 I did confirm with the BTS via email that the times in the dataset were, indeed, in the local timezone of the corresponding airport. The BTS being a government agency that was making the data freely available, I didn't broach the matter of them producing a separate dataset with UTC timestamps. In a contractual relationship with a vendor, however, this is the type of change you might request as a result of EDA.

5 A violin plot is a way of visualizing probability density functions. See *http://seaborn.pydata.org/generated/seaborn.violinplot.html* for examples.

puter (not my laptop) to carry out graph generation. Generating graphics on a cloud computer poses a display challenge because the graphs are being generated on a Compute Engine instance that is headless—that is, it has no input or output devices. A Compute Engine instance has no keyboard, mouse, or monitor, and frequently has no graphics card.[6] Such a machine is accessed purely through a network connection. Fortunately, desktop programs and interactive Read–Eval–Print Loops (REPLs) are no longer necessary to create visualizations. Instead, notebook servers such as Jupyter (*http://jupyter.org/*) (formerly IPython) have become the standard way that data scientists create graphs and disseminate executable reports. On Google Cloud Platform, Cloud Datalab (*https://cloud.google.com/datalab/*) provides a way to run Jupyter notebooks on Compute Engine instances and connect to Google Cloud Platform services.

Loading Flights Data into BigQuery

To be able to carry out exploratory analysis on the flights data, we would like to run arbitrary Cloud SQL queries on it (i.e., without having to create indexes and do tuning). BigQuery is an excellent place to store the flights data for exploratory data analysis. Furthermore, if you tend to use R rather than Python for exploratory data analysis, the dplyr package[7] allows you to write data manipulation code in R (rather than SQL) and translates the R code into efficient SQL on the backend to be executed by BigQuery.

Advantages of a Serverless Columnar Database

Most relational database systems, whether commercial or open source, are row oriented in that the data is stored row by row. This makes it easy to append new rows of data to the database and allows for features such as row-level locking when updating the value of a row. The drawback is that queries that involve table scans (i.e., any aggregation that requires reading every row) can be expensive. Indexing counteracts this expense by creating a lookup table to map rows to column values, so that SELECTs that involve indexed columns do not have to load unnecessary rows from storage into memory. If you can rely on indexes for fast lookup of your data, a traditional Relational Database Management System (RDBMS) works well. For example, if your queries tend to come from software applications, you will know the queries that will come in and can create the appropriate indexes beforehand. This is not an option for use cases like business intelligence for which human users are writing ad hoc queries; therefore, a different architecture is needed.

---

6 Special Graphics Processing Unit (GPU) instances exist (*https://cloud.google.com/gpu/*), but for the graphs in this chapter, CPU instances are sufficient.

7 See *https://cran.rstudio.com/web/packages/dplyr/vignettes/introduction.html*. In this book, for simplicity, I focus on the Python ecosystem of tools for Google Cloud Platform. A parallel R ecosystem also exists.

BigQuery, on the other hand, is a columnar database—data is stored column by column and each column's data is stored in a highly efficient compressed format (*http://bit.ly/2k23ORv*) that enables fast querying. Because of the way data is stored, many common queries can be carried out such that the query processing time is linear on the size of the relevant data (*http://bit.ly/2ACdbiL*). For applications such as data warehousing and business intelligence for which the predominant operations are read-only `SELECT` queries requiring full table scans, columnar databases are a better fit. BigQuery, for example, can scan terabytes of data in a matter of seconds. The trade-off is that `INSERT`, `UPDATE`, and `DELETE`, although possible in BigQuery, are significantly more expensive to process (*http://bit.ly/2zTGc88*) than `SELECT` statements. BigQuery is tuned toward analytics use cases.

BigQuery is serverless, so you don't actually spin up a BigQuery server in your project. Instead, you simply submit a SQL query, and it is executed on the cloud. Queries that you submit to BigQuery are executed on a large number of compute nodes (called *slots*) in parallel. These slots do not need to be statically allocated beforehand—instead, they are "always on," available on demand, and scale to the size of your job. Because data is in situ[8] and not sharded in Google Cloud Platform, the total power of the datacenter can be brought to bear on the problem. Because these resources are elastic and used only for the duration of the query, BigQuery is more powerful and less expensive than a statically preallocated cluster because preallocated clusters will typically be provisioned for the average use case—BigQuery can bring more resources to bear on the above-average computational jobs and utilize fewer resources for below-average ones.

In addition, because you don't need to reserve any compute resources for your data when you are not querying your data, it is extremely cost effective to just keep your data in BigQuery (you'll pay for storage, but storage is inexpensive). Whenever you do need to query the data, the data is immediately available—you can query it without the need to start project-specific compute resources. This on-demand, autoscaling of compute resources is incredibly liberating.

If an on-demand cost structure (you pay per query) makes you concerned about costs that can fluctuate month over month, you can specify a billing cap beyond which users will not be able to go. For even more cost predictability, it is possible to pay a fixed monthly price for BigQuery—flat-rate pricing allows you to get a predictable cost regardless of the number of queries run or data processed by those queries—the fixed monthly price essentially buys you access to a specific number of slots.[9] In short, BigQuery has two pricing models for analysis (*http://bit.ly/2BQX9Se*): an on-demand

---

8 Stored in-place and not sharded onto the compute nodes—see Chapter 2.

9 See *https://cloud.google.com/bigquery/pricing#flat_rate_pricing*. As of this writing, switching to the flat-rate pricing model requires you to contact your Google Cloud Platform account representative.

pricing model in which your cost depends on the quantity of data processed, and a flat-rate model in which you pay a fixed amount per month for an unlimited number of queries that will run on a specific set of compute resources. In either case, storage is a separate cost and depends on data size. In terms of cost, the optimal way of using BigQuery tends to be the default on-demand pricing model, and this is what I'll assume you are using.

In summary, BigQuery is a columnar database, making it particularly effective for read-only queries that process all of the data. Because it is serverless, can autoscale to thousands of compute nodes, and doesn't require clusters to be preallocated, it is also very powerful and quite inexpensive.

Staging on Cloud Storage

The time correction code that we wrote in Chapter 3 took BTS's flight data stored in comma-separated value (CSV) files, corrected the timestamps to UTC, appended some extra columns corresponding to airport location, and wrote the output files as CSV files in Cloud Storage. Let's assume, for the purposes of this section, that the time-corrected data are the files that we obtained from BTS. In this section, we will ingest those CSV files from Cloud Storage into a flights table in BigQuery.

Although it is possible to ingest files from on-premises hardware directly into Big-Query using the bq command-line tool (*http://bit.ly/2zSJLvA*) that comes with the Google Cloud SDK (gcloud), you should use that capability only for small datasets. To retrieve data from outside Google Cloud Platform to BigQuery, it is preferable to first load it into Cloud Storage (see Chapters 2 and 3) and use Cloud Storage as the staging ground for BigQuery, as demonstrated in Figure 5-1.

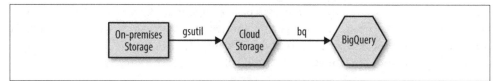

Figure 5-1. Use Cloud Storage as a staging ground to ingest data into BigQuery

For larger files, it is better to ingest the files into Cloud Storage using gsutil first because gsutil takes advantage of multithreaded, resumable uploads and is better suited to the public internet.

Of course, the same Cloud Dataflow pipeline that carried out the time correction also created the events data that were written to BigQuery and used to simulate a real-time stream in Chapter 4. We could have written the flights data from the Cloud Dataflow pipeline directly to BigQuery rather than to CSV files.[10] However, I left it as CSV files just to be able to demonstrate how to ingest data into BigQuery without going through the process of writing a Cloud Dataflow pipeline.

When should you save your data in Cloud Storage, and when should you store it in BigQuery? The answer boils down to what you want to do with the data and the kinds of analyses you want to perform. If you'll mostly be running custom code that expects to read plain files, or your analysis involves reading the entire dataset, use Cloud Storage. On the other hand, if your desired access pattern is to run interactive SQL queries on the data, store your data in BigQuery. In the pre-cloud world, if you would use flat files, use Cloud Storage. If you'd put the data in a database, put it in BigQuery.

Access Control

The first step to ingest data into BigQuery would be to create a BigQuery dataset (all tables in BigQuery must belong to a dataset), but we already have the flights dataset from Chapter 3 that we can continue to use. Datasets in BigQuery are mostly just an organizational convenience—tables are where data resides and it is the columns of the table that dictate the queries we write. Besides providing a way to organize tables, though, datasets also serve as the *access control point*. You can provide view or edit access only at the project or dataset level, not at the table level. So, before we decide to reuse the flights dataset, the key questions we need to answer are whether this table is related to the simevents table that is currently present in that dataset (it is), and whether both tables should share the same access control. The latter question is more difficult to answer—it could be that the simevents table, storing simulated events, is meant for use by a narrower set of roles than the time-corrected data.

Cloud Identity Access Management (Cloud IAM) on Google Cloud Platform provides a mechanism to control *who* can carry out *what* actions on *which* resource (Figure 5-2).

The "who" can be specified in terms of an individual user (identified by his Google account such as a gmail.com address or company email address if the company is a GSuite customer), a Google Group (i.e., all current members of the group), or a GSuite domain (anyone with a Google account in that domain). Google groups and GSuite domains provide a convenient mechanism for aggregating a number of users and providing similar access to all of them.

---

10 See Chapter 8 for an example of how to write to BigQuery from a Dataflow pipeline.

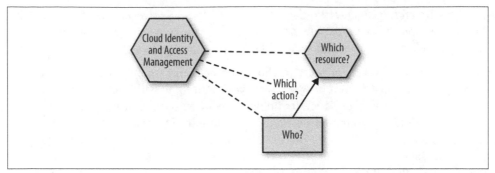

Figure 5-2. Cloud IAM provides a mechanism to control access to resources

In addition, different logical parts of an application can be assigned separate email addresses called *service accounts*. Service accounts are a very powerful concept because they allow different parts of a codebase to have permissions that are independent of the access level of the person running that application. For example, you might want an application to be able to spin up new Compute Engine instances but not provide the raw access to the Compute Engine creation[11] to an end user on behalf of the person for whom the application is spinning up those instances.

You should use service accounts with care for scenarios in which audit records are mandatory. Providing access at the Google Groups level provides more of an audit trail: because Google groups don't have login credentials (only individual users do), the user who made a request or action is always recorded, even if their access is provided at the level of a Google Group or GSuite domain. However, service accounts are themselves login credentials, and so the audit trail turns cold if you provide access to service accounts—you will no longer know which user initiated the application request unless that application in turn logs this information. This is something to keep in mind when granting access to service accounts. Try to avoid providing service account access to resources that require auditability. If you do provide service account access, you should ensure that the application to which you have provided access itself provides the necessary audit trail by keeping track of the user on behalf of whom it is executing the request. The same considerations apply to service accounts that are part of Google Groups or domains. Because audit trails go cold with service accounts,[12] you should restrict Google Groups and GSuite domains to only human

---

11 Especially not Compute Engine instance creation, as this capability will then get hijacked toward bitcoin mining. See *https://www.deepdotweb.com/2014/08/08/mining-cryptocurrency-free-cloud-botnet/*.

12 A service account is tied to a project, but project membership evolves over time. So, even the subset of users who could have invoked the action might not be known unless you have strict governance over who is allowed to be an owner/editor/viewer of a project.

users and service accounts that belong to applications that provide any necessary legal auditability guarantees.

Creating single-user projects is another way to ensure that service accounts map cleanly to users, but this can lead to significant administrative overhead associated with shared resources and departing personnel. Essentially, you would create a project that is billed to the same company billing account, but each individual user would have her own project in which she works. You can use the gcloud command to script the creation of such single-user projects in which the user in question is an editor (not an owner).[13]

In addition to specific users, groups, domains, and service accounts, there are two wildcard options available. Access can be provided to allAuthenticatedUsers, in which case anyone authenticated with either a Google account or a service account is provided access. Because allAuthenticatedUsers includes service accounts, it should be not used for resources for which a clear audit trail is required. The other wildcard option is to provide access to allUsers, in which case anyone on the internet has access—a common use case for this is to provide highly available static web resources by storing them on Cloud Storage. Be careful about doing this indiscriminately—egress of data from Google Cloud Platform is not free, so you will pay for the bandwidth consumed by the download of your cloud-hosted datasets.

The "what" actions depend on the resource access which is being controlled. The resources themselves fall into a policy hierarchy.

Policies can be specified at an organization level (i.e., to all projects in the organization), at the project level (i.e., to all resources in the project), or at the resource level (i.e., to a Compute Engine instance or a BigQuery dataset). As Figure 5-3 shows, policies specified at higher levels are inherited at lower levels, and the policy in effect is the union of all the permissions granted—there is no way to restrict some access to a dataset to a user who has that access inherited from the project level. Moving a project from one organization to another automatically updates that project's Cloud IAM policy and ends up affecting all the resources owned by that project.

---

13 See *http://bit.ly/2iviEPO* for a gcloud script that will create single-user projects. The users will be editors on the project, but project ownership will reside with the person who has billing administrator rights.

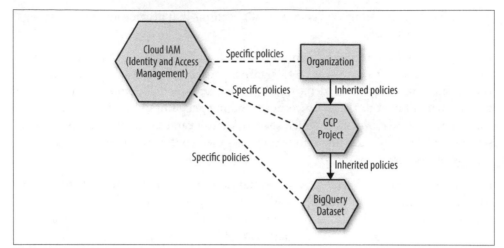

Figure 5-3. Policies specified at higher levels are inherited at lower levels

What type of actions can be carried out depends on the resource in question. Before Cloud IAM was introduced on the Google Cloud Platform, there were only three roles: owner, editor, and viewer/reader for all resources. Cloud IAM brought with it much finer-grained roles, but the original three roles were grandfathered in as primitive roles. Table 5-1 lists the roles that are possible for BigQuery datasets.

Table 5-1. Available roles in BigQuery

Role	Capabilities	Inherits from
Project Viewer	Execute a query List datasets	
Project Editor	Create a new dataset	Project Viewer
Project Owner	List/delete datasets View jobs run by other project users	Project Editor
bigquery.user	Execute a query List datasets	
bigquery.dataViewer	Read, query, copy, export tables in the dataset	
bigquery.dataEditor	Append, load data into tables in the dataset	Project Editor bigquery.dataViewer
bigquery.dataOwner	Update, delete on tables in dataset	Project Owner bigquery.dataEditor
bigquery.admin	All	

Neither the `simevents` table nor the `flights` table holds personally identifiable or confidential information. Therefore, there is no compelling access-control reason to create a separate dataset for the flight information. We will reuse the `flights` dataset that was created in Chapter 3, and we can make everyone in the organization a big query.user so that they can carry out queries on this dataset.

Browse to *bigquery.cloud.google.com*, find the flights dataset, and then click the options menu to be able to share the dataset. In the dialog box that opens (Figure 5-4), I selected the domain option and typed in google.com to allow view access to anyone in my organization.

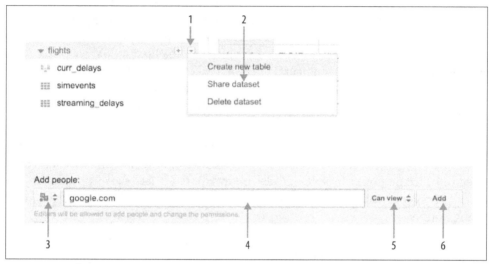

Figure 5-4. Sharing a BigQuery dataset

In some cases, you might find that your dataset contains certain columns that have personally identifying or confidential information. You might need to restrict access to those columns[14] while leaving the remainder of the table accessible to a wider audience. Whenever you need to provide access to a subset of a table in BigQuery (whether it is specific columns or specific rows), you can use views. Put the table itself in a dataset that is accessible to a very small set of users. Then, create a view on this table that will pull out the relevant columns and rows and save this view in a separate dataset that has wider accessibility. Your users will query only this view, and because the personally identifying or confidential information is not even present in the view, the chances of inadvertent leakage are lowered.

One of the benefits of a data warehouse is to allow the mashing of datasets across organizational boundaries. So, unless you have a clear reason not to do so, try to make your data widely accessible. Costs of querying are borne by the person submit-

---

14 Or make a copy or view of the table with anonymized column values—we cover safeguarding personally identifiable information in Chapter 7.

ting the query to the BigQuery engine, so you don't need to worry that you are incurring additional costs for your division by doing this.

Federated Queries

We do not need to ingest data into BigQuery's native table format in order to run Cloud SQL queries on the data. We could rely on BigQuery's "federated query" capabilities (*https://cloud.google.com/bigquery/external-data-sources*). This is the ability of BigQuery to query data that is not stored within the data warehouse product, but instead operate on such data sources as Google Sheets (a spreadsheet on Google Drive) or files on Cloud Storage. Thus, we could leave the files as CSV on Cloud Storage, define a table structure on it, and query the CSV files directly. Recall that we suggested using Cloud Storage if your primary analysis pattern involves working with your data at the level of flat files—this is a way of occasionally applying SQL queries to such datasets.

The first step is to get the schema of the time-corrected files on Cloud Storage. We could have BigQuery autodetect the schema had we still retained the header. However, our files no longer have the header information. So, let's start from the schema of the `simevents` table and remove the last three fields that correspond to the event being notified.

To obtain the schema of the `simevents` table in the `flights` dataset of our project, we can use the `bq` command-line tool that comes with the Google Cloud SDK:

```
bq show --format=prettyjson flights.simevents
```

Save the result to a file by redirecting the output to a file:

```
bq show --format=prettyjson flights.simevents > simevents.json
```

Open this file in an editor and remove everything except the array of fields. Within the array of fields, remove the last three fields (EVENT, NOTIFY_TIME, and EVENT_DATA), as illustrated in Figure 5-5.

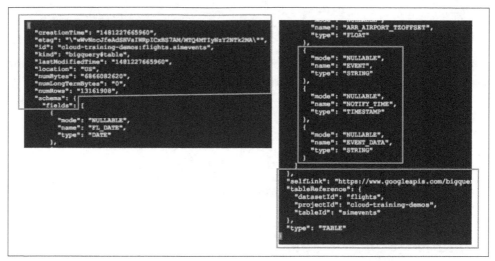

"creationTime": "1481227665960",
"etag": "\"wWvNncJfeAdSHVaIHRpICxBS7AM/MTQ4MTIyNzY2NTk2MA\"",
"id": "cloud-training-demos:flights.simevents",
"kind": "bigquery#table",
"lastModifiedTime": "1481227665960",
"location": "US",
"numBytes": "6866082620",
"numLongTermBytes": "0",
"numRows": "13161908",
"schema": {
    "fields": [
        {
            "mode": "NULLABLE",
            "name": "FL_DATE",
            "type": "DATE"
        },

            "name": "ARR_AIRPORT_TZOFFSET",
            "type": "FLOAT"
        },
        {
            "mode": "NULLABLE",
            "name": "EVENT",
            "type": "STRING"
        },
        {
            "mode": "NULLABLE",
            "name": "NOTIFY_TIME",
            "type": "TIMESTAMP"
        },
        {
            "mode": "NULLABLE",
            "name": "EVENT_DATA",
            "type": "STRING"
        }
    ]
},
"selfLink": "https://www.googleapis.com/bigque
"tableReference": {
    "datasetId": "flights",
    "projectId": "cloud-training-demos",
    "tableId": "simevents"
},
"type": "TABLE"

Figure 5-5. Fields that need to be removed

You should now be left with the schema of the content of the CSV files. The end result of the edit is in the GitHub repository of this book as *05_bqdatalab/tzcorr.json* and looks like this:

```
[
    {
        "mode": "NULLABLE",
        "name": "FL_DATE",
        "type": "DATE"
    },
    {
        "mode": "NULLABLE",
        "name": "UNIQUE_CARRIER",
        "type": "STRING"
    },
    ...
    {
        "mode": "NULLABLE",
        "name": "ARR_AIRPORT_LON",
        "type": "FLOAT"
    },
    {
        "mode": "NULLABLE",
        "name": "ARR_AIRPORT_TZOFFSET",
        "type": "FLOAT"
    }
]
```

Now that we have the schema of the CSV files, we can make a table definition for the federated source, but to keep things zippy, I'll use just one of the 36 files that were written out by the Cloud Dataflow job in Chapter 3:

```
bq mk --
external_table_definition=./tzcorr.json@CSV=
gs://<BUCKET>/flights/tzcorr/all_flights-00030-of-00036 flights.fedtzcorr
```

If you visit the BigQuery web console now, you should see a new table listed in the `flights` dataset (reload the page if necessary). This is a federated data source in that its storage remains the CSV file on Cloud Storage. Yet you can query it just like any other BigQuery table:

```
#standardsql
SELECT
  ORIGIN,
  AVG(DEP_DELAY) as arr_delay,
  AVG(ARR_DELAY) as dep_delay
FROM
  flights.fedtzcorr
GROUP BY
  ORIGIN
```

Don't get carried away by federated queries, though. The most appropriate uses of federated sources involve frequently changing, relatively small datasets that need to be joined with large datasets in BigQuery native tables. There are fundamental advantages to a columnar database design over row-wise storage in terms of the kinds of optimization that can be carried out and, consequently, in the performance that is achievable.[15] Because the columnar storage in BigQuery is so fundamental to its performance, we will load the flights data into BigQuery's native format. Fortunately, the cost of storage in BigQuery is similar to the cost of storage in Cloud Storage, and the discount offered for long-term storage is similar—as long as the table data is not changed (querying the data is okay), the long-term discount starts to apply (*http://bit.ly/2iWVxle*). So, if storage costs are a concern, we could ingest data into BigQuery and get rid of the files stored in Cloud Storage.

Ingesting CSV Files

We can load the data that we created after time correction from the CSV files on Cloud Storage directly into BigQuery's native storage using the same schema:

```
bq load flights.tzcorr \
  "gs://cloud-training-demos-ml/flights/tzcorr/all_flights-*" \
  tzcorr.json
```

If most of our queries would be on the latest data, it is worth considering whether this table should be partitioned by date. If that were the case, we would create the table first, specifying that it should be partitioned by date:

---

15 See "Column-Stores vs. Row-Stores: How Different Are They Really?" by Abadi, Madden, and Hachem in *SIGMOD 2008*. Available online at *http://db.csail.mit.edu/projects/cstore/abadi-sigmod08.pdf*.

```
bq mk --time_partitioning_type=DAY flights.tzcorr
```

When loading the data, we'd need to load each partition separately (partitions are named `flights.tzcorr$20150101`, for example). In our case, `tzcorr` is a historical table that we will query in aggregate, so there is no need to partition it.

A few minutes later, all 21 million flights have been slurped into BigQuery. We can query the data:

```
SELECT
  *
FROM (
  SELECT
    ORIGIN,
    AVG(DEP_DELAY) AS dep_delay,
    AVG(ARR_DELAY) AS arr_delay,
    COUNT(ARR_DELAY) AS num_flights
  FROM
    flights.tzcorr
  GROUP BY
    ORIGIN )
WHERE
  num_flights > 3650
ORDER BY
  dep_delay DESC
```

The inner query is similar to the query we ran on the federated source—it finds average departure and arrival delays at each airport in the US. The outer query, shown in Table 5-2, retains only airports where there were at least 3,650 flights (approximately 10 flights a day) and sorts them by departure delay.

Table 5-2. Average delays at airports, sorted by average departure delay

	ORIGIN	dep_delay	arr_delay	num_flights
1	ASE	16.25387373976589	13.893158898882524	1,4676
2	COU	13.930899908172636	11.105263157894736	4,332
3	EGE	13.907984664110685	9.893413775766714	5,967
4	ORD	13.530937837607377	7.78001398044807	1,062,913
5	TTN	13.481618343755922	9.936269380766669	10,513
6	ACV	13.304634477409348	9.662264517382017	5,149
7	EWR	13.094048007985045	3.5265404459042795	387,258
8	LGA	12.988450786520469	4.865982237475594	371,794
9	CHO	12.760937499999999	8.828187431892479	8,259
10	PBI	12.405778700289266	7.6394356519040665	90,228

The result, to me, is a bit unexpected. Based on personal experience, I expected to see large, busy airports like the New York–area airports (JFK, EWR, LGA) at the top of the list. Although EWR and LGA do show up, and Chicago's airport (ORD) is in the top five, the leaders in terms of departure delay—ASE (Aspen, a ski resort in Colorado), COU (a regional airport in Missouri), and EGE (Vail, another ski resort in Colorado) are smaller airports. Aspen and Vail make sense after they appear on this list—ski resorts are open only in winter, have to load up bulky baggage, and probably suffer more weather-related delays.

Using the average delay to characterize airports is not ideal, though. What if most flights to Columbia, Missouri (COU), were actually on time but a few highly delayed flights (perhaps flights delayed by several hours) are skewing the average? I'd like to see a distribution function of the values of arrival and departure delays. BigQuery itself cannot help us with graphs—instead, we need to tie the BigQuery backend to a graphical, interactive exploration tool. For that, I'll use Cloud Datalab.

Reading a query explanation

Before I move on to Cloud Datalab, though, we want to see if there are any red flags regarding query performance on our table in BigQuery. In the BigQuery console, there is a tab (next to Results) labeled Explanation. Figure 5-6 shows what the explanation turns out to be.

Our query has been executed in three stages:

1. The first stage pulls the origin, departure delay, and arrival delay for each flight; groups them by origin; and writes them to __SHUFFLE0. __SHUFFLE0 is organized by the hash of the ORIGIN.

2. The second stage reads the fields organized by ORIGIN, computes the average delays and count, and filters the result to ensure that the count is greater than 3,650. Note that the query has been optimized a bit—my WHERE clause was actually outside the inner query, but it has been moved here so as to minimize the amount of data written out to __stage2_output.

3. The third stage simply sorts the rows by departure delay and writes to the output.

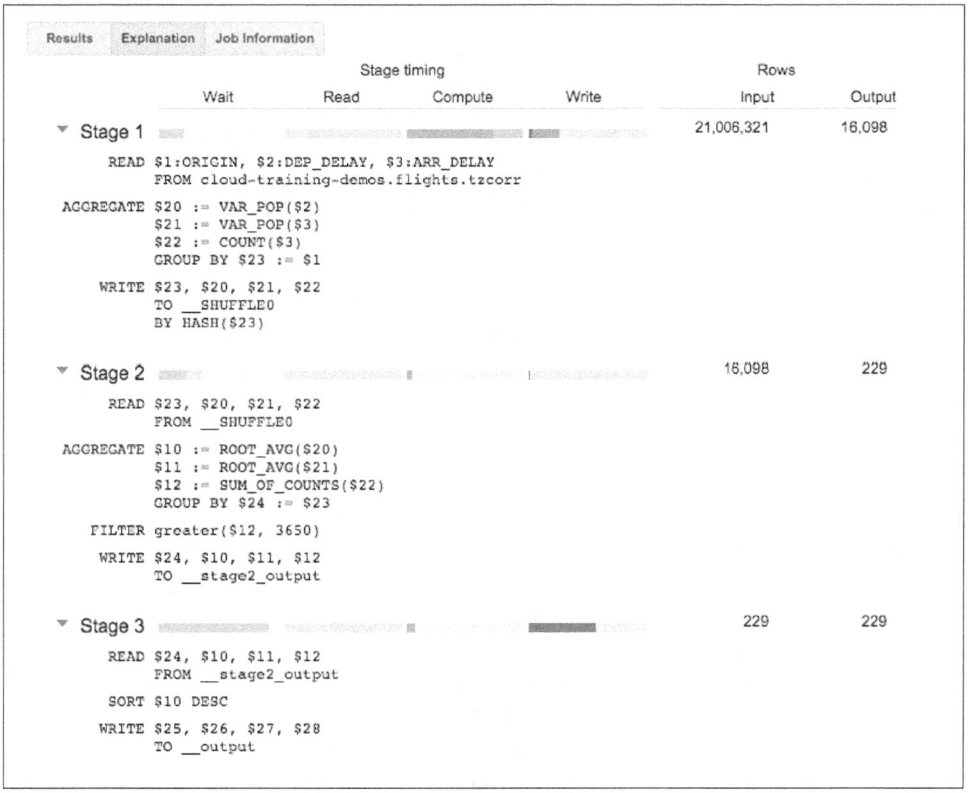

	Stage timing				Rows	
	Wait	Read	Compute	Write	Input	Output
▼ Stage 1					21,006,321	16,098

```
        READ $1:ORIGIN, $2:DEP_DELAY, $3:ARR_DELAY
             FROM cloud-training-demos.flights.tzcorr
   AGGREGATE $20 := VAR_POP($2)
             $21 := VAR_POP($3)
             $22 := COUNT($3)
             GROUP BY $23 := $1
       WRITE $23, $20, $21, $22
             TO __SHUFFLE0
             BY HASH($23)
```

| ▼ Stage 2 | | | | | 16,098 | 229 |

```
        READ $23, $20, $21, $22
             FROM __SHUFFLE0
   AGGREGATE $10 := ROOT_AVG($20)
             $11 := ROOT_AVG($21)
             $12 := SUM_OF_COUNTS($22)
             GROUP BY $24 := $23
      FILTER greater($12, 3650)
       WRITE $24, $10, $11, $12
             TO __stage2_output
```

| ▼ Stage 3 | | | | | 229 | 229 |

```
        READ $24, $10, $11, $12
             FROM __stage2_output
        SORT $10 DESC
       WRITE $25, $26, $27, $28
             TO __output
```

Figure 5-6. The explanation of a query in BigQuery

Based on the preceding second-stage optimization, is it possible to write the query itself in a better way? Yes, by using the HAVING keyword:

```
#standardsql
SELECT
  ORIGIN,
  AVG(DEP_DELAY) AS dep_delay,
  AVG(ARR_DELAY) AS arr_delay,
  COUNT(ARR_DELAY) AS num_flights
FROM
  flights.tzcorr
GROUP BY
  ORIGIN
HAVING
  num_flights > 3650
ORDER BY
  dep_delay DESC
```

In the rest of this chapter, I will use this form of the query that avoids an inner query clause. By using the HAVING keyword, we are not relying on the query optimizer to minimize the amount of data written to __stage2__ output.

What do the graphics mean? Each stage is broken into four parts: wait, read, compute, and write. A colored bar is applied to each of the stages, each of which (regardless of color) has three parts, as shown in Figure 5-7.

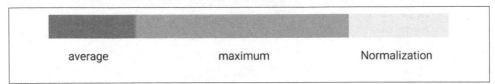

average   maximum   Normalization

Figure 5-7. Each stage in the query explanation is depicted by a color bar that has three parts

The length of the bar is the time taken by the most time-consuming step in this stage. In other words, the bars are all normalized to the time taken by the longest step (wait, read, compute, or write). For example, in stage 1 of our query, the read step takes the longest time and is the one against which the other steps are calibrated. The bars themselves have two colors. The lighter color indicates the time taken by the slowest worker that executed that step, and the darker color indicates the average time taken by all the workers that executed the step. Ideally, the average and the maximum are close to each other. A large difference between the average and the maximum (as in Figure 5-7) indicates a skew—there are some workers who are doing a lot more work than others. Sometimes, it is inherent to the query, but at other times, it might be possible to rework the storage or partitions to reduce such skew.[16]

The wait time is the time spent waiting for the necessary compute resources to become available—a very high value here indicates a job that could not be immediately scheduled on the cluster. A high wait time could occur if you are using the Big-Query flat-rate plan and someone else in your organization is already consuming all of the paid-for capacity. The solution would be to be run your job at a different time, make your job smaller, or negotiate with the group that is using the available resources. The read step reads the data required at this stage from the table or from the output of the previous stage. A high value of read time indicates that you might consider whether you could rework the query so that most of the data is read in the initial stages. The compute step carries out the computation required—if you run into high values here, consider whether you can carry out some of the operations in post-

---

16 Reducing the skew is not just about reducing the time taken by the workers who have a lot to do. You should also see if you can rework the query to combine the work carried out by the underworked workers, so that you have fewer workers overall.

processing or if you could omit the use of user-defined functions (UDFs).[17] The write step writes to temporary storage or to the response and is mainly a function of the amount of data being written out in each stage—optimization of this step typically involves moving filtering options to occur in the innermost query (or earliest stage), although as we saw earlier, the BigQuery optimizer can do some of this automatically.

For all three stages in our query, the read step is what takes the most amount of time, indicating that our query is I/O bound and that the basic cost of reading the data is what dominates the query. It is clear from the numbers in the input column (21 million to 16,000 to 229) that we are already doing quite well at funneling the data through and processing most of the data in earlier stages. We also noticed from the explanation that BigQuery has already optimized things by moving the filtering step to the earliest possible stage—there is no way to move it any earlier because it is not possible to filter on the number of flights until that value is computed. On the other hand, if this is a frequent sort of filter, it might be helpful to add a table indicating the traffic at each airport and join with this table instead of computing the aggregate each time. It might also be possible to achieve an approximation to this by adding a column indicating some characteristic (such as the population) of the metropolitan area that each airport serves. For now, without any idea of the kinds of airports that the typical user of this dataset will be interested in, there is little to be done. We are determined to process all the data, and processing all the data requires time spent reading that data. If we don't need statistics from all the data, we could consider sampling the data and computing our statistics on that sample instead.

From the diagram, we notice that stages 1 and 3 have no wait skew. However, there is a little bit of skew in the wait time for stage 2. Can you guess why? Hint: the write step of stage 1 also has a skew. The answer is that this skew is inherent to the query. Recall that we are grouping by airport, and some airports have many more flights than others. The data corresponding to those busier airports will take longer to write out. There is little to be done here as well, unless we are completely uninterested in the smaller airports. If that is the case, we could filter out the smaller airports from our data, write them to a separate table, and query that table instead from here on.

Exploratory Data Analysis in Cloud Datalab

To see why data scientists have moved en masse to using notebooks, it helps to understand the way exploratory data analysis was carried out and the reports disseminated a few years ago. Take, for example, Figure 5-8, which appears in one of my papers about different ways to track storms in weather radar images (*http://bit.ly/2ABGulv*).

---

[17] BigQuery supports UDFs in JavaScript, but the excessive use of UDFs can slow down your query, and certain UDFs can be high-compute queries (see *https://cloud.google.com/bigquery/pricing#high-compute*).

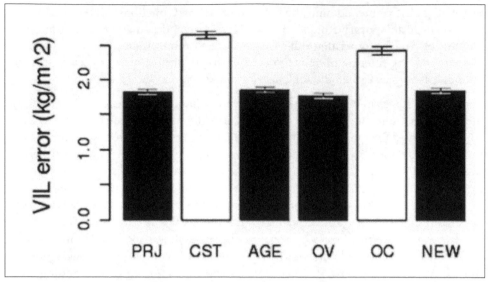

Figure 5-8. This graph was created using a complex workflow

Figure 5-8 was created by running the methods in question (PRJ, CST, etc.) on a large dataset of weather radar imagery and computing various evaluation metrics (VIL error in the graphic). For performance reasons, this was done in C++. The metric for each pair of images was written out to a text file (a different text file for each method), and it is the aggregates of those metrics that are reported in Figure 5-8. The text files had to be wrangled from the cluster of machines on which they were written out, combined by key (the method used to track storms), and then aggregated. This code, essentially a MapReduce operation, was written in Java. The resulting aggregate files were read by an R program that ranked the methods, determined the appropriate shading,[18] and wrote out an image file in PNG format. These PNG images were incorporated into a LaTeX report, and a compiler run to create a shareable document in PDF from the LaTeX and PNG sources. It was this PDF of the paper that we could disseminate to interested colleagues.

If the colleague then suggested a change, we'd go through the process all over again. The ordering of the programs—C++, followed by Java, followed by R, followed by LaTeX, followed by attaching the PDF to an email—was nontrivial, and there were times when we skipped something in between, resulting in incorrect graphics or text that didn't match the graphs.

---

18 Color was not used because color figures in academic journals carried extra costs.

Jupyter Notebooks

Jupyter (*http://jupyter.org/*) is open source software that provides an interactive scientific computing experience in a variety of languages including Python, R, and Scala. The key unit of work is a Jupyter Notebook, which is a web application that serves documents with code, visualizations, and explanatory text. Although the primary output of code in a notebook tends to be graphics and numbers, it is also possible to produce images and JavaScript. Jupyter also supports the creation of interactive widgets for manipulating and visualizing data.

Notebooks have changed the way graphics like this are produced and shared. Had I been doing it today, I might have slurped the score files (created by the C++ program) into a Python notebook. Python can do the file wrangling, ranking, and graph creation. Because the notebook is an HTML document, it also supports the addition of explanatory text to go with the graphs. You can check the notebook itself into a repository and share it. Otherwise, I can run a notebook server and serve the notebook via an HTTP link. Colleagues who want to view the notebook simply visit the URL. Not only can they view the notebook, if they are visiting the live URL, they can change a cell in the notebook and create new graphs.

The difference between a word processor file with graphs and an executable notebook with the same graphs is the difference between a printed piece of paper and a Google Doc in which both you and your collaborators are interacting live. Give notebooks a try—they tie together the functions of an integrated development environment, an executable program, and a report into a nice package.

The one issue with notebooks is how to manage the web servers that serve them. Because the code is executed on the notebook server, bigger datasets often require more powerful machines. You can simplify managing the provisioning of notebook servers by running them on demand in the public cloud.

Cloud Datalab

Cloud Datalab provides a hosted version of Jupyter on Google Cloud Platform; it knows how to authenticate against Google Cloud Platform so as to provide easy access to Cloud Storage, BigQuery, Cloud Dataflow, Cloud ML Engine, and so on. Cloud Datalab is open source, available on GitHub, and consists primarily of add-on modules for Jupyter. If you already have an on-premises Jupyter installation, you can continue using it by installing the Cloud Datalab modules into your Jupyter setup.[19] If you don't have a standardized Jupyter setup in your company, however, I suggest using Cloud Datalab—it gives you the opportunity to get a managed Jupyter installation and access to user-interface improvements over the vanilla Jupyter experience.

---

19 For instructions on how to do this, go to *https://github.com/googledatalab/pydatalab*.

To run Cloud Datalab on a Google Compute Engine instance and connect to it from your local machine, do the following:

1. Open CloudShell and create a compute instance that will run Cloud Datalab, specifying a zone (e.g., us-central1-a) and giving the instance a name (e.g., mydatalabvm):[20]

   ```
   datalab create --zone $ZONE $INSTANCE_NAME
   ```

2. After you get the message that the Cloud Datalab instance is reachable on local-host:8081, use the Web Preview button in CloudShell to navigate to *http://localhost:8081* and begin working with Cloud Datalab.

If the Cloud Datalab command terminates (for example, if the laptop goes to sleep), reconnect to your Cloud Datalab VM using the following:

```
datalab connect --zone $ZONE $INSTANCE_NAME
```

When you are done using the Cloud Datalab VM, delete the instance:

```
datalab delete --zone $ZONE $INSTANCE_NAME
```

After you have launched Cloud Datalab, you can create a new notebook. Click the Home icon if necessary, and then navigate to the folder in which you want this notebook to appear. A *markdown* cell is cell with text content. A *code* cell has Python code —when you run such a cell, the notebook displays the printed output of that cell.

For example, suppose that you type into a notebook the contents of Figure 5-9 (with the first cell a markdown cell, and the second cell a Python cell).

You can run the cell your cursor is in by clicking Run (or use the keyboard shortcut Ctrl+Shift+Enter). You could also run all cells by clicking "Run all cells." When you click this, the cells are evaluated, and the resulting rendered notebook looks like Figure 5-10.

---

20 In this and subsequent connect and delete commands, you can avoid specifying the zone of the instance every time by setting a property: gcloud config set compute/zone $ZONE.

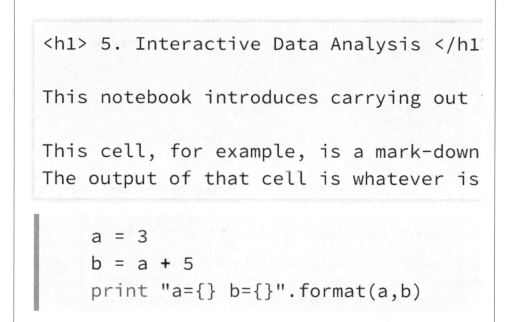

```
<h1> 5. Interactive Data Analysis </h1>

This notebook introduces carrying out

This cell, for example, is a mark-down
The output of that cell is whatever is
```

```
a = 3
b = a + 5
print "a={} b={}".format(a,b)
```

Figure 5-9. What you type into the notebook (compare with Figure 5-10)

5. Interactive Data Analysis

This notebook introduces carrying out interactive data an

This cell, for example, is a mark-down cell. Which is why y

```
1 a = 3
2 b = a + 5
3 print "a={} b={}".format(a,b)
```

```
a=3  b=8
```

Figure 5-10. What happens after you execute the cells (compare with Figure 5-9)

Note that the markdown has been converted into a visual document, and note that the Python code has been evaluated, and the resulting output printed out.

Relative paths in Cloud Datalab are relative to the location of the notebook. Thus, for example, if you type the following into a code cell

```
!pwd
```

you will get the folder in which that notebook appears, but it will begin with */content*, as demonstrated in Figure 5-11.

Figure 5-11. Running a shell command to get the current working directory

The */content* path is mapped to a local folder on the machine running Datalab. You should determine where */content* is mapped to—as of this writing, this is specified at the time the Docker container is launched and is typically mapped to *$HOME*. I tend to map */content* to a folder in which I have checked out a copy of my Git repository. Doing this will get you into the habit of practicing source-code control on changed notebooks.[21]

The use of the exclamation point (when you typed `!pwd` into a code cell) is an indication to Jupyter that the line is not Python code, but is instead a shell command. If you have multiple lines of a shell command, you can start a shell with `%bash`, for example:

```
%bash
wget tensorflow …
pip install …
```

Installing Packages in Cloud Datalab

Which Python packages are already installed in Cloud Datalab, and which ones will we have to install? One way to check which packages are installed is to type the following:

```
!pip freeze
```

This lists the Python packages installed. Another option is to add in imports for packages and see if they work. Let's do that with packages that I know that we'll need:

---

21 If your notebooks are stored on Google Drive, Drive can, of course, take care of collaboration and versioning.

```
import matplotlib.pyplot as plt
import seaborn as sb
import pandas as pd
import numpy as np
```

numpy is the canonical numerical Python library that provides efficient ways of working with arrays of numbers. Pandas is an extremely popular data analysis library that provides a way to do operations such as group by and filter on in-memory data-frames. matplotlib is a Matlab-inspired module to create graphs in Python. seaborn provides extra graphics capabilities built on top of the basic functionality provided by matplotlib. All these are open source packages that are installed in Cloud Datalab by default.

Had I needed a package that is not already installed in Cloud Datalab, I could have installed it in one of two ways: using pip or using apt-get. You can install many Python modules by using pip. For example, to install the Cloud Platform APIs that we used in Chapter 3, execute this code within a cell:

```
!pip install google-cloud
```

Some modules are installed as Linux packages because they might involve the installation of not only Python wrappers, but also the underlying C libraries. For example, to install basemap, a geographic plotting package that uses the C library proj.4 to convert between map projections, you'd run this code within a cell:

```
%bash
apt-get update
apt-get -y install python-mpltoolkits.basemap
```

There is no need to sudo (i.e., run as root) because the entire Cloud Datalab Docker container is running as root (*gulp*). Be careful, therefore, about what you do in bash—there are no guardrails because you are running as root.

Finally, there is a difference between pip and apt-get in terms of whether they update the notebook's Python kernel. Using pip updates the Python kernel of the notebook with the new package. So, you can directly begin using a package that has been installed using pip. However, because apt-get is a system-level update, you need to restart the Python kernel for the new package to be picked up (you can do this using the Reset Kernel button on the Cloud Datalab notebook user interface). At this point, if you run apt-get again, you should see a message indicating that the package is already installed.

Jupyter Magic for Google Cloud Platform

When we used %bash in the previous section, we were using a Jupyter *magic*, a syntactic element that marks what follows as special.[22] This is how Jupyter can support multiple interpreters or engines. Jupyter knows what language a cell is in by looking at the magic at its beginning. For example, try typing the following into a code cell:

```
%html
This cell will print out a <b> HTML </b> string.
```

You should see the HTML rendering of that string being printed out on evaluation, as depicted in Figure 5-12.

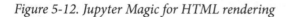

```
%html
This cell will print out a <b> HTML </b> string.
```

This cell will print out a **HTML** string.

Figure 5-12. Jupyter Magic for HTML rendering

Jupyter magics provide a mechanism to run a wide variety of languages, and ways to add some more. Cloud Datalab itself has added a few magics to make the interaction with Google Cloud Platform convenient. To use them, ensure that you are signed into Google Cloud Platform by looking at the upper-right ribbon of Cloud Datalab and clicking the profile-like icon. If you are not signed in, do so at this time.

For example, you can view the schema of your BigQuery table using the %bigquery magic environment that comes with Cloud Datalab:

```
%bigquery schema --table flights.tzcorr
```

If you get the schema back, as shown in Figure 5-13, all is well.

If not, look at the error message and carry out appropriate remedial actions. You might need to authenticate yourself, set the project you are working in, or change permissions on the BigQuery table.

---

22 Magics use a syntax element that is not valid in the underlying language. In the case of notebooks in Python, this is the % symbol.

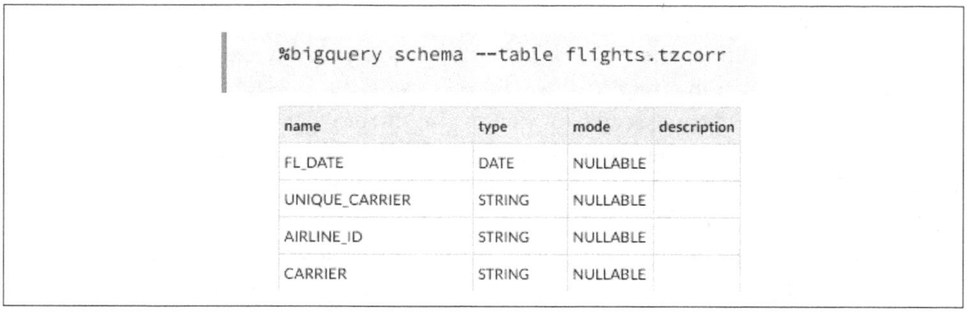

```
%bigquery schema --table flights.tzcorr
```

name	type	mode	description
FL_DATE	DATE	NULLABLE	
UNIQUE_CARRIER	STRING	NULLABLE	
AIRLINE_ID	STRING	NULLABLE	
CARRIER	STRING	NULLABLE	

Figure 5-13. The %biqquery magic environment that comes with Datalab

The fact that we refer to %bigquery as a Jupyter magic should indicate that this is not pure Python—you can execute this only within a notebook environment. The magic, however, is simply a wrapper function for Python code.[23] If there is a piece of code that you'd ultimately want to run outside a notebook (perhaps as part of a scheduled script), it's better to use the underlying Python and not the magic pragma.

One way to use the underlying Python is to use the datalab.bigquery package—this allows us to use code independent of the notebook environment. The bigquery package in Cloud Datalab is different from the bigquery package in the Google Cloud Platform API library that we used in Chapters 3 and 4. Whereas the Google Cloud Python API is primarily about providing convenient mechanisms to invoke REST APIs to communicate with BigQuery, the Cloud Datalab bigquery package adds interconnections between BigQuery results and numpy/Pandas to simplify the creation of graphics.

Exploring arrival delays

To pull the arrival delays corresponding to the model created in Chapter 3 (i.e., of the arrival delay for flights that depart more than 10 minutes late), we can do the following:

```
import google.datalab.bigquery as bq
sql = """
SELECT ARR_DELAY, DEP_DELAY
FROM `flights.tzcorr`
WHERE DEP_DELAY  10 AND RAND() < 0.01
"""
df = bq.Query(sql).execute().result().to_dataframe()
```

---

23 See *https://github.com/googledatalab/pydatalab/tree/master/datalab/bigquery* for the Python code being wrapped.

This code uses the `datalab.bigquery` package (imported as bq) to run the Cloud SQL statement given in the `sql` variable and converts the result set into a Pandas dataframe. Recall that in Chapter 4, we did this using the Google Cloud Platform API but had to handle different scenarios like paging through the query, or timeouts. All this is handled for us by the higher-level functionality provided by the Cloud Datalab package. Converting the results into a Pandas dataframe (represented here as the variable df) is a nice touch because it opens up the rest of the Python data science ecosystem. The statistics will not be exact because our query pulls a random 1% of the complete dataset by specifying that `RAND()`, a function that returns a random number uniformly distributed between 0 and 1, had to be less than 0.01. In exploratory data analysis, however, it is not critical to use the entire dataset, just a large enough one.

After we have the dataframe, getting fundamental statistics about the two columns returned by the query is as simple as this:

```
df.describe()
```

This gives us the mean, standard deviation, minimum, maximum, and quartiles of the arrival and departure delays given that departure delay is more than 10 minutes, as illustrated in Figure 5-14 (see the WHERE clause of the query).

df.describe()

	ARR_DELAY	DEP_DELAY
count	45792.000000	46057.000000
mean	45.797650	50.822068
std	62.863612	61.079590
min	-46.000000	10.000000
25%	11.000000	17.000000
50%	27.000000	30.000000
75%	59.000000	60.000000
max	1321.000000	1330.000000

Figure 5-14. Getting the fundamental statistics of a Pandas dataframe

Beyond just the statistical capabilities of Pandas, we can also pass the Pandas dataframes and underlying numpy arrays to plotting libraries like seaborn. For example, to plot a violin plot of our decision surface from the previous chapter (i.e., of the arrival delay for flights that depart more than 10 minutes late), we can do the following:

```
sns.set_style("whitegrid")
ax = sns.violinplot(data=df, x='ARR_DELAY', inner='box', orient='h')
```

This produces the graph shown in Figure 5-15.

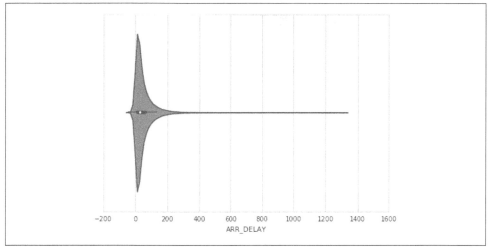

Figure 5-15. Violin plot of arrival delay

A violin plot is a *kernel density plot*;[24] that is, it is an estimate of the probability distribution function (PDF[25]). It carries a lot more information than simply a *box-and-whiskers* plot because it does not assume that the data is normally distributed. Indeed, we see that even though the distribution peaks around 10 minutes (which is the mode), deviations around this peak are skewed toward larger delays than smaller ones. Importantly, we also notice that there is only one peak—the distribution is not, for example, bimodal.

Let's compare the violin plot for flights that depart more than 10 minutes late with the violin plot for flights that depart less than 10 minutes late and zoom in on the x-axis close to our 15-minute threshold. First, we pull all of the delays using the following:

```
sql = """
SELECT ARR_DELAY, DEP_DELAY
FROM `flights.tzcorr`
WHERE RAND() < 0.001
"""
df = bq.Query(sql).execute().result().to_dataframe()
```

---

24 A kernel density plot is just a smoothed histogram—the challenge lies in figuring out how to smooth the histogram while balancing interpretability with loss of information. Here, I'm just letting seaborn use its default settings for the smoothing bandwidth. For more information, see *https://en.wikipedia.org/wiki/ Kernel_density_estimation*.

25 See the discussion of the PDF in Chapter 1.

In this query, I have dropped the WHERE clause. Instead, we will rely on Pandas to do the thresholding. Because Cloud Datalab runs totally in-memory, I pull only 1 in 1,000 flights (using RAND() < 0.001). I can now create a new column in the Pandas dataframe that is either True or False depending on whether the flight departed less than 10 minutes late:

```
df['ontime'] = df['DEP_DELAY'] < 10
```

We can graph this new Pandas dataframe using seaborn:

```
ax = sns.violinplot(data=df, x='ARR_DELAY', y='ontime',
                    inner='box', orient='h')
ax.set_xlim(-50, 200)
```

The difference between the previous violin plot and this one is the inclusion of the ontime column. This results in a violin plot (see Figure 5-16) that illustrates how different flights that depart 10 minutes late are from flights that depart early.

The squashed top of the top violin plot indicates that the seaborn default smoothing was too coarse. You can fix this by passing in a gridsize parameter:

```
ax = sns.violinplot(data=df, x='ARR_DELAY', y='ontime',
inner='box', orient='h', gridsize=1000)
```

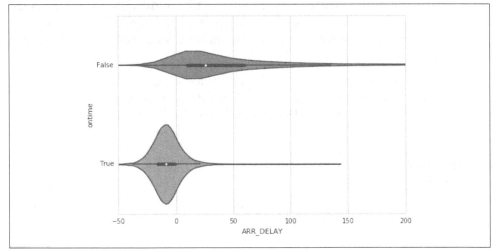

Figure 5-16. Difference between violin plots of all late flights (top) versus on-time flights (bottom)

As we discussed in Chapter 3, it is clear that the 10-minute threshold separates the dataset into two separate statistical regimes, so that the typical arrival delay for flights that depart more than 10 minutes late is skewed toward much higher values than for flights that depart more on time. We can see this in Figure 5-17, both from the shape of the violin plot and from the box plot that forms its center. Note how centered the on-time flights are versus the box plot (the dark line in the center) for delayed flights.[26]

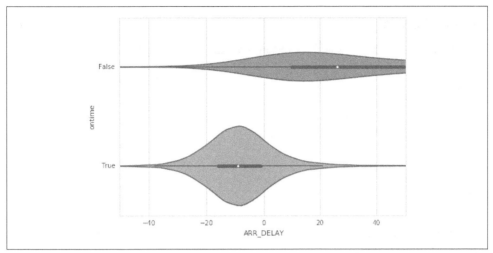

Figure 5-17. Zoomed-in look at Figure 5-16

However, the extremely long skinny tail of the violin plot is a red flag—it is an indication that the dataset might pose modeling challenges. Let's investigate what is going on.

Quality Control

We can continue writing queries in Cloud Datalab, but doing so on the BigQuery console gives me immediate feedback on syntax and logic errors. So, I switch over to *https://bigquery.cloud.google.com/* and type in my first query:

```
#standardsql
SELECT
  AVG(ARR_DELAY) AS arrival_delay
FROM
  flights.tzcorr
GROUP BY
  DEP_DELAY
ORDER BY
  DEP_DELAY
```

---

26 I created this second, zoomed-in violin plot by adding ax.set_xlim(-50, 50).

This should give me the average arrival delay associated with every value of departure delay (which, in this dataset, is stored as an integer number of minutes). I get back more than 1,000 rows. Are there really more than 1,000 unique values of DEP_DELAY? What's going on?

Oddball Values

To look at this further, let's add more elements to my initial query:

```
#standardsql
SELECT
  DEP_DELAY,
  AVG(ARR_DELAY) AS arrival_delay,
  COUNT(ARR_DELAY) AS numflights
FROM
  `flights.tzcorr`
GROUP BY
  DEP_DELAY
ORDER BY
  DEP_DELAY
```

The resulting table explains what's going on. The first few rows have only a few flights each, as shown in Figure 5-18.

However, departure delay values of a few minutes have tens of thousands of flights, which we can see in Figure 5-19.

Row	DEP_DELAY	arrival_delay	numflights
1	null	null	0
2	-82.0	-80.0	3
3	-68.0	-87.0	3
4	-61.0	-77.0	3
5	-56.0	-35.0	6
6	-55.0	-60.0	3
7	-52.0	-57.5	6
8	-51.0	-49.0	6
9	-49.0	-50.0	3
10	-48.0	-32.87500000000001	8

Figure 5-18. Number of flights at each departure delay

Row	DEP_DELAY	arrival_delay	numflights
56	-2.0	-7.7558555586246385	1563984
57	-1.0	-6.6431868782882875	1389209
58	0.0	-5.251858718686436	1176886
59	1.0	-4.347512076407868	571983
60	2.0	-3.3793214020420677	433482
61	3.0	-2.340170403298544	372528
62	4.0	-1.3548879529849038	331468
63	5.0	-0.2993271528115161	300514
64	6.0	0.6396729702723887	269211

Figure 5-19. Low values of departure delay have large numbers of flights

Oddball values that are such a small proportion of the data can probably be ignored. Moreover, if the flight does really leave 82 minutes early, I'm quite sure that you won't be on the flight, and if you are, you know that you will make the meeting. There is no reason to complicate our statistical modeling with such odd values.

Outlier Removal: Big Data Is Different

How can you remove such outliers? There are two ways to filter the data: one would be based on the departure delay variable itself, keeping only values that met a condition such as this:

```
WHERE dep_delay > -15
```

A second method would be to filter the data based on the number of flights:

```
WHERE numflights > 300
```

The second method—using a quality-control filter that is based on removing data for which we have insufficient examples—is preferable.

This is an important point and gets at the key difference between statistics on "normal" datasets and statistics on big data. Although I agree that the term *big data* has become completely hyped, people who claim that big data is just data are missing a key point—the fundamental approach to problems becomes different when datasets grow sufficiently large. The way we detect outliers is just one such example.

For a dataset that numbers in the hundreds to thousands of examples, you would filter the dataset and remove values outside, say, $\mu \pm 3\sigma$ (where μ is the mean and σ the standard deviation). We can find out what the range would be by running a BigQuery query on the table:

```
#standardsql
SELECT
  AVG(DEP_DELAY) - 3*STDDEV(DEP_DELAY) AS filtermin,
  AVG(DEP_DELAY) + 3*STDDEV(DEP_DELAY) AS filtermax
FROM
  `flights.tzcorr`
```

This yields the range [−102, 120] minutes so that the WHERE clause would become as follows:

```
WHERE dep_delay > -102 AND dep_delay < 120
```

Of course, a filter that retains values in the range $\mu \pm 3\sigma$ is based on an implicit assumption that the distribution of departure delays is Gaussian. We can avoid such an assumption by using percentiles, perhaps by omitting the top and bottom 5% of values:

```
#standardsql
SELECT
  APPROX_QUANTILES(DEP_DELAY, 20)
FROM
  `flights.tzcorr`
```

This would lead us to retain values in the range [−9, 66]. Regardless of how we find the range, though, the range is based on an assumption that unusually high and low values are outliers.

On datasets that number in the hundreds of thousands to millions of examples, thresholding your input data based on value is dangerous because you can very well be throwing out valuable nuance—if there are sufficient examples of a delay of 150 minutes, it is worth modeling such a value regardless of how far off the mean it is. Customer satisfaction and "long-tail" business strategies might hinge on our systems coping well with usually small or large values. There is, therefore, a world of difference between filtering our data using

```
WHERE dep_delay > -15
```

versus filtering it using:

```
WHERE numflights > 370
```

The first method imposes a threshold on the input data and is viable only if we are sure that a departure delay of less than −15 minutes is absurd. The second method, on the other hand, is based on how often certain values are observed—the larger our dataset grows, the less unusual any particular value becomes.

The term *outlier* is, therefore, somewhat of a misnomer when it comes to big data. An outlier implies a range within which values are kept, with outliers being values that lie outside that range. Here, we are keeping data that meets a criterion involving frequency of occurrence—any value is acceptable as long as it occurs often enough in our data.[27]

Filtering Data on Occurrence Frequency

To filter the dataset based on frequency of occurrence, we first need to compute the frequency of occurrence and then threshold the data based on it. We can accomplish this by using a HAVING clause:

```
#standardsql
SELECT
  DEP_DELAY,
  AVG(ARR_DELAY) AS arrival_delay,
  STDDEV(ARR_DELAY) AS stddev_arrival_delay,
  COUNT(ARR_DELAY) AS numflights
FROM
  `flights.tzcorr`
GROUP BY
  DEP_DELAY
HAVING
  numflights > 370
ORDER BY
  DEP_DELAY
```

Why threshold the number of flights at 370? This number derives from a guideline called the *three-sigma rule*,[28] which is traditionally the range within which we consider "nearly all values"[29] to lie. If we assume (for now; we'll verify it soon) that at any departure delay, arrival delays are normally distributed, we can talk about things that are true for "almost every flight" if our population size is large enough—filtering our dataset so that we have at least 370[30] examples of each input value is a rule of thumb that achieves this.

---

27 In this dataset, floating-point numbers have already been discretized. For example, arrival delays have been rounded to the nearest minute. If this is not the case, you will have to discretize continuous data before computing frequency of occurrence.

28 For a normal distribution (at each departure delay, the number of flights is in the hundreds to thousands, so usual statistical thinking applies), 68.27% of values lie in the $\mu \pm \sigma$ range, 95.45% of values lie in the $\mu \pm 2\sigma$ range, and 99.73% of values lie in the $\mu \pm 3\sigma$ range. That last range is termed the three-sigma rule. For more information, go to *https://www.encyclopediaofmath.org/index.php/Three-sigma_rule*.

29 Traditions, of course, are different in different fields and often depend on how much data you can reasonably collect in that field. In business statistics, this three-sigma rule is quite common. In the social sciences and in medicine, two-sigma is the typical significance threshold. Meanwhile, when the Higgs Boson discovery announcement was made, the significance threshold to classify it as a true discovery and not just a statistical artifact was five-sigma or 1 in 3.5 million (see *https://blogs.scientificamerican.com/observations/five-sigmawhats-that/*).

30 $1 / (1 - 0.9973) = 370$.

How different would the results be if we were to choose a different threshold? We can look at the number of flights that are removed by different quality-control thresholds by replacing `SELECT *` in the previous query by `20604235 - SUM(numflights)`[31] and look at the slope of a linear model between arrival delay and departure delay using this query:

```
#standardsql
SELECT
  20604235 - SUM(numflights) AS num_removed,
  AVG(arrival_delay * numflights)/AVG(DEP_DELAY * numflights) AS lm
FROM (
  as before )
WHERE
  numflights > 1000
```

Running this query for various different thresholds on `numflights`, we get the results shown in Table 5-3.

Table 5-3. Impact of different thresholds on numflights

Threshold on numflights	Number of flights removed	Linear model slope (lm)
1,000	86,787	0.35
500	49,761	0.38
370 (three-σ rule)	38,139	0.39
300	32,095	0.40
200	23,892	0.41
100	13,506	0.42
22 (two-σ rule)	4990	0.43
10	2,243	0.44
5	688	0.44

As you can see, the slope varies extremely slowly as we remove fewer and fewer flights by decreasing the threshold. Thus, the differences in the model created for thresholds of 300, 370, or 500 are quite minor. However, that model is quite different from that created if the threshold were 5 or 10. The order of magnitude of the threshold matters, but perhaps not the exact value.

Arrival Delay Conditioned on Departure Delay

Now that we have a query that cleans up oddball values of departure delay from the dataset, we can take the query over to the Cloud Datalab notebook to continue our exploratory analysis and to develop a model to help us make a decision on whether to

---

31 20,604,235 is the total number of flights in the dataset.

cancel our meeting. I simply copy and paste from the BigQuery console to Cloud Datalab and give the query a name, as shown here:

```
depdelayquery = """
SELECT
  DEP_DELAY,
  arrival_delay,
  stddev_arrival_delay,
  numflights
FROM (
  SELECT
    DEP_DELAY,
    AVG(ARR_DELAY) AS arrival_delay,
    STDDEV(ARR_DELAY) AS stddev_arrival_delay,
    COUNT(ARR_DELAY) AS numflights
  FROM
    `flights.tzcorr`
  GROUP BY
    DEP_DELAY )
WHERE
  numflights > 370
ORDER BY
  DEP_DELAY
"""
```

We can supply it to the Query constructor and run the query as usual to obtain a Pandas dataframe:

```
depdelay = bq.Query(depdelayquery).execute().result().to_dataframe()
depdelay[:5]
```

The [:5] slices it to show the first five rows. Figure 5-20 shows the result.

	DEP_DELAY	arrival_delay	stddev_arrival_delay	numflights
0	-27.0	-26.793548	10.785545	465
1	-26.0	-24.438375	11.403709	714
2	-25.0	-25.185224	10.598301	961
3	-24.0	-24.090560	12.087346	1303
4	-23.0	-24.016630	11.008934	1804

Figure 5-20. Pandas dataframe for departure delays with more than 370 flights

Let's plot this data to see what insight we can get. Even though we have been using seaborn so far, Pandas itself has plotting functions built in:

```
ax = depdelay.plot(kind='line', x='DEP_DELAY',
                y='arrival_delay', yerr='stddev_arrival_delay')
```

This yields the plot shown in Figure 5-21.

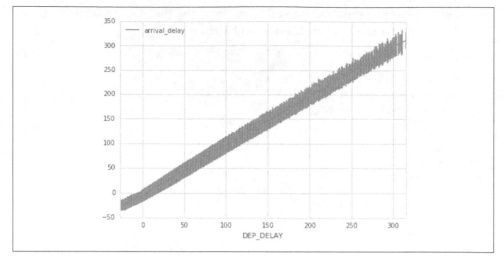

Figure 5-21. Relationship between departure delay and arrival delay

It certainly does appear as if the relationship between departure delay and arrival delay is quite linear. The width of the standard deviation of the arrival delay is also pretty constant, on the order of 10 minutes.

There are a variety of `%bigquery` and `%sql` magics available in Cloud Datalab. Together, they form a very convenient "fat SQL" client suitable for running entire Cloud SQL workflows. Particularly useful is the ability to create a temporary dataset and send the results of a query (such as the `depdelayquery` we just carried out) to a table in that dataset using the following:

```
%bigquery create dataset -n temp_dataset
%bigquery execute -q depdelayquery -t my_temp_dataset.delays
```

Now, we can use this table as the input for queries further down in the notebook. At the end of the workflow, after all the necessary charts and graphs are created, we can delete the dataset using Python:

```
for table in bq.Dataset("temp_dataset").tables():
  table.delete()
bq.Dataset("temp_dataset").delete()
```

Applying Probabilistic Decision Threshold

Recall from Chapter 1 that our decision criterion is 15 minutes and 30%. If the plane is more than 30% likely to be delayed (on arrival) by more than 15 minutes, we want to send a text message asking to postpone the meeting. At what departure delay does this happen?

By computing the standard deviation of the arrival delays corresponding to each departure delay, we implicitly assumed that arrival delays are normally distributed. For now, let's continue with that assumption. I can examine a complementary cumulative distribution table (*http://bit.ly/2jltOrs*) and find where 0.3 happens. From the table, this happens at Z = 0.52.

Let's now go back to Cloud Datalab to plug this number into our dataset:

```
Z_30 = 0.52
depdelay['arr_delay_30'] = (Z_30 * depdelay['stddev_arrival_delay']) \
            + depdelay['arrival_delay']
plt.axhline(y=15, color='r')
ax = plt.axes()
depdelay.plot(kind='line', x='DEP_DELAY', y='arr_delay_30',
            ax=ax, ylim=(0,30), xlim=(0,30), legend=False)
ax.set_xlabel('Departure Delay (minutes)')
ax.set_ylabel('> 30% likelihood of this Arrival Delay (minutes)')
```

The plotting code yields the plot depicted in Figure 5-22.

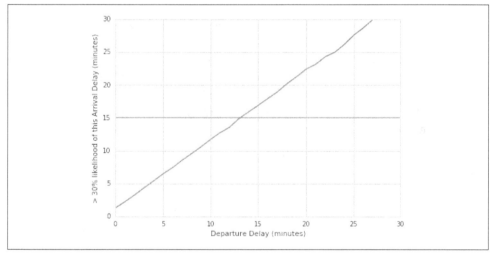

Figure 5-22. Choosing the departure delay threshold that results in a 30% likelihood of an arrival delay of <15 minutes

It appears that your decision criterion translates to a departure delay of 13 minutes. If your departure delay is 13 minutes or more, you are more than 30% likely to be delayed by 15 minutes or more.

Empirical Probability Distribution Function

What if we drop the assumption that the distribution of flights at each departure delay is normally distributed? We then will need to empirically determine the 30% likelihood at each departure delay. Happily, we do have at least 370 flights at each departure delay (the joys of working with large datasets!), so we can simply compute the 30th percentile for each departure delay.

We can compute the 30th percentile in BigQuery by discretizing the arrival delays corresponding to each departure delay into 100 bins and picking the arrival delay that corresponds to the 70th bin:

```
#standardsql
SELECT
  DEP_DELAY,
  APPROX_QUANTILES(ARR_DELAY, 101)[OFFSET(70)] AS arrival_delay,
  COUNT(ARR_DELAY) AS numflights
FROM
  `flights.tzcorr`
GROUP BY
  DEP_DELAY
HAVING
  numflights > 370
ORDER BY
  DEP_DELAY
```

The function `APPROX_QUANTILES()` takes the `ARR_DELAY` and divides it into $N + 1$ bins (here we specified $N = 101$).[32] The first bin is the approximate minimum, the last bin the approximate maximum, and the rest of the bins are what we'd traditionally consider the bins. Hence, the 70th percentile is the 71st element of the result. The [ ] syntax finds the *n*th element of that array—`OFFSET(70)` will provide the 71st element because `OFFSET` is zero-based.[33] Why 70 and not 30? Because we want the arrival delay that could happen with 30% likelihood and this implies the larger value.

The results of this query provide the empirical 30th percentile threshold for every departure delay, which you can see in Figure 5-23.

---

32 For an explanation of the parameters, go to *https://cloud.google.com/bigquery/docs/reference/standard-sql/functions-and-operators#approx_quantiles*. This function computes the approximate quantiles because computing the exact quantiles on large datasets, especially of floating-point values, can be very expensive in terms of space. Instead, most big data databases use some variant of Greenwald and Khanna's algorithm, described in *http://dl.acm.org/citation.cfm?doid=375663.375670*, to compute approximate quantiles.

33 Had I used `ORDINAL` instead of `OFFSET`, it would have been 1-based.

Results	Explanation	Job Information	
Row	DEP_DELAY	arrival_delay	numflights
1	-27.0	-24.0	465
2	-26.0	-21.0	714
3	-25.0	-22.0	961
4	-24.0	-21.0	1303
5	-23.0	-20.0	1804

Figure 5-23. Empirical 30% likelihood arrival delay for each possible departure delay

Plugging the query back into Cloud Datalab, we can avoid the Z-lookup and Z-score calculation associated with Gaussian distributions:

```
depdelay = bq.Query(depdelayquery2).execute().result().to_dataframe()
plt.axhline(y=15, color='r')
ax = plt.axes()
depdelay.plot(kind='line', x='DEP_DELAY', y='arrival_delay',
              ax=ax, ylim=(0,30), xlim=(0,30), legend=False)
ax.set_xlabel('Departure Delay (minutes)')
ax.set_ylabel('> 30% likelihood of this Arrival Delay (minutes)')
```

We now get the chart shown in Figure 5-24.

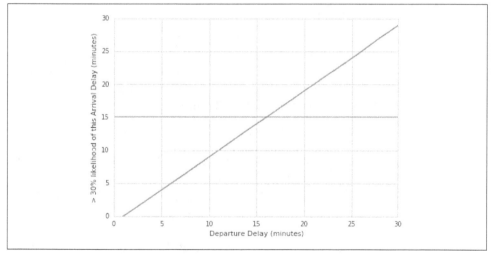

Figure 5-24. Departure delay threshold that results in a 30% likelihood of an arrival delay of <15 min

The Answer Is...

From the chart in Figure 5-24, your decision threshold, without the assumption of normal distribution, is 16 minutes. If your flight is delayed by more than 16 minutes, there is a greater than 30% likelihood that you will arrive more than 15 minutes late.

Recall that the aforementioned threshold is conditioned on rather conservative assumptions—you are going to cancel the meeting if there is more than 30% likelihood of being late by 15 minutes. What if you are a bit more audacious in your business dealings, or if this particular customer will not be annoyed by a few minutes' wait? What if you won't cancel the meeting unless there is a greater than 70% chance of being late by 15 minutes? The good thing is that it is easy enough to come up with a different decision threshold for different people and different scenarios out of the same basic framework.

Another thing to notice is that the addition of the actual departure delay in minutes has allowed us to make a better decision than going with just the contingency table. Using just the contingency table, we would cancel meetings whenever flights were just 10 minutes late. Using the actual departure delay and a probabilistic decision framework, we were able to avoid canceling our meeting unless flights were delayed by 16 minutes or more.

Evaluating the Model

But how good is this advice? How many times will my advice to cancel or not cancel the meeting be the correct one? Had you asked me that question, I would have hemmed and hawed—I don't know how accurate the threshold is because we have no independent sample. Let's address that now—as our models become more sophisticated, an independent sample will be increasingly required.

There are two broad approaches to finding an independent sample:

- Collect new data. For example, we could go back to BTS and download 2016 data and evaluate the recommendation on that dataset.

- Split the 2015 data into two parts. Create the model on the first part (called the *training set*), and evaluate it on the second part (called the *test set*).

The second approach is more common because datasets tend to be finite. In the interest of being practical here, let's do the same thing even though, in this instance, we could go back and get more data.[34]

---

34 By the time we get to Chapter 10, I will have based so many decisions on the split dataset that I will get 2016 data to act as a truly independent test set.

When splitting the data, we must be careful. We want to ensure that both parts are representative of the full dataset (and have similar relationships to what you are predicting), but at the same time we want to make sure that the testing data is independent of the training data. To understand what this means, let's take a few reasonable splits and talk about why they won't work.

Random Shuffling

We might split the data by randomly shuffling all the rows in the dataset and then choosing the first 70% as the training set, and the remaining 30% as the test set. In BigQuery, you could do that using the RAND() function:

```
#standardsql
SELECT
  ORIGIN, DEST,
  DEP_DELAY,
  ARR_DELAY
FROM
  flights.tzcorr
WHERE
  RAND() < 0.7
```

The RAND() function returns a value between 0 and 1, so approximately 70% of the rows in the dataset will be selected by this query. However, there are several problems with using this sampling method for machine learning:

- It is not nearly as easy to get the 30% of the rows that were not selected to be in the training set to use as the test dataset.

- The RAND() function returns different things each time it is run, so if you run the query again, you will get a different 70% of rows. In this book, we are experimenting with different machine learning models, and this will play havoc with comparisons between models if each model is evaluated on a different test set.

- The order of rows in a BigQuery result set is not guaranteed—it is essentially the order in which different workers return their results. So, even if you could set a random seed to make RAND() repeatable, you'll still not get repeatable results. You'd have to add an ORDER BY clause to explicitly sort the data (on an ID field, a field that is unique for each row) before doing the RAND(). This is not always going to be possible.

Further, on this particular dataset, random shuffling is problematic for another reason. Flights on the same day are probably subject to the same weather and traffic factors. Thus, the rows in the training set, and test sets will not be independent if we simply shuffle the data. This consideration is relevant only for this particular dataset —shuffling the data and taking the first 70% will work for other datasets that don't have this inter-row dependence, as long as you have an id field.

We could split the data such that Jan–Sep 2015 is training data and Oct–Dec is testing data. But what if delays can be made up in summer but not in winter? This split fails the representativeness test. Neither the training dataset nor the test dataset will be representative of the entire year if we split the dataset by months.

Splitting by Date

The approach that we will take is to find all the unique days in the dataset, shuffle them, and use 70% of these days as the training set and the remainder as the test set. For repeatability, I will store this division as a table in BigQuery.

The first step is to get all the unique days in the dataset:

```
#standardsql
SELECT
  DISTINCT(FL_DATE) AS FL_DATE
FROM
  flights.tzcorr
ORDER BY
  FL_DATE
```

The next step is to select a random 70% of these to be our training days:

```
#standardsql
SELECT
  FL_DATE,
  IF(MOD(ABS(FARM_FINGERPRINT(CAST(FL_DATE AS STRING))), 100) < 70,
     'True', 'False') AS is_train_day
FROM (
  SELECT
    DISTINCT(FL_DATE) AS FL_DATE
  FROM
    `flights.tzcorr`)
ORDER BY
  FL_DATE
```

In the preceding query, the hash value of each of the unique days from the inner query is computed using the FarmHash library[35] and the is_train_day field is set to True if the last two digits of this hash value are less than 70. Figure 5-25 shows the resulting table.

---

35 See *https://opensource.googleblog.com/2014/03/introducing-farmhash.html* for a description, and *https://github.com/google/farmhash* for the code.

Row	FL_DATE	is_train_day
1	2015-01-01	True
2	2015-01-02	False
3	2015-01-03	False
4	2015-01-04	True
5	2015-01-05	True
6	2015-01-06	False
7	2015-01-07	True
8	2015-01-08	True
9	2015-01-09	True
10	2015-01-10	True

Figure 5-25. Selecting training days

The final step is to save this result as a table in BigQuery. We can do this from the BigQuery console using the "Save as Table" button. I'll call this table `trainday`; we can join with this table whenever we want to pull out training rows.

In some chapters, we won't be using BigQuery. Just in case we aren't using BigQuery, I will also export the table as a CSV file—we can do this by clicking the blue arrow next to the table name, as demonstrated in Figure 5-26.

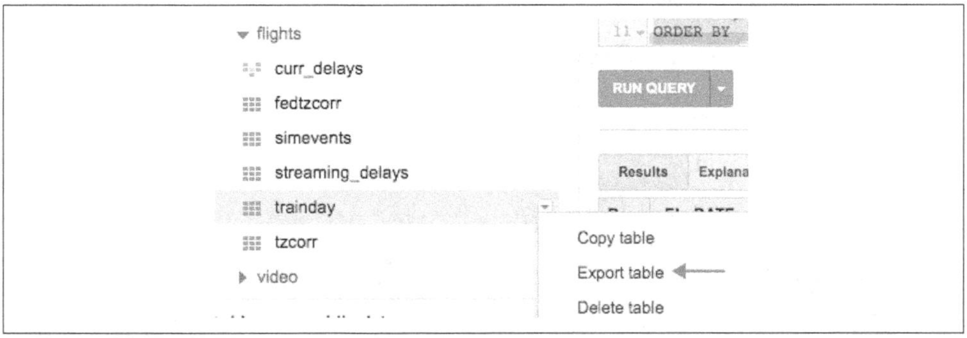

Figure 5-26. Exporting a BigQuery table as a CSV file

Next, select the "Export table" option. For this exercise, I choose to store it on Cloud Storage as *gs://cloud-training-demos-ml/flights/trainday.csv* (you should use your own bucket, of course).

Training and Testing

Now, I can go back and edit my original query to carry out the percentile using only data from my training days. To do that, I will change this string in my original query

```
FROM
  `flights.tzcorr`
```

to:

```
FROM
  `flights.tzcorr` f
JOIN
  `flights.trainday` t
ON
  f.FL_DATE = t.FL_DATE
WHERE
  t.is_train_day = 'True'
```

Now, the query is carried only on days for which is_train_day is True.

Here's the new query in Cloud Datalab:

```
%sql --dialect standard --module depdelayquery3
#standardsql
SELECT
  *
FROM (
  SELECT
    DEP_DELAY,
    APPROX_QUANTILES(ARR_DELAY,
      101)[OFFSET(70)] AS arrival_delay,
    COUNT(ARR_DELAY) AS numflights
  FROM
    `cloud-training-demos.flights.tzcorr` f
  JOIN
    `flights.trainday` t
  ON
    f.FL_DATE = t.FL_DATE
  WHERE
    t.is_train_day = 'True'
  GROUP BY
    DEP_DELAY )
WHERE
  numflights > 370
ORDER BY
  DEP_DELAY
```

The code to create the plot remains the same (other than the change in query name on the first line):

```
depdelay = bq.Query(depdelayquery3).to_dataframe()
plt.axhline(y=15, color='r')
ax = plt.axes()
depdelay.plot(kind='line', x='DEP_DELAY', y='arr_delay_30',
              ax=ax, ylim=(0,30), xlim=(0,30), legend=False)
ax.set_xlabel('Departure Delay (minutes)')
ax.set_ylabel('> 30% likelihood of this Arrival Delay (minutes)')
```

The threshold (the x-axis value of the intersection point) remains consistent, as depicted in Figure 5-27.

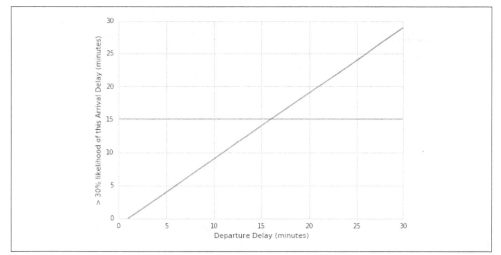

Figure 5-27. The departure delay threshold remains consistent with earlier methods

This is gratifying because we get the same answer—16 minutes—after creating the empirical probabilistic model on just 70% of the data.

Let's formally evaluate how well our recommendation of 16 minutes does in terms of predicting an arrival delay of 15 minutes or more. To do that, we have to find the number of times that we would have wrongly canceled a meeting or missed a meeting. We can compute these numbers using this query on days that are not training days:

```
#standardsql
SELECT
  SUM(IF(DEP_DELAY < 16
     AND arr_delay < 15, 1, 0)) AS correct_nocancel,
  SUM(IF(DEP_DELAY < 16
     AND arr_delay >= 15, 1, 0)) AS wrong_nocancel,
  SUM(IF(DEP_DELAY >= 16
     AND arr_delay < 15, 1, 0)) AS wrong_cancel,
  SUM(IF(DEP_DELAY >= 16
     AND arr_delay >= 15, 1, 0)) AS correct_cancel
FROM (
  SELECT
    DEP_DELAY,
    ARR_DELAY
  FROM
    `flights.tzcorr` f
  JOIN
    `flights.trainday` t
  ON
```

```
    f.FL_DATE = t.FL_DATE
  WHERE
    t.is_train_day = 'False' )
```

Note that unlike when I was computing the decision threshold, I am not removing outliers (i.e., thresholding on 370 flights at a specific departure delay) when evaluating the model—outlier removal is part of my training process and the evaluation needs to be independent of that. The second point to note is that this query is run on days that are not in the training dataset. Running this query in BigQuery, I get the result shown in Figure 5-28.

	correct_nocancel	wrong_nocancel	wrong_cancel	correct_cancel
0	4493692	238360	188140	773612

Figure 5-28. Confusion matrix on independent test dataset

We will cancel meetings corresponding to a total of 188,140 + 773,612 = 961,752 flights. What fraction of the time are these recommendations correct? We can do the computation in Cloud Datalab:

```
eval = bq.Query(evalquery).to_dataframe(dialect='standard')
print eval['correct_nocancel'] / (eval['correct_nocancel'] + \
eval['wrong_nocancel'])
print eval['correct_cancel'] / (eval['correct_cancel'] + \
eval['wrong_cancel'])
```

Figure 5-29 presents the results.

```
eval = bq.Query(evalquery).to_dataframe(dialect='standard')
print eval['correct_nocancel'] / (eval['correct_nocancel'] + \
eval['wrong_nocancel'])
print eval['correct_cancel'] / (eval['correct_cancel'] + \
eval['wrong_cancel'])

0    0.949629
dtype: float64
0    0.804378
dtype: float64
```

Figure 5-29. Computing accuracy on independent test dataset

It turns out when I recommend that you not cancel your meeting, I will be correct 95% of the time, and when I recommend that you cancel your meeting, I will be correct 80% of the time.

Why is this not 70%? Because the populations are different. In creating the model, we found the 70th percentile of arrival delay given a specific departure delay. In evaluating the model, we looked at the dataset of all flights. One's a marginal distribution, and the other's the full one. Another way to think about this is that the 81% figure is padded by all the departure delays of more than 20 minutes when canceling the meeting is an easy call.

We could, of course, evaluate right at the decision boundary by changing our scoring function:

```
%sql --dialect standard --module evalquery2
#standardsql
SELECT
  SUM(IF(DEP_DELAY = 15
      AND arr_delay < 15, 1, 0)) AS correct_nocancel,
  SUM(IF(DEP_DELAY = 15
      AND arr_delay >= 15, 1, 0)) AS wrong_nocancel,
  SUM(IF(DEP_DELAY = 16
      AND arr_delay < 15, 1, 0)) AS wrong_cancel,
  SUM(IF(DEP_DELAY = 16
      AND arr_delay >= 15, 1, 0)) AS correct_cancel
...
```

If we do that, evaluating only at departure delays of 15 and 16 minutes, the contingency table looks like Figure 5-30.

```
eval = bq.Query(evalquery2).to_dataframe(dialect='standard')
eval.head()
```

	correct_nocancel	wrong_nocancel	wrong_cancel	correct_cancel
0	27200	10391	24005	10408

```
print eval['correct_nocancel'] / (eval['correct_nocancel'] + \
eval['wrong_nocancel'])
print eval['correct_cancel'] / (eval['correct_cancel'] + \
eval['wrong_cancel'])
```
```
        0     0.723577
        dtype: float64
        0     0.302444
        dtype: float64
```

Figure 5-30. Evaluating only at marginal decisions

As expected, we are correct to cancel the meeting only 30.2% of the time, close to our target of 30%. This model achieves the 70% correctness measure that was our target but does so by canceling fewer flights than the contingency-table-based model of Chapter 3.

Summary

In this chapter, we began to carry out exploratory data analysis. To be able to interactively analyze our large dataset, we loaded the data into BigQuery, which gave us the ability to carry out queries on millions of rows in a matter of seconds. We required sophisticated statistical plotting capabilities, and we obtained that by using a Jupyter notebook in the form of Cloud Datalab.

In terms of the model itself, we were able to use nonparametric estimation of the 30th percentile of arrival delays to pick the departure delay threshold. We discovered that doing this allows us to cancel fewer meetings while attaining the same target correctness. We evaluated our decision threshold on an independent set of flights by dividing our dataset into two parts—a training set and a testing set—based on randomly partitioning the distinct days that comprise our dataset.

## CHAPTER 6

Bayes Classifier on Cloud Dataproc

Having become accustomed to running queries in BigQuery where there were no clusters to manage, I'm dreading going back to configuring and managing Hadoop clusters. But I did promise you a tour of data science on the cloud, and in many companies, Hadoop plays an important role in that. Fortunately, Google Cloud Dataproc (*http://cloud.google.com/dataproc*) makes it convenient to spin up a Hadoop cluster that is capable of running MapReduce, Pig, Hive, and Spark. Although there is no getting away from cluster management and diminished resources,[1] I can at least avoid the programming drudgery of writing low-level MapReduce jobs by using Apache Spark and Apache Pig.

In this chapter, we tackle the next stage of our data science problem, by creating a Bayesian model to predict the likely arrival delay of a flight. We will do this through an integrated workflow that involves BigQuery, Spark SQL, and Apache Pig. Along the way, we will also learn how to create, resize, and delete job-specific Hadoop clusters using Cloud Dataproc.

MapReduce and the Hadoop Ecosystem

MapReduce was described in a paper by Jeff Dean and Sanjay Ghemawat (*https://research.google.com/archive/mapreduce.html*) as a way to process large datasets on a cluster of machines. They showed that many real-world tasks can be decomposed into a sequence of two types of functions: *map* functions that process key-value pairs

---

1 I suppose that I *could* create a 1,000-node cluster to run my Spark job so that I have as much compute resources at my disposal as I did when using BigQuery, but it would be sitting idle most of the time. The practical thing to do would be to create a three-node cluster for development, and then resize it to 20 workers when I'm about to run it on the full dataset.

to generate intermediate key-value pairs, and *reduce* functions that merge all the intermediate values associated with the same key. A flexible and general-purpose framework can run programs that are written following this MapReduce model on a cluster of commodity machines. Such a MapReduce framework will take care of many of the details that make writing distributed system applications so difficult—the framework, for example, will partition the input data appropriately, schedule running the program across a set of machines, and handle job or machine failures.

How MapReduce Works

Imagine that you have a large set of documents and you want to compute word frequencies on that dataset. Before MapReduce, this was an extremely difficult problem. One approach you might take would be to scale up—that is, to get an extremely large, powerful machine.[2] The machine will hold the current word frequency table in memory, and every time a word is encountered in the document, this word frequency table will be updated. Here it is in pseudocode:

```
wordcount(Document[] docs):
    wordfrequency = {}
    for each document d in docs:
        for each word w in d:
            wordfrequency[w] += 1
    return wordfrequency
```

We can make this a multithreaded solution by having each thread work on a separate document, sharing the word frequency table between the threads, and updating this in a thread-safe manner. You will at some point, though, run into a dataset that is beyond the capabilities of a single machine. At that point, you will want to scale out, by dividing the documents among a cluster of machines. Each machine on the cluster then processes a fraction of the complete document collection. The programmer implements two methods, map and reduce:

```
map(String docname, String content):
    for each word w in content:
        emitIntermediate(w, 1)

reduce(String word, Iterator<int> intermediate_values):
    int result = 0;
    for each v in intermediate_values:
        result += v;
    emit(result);
```

---

2 In Chapter 2, we discussed scaling up, scaling out, and data in situ from the perspective of datacenter technologies. This is useful background to have here.

The framework manages the orchestration of the maps and reduces and interposes a group-by-key in between; that is; the framework makes these calls (not the programmer):

```
wordcount(Document[] docs):
    for each doc in docs:
        map(doc.name, doc.content)
    group-by-key(key-value-pairs)
    for each key in key-values:
        reduce(key, intermediate_values)
```

To improve speed in an environment in which network bisection bandwidth is low,[3] the documents are stored on local drives attached to the compute instance. The map operations are then scheduled by the MapReduce infrastructure in such a way that each map operation runs on a compute instance that already has the data it needs (this assumes that the data has been presharded on the cluster), as shown in Figure 6-1.

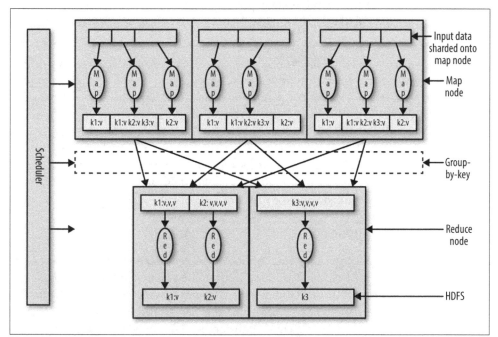

Figure 6-1. MapReduce is an algorithm for distributed processing of datasets in which the data are presharded onto compute instances such that each map operation can access the data it needs using a local filesystem call

---

3 See slide 6 of Dean and Ghemawat's original presentation here: *https://research.google.com/archive/mapreduce-osdi04-slides/index-auto-0006.html*—the MapReduce architecture they proposed assumes that the cluster has limited bisection bandwidth and local, rather slow drives.

As the diagram indicates, there can be multiple map and reduce jobs assigned to a single machine. The key capability that the MapReduce framework provides is the orchestration and massive group-by-key after the map tasks complete and before the reduce jobs can begin.

Apache Hadoop

When Dean and Ghemawat published the MapReduce paper, they did not make Google's MapReduce implementation open source.[4] Hadoop (*http://hadoop.apache.org/*) is open source software that was created from parts of Apache Nutch (*http://nutch.apache.org/*), an open source web crawler created by Doug Cutting based on a couple of Google papers (*http://bit.ly/2BNXh4X*). Cutting modeled the distributed filesystem in his crawler on Google's descriptions of the Google File System (*https://research.google.com/archive/gfs.html*) (a predecessor of the Colossus filesystem (*http://bit.ly/2AXoa8U*) that is in use within Google Cloud Platform today) and the data processing framework on the MapReduce paper. These two parts were then factored out into Hadoop in 2006 as the Hadoop Distributed File System (HDFS) and the MapReduce engine.

Hadoop today is managed by the Apache Software Foundation. It is a framework that runs applications using the MapReduce algorithm, enabling these applications to process data in parallel on a cluster of commodity machines. Apache Hadoop provides Java libraries necessary to write MapReduce applications (i.e., the `map` and `reduce` methods) that will be run by the framework. In addition, it provides a scheduler, called YARN, and a distributed filesystem (HDFS). To run a job on Hadoop, the programmer submits a job by specifying the location of the input and output files (typically, these will be in HDFS) and uploading a set of Java classes that provide the implementation of the `map` and `reduce` methods.

Google Cloud Dataproc

Normally, the first step in writing Hadoop jobs is to get a Hadoop installation going. This involves setting up a cluster, installing Hadoop on it, and configuring the cluster so that the machines all know about one another and can communicate with one another in a secure manner. Then, you'd start the YARN and MapReduce processes and finally be ready to write some Hadoop programs. On Google Cloud Platform, we can create a fully configured Hadoop cluster by using the following single `gcloud` command:[5]

---

4 Now, research papers from Google are often accompanied by open source implementations—Kubernetes, Apache Beam, TensorFlow, and Inception are examples.

5 As discussed in Chapter 3, the `gcloud` command makes a REST API call and so this can be done programmatically. You could also use the Google Cloud Platform web console.

```
gcloud dataproc clusters create \
    --num-workers=2 \
    --scopes=cloud-platform \
    --worker-machine-type=n1-standard-2 \
    --master-machine-type=n1-standard-4 \
    --zone=us-central1-a \
    ch6cluster
```

A minute or so later, the Cloud Dataproc cluster is created, all ready to go. The parameters above are all quite self-evident except for a couple. The `scopes` parameter indicates what Cloud Identity Access Management (IAM) roles this cluster's service account should have. For example, to create a cluster that will run programs that will need to administer Cloud Bigtable and invoke BigQuery queries, you could specify the scope as follows:

```
--scopes=https://www.googleapis.com/auth/bigtable.admin,bigquery
```

Here, I'm allowing the cluster to work with all Google Cloud Platform products. Finally, if your data (that will be processed by the cluster) is in a single-region bucket on Google Cloud Storage, you should create your cluster in that same zone to take advantage of the high bisection bandwidth within a Google datacenter; that's what the `--zone` specification does that we saw in the example we looked at just a moment ago.

Although the cluster creation command supports a `--bucket` option to specify the location of a staging bucket to store such things as configuration and control files, best practice is to allow Cloud Dataproc to determine its own staging bucket. This allows you to keep your data separate from the staging information needed for the cluster to carry out its tasks. Cloud Dataproc will create a separate bucket in each geographic region, choose an appropriate bucket based on the zone in which your cluster resides, and reuse such Cloud Dataproc–created staging buckets between cluster create requests if possible.[6]

We can verify that Hadoop exists by connecting to the cluster using Secure Shell (SSH). You can do this by visiting the Cloud Dataproc section of the Google Cloud Platform web console, and then, on the newly created cluster, click the SSH button next to the master node. In the SSH window, type the following:

```
hdfs dfsadmin -report
```

You should get a report about all the nodes that are running.

---

6 To find the name of the staging bucket created by Cloud Dataproc, run **gcloud dataproc clusters describe**.

Need for Higher-Level Tools

We can improve the efficiency of the basic MapReduce algorithm by taking advantage of local aggregation. For example, we can lower network traffic and the number of intermediate value pairs by carrying out the reduce operation partially on the map nodes (i.e., the word frequency for each document can be computed and then emitted to the reduce nodes). This is called a *combine operation*. This is particularly useful if we have *reduce stragglers*—reduce nodes that need to process a lot more data than other nodes. For example, the reduce node that needs to keep track of frequently occurring words like *the* will be swamped in a MapReduce architecture consisting of just map and reduce processes. Using a combiner helps equalize this because the most number of values any reduce node will have to process is limited by the number of map nodes. The combine and reduce operations cannot always be identical—if, for example, we are computing the mean, it is necessary for the combine operator to not compute the intermediate mean,[7] but instead emit the intermediate sum and intermediate count. Therefore, the use of combine operators cannot be automatic—you can employ it only for specific types of aggregations, and for other types, you might need to use special tricks. The combine operation, therefore, is best thought of as a local optimization that is best carried out by higher-level abstractions in the framework.

The word count example is embarrassingly parallel, and therefore trivial to implement in terms of a single map and a single reduce operation. However, it is nontrivial to cast more complex data processing algorithms into sequences of map and reduce operations. For example, if we need to compute word co-occurrence in a corpus of documents,[8] it is necessary to begin keeping joint track of events. This is usually done using pairs or stripes. In the pairs technique, the mapper emits a key consisting of every possible pair of words and the number 1. In the stripes technique, the mapper emits a key, which is the first word, and the value is the second word and the number 1, so that the reducer for word1 aggregates all the co-occurrences (termed stripes) involving word1. The pairs algorithm generates far more key-value pairs than the stripes approach, but the stripes approach involves a lot more serialization and deserialization because the values (being lists) are more complex. Problems involving sorting pose another form of complexity—the MapReduce framework distributes keys, but what about values? One solution is to move part of the value into the key, thus using the framework itself for sorting. All these design patterns need to be put together carefully in any reasonably real-world solution. For example, the first step of the Bayes classifier that we are about to develop in this chapter involves computing

---

7 Because the average of partial averages is not necessarily the average of the whole (it will be equal to the whole only if the partials are all the same size).

8 This discussion applies to any joint distribution such as "people who buy item1 also buy item2."

quantiles—this involves partial sorting and counting. Doing this with low-level MapReduce operations can become quite a chore.

For these reasons and others, decomposing a task into sequences of MapReduce programs is not trivial. Higher-level solutions are called for, and as different organizations implemented add-ons to the basic Hadoop framework and made these additions available as open source, the Hadoop ecosystem was born.

Apache Pig (*http://pig.apache.org/*) provided one of the first ways to simplify the writing of MapReduce programs to run on Hadoop. Apache Pig requires you to write code in a language called *Pig Latin*; these programs are then converted to sequences of MapReduce programs, and these MapReduce programs are executed on Apache Hadoop. Because Pig Latin comes with a command-line interpreter, it is very conducive to interactive creation of programs meant for large datasets. At the same time, it is possible to save the interactive commands and execute the script on demand. This provides a way to achieve both embarrassingly parallel data analysis and data flow sequences consisting of multiple interrelated data transformations. Pig can optimize the execution of MapReduce sequences, thus allowing the programmer to express tasks naturally without worrying about efficiency.

Apache Hive (*https://hive.apache.org/*) provides a mechanism to project structure onto data that is already in distributed storage. With the structure (essentially a table schema) projected onto the data, it is possible to query, update, and manage the dataset using SQL. Typical interactions with Hive use a command-line tool or a Java Database Connectivity (JDBC) driver.

Pig and Hive both rely on the distributed storage system to store intermediate results. Apache Spark (*http://spark.apache.org/*), on the other hand, takes advantage of in-memory processing and a variety of other optimizations. Because many data pipelines start with large, out-of-memory data, but quickly aggregate to it to something that can be fit into memory, Spark can provide dramatic speedups when compared to Pig and Spark SQL when compared to Hive.[9] In addition, because Spark (like Pig and BigQuery) optimizes the directed acyclic graph (DAG) of successive processing stages, it can provide gains over handwritten Hadoop operations. With the growing popularity of Spark, a variety of machine learning, data mining, and streaming packages have been written for it. Hence, in this chapter, we focus on Spark and Pig solutions. Cloud Dataproc, though, provides an execution environment for Hadoop jobs regardless of the abstraction level (i.e., whether you submit jobs in Hadoop, Pig, Hive, or Spark).

---

9 Hive has been sped up in recent years through the use of a new application framework (Tez) and a variety of optimizations for long-lived queries. See *https://cwiki.apache.org/confluence/display/Hive/Hive+on+Tez* and *https://cwiki.apache.org/confluence/display/Hive/LLAP*.

All these software packages are installed by default on Cloud Dataproc. For example, you can verify that Spark exists on your cluster by connecting to the master node via SSH and then, on the command line, typing **pyspark**.

Jobs, Not Clusters

We will look at how to submit jobs to the Cloud Dataproc clusters shortly, but after you are done with the cluster, delete it by using the following:[10]

```
gcloud dataproc clusters delete ch6cluster
```

This is not the typical Hadoop workflow—if you are used to an on-premises Hadoop installation, you might have set up the cluster a few months ago and it has remained up since then. The better practice on Google Cloud Platform, however, is to delete the cluster after you are done. The reasons are two-fold. First, it typically takes less than two minutes to start a cluster. Because cluster creation is fast and can be automated, it is wasteful to keep unused clusters around—you are paying for a cluster of machines if the machines are up, regardless of whether you are running anything useful on them. Second, one reason that on-premises Hadoop clusters are kept always on is because the data is stored on HDFS. Although you can use HDFS in Cloud Dataproc (recall that we used an hdfs command to get the status of the Hadoop cluster), it is not recommended. Instead, it is better to keep your data on Google Cloud Storage and directly read from Cloud Storage in your MapReduce jobs—the original Map-Reduce practice of assigning map processes to nodes that already have the necessary data came about in an environment in which network bisection speeds were low. On the Google Cloud Platform, for which network bisection speeds are on the order of a petabit per second, best practice changes. Instead of sharding your data onto HDFS, keep your data on Cloud Storage and read the data from an ephemeral cluster, as demonstrated in Figure 6-2.

Because of the high network speed that prevails within the Google datacenter, reading from Cloud Storage is competitive with HDFS in terms of speed for sustained reads of large files (the typical Hadoop use case). If your use case involves frequently read-ing small files, reading from Cloud Storage could be slower than reading from HDFS. However, even in this scenario, you can counteract this lower speed by simply creat-ing more compute nodes—because storage and compute are separate, you are not limited to the number of nodes that happen to have the data. Because Hadoop clus-ters tend to be underutilized, you will often save money by creating an ephemeral cluster many times the size of an always-on cluster with a HDFS filesystem. Getting the job done quickly with a lot more machines and deleting the cluster when you are done is often the more frugal option (you should measure this on your particular

---

[10] As this book was heading to print, the Dataproc team announced a new feature—you can now automatically schedule a cluster for deletion after, say, 10 minutes of idle time.

workflow, of course, and estimate the cost[11] of different scenarios). This method of operating with short-lived clusters is also quite conducive to the use of preemptible instances (*https://cloud.google.com/preemptible-vms/*)—you can create a cluster with a given number of standard instances and many more preemptible instances, thus getting a lower cost for the full workload.

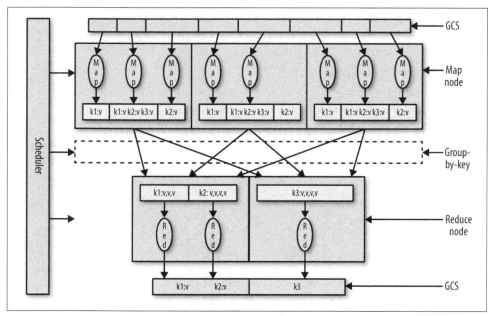

Figure 6-2. Because network bisection speeds on Google Cloud are on the order of a petabit per second, best practice is to keep your data on Cloud Storage and simply spin up short-lived compute nodes to perform the map operations. These nodes will read the data across the network. In other words, there is no need to preshard the data.

Initialization Actions

Creating and deleting clusters on demand is fine if you want a plain, vanilla Hadoop cluster, but what if you need to install specific software on the individual nodes? If you need the master and slave nodes of the Cloud Dataproc cluster set up in a specific way, you can use initialization actions. These are simply startup executables, stored on Cloud Storage, that will be run on the nodes of the cluster. For example, suppose that we want the GitHub repository for this course installed on the cluster's master node, you would do three things:

---

11 For a tool to estimate costs quickly, go to *https://cloud.google.com/products/calculator/*.

1. Create a script to carry out whatever software we want preinstalled:[12]

```
#!/bin/bash
USER=vlakshmanan    # change this ...
ROLE=$(/usr/share/google/get_metadata_value attributes/dataproc-role)
if [[ "${ROLE}" == 'Master' ]]; then
  cd home/$USER
  git clone \
     https://github.com/GoogleCloudPlatform/data-science-on-gcp
fi
```

2. Save the script on Cloud Storage:

```
#!/bin/bash
BUCKET=cloud-training-demos-ml
ZONE=us-central1-a
INSTALL=gs://$BUCKET/flights/dataproc/install_on_cluster.sh

# upload install file
gsutil cp install_on_cluster.sh $INSTALL
```

3. Supply the script to the cluster creation command:[13]

```
gcloud dataproc clusters create \
    --num-workers=2 \
    --scopes=cloud-platform \
    --worker-machine-type=n1-standard-2 \
    --master-machine-type=n1-standard-4 \
    --zone=$ZONE \
    --initialization-actions=$INSTALL \
    ch6cluster
```

Now, when the cluster is created, the GitHub repository will exist on the master node.

Quantization Using Spark SQL

So far, we have used only one variable in our dataset—the departure delay—to make our predictions of the arrival delay of a flight. However, we know that the distance the aircraft needs to fly must have some effect on the ability of the pilot to make up delays en route. The longer the flight, the more likely it is that small delays in departure can be made up in the air. So, let's build a statistical model that uses two variables—the departure delay and the distance to be traveled.

One way to do this is to put each flight into one of several bins, as shown in Table 6-1.

---

12 One efficient use of installation actions is to preinstall all the third-party libraries you might need, so that they don't have to be submitted with the job.

13 This script is in the GitHub repository of this book as *06_dataproc/create_cluster.sh*.

Table 6-1. Quantizing distance and departure delay to carry out Bayesian classification over two variables

	<10 min	10–12 minutes	12–15 minutes	>15 minutes
<100 miles	For example: Arrival Delay ≥ 15 min: 150 flights. Arrival Delay < 15min: 850 flights. 85% of flights have arrival delay < 15 minutes			
100–500 miles				
>500 miles				

For each bin, I can look at the number of flights within the bin that have an arrival delay of more than 15 minutes, and the number of flights with an arrival delay of less than 15 minutes and determine which category is higher. The majority vote then becomes our prediction for that entire bin. Because our threshold for decisions is 70% (recall that we want to cancel the meeting if there is a 30% likelihood that the flight will be late), we'll recommend canceling flights that fall into a bin if the fraction of arrival delays of less than 15 minutes is less than 0.7. This method is called *Bayes classification* and the statistical model is simple enough that we can build it from scratch with a few lines of code.

Within each bin, we are calculating the conditional probability $P(C_{ontime} \mid x_0, x_1)$ and $P(C_{late} \mid x_0, x_1)$ where (x_0, x_1) is the pair of predictor variables (mileage and departure delay) and C_k is one of two classes depending on the value of the arrival delay of the flight. $P(C_k \mid x_i)$ is called the conditional probability—for example, the probability that the flight will be late given that (x_0, x_1) is (120 miles, 8 minutes). As we discussed in Chapter 1, the probability of a specific value of a continuous variable is zero—we need to estimate the probability over an interval, and, in this case, the intervals are given by the bins. Thus, to estimate $P(C_{ontime} \mid x_0, x_1)$, we find the bin that (x_0, x_1) falls into and use that as the estimate of $P(C_{ontime})$. If this is less than 70%, our decision will be to cancel the meeting.

Of all the ways of estimating a conditional probability, the way we are doing it—by divvying up the dataset based on the values of the variables—is the easiest, but it will work only if we have large enough populations in each of the bins. This method of directly computing the probability tables works with two variables, but will it work with 20 variables? How likely is it that there will be enough flights for which the departure airport is TUL, the distance is about 350 miles, the departure delay is about 10 minutes, the taxi-out time is about 4 minutes, and the hour of day that the flight departs is around 7 AM?

As the number of variables increases, we will need more sophisticated methods in order to estimate the conditional probability. A scalable approach that we can employ if the predictor variables are independent is a method called *Naive Bayes*. In the Naive Bayes approach, we compute the probability tables by taking each variable in isolation (i.e., computing $P(C_{ontime} \mid x_0)$ and $P(C_{ontime} \mid x_1)$ separately) and then multiplying them to come up with $P(C_k \mid x_i)$. However, for just two variables, for a dataset this big, we can get away with binning the data and directly estimating the conditional probability.

Google Cloud Datalab on Cloud Dataproc

Developing the Bayesian classification from scratch requires being able to interactively carry out development. Although we could spin up a Cloud Dataproc cluster, connect to it via SSH, and do development on the Spark Read–Eval–Print Loop (REPL), it would be better to use Cloud Datalab or Jupyter and get a notebook experience similar to how we worked with BigQuery in Chapter 5.

Fortunately, we don't need to roll out an installation script for Cloud Datalab. There is a GitHub repository of Cloud Dataproc initialization actions (*http://bit.ly/2nyCdwj/*), and those actions are also stored in a public bucket on Cloud Storage in *gs://dataproc-initialization-actions/*. Thus, we can start a cluster that has Cloud Datalab installed by specifying the initialization action, as follows:

```
--initialization-actions=gs://dataproc-initialization-actions/datalab/datalab.sh
```

Connecting to Cloud Datalab on this cluster, though, is more complex than connecting to a local Docker container. To avoid security issues, the port 8080 is not open to anyone who happens to know the IP address of your Cloud Dataproc master node. Instead, we need to connect through an SSH tunnel. This requires two steps:

1. Start the SSH tunnel on your local machine (not Cloud Shell) using the following commands:

    ```
    ZONE=us-central1-a
    gcloud compute ssh  --zone=$ZONE \
          --ssh-flag="-D 1080" --ssh-flag="-N" --ssh-flag="-n" \
          ch6cluster-m
    ```

2. Start a new Chrome session that delegates to this proxy (you can leave your other Chrome windows running):

    ```
    rm -rf /tmp/junk
    /usr/bin/chrome \
      --proxy-server="socks5://localhost:1080" \
      --host-resolver-rules="MAP * 0.0.0.0 , EXCLUDE localhost" \
      --user-data-dir=/tmp/junk
    ```

    Change the path to your Chrome executable and specify a nonexistent user data directory (I'm using */tmp/junk*) appropriately.

3. In the browser window, navigate to *http://ch6cluster-m:8080/*. If you have corporate proxy settings, you might need to disable them in Chrome settings.

After Cloud Datalab starts, use the "ungit" icon to clone the GitHub repository for this book.[14] Then, you can navigate into the repository to open up a notebook containing the code in this chapter.[15]

Independence Check Using BigQuery

Before we can get to computing the proportion of delayed flights in each bin, we need to decide how to quantize the delay and distance. What we do not want are bins with very few flights—in such cases, statistical estimates will be problematic. In fact, if we could somehow spread the data somewhat evenly between bins, it would be ideal.

For simplicity, we would like to choose the quantization thresholds for distance and for departure delay separately, but we can do this only if they are relatively independent. Let's verify that this is the case. Cloud Dataproc is integrated with the managed services on Google Cloud Platform, so even though we have our own Hadoop cluster, we can still call out to BigQuery from the notebook that is running on Cloud Dataproc. Using BigQuery, Pandas, and seaborn as we did in Chapter 5, here's what the query looks like:

```
sql = """
SELECT DISTANCE, DEP_DELAY
FROM `flights.tzcorr`
WHERE RAND() < 0.001 AND dep_delay > -20
    AND dep_delay < 30 AND distance < 2000
"""
df = bq.Query(sql).to_dataframe(dialect='standard')
sns.set_style("whitegrid")
g = sns.jointplot(df['DISTANCE'], df['DEP_DELAY'], kind="hex",
                  size=10, joint_kws={'gridsize':20})
```

The query samples the full dataset, pulling in 1/1,000 of the flights' distance and departure delay fields (that lie within reasonable ranges) into a Pandas dataframe. This sampled dataset is sent to the seaborn plotting package and a hexbin plot is created. The resulting graph is shown in Figure 6-3.

---

14 The repository URL is *http://github.com/GoogleCloudPlatform/data-science-on-gcp*; an alternate way to clone the repository is to start a new notebook and, in a cell in that new notebook, type `!git clone http:// github.com/GoogleCloudPlatform/data-science-on-gcp`.

15 Look in the GitHub repository for this book at *06_dataproc/quantization.ipynb*.

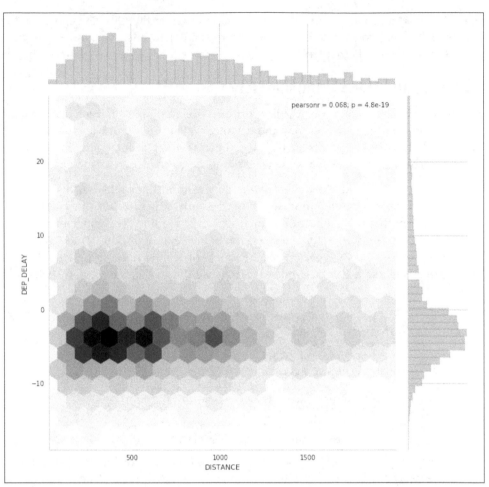

Figure 6-3. The hexbin plot shows the joint distribution of departure delay and the distance flown. You can use such a plot to verify whether the fields in question are independent.

Each hexagon of a hexagonal bin plot is colored based on the number of flights in that bin, with darker hexagons indicating more flights. It is clear that at any distance, a wide variety of departure delays is possible and for any departure delay, a wide variety of distances is possible. The distribution of distances and departure delays in turn is similar across the board. There is no obvious trend between the two variables, indicating that we can treat them as independent.

The distribution plots at the top and right of the center panel of the graph show how the distance and departure delay values are distributed. This will affect the technique that we can use to carry out quantization. Note that the distance is distributed relatively uniformly until about 1,000 miles, beyond which the number of flights begins to taper off. The departure delay, on the other hand, has a long tail and is clustered around −5 minutes. We might be able to use equispaced bins for the distance variable (at least in the 0- to 1,000-mile range), but for the departure delay variable, our bin size must be adaptive to the distribution of flights. In particular, our bin size must be wide in the tail areas and relatively narrow where there are lots of points.

There is one issue with the hexbin plot in Figure 6-3: we have used data that we are not allowed to use. Recall that our model must be developed using only the training data. While we used it only for some light exploration, it is better to be systematic about excluding days that will be part of our evaluation dataset from all model development. To do that, we need to join with the traindays table and retain only days for which is_train_day is True. We could do that in BigQuery, but even though Cloud Dataproc is integrated with other Google Cloud Platform services, invoking Big-Query from a Hadoop cluster feels like a cop-out. So, let's try to re-create the same plot as before, but this time using Spark SQL, and this time using only the training data.

Spark SQL in Google Cloud Datalab

A Spark session already exists in Cloud Datalab; you can verify this by typing the following into a code cell:

```
print spark
```

In a standalone script, though, we'd need to create the Spark session using this:

```
from pyspark.sql import SparkSession
spark = SparkSession \
    .builder \
    .appName("Bayes classification using Spark") \
    .getOrCreate()
```

With the spark variable in hand, we can read in the comma-separated value (CSV) files on Google Cloud Storage:

```
inputs = 'gs://cloud-training-demos-ml/flights/tzcorr/all_flights-*')
flights = spark.read\
            .schema(schema)\
            .csv(inputs)
```

The schema to be specified is the schema of the CSV files. By default, Spark will assume that all columns are strings, so we'll correct the types for the three columns we are interested in—arr_delay, dep_delay, and distance:

```
from pyspark.sql.types import *

def get_structfield(colname):
    if colname in ['ARR_DELAY', 'DEP_DELAY', 'DISTANCE']:
        return StructField(colname, FloatType(), True)
    else:
```

```
                return StructField(colname, StringType(), True)

    schema = StructType([get_structfield(colname) \
                        for colname in header.split(',')])
```

Even though we do want to ultimately read all the flights and create our model from all of the data, we will find that development goes faster if we read a fraction of the dataset. So, let's change the input from all_flights-* to all_flights-00000-*.

```
    inputs = 'gs://${BUCKET}/flights/tzcorr/all_flights-00000-*')
```

Because I had 31 CSV files, doing this change means that I will be processing just the first file, and we will notice an increase in speed of 30 times during development. Of course, we should not draw any conclusions from processing such a small sample[16] other than that the code works as intended. After the code has been developed on 3% of the data, we'll change the string so as to process all data and increase the cluster size so that this is also done in a timely manner. Doing development on a small sample on a small cluster ensures that we are not underutilizing a huge cluster of machines while we are developing the code.

With the flights dataframe created as shown previously, we can employ SQL on the dataframe by creating a temporary view (it is available only within this Spark session):

```
    flights.createOrReplaceTempView('flights')
```

Now, we can employ SQL to query the flights view, for example by doing this:

```
    results = spark.sql('SELECT COUNT(*) FROM flights WHERE dep_delay >
    -20 AND distance < 2000')
    results.show()
```

On my development subset, this yields the following result:

```
    +--------+
    |count(1)|
    +--------+
    |  384687|
    +--------+
```

Even this is too large to comfortably fit in memory,[17] but I dare not go any smaller than 3% of the data, even in development.

To create the traindays dataframe, we can follow the same steps, but because *train-day.csv* still has its header, we can take a shortcut, instructing Spark to name the columns based on that header in the data file. Also, because *trainday.csv* is quite small

---

16 Just as an example, the Google Cloud Dataflow job that wrote out this code could have ordered the CSV file by date, and in that case, this file will contain only the first 12 days of the year.

17 Around 50,000 would have been just right.

(only 365 lines of data), we can also ask Spark to infer the column types. Inferring the schema requires a second pass through the dataset, and, therefore, you should not do it on very large datasets.

```
traindays = spark.read \
    .option("header", "true") \
    .option("inferSchema", "true") \
    .csv('gs://cloud-training-demos-ml/flights/trainday.csv')
traindays.createOrReplaceTempView('traindays')
```

A quick check illustrates that traindays has been read, and the column names and types are correct:

```
results = spark.sql('SELECT * FROM traindays')
results.head(5)
```

This yields the following:

```
[Row(FL_DATE=datetime.datetime(2015, 1, 1, 0, 0), is_train_day=True),
 Row(FL_DATE=datetime.datetime(2015, 1, 2, 0, 0), is_train_day=False),
 Row(FL_DATE=datetime.datetime(2015, 1, 3, 0, 0), is_train_day=False),
 Row(FL_DATE=datetime.datetime(2015, 1, 4, 0, 0), is_train_day=True),
 Row(FL_DATE=datetime.datetime(2015, 1, 5, 0, 0), is_train_day=True)]
```

To restrict the flights dataframe to contain only training days, we can do a SQL join:

```
statement = """
SELECT
  f.FL_DATE AS date,
  distance,
  dep_delay
FROM flights f
JOIN traindays t
ON f.FL_DATE == t.FL_DATE
WHERE
  t.is_train_day AND
  f.dep_delay IS NOT NULL
ORDER BY
  f.dep_delay DESC
"""
flights = spark.sql(statement)
```

Now, we can use the flights dataframe for the hexbin plots after clipping the x-axis and y-axis to reasonable limits:

```
df = flights[(flights['distance'] < 2000) & \
    (flights['dep_delay'] > -20) & \
    (flights['dep_delay'] < 30)]
df.describe().show()
```

On the development dataset, this yields the following:

```
+-------+------------------+------------------+
|summary|          distance|         dep_delay|
+-------+------------------+------------------+
|  count|            207245|            207245|
|   mean|703.3590581196169|0.853024198412507|
| stddev| 438.365126616063|8.859942819934993|
|    min|              31.0|             -19.0|
|    max|            1999.0|              29.0|
+-------+------------------+------------------+
```

When we drew the hexbin plot in the previous section, we sampled the data to 1/1,000, but that was because we were passing in a Pandas dataframe to seaborn. This sampling was done so that the Pandas dataframe would fit into memory. However, whereas a Pandas dataframe must fit into memory, a Spark dataframe does not. As of this writing, though, there is no way to directly plot a Spark dataframe either—you must convert it to a Pandas dataframe and therefore, we will still need to sample it, at least when we are processing the full dataset.

Because there are about 200,000 rows on 1/30 of the data, we expect the full dataset to have about 6 million rows. Let's sample this down to about 100,000 records, which would be about 0.02 of the dataset:

```
pdf = df.sample(False, 0.02, 20).toPandas()
g = sns.jointplot(pdf['distance'], pdf['dep_delay'], kind="hex",
                  size=10, joint_kws={'gridsize':20})
```

This yields a hexbin plot that is not very different from the one we ended up with in the previous section. The conclusion—that we need to create adaptive-width bins for quantization—still applies. Just to be sure, though, this is the point at which I'd repeat the analysis on the entire dataset to ensure our deductions are correct had I done only the Spark analysis. However, we did do it on the entire dataset in BigQuery, so let's move on to creating adaptive bins.

Histogram Equalization

To choose the quantization thresholds for the departure delay and the distance in an adaptive way (wider thresholds in the tails and narrower thresholds where there are a lot of flights), we will adopt a technique from image processing called *histogram equalization*.[18]

Low-contrast digital images have histograms of their pixel values distributed such that most of the pixels lie in a narrow range. Take, for example, the photograph in Figure 6-4.[19]

---

[18] For examples of histogram equalization applied to improve the contrast of images, go to *http://docs.opencv.org/3.1.0/d5/daf/tutorial_py_histogram_equalization.html*.

[19] Photograph by the author.

Figure 6-4. Original photograph of the pyramids of Giza used to demonstrate histogram equalization

As depicted in Figure 6-5, the histogram of pixel values in the image is clustered around two points: the dark pixels in the shade, and the bright pixels in the sun.

Figure 6-5. Histogram of pixel values in photograph of the pyramids

Let's remap the pixel values such that the full spectrum of values is present in the image, so that the new histogram looks like that shown in Figure 6-6.

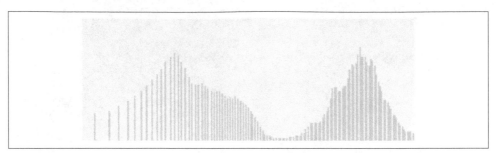

Figure 6-6. Histogram of pixels after remapping the pixels to occupy the full range

The remapping is of pixel values and has no spatial component. For example, all pixel values of 125 in the old image might be changed to a pixel value of 5 in the new image. Figure 6-7 presents the remapped image.

Figure 6-7. Note that after the histogram equalization, the contrast in the image is enhanced

Histogram equalization has helped to enhance the contrast in the image and bring out finer details. Look, for example, at the difference in the rendering of the sand in front of the pyramid or of the detail of the mid-section of Khafre's pyramid (the tall one in the middle[20]).

How is this relevant to what we want to do? We are also looking to remap values when we seek to find quantization intervals. For example, we'd like to remap a distance value of 422 miles to a quantized value of perhaps 3. As in histogram equalization, we want these values to be uniformly distributed between the bins. We can, therefore, apply the same technique as is employed in the image processing filter to achieve this.

What we want to do is to divide the spectrum of distance values into, say, 10 bins. The first bin will contain all values in $[0, d_0)$, the second will contain values in $[d_0, d_1]$, and so on, until the last bin contains values in $[d_9, \infty)$. Histogram equalization requires that d_0, d_1, and so on be such that the number of flights in each bin is approximately equal—that is, for the data to be uniformly distributed after quantization. As in the example photograph of the pyramids, it won't be perfectly uniform because the input values are also discrete. However, the goal is to get as close to an equalized histogram as possible.

Assuming independence and 6 million total flights, if we divvy up the data into 100 bins (10 bins per variable), we will still have about 60,000 flights in each bin. Therefore, with histogram equalization, at any specific departure delay, the number of flights at each distance and delay bin should remain large enough that our conclusions are statistically valid. Divvying up the data into 10 bins implies a probability range of 0, 0.1, 0.2, ..., 0.9 or 10 probabilistic thresholds:

```
np.arange(0, 1.0, 0.1)
```

Finding thresholds that make the two quantized variables uniformly distributed is quite straightforward using the approximate quantiles method discussed in Chapter 5. There is an approxQuantile() method available on the Spark dataframe also:

```
distthresh = flights.approxQuantile('distance',
                list(np.arange(0, 1.0, 0.1)), 0.02)
delaythresh = flights.approxQuantile('dep_delay',
                list(np.arange(0, 1.0, 0.1)), 0.02)
```

On the development dataset, here's what the distance thresholds turn out to be:

```
[31.0, 228.0, 333.0, 447.0, 557.0, 666.0, 812.0, 994.0, 1184.0, 1744.0]
```

Here are the delay thresholds:

```
[-61.0, -7.0, -5.0, -4.0, -2.0, -1.0, 3.0, 8.0, 26.0, 42.0]
```

---

20 Not the tallest, though. Khufu's pyramid (the tall pyramid in the forefront) is taller and larger, but has been completely stripped of its alabaster topping and is situated on slightly lower ground.

The zeroth percentile is essentially the minimum, so we can ignore the first threshold. All departure delays of less than 7 minutes are lumped together, as are departure delays of greater than 42 minutes. About 1/10 of all flights have departure delays between three and eight minutes. We can check that about 1/100 of the flights do have a distance between 447 and 557 miles and departure delay of between three and eight minutes:

```
results = spark.sql('SELECT COUNT(*) FROM flights' +
    ' WHERE dep_delay >= 3 AND dep_delay < 8 AND' +
    ' distance >= 447 AND distance < 557')
results.show()
```

The result on my development dataset, which had about 200,000-plus rows, is as follows:

```
+--------+
|count(1)|
+--------+
|    2750|
+--------+
```

Note that the intervals are wide at the tails of the distribution and quite narrow near the peak—these intervals have been learned from the data. Other than setting the policy ("histogram equalization"), we don't need to be in the business of choosing thresholds. This automation is important because it allows us to dynamically update thresholds if necessary[21] on the most recent data, taking care to use the same set of thresholds in prediction as was used in training.

Dynamically Resizing Clusters

Remember, however, that these thresholds have been computed on about 1/30 of the data (recall that our input was all-flights-00000-of-*). So, we should find the actual thresholds that we will want to use by repeating the processing on all of the training data at hand. To do this in a timely manner, we will also want to increase our cluster size. Fortunately, we don't need to bring down our Cloud Dataproc cluster in order to add more nodes.

Let's add machines to the cluster so that it has 20 workers, 15 of which are preemptible and so are heavily discounted in price:

```
gcloud dataproc clusters update ch6cluster\
    --num-preemptible-workers=15 --num-workers=5
```

---

21 If, for example, there is a newfangled technological development that enables pilots to make up time in the air better or, more realistically, if new regulations prompt airline schedulers to start padding their flight-time estimates.

Preemptible machines are machines that are provided by Google Cloud Platform at a heavy (fixed) discount to standard Google Compute Engine instances in return for users' flexibility in allowing the machines to be taken away at very short notice.[22] They are particularly helpful on Hadoop workloads because Hadoop is fault-tolerant and can deal with machine failure—it will simply reschedule those jobs on the machines that remain available. Using preemptible machines on your jobs is a frugal choice—here, the five standard workers are sufficient to finish the task in a reasonable time. However, the availability of 15 more machines means that our task could be completed four times faster and much more inexpensively[23] than if we have only standard machines in our cluster.

We can navigate to the Google Cloud Platform console in a web browser and check that our cluster now has 20 workers, as illustrated in Figure 6-8.

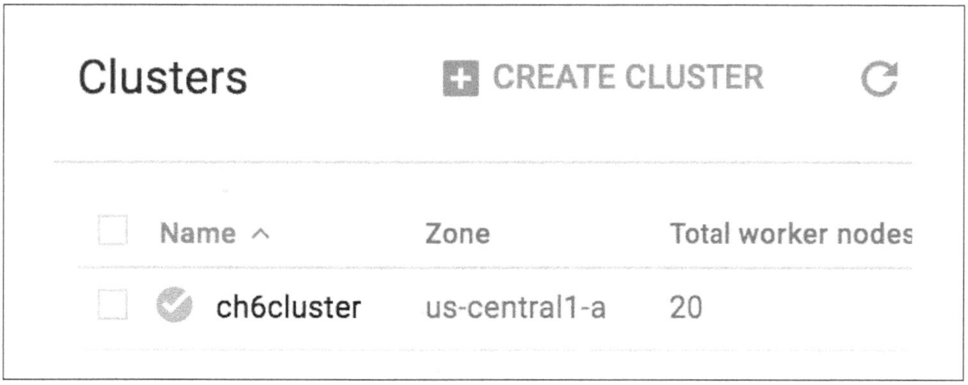

Clusters	**+** CREATE CLUSTER		C
Name ^	Zone	Total worker nodes	
✓ ch6cluster	us-central1-a	20	

Figure 6-8. The cluster now has 20 workers

Now, go to the Datalab notebook and change the input variable to process the full dataset, as shown in Figure 6-9.

---

22 Less than a minute's notice as of this writing.

23 If the preemptible instances cost 20% of a standard machine (as they do as of this writing), the 15 extra machines cost us only as much as three standard machines.

```
#inputs = 'gs://cloud-training-demos-ml/flights/tzcorr/all_flights-00000-*'  # 1/30th
inputs = 'gs://cloud-training-demos-ml/flights/tzcorr/all_flights-*'   # FULL
flights = spark.read\
            .schema(schema)\
            .csv(inputs)

# this view can now be queried ...
flights.createOrReplaceTempView('flights')
```

Figure 6-9. Changing the wildcard in inputs to process the entire dataset

Next, in the Cloud Datalab notebook, click "Clear all Cells" (Figure 6-10) to avoid mistakenly using a value corresponding to the development dataset. To be doubly sure of not using any value that is lying around from our earlier work, also click Reset Session.

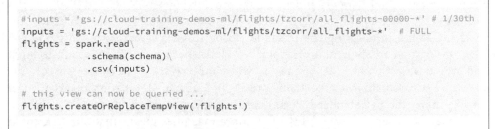

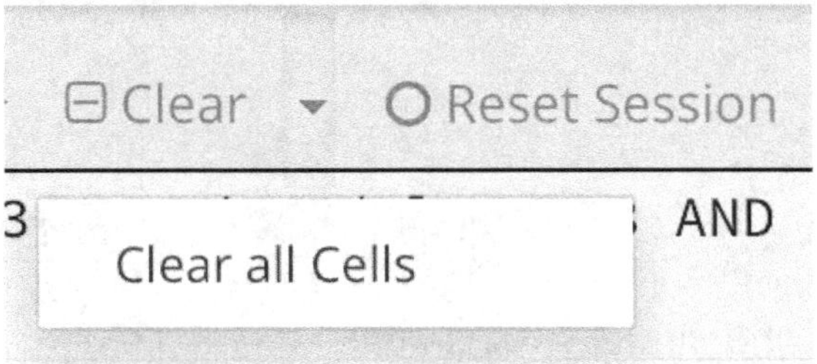

Figure 6-10. You can find Clear all Cells by clicking the down arrow next to the Clear menu item

Finally, click "Run all Cells," as depicted in Figure 6-11.

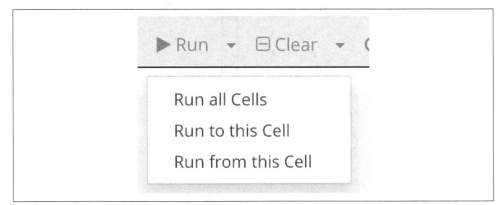

Figure 6-11. You can find the Run all Cells by clicking the down arrow next to the Run menu item

All the graphs and charts are updated. The key results, though, are the quantization thresholds that we will need to compute the conditional probability table:

```
[30.0, 251.0, 368.0, 448.0, 575.0, 669.0, 838.0, 1012.0, 1218.0, 1849.0]
[-82.0, -6.0, -5.0, -4.0, -3.0, 0.0, 3.0, 5.0, 11.0, 39.0]
```

Recall that the first threshold is the minimum and can be ignored. The actual thresholds start with 251 miles and –6 minutes.

After we have the results, let's resize the cluster back to something smaller so that we are not wasting cluster resources while we go about developing the program to compute the conditional probabilities:

```
gcloud dataproc clusters update ch6cluster\
    --num-preemptible-workers=0 --num-workers=2
```

I have been recommending that you create ephemeral clusters, run jobs on them, and then delete them when you are done. Your considerations might change, however, if your company owns a Hadoop cluster. In that case, you will submit Spark and Pig jobs to that long-lived cluster and will typically be concerned with ensuring that the cluster is not overloaded. For the scenario in which you own an on-premises cluster, you might want to consider using a public cloud as spillover in those situations for which there are more jobs than your cluster can handle. You can achieve this by monitoring YARN jobs and sending such spillover jobs to Cloud Dataproc. Apache Airflow provides the necessary plug-ins to able to do this, but discussing how to set up such a hybrid system is beyond the scope of this book.

Bayes Classification Using Pig

Now that we have the quantization thresholds, what we need to do is find out the recommendation (whether to cancel the meeting) for each bin based on whether 70% of flights in that bin are on time or not.

We could do this in Spark SQL, but just to show you another tool that we could use, let's use Pig. First, we will log into the master node via SSH and write Pig jobs using the command-line interpreter. After we have the code working, we'll increase the size of the cluster and submit a Pig script to the Cloud Dataproc cluster (you can submit Spark jobs to the Cloud Dataproc cluster in the same way) from CloudShell or any machine on which you have the gcloud SDK installed.

Log in to the master node of your cluster and start a Pig interactive session by typing **pig**.

Let's begin by loading up a single CSV file into Pig to make sure things work:

```
REGISTER /usr/lib/pig/piggybank.jar;

FLIGHTS =
```

```
LOAD 'gs://cloud-training-demos-ml/flights/tzcorr/all_flights-00000-*'
using org.apache.pig.piggybank.storage.CSVExcelStorage(
    ',', 'NO_MULTILINE', 'NOCHANGE')
  AS
(FL_DATE:chararray,UNIQUE_CARRIER:chararray,AIRLINE_ID:chararray,
CARRIER:chararray,FL_NUM:chararray,ORIGIN_AIRPORT_ID:chararray,
ORIGIN_AIRPORT_SEQ_ID:int,ORIGIN_CITY_MARKET_ID:chararray,
ORIGIN:chararray,DEST_AIRPORT_ID:chararray,DEST_AIRPORT_SEQ_ID:int,
DEST_CITY_MARKET_ID:chararray,DEST:chararray,CRS_DEP_TIME:datetime,
DEP_TIME:datetime,DEP_DELAY:float,TAXI_OUT:float,WHEELS_OFF:datetime,
WHEELS_ON:datetime,TAXI_IN:float,CRS_ARR_TIME:datetime,ARR_TIME:datetime,
ARR_DELAY:float,CANCELLED:chararray,CANCELLATION_CODE:chararray,
DIVERTED:chararray,DISTANCE:float,DEP_AIRPORT_LAT:float,
DEP_AIRPORT_LON:float,DEP_AIRPORT_TZOFFSET:float,ARR_AIRPORT_LAT:float,
ARR_AIRPORT_LON:float,ARR_AIRPORT_TZOFFSET:float,EVENT:chararray,
NOTIFY_TIME:datetime);
```

The schema itself is the same as the schema for the CSV files that we supplied to Big-Query. The difference is that Pig calls strings chararray, integers simply as int, and the timestamp in BigQuery is a datetime in Pig.

After we have the FLIGHTS, we can use Spark to bin each flight based on the thresholds we found:[24]

```
FLIGHTS2 = FOREACH FLIGHTS GENERATE
    (DISTANCE < 251? 0:
    (DISTANCE < 368? 1:
    (DISTANCE < 448? 2:
    (DISTANCE < 575? 3:
    (DISTANCE < 669? 4:
    (DISTANCE < 838? 5:
    (DISTANCE < 1012? 6:
    (DISTANCE < 1218? 7:
    (DISTANCE < 1849? 8:
        9)))))))) AS distbin:int,
    (DEP_DELAY < -6? 0:
    (DEP_DELAY < -5? 1:
    (DEP_DELAY < -4? 2:
    (DEP_DELAY < -3? 3:
    (DEP_DELAY < 0? 4:
    (DEP_DELAY < 3? 5:
    (DEP_DELAY < 5? 6:
    (DEP_DELAY < 11? 7:
    (DEP_DELAY < 39? 8:
        9)))))))) AS depdelaybin:int,
    (ARR_DELAY < 15? 1:0) AS ontime:int;
```

---

24 Yes, if we had been using Python, we could have used the numpy library to find the bin more elegantly.

Having binned each flight and found the category (on time or not) of the flight, we can group the data based on the bins and compute the on-time fraction within each bin:

```
grouped = GROUP FLIGHTS2 BY (distbin, depdelaybin);
result = FOREACH grouped GENERATE
    FLATTEN(group) AS (dist, delay),
      ((double)SUM(FLIGHTS2.ontime))/COUNT(FLIGHTS2.ontime)
                    AS ontime:double;
```

At this point, we now have a three-column table: the distance bin, the delay bin, and the fraction of flights that are on time in that bin. Let's write this out to Cloud Storage with a STORE so that we can run this script noninteractively:

```
STORE result into 'gs://cloud-training-demos-ml/flights/pigoutput/'
      using PigStorage(',','-schema');
```

Running a Pig Job on Cloud Dataproc

After increasing the size of the cluster, I can submit this Pig job to Cloud Dataproc using the gcloud command from CloudShell:

```
gcloud dataproc jobs submit pig \
      --cluster ch6cluster --file bayes.pig
```

The name of my Dataproc cluster is ch6cluster, and the name of my Pig script is *bayes.pig*.

I get a bunch of seemingly correct output, and when the job finishes, I can look at the output directory on Google Cloud Storage:

```
gsutil ls gs://cloud-training-demos-ml/flights/pigoutput/
```

The actual output file is *part-r-00000*, which we can print out using the following:

```
gsutil cat gs://cloud-training-demos-ml/flights/pigoutput/part-*
```

The result for one of the distance bins

```
5,0,0.9726378794356563
5,1,0.9572953736654805
5,2,0.9693486590038314
5,3,0.9595657057281917
5,4,0.9486424180327869
5,5,0.9228643216080402
5,6,0.9067321178120618
5,7,0.8531653960888299
5,8,0.47339027595269384
5,9,0.0053655264922870555
```

seems quite reasonable. The on-time arrival percentage is more than 70% for delay bins 0 to 7, but bins 8 and 9 require the flight to be canceled.

There are three issues with this script that I need to fix:

- It is being run on all the data. It should be run only on training days.
- The output is quite verbose because I am printing out all the bins and probabilities. It is probably enough if we know the bins for which the recommendation is that you need to cancel your meeting.
- I need to run it on all the data, not just the first flights CSV file.

Let's do these things.

Limiting to Training Days

Because the training days are stored as a CSV file on Cloud Storage, I can read it from our Pig script (the only difference in the read here is that we are skipping the input header) and filter by the Boolean variable to get a relation that corresponds only to training days:

```
alldays = LOAD 'gs://cloud-training-demos-ml/flights/trainday.csv'
    using org.apache.pig.piggybank.storage.CSVExcelStorage(
        ',', 'NO_MULTILINE', 'NOCHANGE', 'SKIP_INPUT_HEADER')
    AS (FL_DATE:chararray, is_train_day:boolean);
traindays = FILTER alldays BY is_train_day == True;
```

Then, after renaming the full dataset ALLFLIGHTS, I can do a join to get just the flights on training days:

```
FLIGHTS = JOIN ALLFLIGHTS BY FL_DATE, traindays BY FL_DATE;
```

The rest of the Pig script[25] remains the same because it operates on FLIGHTS.

Running it, though, I realize that Pig will not overwrite its output directory, so I remove the output directory on Cloud Storage:

```
gsutil -m rm -r gs://cloud-training-demos-ml/flights/pigoutput
gcloud dataproc jobs submit pig \
        --cluster ch6cluster --file bayes2.pig
```

The resulting output file looks quite similar to what we got when we ran on all the days, not just the training ones. The first issue—of limiting the training to just the training days—has been fixed. Let's fix the second issue.

The Decision Criteria

Instead of writing out all the results, let's filter the result to keep only the distance and departure delay identifiers for the bins for which we are going to suggest canceling

---

25 See *06_dataproc/bayes2.pig* in the GitHub repository for this book.

the meeting. Doing this will make it easier for a downstream programmer to program this into an automatic alerting functionality.

To do this, let's add a few extra lines to the original Pig script before STORE, renaming the original result at probs and filtering it based on number of flights and likelihood of arriving less than 15 minutes late:[26]

```
grouped = GROUP FLIGHTS2 BY (distbin, depdelaybin);

probs = FOREACH grouped GENERATE
          FLATTEN(group) AS (dist, delay),
          ((double)SUM(FLIGHTS2.ontime))/COUNT(FLIGHTS2.ontime) AS ontime:double,
          COUNT(FLIGHTS2.ontime) AS numflights;

result = FILTER probs BY (numflights > 10) AND (ontime < 0.7);
```

The result, as before, is sent to Cloud Storage and looks like this:

```
0,8,0.3416842105263158,4750
0,9,7.351139426611125E-4,4081
1,8,0.3881127160786171,4223
1,9,3.0003000300030005E-4,3333
2,8,0.4296875,3328
2,9,8.087343307723412E-4,2473
3,8,0.4080819578827547,3514
3,9,0.001340033500837521,2985
4,8,0.43937644341801385,3464
4,9,0.002002402883460152,2497
5,8,0.47252208047105004,4076
5,9,0.004490057729313663,3118
6,8,0.48624950179354326,5018
6,9,0.00720192051213657,3749
7,8,0.48627167630057805,4152
7,9,0.010150722854506305,3251
8,8,0.533605720122574,4895
8,9,0.021889055472263868,3335
9,8,0.6035689293212037,2858
9,9,0.03819444444444445,2016
```

In other words, it is always delay bins 8 and 9 that require cancellation. It appears that we made a mistake in choosing the quantization thresholds. Our choice of quantization threshold was predicated on the overall distribution of departure delays, but our decision boundary is clustered in the range 10 to 20 minutes. Therefore, although we were correct in using histogram equalization for the distance, we should probably just try out every departure delay threshold in the range of interest. Increasing the resolution of the departure delay quantization means that we will have to keep an eagle eye on the number of flights to ensure that our results will be statistically valid.

---

26 See *06_dataproc/bayes3.pig* in the GitHub repository for this book.

Let's make the change to be finer-grained in departure delay around the decision boundary:[27]

```
(DEP_DELAY < 11? 0:
 (DEP_DELAY < 12? 1:
 (DEP_DELAY < 13? 2:
 (DEP_DELAY < 14? 3:
 (DEP_DELAY < 15? 4:
 (DEP_DELAY < 16? 5:
 (DEP_DELAY < 17? 6:
 (DEP_DELAY < 18? 7:
 (DEP_DELAY < 19? 8:
       9))))))))) AS depdelaybin:int,
```

Taking two of the distance bins as an example, we notice that the delay bins corresponding to canceled flights vary:

```
3,2,0.6893203883495146,206
3,3,0.6847290640394089,203
3,5,0.6294416243654822,197
3,6,0.5863874345549738,191
3,7,0.5521472392638037,163
3,8,0.6012658227848101,158
3,9,0.0858412441930923,4951
4,4,0.6785714285714286,196
4,5,0.68125,160
4,6,0.6162162162162163,185
4,7,0.5605095541401274,157
4,8,0.5571428571428572,140
4,9,0.11853832442067737,4488
```

As expected, the probability of arriving on time drops as the departure delay increases for any given distance. Although this drop is not quite monotonic, we expect that it will become increasingly monotonic as the number of flights increases (recall that we are processing only 1/30 of the full dataset). However, let's also compensate for the finer resolution in the delay bins by making the distance bins more coarse grained. Fortunately, we don't need to recompute the quantization thresholds—we already know the 20th, 40th, 60th, and so on percentiles because they are a subset of the 10th, 20th, 30th, and so forth percentiles.

If the departure delay is well behaved, we need only to know the threshold at which we must cancel the meeting depending on the distance to be traveled. For example, we might end up with a matrix like that shown in Table 6-2.

---

27 See *06_dataproc/bayes4.pig* in the GitHub repository for this book.

Table 6-2. Decision table of departure delay thresholds by distance

Distance bin	Departure delay (minutes)
<300 miles	13
300–500 miles	14
500–800 miles	15
800–1200 miles	14
>1200 miles	17

Of course, we don't want to hand-examine the resulting output and figure out the departure delay threshold. So, let's ask Pig to compute that departure delay threshold for us:

```
cancel = FILTER probs BY (numflights > 10) AND (ontime < 0.7);
bydist = GROUP cancel BY dist;
result = FOREACH bydist GENERATE group AS dist,
                        MIN(cancel.delay) AS depdelay;
```

We are finding the delay beyond which we need to cancel flights for each distance and saving just that threshold. Because it is the threshold that we care about, let's also change the bin number to reflect the actual threshold. With these changes, the FLIGHTS2 relation becomes as follows:

```
FLIGHTS2 = FOREACH FLIGHTS GENERATE
    (DISTANCE < 368? 368:
    (DISTANCE < 575? 575:
    (DISTANCE < 838? 838:
    (DISTANCE < 1218? 1218:
        9999)))) AS distbin:int,
    (DEP_DELAY < 11? 11:
    (DEP_DELAY < 12? 12:
    (DEP_DELAY < 13? 13:
    (DEP_DELAY < 14? 14:
    (DEP_DELAY < 15? 15:
    (DEP_DELAY < 16? 16:
    (DEP_DELAY < 17? 17:
    (DEP_DELAY < 18? 18:
    (DEP_DELAY < 19? 19:
        9999))))))))) AS depdelaybin:int,
    (ARR_DELAY < 15? 1:0) AS ontime:int;
```

Let's now run this on all the training days by changing the input to all-flights-*.[28] It takes a few minutes for me to get the following output:

```
368,15
575,17
838,18
```

---

28 See *06_dataproc/bayes_final.pig* in the GitHub repository for this book.

```
1218,18
9999,19
```

As the distance increases, the departure delay threshold also increases and a table like this is quite easy to base a production model on. The production service could simply read the table from the Pig output bucket on Cloud Storage and carry out the appropriate thresholding.

For example, what is the appropriate decision for a flight with a distance of 1,000 miles that departs 15 minutes late? The flight falls into the 1218 bin, which holds flights with distances between 838 and 1,218 miles. For such flights, we need to cancel the meeting only if the flight departs 18 or more minutes late. The 15-minute departure delay is something that can be made up en route.

Evaluating the Bayesian Model

How well does this new two-variable model perform? We can modify the evaluation query from Chapter 5 to add in a distance criterion and supply the appropriate threshold for that distance:

```
#standardsql
SELECT
  SUM(IF(DEP_DELAY = 15
      AND arr_delay < 15,
      1,
      0)) AS wrong_cancel,
  SUM(IF(DEP_DELAY = 15
      AND arr_delay >= 15,
      1,
      0)) AS correct_cancel
FROM (
  SELECT
    DEP_DELAY,
    ARR_DELAY
  FROM
    flights.tzcorr f
  JOIN
    flights.trainday t
  ON
    f.FL_DATE = t.FL_DATE
  WHERE
    t.is_train_day = 'False'
    AND f.DISTANCE < 368)
```

In this query, 15 is the newly determined threshold for distances under 368 miles and the WHERE clause is now limited to flights over distances of less than 368 miles. Figure 6-12 shows the result.

Row	wrong_cancel	correct_cancel
1	5049	2593

Figure 6-12. Result when WHERE clause is limited to distances of less than 368 miles

This indicates that we cancel meetings when it is correct to do so 2,593 / (2,593 + 5,049) or 34% of the time—remember that our goal was 30%. Similarly, we can do the other four distance categories. Both with this model, and with a model that took into account only the departure delay (as in Chapter 5), we are able to get reliable predictions—canceling meetings when the flight has more than a 30% chance of being delayed.

So, why go with the more complex model? The more complex model is worthwhile if we end up canceling fewer meetings or if we can be more fine-grained in our decisions (i.e., change which meetings we cancel). What we care about, then, is the sum of correct_cancel and wrong_cancel over all flights. In the case of using only departure delay, this number was about 962,000. How about now? Let's look at the total number of flights in the test set that would cause us to cancel our meetings:

```
SELECT
  SUM(IF(DEP_DELAY >= 15 AND DISTANCE < 368, 1, 0)) +
  SUM(IF(DEP_DELAY >= 17 AND DISTANCE >= 368 AND DISTANCE < 575, 1, 0)) +
  SUM(IF(DEP_DELAY >= 18 AND DISTANCE >= 575 AND DISTANCE < 838, 1, 0)) +
  SUM(IF(DEP_DELAY >= 18 AND DISTANCE >= 838 AND DISTANCE < 1218, 1, 0)) +
  SUM(IF(DEP_DELAY >= 19 AND DISTANCE >= 1218, 1, 0))
  AS cancel
FROM (
  SELECT
    DEP_DELAY,
    ARR_DELAY,
    DISTANCE
  FROM
    flights.tzcorr f
  JOIN
    flights.trainday t
  ON
    f.FL_DATE = t.FL_DATE
  WHERE
    t.is_train_day = 'False')
```

This turns out to be 920,355. This is about 5% fewer canceled meetings as when we use a threshold of 16 minutes across the board. How many of these cancellations are correct? We can find out by adding ARR_DELAY >= 15 to the WHERE clause, and we get 760,117, indicating that our decision to cancel a meeting is correct 83% of the time.

It appears, then, that our simpler univariate model got us pretty much the same results as this more complex model using two variables. However, the decision surfaces are different—in the single-variable threshold, we cancel meetings whenever the flight is delayed by 16 minutes or more. However, when we take into account distance, we cancel more meetings corresponding to shorter flights (threshold is now 15 minutes) and cancel fewer meetings corresponding to longer flights (threshold is now 18 or 19 minutes). One reason to use this two-variable Bayes model over the one-variable threshold determined empirically is to make such finer-grained decisions. This might or might not be important.

Why did we get only a 5% improvement? Perhaps the round-off in the delay variables (they are rounded off to the nearest minute) has hurt our ability to locate more precise thresholds. Also, maybe the extra variable would have helped if I'd used a more sophisticated model—direct evaluation of conditional probability on relatively coarse-grained quantization bins is a very simple method. In Chapter 7, we explore a more complex approach.

Summary

In this chapter, we explored how to create a two-variable Bayesian model to provide insight as to whether to cancel a meeting based on the likely arrival delay of a flight. We quantized the two variables (distance and departure delay), created a conditional probability lookup table, and examined the on-time arrival percentage in each bin. We carried out the quantization using histogram equalization in Spark, and carried out the on-time arrival percentage computation in Pig.

Upon discovering that equalizing the full distribution of departure delays resulted in a very coarse sampling of the decision surface, we chose to go with the highest possible resolution in the crucial range of departure delay. However, to ensure that we would have statistically valid groupings, we also made our quantization thresholds coarser in distance. On doing this, we discovered that the probability of the arrival delay being less than 15 minutes varied rather smoothly. Because of this, our conditional probability lookup reduced to a table of thresholds that could be applied rather simply using IF-THEN rules.

On evaluating the two-variable model, we found that we would be canceling about 5% fewer meetings than with the single-variable model while retaining the same overall accuracy. We hypothesize that the improvement isn't higher because the departure delay variable has already been rounded off to the nearest minute, limiting the scope of any improvement we can make.

In terms of tooling, we created a three-node Cloud Dataproc cluster for development and resized it on the fly to 20 workers when our code was ready to be run on the full dataset. Although there is no getting away from cluster management when using

Hadoop, Cloud Dataproc goes a long way toward making this a low-touch endeavor. The reason that we can create, resize, and delete Cloud Dataproc clusters is that our data is held not in HDFS, but on Google Cloud Storage. We carried out development both on the Pig interpreter and in Cloud Datalab, which gives us an interactive notebook experience. We also found that we were able to integrate BigQuery, Spark SQL, and Apache Pig into our workflow on the Hadoop cluster.

## CHAPTER 7

Machine Learning: Logistic Regression on Spark

In Chapter 6, we created a model based on two variables—distance and departure delay—to predict the probability that a flight will be more than 15 minutes late. We found that we could get a finer-grained decision if we used a second variable (distance) instead of using just one variable (departure delay).

Why not use all the variables in the dataset? Or at least many more of them? In particular, I'd like to use the `TAXI_OUT` variable—if it is too high, the flight was stuck on the runway waiting for the airport tower to allow the plane to take off, and so the flight is likely to be delayed. Our approach in Chapter 6 was quite limiting in terms of being able to incorporate additional variables. As we add variables, we would need to continue slicing the dataset into smaller and smaller bins. We would then find that many of our bins would contain very few samples, and the resulting decision surfaces would not be well behaved. Remember that after we binned the data by distance, we found that the departure delay decision boundary was quite well behaved—departure delays above a certain threshold were associated with the flight not arriving on time. Our simplification of the Bayesian classification surface to a simple threshold that varied by bin would not have been possible if the decision boundary had been noisier.[1] The more variables we use, the more bins we will have, and this good behavior will begin to break down. This sort of breakdown in good behavior as the number of variables (or *dimensions*) increases is called the *curse of dimensionality*; it affects many statistical and machine learning techniques, not just the quantization-based Bayesian approach of Chapter 6.

---

[1] We also put our thumb on the scale a little. Recall that we quantized the distance variable quite coarsely. Had we quantized distance into many more bins, there would have been fewer flights in each bin.

Logistic Regression

One way to address the breakdown in behavior as the number of variables increases is to change the approach from that of directly evaluating the probability based on the input dataset. Instead, we could attempt to fit a smooth function on the variables in the dataset (a multidimensional space) to the probability of a flight arriving late (a single-dimensional space) and use the value of that function as the estimate of the probability. In other words, we could try to find a function f, such that:

$$P(Y) \approx f\left(x_0, x_1, ..., x_{n-1}\right)$$

In our case, s_0 could be departure delay, x_1 the taxi out time, x_2 the distance, and so on. Each row will have different values for the x's and represent different flights. The idea is that we have a function that will take these x's and somehow transform them to provide a good estimate of the probability that the flight corresponding to that row's input variables is on time.

One of the simplest transformations of a multidimensional space to a single-dimensional one is to compute a weighted sum of the input variables, as demonstrated here:

$$L = w_0 x_0 + w_1 x_1 + ... + w_{n-1} x_{n-1} + b$$

The w's (called the weights) and the constant b (called the intercept) are constants, but we don't initially know what they are. We need to find "good" values of the w's and b such that the weighted sum for any row closely approximates either 1 (when the flight is on time) or 0 (when the flight is late). Because this process of finding good values is averaged over a large dataset, the value L is the prediction that flights with a specific departure delay, taxi-out time, and so on will arrive on time. If that number is 0.8, we would like it to be that 80% of such flights would arrive on time, and 20% would be late. In other words, rather than L be simply 1 or 0, we'd like it to be the likelihood that the flight will arrive on time. We would like it to be a probability.

There is a problem, though. The weighted sum above cannot function as a probability. This is because the linear combination (L) can take any value, whereas a probability will need to lie between 0 and 1. One common solution for this problem is to transform the linear combination using the *logistic* function:

$$P(Y) = \frac{1}{1 + e^{-L}}$$

Fitting a logistic function of a linear combination of variables to binary outcomes (i.e., finding "good" values for the w's and b such that the estimated $P(Y)$ are close to the actual recorded outcome of the flight being on time) is called *logistic regression*.

In machine learning, the original linear combination, L, which lies between $-\infty$ and ∞, is called the *logit*. You can see that if the logit adds up to ∞, e^{-L} will be 0 and so, $P(Y)$ will be 1. If the original linear combination adds up to $-\infty$, then e^{-L} will be ∞ and so, $P(Y)$ will be 0. Therefore, Y could be an event such as the flight arriving on time and $P(Y)$, the probability of that event happening. Because of the transformation, $P(Y)$ will lie between 0 and 1 as required for anything to be a probability.

If $P(Y)$ is the probability, the logit, L, is given by the following:

$$\log_e \frac{P(Y)}{1 - P(Y)}$$

The *odds* is the ratio of the probability of the event happening, $P(Y)$, to the event not happening, $1 - P(Y)$. Therefore, the logit can also be interpreted as the log-odds where the base of the logarithm is e.

Figure 7-1 depicts the relationship between the logit, the probability, and the odds.

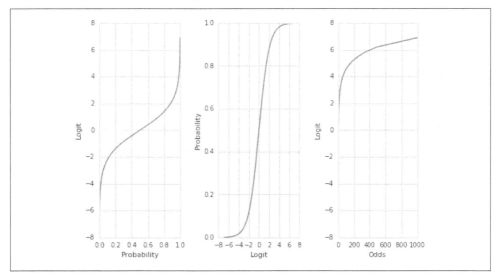

Figure 7-1. The relationships between the probability, the logit, and the odds

Spend some time looking at the graphs in Figure 7-1 and gaining an intuitive understanding for what the relationships mean. For example, see if you can answer this set of questions (feel free to sketch out the curves as you do your reasoning[2]):

1. At equal odds (i.e., the flight is as likely to be late as not), what is the logit? How about if the odds are predominantly in favor of flight being on time?

2. At what probability does the logit function change most rapidly?

3. Where is the gradient (rate of change) of the logit function slowest?

4. Which logit change, from 2 to 3 or from 2 to 1, will result in a greater change in probability?

5. How does the value of the intercept, b, affect the answer to question 4?

6. Suppose that the intercept is 0. If all the input variables double, what happens to the logit?

7. If the logit value doubles, what happens to the probability? How does this depend on the original value of the logit?

8. What logits value does it take to provide a probability of 0.95? How about 0.995?

9. How extreme do the input variables need to be to attain probabilities that are close to 0 or 1?

Many practical considerations in classification problems in machine learning derive from this set of relationships. So, as simple as these curves are, it is important that you understand their implications.

The name *logistic regression* is a little confusing—regression is normally a way of fitting a real-valued number, whereas classification is a way of fitting to a categorical outcome. Here, we fit the observed variables (the x's) to a logit (which is real-valued) —this is the regression that is being referred to in the name. However, we then use

---

2 Answers (but don't take my word for it):
   1. At equal odds, the probability is 0.5 and the logit is 0.
   2. The logit function changes fastest at probabilities near 0 and 1.
   3. The gradient of the logit function is slowest near a probability of 0.5.
   4. The change from 2 to 1 will result in a greater change in probability. Near probabilities of 0 and 1, larger logit changes are required to have the same impact on probability. As you get nearer to a probability of 0.5, smaller logit changes suffice.
   5. The intercept directly impacts the value of the logit, so it moves the first curve upward or downward.
   6. The logit doubles.
   7. If the original probability is near 0 or 1, doubling of the logit has negligible impact (look at what happens if the logit changes from 4 to 8, for example). If the original probability is between about 0.3 and 0.7, the relationship is quite linear: doubling of the logit ends up causing a proportional increase in probability.
   8. About 3, and about 5.
   9. Doubling of the logit value at 0.95 is required to reach 0.995. Lots of "energy" in the input variables is required to move the probability needle at the extremes.

the logistic function that has no free parameters (no weights to tune) to transform the real-valued number to a probability. Overall, therefore, logistic regression functions as a classification method.

Spark ML Library

Given a multivariable dataset, Spark has the ability to carry out logistic regression and give us the optimal weight for each variable. Spark's logistic regression module will give us the w's and b if we show it a bunch of x's and the corresponding Ys. The logistic regression module is part of Apache Spark's machine learning library, MLlib, which you can program against in Java, Scala, Python, or R. Spark MLlib (colloquially known as Spark ML) includes implementations of many canonical machine learning algorithms: decision trees, random forests, alternating least squares, k-means clustering, association rules, support vector machines, and so on. Spark can execute on a Hadoop cluster; thus, it can scale to large datasets.

The problem we are solving—to find a set of weights that optimizes model predictions based on known outcomes, is an instance of a *supervised* learning problem—is the kind of machine learning problem for which the actual answers, called *labels*, are known for some dataset. As illustrated in Figure 7-2, first you ask the machine (here, Spark) to learn (the w's) from data (the x's) that have labels (the Y's). This is called *training*.

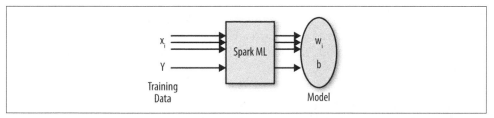

Figure 7-2. In supervised learning, the machine (here, Spark) learns a set of parameters (the w's and b's) from training data that consists of inputs (x's) and their corresponding labels (Y's)

The learned set of weights, along with the original equation (the logistic function of a linear combination of x's), is called a *model*. After you have learned a model from the training data, you can save it to a file. Then, whenever you want to make a prediction for a new flight, you can re-create the model from that file, pass in the x's in the same order, and compute the logistic function and obtain the estimate $P(Y)$. This process, called *prediction* or *serving*, might be carried out in real time in response to a request that includes the input variables, whereas the training of the model might happen less frequently, as shown in Figure 7-3.

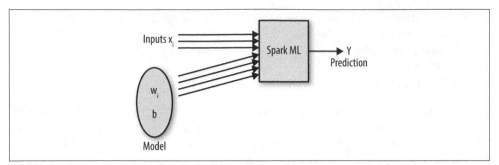

Figure 7-3. You can use the learned set of weights to predict the value of Y for new data (x's)

Of course, the prediction can be carried outside of Spark—all that we'd need to do is compute the weighted sum of the inputs and the intercept, and then compute the logistic function of the weighted sum. In general, though, you should seek to use the same libraries for prediction as you use for training. This helps to mitigate training–serving skew, the situation that we talked about in Chapter 1 in which the input variables in prediction are subtly different from those used in training and which leads to poorly performing models.

Getting Started with Spark Machine Learning

To run Spark conveniently, I will continue to use the Cloud Dataproc cluster that I launched in the previous chapter. In particular, I will use the same creation and resizing scripts, and use Cloud Datalab on the cluster to develop in a notebook environment.

 For complete setup instructions, see Chapter 6.

Although I prefer the notebook environment, another option is to use Spark's interactive shell after using Secure Shell to connect to the master node. We could try out single lines of Spark code in Python (PySpark), and when we are happy with what it does, copy and paste those lines into a script that we can run whenever we want to repeat the data analysis. Even when using the notebook, we should keep in mind that our end goal is to run the machine jobs routinely. To achieve that goal, it is important to keep a notebook with the final machine learning workflow and export this notebook into a standalone program. You can submit the standalone program to the cluster whenever the machine learning needs to be repeated on new datasets.

One complication is that both the interactive shell and the Cloud Datalab notebook come with the `SparkContext` variable `sc` and the `SparkSession` variable `spark`. You will need to create these explicitly in the standalone, submittable program.[3] So, this code will be extra in the submittable program, but won't be needed in the notebook or in an interactive session:

```
from pyspark.sql import SparkSession
from pyspark import SparkContext
sc = SparkContext('local', 'logistic')
spark = SparkSession \
    .builder \
    .appName("Logistic regression w/ Spark ML") \
    .getOrCreate()
```

After we do this, any line that works in the Cloud Datalab notebook *logistic.ipynb* will also work when launched from the script *logistic.py*. The application name (`logistic`) will show up in logs when the script is run.

Let's begin by adding `import` lines for the Python classes that we'll need:

```
from pyspark.mllib.classification import LogisticRegressionWithLBFGS
from pyspark.mllib.regression import LabeledPoint
```

Spark Logistic Regression

Note that there are two logistic regression implementations in Spark: one in *pyspark.ml* and another in *pyspark.mllib*. The ML-library one is more current, and that's the one we'll use. L-BFGS stands for the initials of the independent inventors (Broyden, Fletcher, Goldfarb, and Shanno)[4] of a popular, iterative, fast-converging optimization algorithm. The L-BFGS algorithm is used by Spark to find the weights that minimize the *logistic loss* function

$$\Sigma \ \log \ \left(1 + e^{-yL}\right)$$

over the training dataset, where y, the training label, is either -1 or 1 and L is the logit computed from the input variables, the weights, and the intercept.

Knowing the details of the logistic formulation and loss function used by Spark is important. This is because different machine learning libraries use equivalent (but not identical) versions of these formulae. For example, another common approach taken by machine learning frameworks is to minimize the *cross-entropy*:

---

3 See *logistic.py* and *logistic.ipynb* in *flights_data_analysis/07_sparkml* of the GitHub repository for this book.

4 The *L* stands for low-memory—this is a limited-memory variant of the BFGS algorithm.

$$\Sigma - y \log P(Y) - (1 - y) \log (1 - P(Y)))$$

Here, y is the training label, and $P(Y)$ is the probabilistic output of the model. In that case, the training label will need to be 0 or 1. I won't go through the math, but even though the two loss functions look very different, minimizing the logistic loss and minimizing the cross-entropy loss turn out to be equivalent.

Rather confusingly, the Spark documentation notes that[5] "a binary label y is denoted as either +1 (positive) or –1 (negative), which is convenient for the formulation. However, the negative label is represented by 0 in *spark.mllib* instead of –1, to be consistent with multiclass labeling." In other words, Spark ML uses the logistic loss function, but requires that the labels we provide be 0 or 1. There really is no substitute for reading the documentation!

To summarize, the preprocessing that you might need to do to your input data depends on the formulation of the loss function employed by the machine leaning framework you are using. Suppose that we decide to do this:

y = 0 if arrival delay ≥ 15 minutes and

y = 1 if arrival delay < 15 minutes

Because we have mapped on-time flights to 1, the machine learning algorithm (after training) will predict the probability that the flight is on time.

Creating a Training Dataset

As we did in Chapter 6, let's launch a minimal Cloud Dataproc cluster with initialization actions for Datalab.[6] We can then start an SSH tunnel, a Chrome session via the network proxy, and browse to port 8080 on the master node of the cluster. In Cloud Datalab, we then can use ungit (*https://github.com/FredrikNoren/ungit*) to clone the GitHub repository and start off a new Cloud Datalab notebook.[7]

First, let's read in the list of training days. To do that, we need to read *trainday.csv* from Cloud Storage, remembering that the comma-separated value (CSV) file has a header that will help with inferring its schema:

```
traindays = spark.read \
    .option("header", "true") \
    .csv('gs://{}/flights/trainday.csv'.format(BUCKET))
```

For convenience, I'll make this a Spark SQL view, as well:

```
traindays.createOrReplaceTempView('traindays')
```

---

5 See the section on logistic loss in *https://spark.apache.org/docs/latest/mllib-linear-methods.html*.

6 See *start_cluster.sh*, *start_tunnel.sh*, and *start_chrome.sh* in *06_dataproc*. These were explained in Chapter 6.

7 The notebook is *logistic_regression.ipynb* in *07_sparkml* and these steps are described in detail in Chapter 6.

We can print the first few lines of this file:

```
spark.sql("SELECT * from traindays LIMIT 5").show()
```

This obtains the following eminently reasonable result:

```
+----------+-----------+
|   FL_DATE|is_train_day|
+----------+-----------+
|2015-01-01|       True|
|2015-01-02|      False|
|2015-01-03|      False|
|2015-01-04|       True|
|2015-01-05|       True|
+----------+-----------+
```

Now that we have the training days, we can read in the `flights` dataset. So that our queries are understandable, it is preferable to set up an appropriate schema. To do that, we define the header and read almost all the columns as strings except the four numeric ones that we care about:

```
from pyspark.sql.types \
    import StringType, FloatType, StructType, StructField
header = \
'FL_DATE,UNIQUE_CARRIER,AIRLINE_ID,CARRIER,FL_NUM,ORIGIN_AIRPORT_ID,
ORIGIN_AIRPORT_SEQ_ID,ORIGIN_CITY_MARKET_ID,ORIGIN,DEST_AIRPORT_ID,
DEST_AIRPORT_SEQ_ID,DEST_CITY_MARKET_ID,DEST,CRS_DEP_TIME,DEP_TIME,
DEP_DELAY,TAXI_OUT,WHEELS_OFF,WHEELS_ON,TAXI_IN,
CRS_ARR_TIME,ARR_TIME,ARR_DELAY,CANCELLED,
CANCELLATION_CODE,DIVERTED,DISTANCE,DEP_AIRPORT_LAT,
DEP_AIRPORT_LON,DEP_AIRPORT_TZOFFSET,ARR_AIRPORT_LAT,ARR_AIRPORT_LON,
ARR_AIRPORT_TZOFFSET,EVENT,NOTIFY_TIME'

def get_structfield(colname):
  if colname in ['ARR_DELAY', 'DEP_DELAY', 'DISTANCE', 'TAXI_OUT']:
    return StructField(colname, FloatType(), True)
  else:
    return StructField(colname, StringType(), True)

schema = StructType([get_structfield(colname) for colname in header.split(',')])
```

While we're developing the code (on my minimal Hadoop cluster that is running Cloud Datalab), it would be easier to read only a small part of the dataset. Hence, we define the `inputs` variable to be just one of the shards:

```
inputs = 'gs://{}/flights/tzcorr/all_flights-00000-*'.format(BUCKET)
```

After we have developed all of the code, we can change the inputs:

```
#inputs = 'gs://{}/flights/tzcorr/all_flights-*'.format(BUCKET)  # FULL
```

For now, though, let's leave the latter line commented out.

When we have a schema, creating a `flights` view for Spark SQL is straightforward:

```
flights = spark.read\
            .schema(schema)\
            .csv(inputs)
flights.createOrReplaceTempView('flights')
```

Training will need to be carried out on the flights that were on days for which is_train_day is True:

```
trainquery = """
SELECT
  f.*
FROM flights f
JOIN traindays t
ON f.FL_DATE == t.FL_DATE
WHERE
  t.is_train_day == 'True'
"""
traindata = spark.sql(trainquery)
```

Dealing with Corner Cases

Let's verify that traindata does contain the data we need. We can look at the first few (here, the first two) rows of the data frame using the following:

```
traindata.head(2)
```

The result seems quite reasonable:

```
[Row(FL_DATE=u'2015-02-02', UNIQUE_CARRIER=u'EV', AIRLINE_ID=u'20366',
CARRIER=u'EV', FL_NUM=u'4410', ORIGIN_AIRPORT_ID=u'12266',
ORIGIN_AIRPORT_SEQ_ID=u'1226603', …
```

Date fields are dates, and airport codes are reasonable, as are the latitudes and longitudes. But eyeballing is no substitute for truly verifying that all of the values exist. Knowing that the four variables we are interested in are all floats, we can ask Spark to compute simple statistics over the full dataset:

```
traindata.describe().show()
```

The describe() method computes column-by-column statistics, and the show() method causes those statistics to be printed. We now get the following:[8]

---

8 Your results might be different because the actual flight records held in your first shard (recall that the input is all_flights-00000-*) are possibly different.

```
+-------+---------+---------+---------+---------+
|summary| DEP_DELAY| TAXI_OUT| ARR_DELAY| DISTANCE|
+-------+---------+---------+---------+---------+
|  count|   259692|   259434|   258706|   275062|
|   mean|   13.178|  16.9658|   9.7319| 802.3747|
| stddev|  41.8886|  10.9363|  45.0384|  592.254|
|    min|    -61.0|      1.0|    -77.0|     31.0|
|    max|   1587.0|    225.0|   1627.0|   4983.0|
+-------+---------+---------+---------+---------+
```

Notice anything odd?

Notice the `count` statistic. There are 275,062 `DISTANCE` values, but only 259,692 `DEP_DELAY` values, and even fewer `TAXI_OUT` values. What is going on? This is the sort of thing that you will need to chase down to find the root cause. In this case, the reason has to do with flights that are scheduled, but never leave the gate, and flights that depart the gate but never take off. Similarly, there are flights that take off (and have a `TAXI_OUT` value) but are diverted and do not have an `ARR_DELAY`. In the data, these are denoted by `NULL`, and Spark's `describe()` method doesn't count nulls.

We don't want to use canceled and diverted flights for training either. One way to tighten up the selection of our training dataset would be to simply remove `NULL`s, as shown here:

```
trainquery = """
SELECT
  DEP_DELAY, TAXI_OUT, ARR_DELAY, DISTANCE
FROM flights f
JOIN traindays t
ON f.FL_DATE == t.FL_DATE
WHERE
  t.is_train_day == 'True' AND
  f.dep_delay IS NOT NULL AND
  f.arr_delay IS NOT NULL
"""
traindata = spark.sql(trainquery)
traindata.describe().show()
```

Running this gets us a consistent value of the count across all the columns:

```
|summary| DEP_DELAY|  TAXI_OUT| ARR_DELAY| DISTANCE|
|  count|   258706|    258706|   258706|   258706|
```

However, I strongly encourage you not to do this. Removing `NULL`s is merely fixing the symptom of the problem. What we really want to do is to address the root cause. In this case, you'd do that by removing flights that have been canceled or diverted, and fortunately, we do have this information in the data. So, we can change the query to be the following:

```
trainquery = """
SELECT
```

```
    DEP_DELAY, TAXI_OUT, ARR_DELAY, DISTANCE
FROM flights f
JOIN traindays t
ON f.FL_DATE == t.FL_DATE
WHERE
    t.is_train_day == 'True' AND
    f.CANCELLED == '0.00' AND
    f.DIVERTED == '0.00'
"""
traindata = spark.sql(trainquery)
traindata.describe().show()
```

This, too, yields the same counts as when we threw away the NULLs, thereby demonstrating that our diagnosis of the problem was correct.

Discovering corner cases and problems with an input dataset at the time we begin training a machine learning model is quite common. In this case, I knew this problem was coming, and was careful to select the CANCELLED and DIVERTED columns to be part of my input dataset (in Chapter 2). In real life, you will need to spend quite a bit of time troubleshooting this, potentially adding new logging operations to your ingest code to uncover the reason that underlies a simple problem. What you should not do is to simply throw away bad values.

Creating Training Examples

Now that we have the training data, we can look at the documentation for Logisti cRegressionModel (*http://bit.ly/2AYmn3p*) to determine the format of its input. The documentation indicates that each row of the training data needs to be transformed to a LabeledPoint (*http://bit.ly/2AzVm5A*) whose documentation in turn indicates that its constructor requires a label and an array of features, all of which need to be floating-point numbers.

Let's create a method that will convert each data point of our DataFrame into a *training example* (an example is a combination of the input features and the true answer):

```
def to_example(raw_data_point):
  return LabeledPoint(\
            float(raw_data_point['ARR_DELAY'] < 15), # on-time? \
            [ \
                raw_data_point['DEP_DELAY'], \
                raw_data_point['TAXI_OUT'], \
                raw_data_point['DISTANCE'], \
            ])
```

Note that we have created a label and an array of features. Here, the features consist of three numeric fields that we pass in as-is. It is good practice to create a separate method that takes the raw data and constructs a training example because this allows us to fold in other operations as well. For example, we begin to do preprocessing of the feature values, and having a method to construct training examples allows us to reuse the code between training and evaluation.

After we have a way to convert each raw data point into a training example, we need to apply this method to the entire training dataset. We can do this by mapping the dataset row by row:

```
examples = traindata.rdd.map(to_example)
```

Training

Now that we have a DataFrame in the requisite format, we can ask Spark to fit the training dataset to the labels:

```
lrmodel = LogisticRegressionWithLBFGS.train(examples, intercept=True)
```

We'd have specified intercept=False if we believed that when all x = 0, the prediction needed to be 0. We have no reason to expect this, so we ask the model to find a value for the intercept.

When the train() method completes, the lrmodel will have the weights and intercept, and we can print them out:

```
print lrmodel.weights,lrmodel.intercept
```

This yields the following:[9]

```
[-0.164,-0.132,0.000294] 5.1579
```

The weights is an array, one for each variable. These numbers, plus the formula for logistic regression, are enough to set up code for the model in any language we choose. Remember that in our labeled points, 0 indicated late arrivals and 1 indicated on-time arrivals. So, applying these weights to the departure delay, taxi-out time, and flight distance of a flight will yield the probability that the flight will be on time.

In this case, it appears that the departure delay has a weight of –0.164. The negative sign indicates that the higher the departure delay, the lower the likelihood that the flight will be on time (which sounds about right). On the other hand, the sign on the distance is positive, indicating that higher distances are associated with more on-time behavior. Even though we are able to look at the weights and reason with them on this dataset, such reasoning will begin to break down if the variables are not independent. If you have highly correlated input variables, the magnitudes and signs of the weights are no longer interpretable.

Let's try out a prediction:

---

9 Because of random seeds used in the optimization process, and different data in shards, your results will be different.

```
lrmodel.predict([6.0,12.0,594.0])
```

The result is 1—that is, the flight will be on time when the departure delay is 6 minutes, the taxi-out time is 12 minutes, and the flight is for 594 miles. Let's change the departure delay to 36 minutes (from 6):

```
lrmodel.predict([36.0,12.0,594.0])
```

The result now is 0—the flight won't arrive on time.

But wait a minute. We want the output to be a probability, not 0 or 1 (the final label). To do that, we can remove the implicit threshold of 0.5:

```
lrmodel.clearThreshold()
```

With the thresholding removed, we get probabilities. The probability of arriving late increases as the departure delay increases.

By keeping two of the variables constant, it is possible to study how the probability varies as a function of one of the variables. For example, at a departure delay of 20 minutes and a taxi-out time of 10 minutes, this is how the distance affects the probability that the flight is on time:

```
dist = np.arange(10, 2000, 10)
prob = [lrmodel.predict([20, 10, d]) for d in dist]
plt.plot(dist, prob)
```

Figure 7-4 shows the plot.

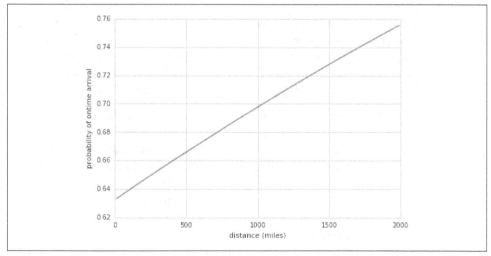

Figure 7-4. How the distance of the flight affects the probability of on-time arrival. According to our model, longer flights tend to have higher likelihoods of arriving on time, but the effect is rather minor.

As you can see, the effect is relatively minor. The probability increases from about 0.63 to about 0.76 as the distance changes from a very short hop to a cross-continent flight. On the other hand, if we hold the taxi-out time and distance constant and examine the dependence on departure delay, we see a more dramatic impact (see Figure 7-5):

```
delay = np.arange(-20, 60, 1)
prob = [lrmodel.predict([d, 10, 500]) for d in delay]
ax = plt.plot(delay, prob)
```

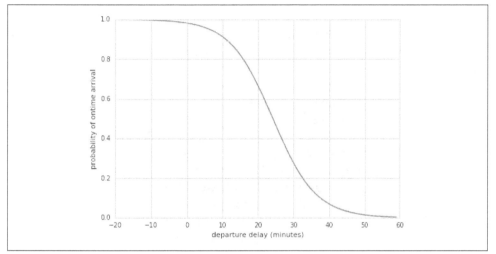

Figure 7-5. How the departure delay of the flight affects the probability of on-time arrival. The effect of the departure delay is rather dramatic.

Although the probabilities are useful to be able to plot the behavior of the model in different scenarios, we do want a specific decision threshold. Recall that we want to cancel the meeting if the probability of the flight arriving on time is less than 70%. So, we can change the decision threshold:

```
lrmodel.setThreshold(0.7)
```

Now, the predictions are 0 or 1, with the probability threshold set at 0.7.

Predicting by Using a Model

Now that we have a trained model, we can save it to Cloud Storage and retrieve it whenever we need to make a prediction. To save the model, we provide a location on Cloud Storage:

```
MODEL_FILE='gs://' + BUCKET + '/flights/sparkmloutput/model'
lrmodel.save(sc, MODEL_FILE)
```

To retrieve the model, we load it from the same location:

```
from pyspark.mllib.classification import LogisticRegressionModel
lrmodel = LogisticRegressionModel.load(sc, MODEL_FILE)
lrmodel.setThreshold(0.7)
```

Note that we must take care to set the decision threshold; it is not part of the model.

Now, we can use the `lrmodel` variable to carry out predictions:

```
print lrmodel.predict([36.0,12.0,594.0])
```

Obviously, this code could be embedded into a Python web application to create a prediction web service or API.

A key point to realize is that whereas model training in Spark is distributed and requires a cluster, model prediction is a pretty straightforward mathematical computation. Model training is a batch operation and requires the ability to scale out to multiple processors, but online prediction requires fast computation on a single processor. When the machine learning model is relatively small (as in our logistic regression workflow[10]), hardware optimizations (like Graphics Processing Units [GPUs]) are not needed in the training stage. However, even for small models, they are potentially needed in the prediction stage. GPUs become useful in prediction even for small models if the system needs to provide for low latency and a high number of queries per second (QPS). Thus, when choosing how to resize the cluster to run our machine learning training job over the full dataset, it is more cost-effective to simply add more CPUs. Of course, had we been training a deep learning model for image classification with hundreds of layers, GPUs would have been called for both in training and in prediction.

Evaluating a Model

Now that we have a trained model, we can evaluate its performance on the test days, a set of days that were not used in training (we created this test dataset in Chapter 5). To do that, we change the query to pull out the test days:

```
testquery = trainquery.replace(\
        "t.is_train_day == 'True'","t.is_train_day == 'False'")
print testquery
```

Here is the resulting query:

```
SELECT
  DEP_DELAY, TAXI_OUT, ARR_DELAY, DISTANCE
FROM flights f
JOIN traindays t
ON f.FL_DATE == t.FL_DATE
```

---

10 Very large deep neural networks, such as those used for image classification, are another story. Such models can have hundreds of layers, each with hundreds of weights. Here, we have three weights—four if you count the intercept.

```
WHERE
    t.is_train_day == 'False' AND
    f.CANCELLED == '0.00' AND
    f.DIVERTED == '0.00'
```

We then carry out the same ML pipeline as we did during training:

```
testdata = spark.sql(testquery)
examples = testdata.rdd.map(to_example)
```

Note how useful it was that we made the process of going from the raw data to the training examples modular by creating a function for it.

As soon as we have the examples, we can have the model predict the label for each set of features, and then create a data frame that contains the true label and the model prediction for each row:

```
labelpred = examples.map(lambda p: \
        (p.label, lrmodel.predict(p.features)))
```

To evaluate the performance of the model, we first find out how many flights we will need to cancel and how accurate we are in terms of flights we cancel and flights we don't cancel:

```
def eval(labelpred):
    cancel = labelpred.filter(lambda (label, pred): pred == 1)
    nocancel = labelpred.filter(lambda (label, pred): pred == 0)
    corr_cancel = cancel.filter(lambda (label, pred): \
                                        label == pred).count()
    corr_nocancel = nocancel.filter(lambda (label, pred): \
                                        label == pred).count()
    return {'total_cancel': cancel.count(), \
            'correct_cancel': float(corr_cancel)/cancel.count(), \
            'total_nocancel': nocancel.count(), \
            'correct_noncancel': float(corr_nocancel)/nocancel.count()\
           }
```

Here's what the resulting statistics turn out to be:

```
{'correct_cancel': 0.7917474551623849, 'total_noncancel': 115949,
 'correct_noncancel': 0.9571363271783284, 'total_cancel': 33008}
```

As discussed in Chapter 5, the reason the correctness percentages are not 70% is because the 70% threshold is on the marginal distribution—the accuracy percentages here are computed on the total distribution and so are padded by the easy decisions. However, let's go back and modify the evaluation function to explicitly print out statistics around the decision threshold—this is important to ensure that we are, indeed, making a probabilistic decision.

We should clear the threshold so that the model returns probabilities and then carry out the evaluation twice: once on the full dataset, and next on only those flights that fall near the decision threshold of 0.7:

```
lrmodel.clearThreshold() # so it returns probabilities
labelpred = examples.map(lambda p: \
                         (p.label, lrmodel.predict(p.features)))
print eval(labelpred)
# keep only those examples near the decision threshold
labelpred = labelpred.filter(lambda (label, pred):\
                     pred > 0.65 and pred < 0.75)
print eval(labelpred)
```

Of course, we must change the evaluation code to work with probabilities instead of with categorical predictions. The four variables now become as follows:

```
cancel = labelpred.filter(lambda (label, pred): pred < 0.7)
nocancel = labelpred.filter(lambda (label, pred): pred >= 0.7)
corr_cancel = cancel.filter(lambda (label, pred): \
                       label == int(pred >= 0.7)).count()
corr_nocancel = nocancel.filter(lambda (label, pred): \
                       label == int(pred >= 0.7)).count()
```

When run, the first set of results remains the same, and the second set of results now yields this:

```
{'correct_cancel': 0.30886504799548276, 'total_noncancel': 2224,
 'correct_noncancel': 0.7383093525179856, 'total_cancel': 1771}
```

Note that we are correct about 74% of the time in our decision to go ahead with a meeting (our target was 70%). Although useful to verify that the code is working as intended, the actual results are meaningless because we are not running on the entire dataset, just one shard of it. Therefore, the final step is to export the code from the notebook, remove the various show() and plot() functions, and create a submittable script.[11]

We can submit the script to the Cloud Dataproc cluster from a laptop with the Cloud SDK installed, from CloudShell, or from the Cloud Dataproc section of the Google Cload Platform web console at *https://console.cloud.google.com/*. Before we submit the script, we need to resize the cluster, so that we can process the entire dataset on a larger cluster than the one on which we did development. So, what we need to do is to increase the size of the cluster, submit the script, and decrease the size of the cluster after the script is done.[12]

Running *logistic.py* on the larger cluster, we create a model and then evaluate it on the test days. We now get these results on the entire dataset:

```
{'correct_cancel': 0.8141780686099543, 'total_noncancel': 1574550,
 'correct_noncancel': 0.9635584770251818, 'total_cancel': 353010}
```

---

11 See *logistic.py* in *07_sparkml*.

12 See the scripts *increase_cluster.sh* and *decrease_cluster.sh* in *06_dataproc* and the script *submit_spark.sh* in *07_sparkml*. You will need to shut down any running notebooks before submitting a Spark job.

Looking at these overall results, notice that we are canceling about 350,000 meetings. We are accurate 96.3% of the time we don't cancel a meeting and 81.4% of the time we decide to cancel. Remember that we canceled 920,355 meetings when using the Bayesian classifier and were correct 83% of the time that we decided to cancel. Here, we get nearly the same correctness, but cancel far fewer meetings—using a third variable and a more sophisticated model seems to have helped dramatically.

The first set of results is on the entire dataset and the second set is on the marginal distribution (i.e., on flights for which our probability is near 0.7). The second set indicates that we are, indeed, making an appropriately probabilistic decision—our decision to go ahead with a meeting is correct 72% of the time:

```
{'correct_cancel': 0.33481603514552444, 'total_noncancel': 22242,
 'correct_noncancel': 0.7212930491862243, 'total_cancel': 18210}
```

Machine learning using logistic regression on three variables has enabled us to attain performance three times that which we did using hand-tuned heuristics. Machine learning, besides providing a better model, also allows us to be more agile—we can quickly retrain on newer datasets. Indeed, one could imagine continually retraining on the latest year of data so that as pilots' behavior changes and airlines' scheduling practices change, the machine learning model continually adapts.

Feature Engineering

Still, it is unclear whether we really needed all three variables in the logistic regression model. Any variable you include in a machine learning model brings with it an increased danger of overfitting. Known as the principle of parsimony (*http://bit.ly/2nAggN5*) (often referred to as Occam's razor[13]), the idea is that it is preferable to use a simpler model to a more complex model that has similar accuracy—the fewer variables we have in our model, the better it is.

One manifestation of the principle of parsimony is that there are practical considerations involved with every new variable in a machine learning model. A handcoded system of rules can deal with the presence or absence of values (for example, if the variable in question was not collected) for specific variables relatively easily—simply write a new rule to handle the case. On the other hand, machine learning models require the presence of enough data when that variable value is absent. Thus, a machine learning model will often be unusable if all of its variable values are not present in the data. Even if a variable value is present in some new data, it might be defined differently or computed differently, and we might have to go through an expensive retraining effort in order to use it. Thus, extra variable values pose issues

---

13 See *http://bit.ly/2ixofW8*, for example. Occam, who was a bishop in medieval England, actually wrote *"Pluralitas non est ponenda sine necessitate,"* which translates to "Entities should not be multiplied unnecessarily."

around the applicability of a machine learning model to new situations. We should attempt to use as few variables as possible.

Experimental Framework

It is also unclear whether the three variables we chose are the only ones that matter. Perhaps we could use more variables from the dataset besides the three we are using. In machine learning terminology, the inputs to the model are called *features*. The features could be different from the raw input variables, because the input variables could be transformed in some way before being provided to the model. The process of designing the transforms that are carried out on the raw input variables is called *feature engineering*.

To test whether a feature provides value to the model, we need to build an experimental framework. We could begin with one feature (departure delay, for example) and test whether the incorporation of a new feature (perhaps the distance) improves model performance. If it does, we keep it and try out one more feature. If not, we discard it and try the next feature on our list. This way, we get to select a subset of features and ensure that they do matter. Another approach is to train a model with all possible features, remove a feature, and retrain. If performance doesn't go down, leave the feature out. At the end, as before, we will be left with a subset of features that matter. The second approach is preferable because it allows us to capture interactions—perhaps a feature by itself doesn't matter, but its presence alongside another is powerful. Choosing the set of features through a systematic process is called *feature selection*.

For both feature engineering and feature selection, it is important to devise an experimental framework to test out our hypotheses as to whether a feature is needed. On which dataset should we evaluate whether a feature is important? We cannot evaluate how much it improves accuracy on the training dataset itself, because the model might be fitting noise in the training data. Instead, we need an independent dataset in order to carry out feature selection. However, we cannot use the test dataset, because if we use the test dataset in our model creation process, it is no longer independent and cannot be used as a good indicator of model performance. Therefore, we will split the training dataset itself into two parts—one part will be used for training, whereas the other will be held out and used to evaluate different models.

Figure 7-6 shows what our experimentation framework is going to look like.

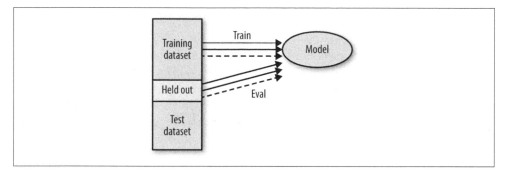

Figure 7-6. We often split a dataset into three parts. The training dataset is used to tune the weights of a model, and the held-out dataset is used to evaluate the impact of model changes, such as feature selection. The independent test dataset is used only to gauge the performance of the final, selected model.

First, we break the full dataset into two parts and keep one part of it for the final evaluation of models (we did this in Chapter 5 when we created the `traindays` dataset). This part is called the test dataset and is what we have been using for end-of-chapter evaluations. However, when we are creating several models and need to choose among them, we cannot use the test dataset. Therefore, we will split our original training dataset itself into two parts. We'll retain the larger part of it for actual training and use the held-out portion to evaluate the model. In Figure 7-6, for example, we are deciding whether to use the third input variable. We do this based on whether that feature improves model performance enough.

What metric should we evaluate in order to choose between two models? *Not* the number of canceled flights! It is easy to game metrics computed from the contingency table because it is possible to change the probability threshold to get a wide range of accuracy, precision, or recall metrics.[14] A contingency-table-based metric is a good way to understand the performance of a model, but not to choose between two models unless care is taken to ensure that the measure is not tuneable by changing the threshold. One way to do this would be to, for example, compare precision at a fixed recall rate, but you should do this only if that fixed recall is meaningful. In our problem, however, it is the probability that is meaningful, not the precision or recall.

---

14 Recall that we need to threshold the probabilistic output of the model to get the entries in the contingency table. A correct cancel, for example, is the situation that the flight arrived more than 15 minutes late, and the predicted probability of on-time arrival was less than 0.7. The metrics evaluated on the contingency table are extremely sensitive to this choice of threshold. Different models will be different at thresholds of 0.65, 0.68, or 0.70, especially for models whose performance is quite comparable. If, for example, we want the overall correct cancel percentage to be 80%, we can change the threshold to get this. We can also change the threshold to get an overall correct cancel percentage of 20% if that is what we desire.

Hence, it is not possible to fix either of them, and we are left comparing two pairs of numbers.

Another way to avoid the problem that the metric can be gamed is to use a measure that uses the full distribution of probabilities that are output by the model. When carrying out feature selection or any other form of hyperparameter tuning, we could use a measure such as the logistic loss or cross-entropy that conveys this full distribution. As a simpler, more intuitive measure that nevertheless uses the full distribution of probabilities, let's use the Root Mean Squared Error (RMSE) between the true labels and the probabilistic predictions:

```
totsqe = labelpred.map(lambda (label, pred): \
                       (label-pred)*(label-pred)).sum()
'rmse': np.sqrt(totsqe/float(cancel.count() + nocancel.count()))
```

What is "enough" of an improvement when it comes to RMSE? There are no hard-and-fast rules. We need the model performance to improve enough to outweigh the drawbacks involved with additional inputs and the loss of agility and model runtime speed that additional input features entail. Here, I will choose to use 0.5% as my threshold. If the model performance, based on some metric we decide upon, isn't reduced by at least 0.5% by removing a variable, I won't use the extra variable.

Creating the Held-Out Dataset

Because the held-out dataset is going to be used only for model evaluation and only within Spark, we do not need to create the held-out dataset as rigorously as when we created the test dataset in Chapter 5. For example, we do not need to store the held-out days as a separate dataset that can be read from multiple frameworks.[15] However, the principle of repeatability still applies—every time we run our Spark program, we should get the same set of held-out days. Otherwise, it will not be possible to compare the performance of different models (because evaluation metrics depend on the dataset on which they are evaluated).

After I read the `traindays` dataset, I will add in a new temporary column called `hold out` that will be initialized from a random array:[16]

```
from pyspark.sql.functions import rand
SEED = 13
traindays = traindays.withColumn("holdout", rand(SEED) > 0.8)  # 20%
traindays.createOrReplaceTempView('traindays')
```

---

15 Recall that we stored the training versus test days both as a BigQuery table and as a CSV file on Cloud Storage. We had to save the `traindays` dataset to persistent storage because otherwise we would have run into the problem of different hash function implementations in Spark, Pig, and Tensorflow. There would have been no way to evaluate model performance on the same dataset.

16 See *experimentation.ipynb* and *experiment.py* in *07_sparkml*.

I am passing in a seed so that I get the exact same array (and hence the same set of held-out days) every time I run this Spark code.

The first few rows of the `traindays` table are now as follows:

```
Row(FL_DATE=u'2015-01-01', is_train_day=u'True', holdout=False),
Row(FL_DATE=u'2015-01-02', is_train_day=u'False', holdout=True),
Row(FL_DATE=u'2015-01-03', is_train_day=u'False', holdout=False),
Row(FL_DATE=u'2015-01-04', is_train_day=u'True', holdout=False),
Row(FL_DATE=u'2015-01-05', is_train_day=u'True', holdout=True),
```

Note that we have both `is_train_day` and `holdout`—obviously, we are not going to be holding out any *test* data, so the query to pull training samples is as follows:

```
SELECT
  *
FROM flights f
JOIN traindays t
ON f.FL_DATE == t.FL_DATE
WHERE
  t.is_train_day == 'True' AND
  t.holdout == False AND
  f.CANCELLED == '0.00' AND
  f.DIVERTED == '0.00'
```

After we have trained the model, we evaluate it not on the test data as before, but on the held-out data:

```
evalquery = trainquery.replace("t.holdout == False", \
                               "t.holdout == True")
```

After we have developed this code, we can export it out of the notebook into a stand-alone script so that it can be submitted conveniently.

Feature Selection

Let's use this experimental framework and the held-out dataset to decide whether all three input variables are important. As explained earlier, we will remove one variable at a time and check the RMSE on the evaluation dataset. Conveniently, this involves changing only the `to_example()` method from:

```
def to_example(raw_data_point):
  return LabeledPoint(\
             float(raw_data_point['ARR_DELAY'] < 15), #ontime \
             [ \
                raw_data_point['DEP_DELAY'], # DEP_DELAY \
raw_data_point['DEP_DISTANCE'], # DEP_DELAY \
     raw_data_point['TAXI_OUT'], # TAXI_OUT \
             ])
```

to:

```
def to_example(raw_data_point):
    return LabeledPoint(\
                float(raw_data_point['ARR_DELAY'] < 15), #ontime \
                [ \
                    raw_data_point['DEP_DELAY'], # DEP_DELAY \
                    raw_data_point['DISTANCE'], # TAXI_OUT \
                ])
```

We would like to quickly experiment with code changes. My 20-node cluster of n1-standard-2 machines took about 20 minutes to process the dataset, which is far too long. Therefore, I replaced the cluster by a cluster consisting of 50 machines:[17]

```
#!/bin/bash
ZONE=us-central1-a
# create cluster
gcloud dataproc clusters create \
    --num-workers=35 \
    --num-preemptible-workers=15 \
    --scopes=cloud-platform \
    --worker-machine-type=n1-standard-4 \
    --master-machine-type=n1-standard-8 \
    --worker-boot-disk-size=10 \
    --preemptible-worker-boot-disk-size=10 \
    --zone=$ZONE \
    ch6cluster
```

When you're using a large cluster and submitting jobs one after the other, it is a good idea to monitor the Hadoop nodes to ensure that all the machines are available and that jobs are being spread over the entire cluster. You can access the monitoring web interface using the same *start_tunnel.sh* and *start_chrome.sh* as you used when accessing Cloud Datalab. This time, though, navigate to the YARN (8088) and HDFS (50070) web interfaces, as demonstrated in Figure 7-7.

---

17 Trying to increase the number of workers might have you hitting against (soft) quotas on the maximum number of CPUs, drives, or addresses. If you hit any of these soft quotas, request an increase from the Google Cloud Platform console's section on Compute Engine quotas: *https://console.cloud.google.com/compute/quotas*. I already had the necessary CPU quota, but I needed to ask for an increase in DISKS_TOTAL_GB and IN_USE_ADDRESSES. Because a Cloud Dataproc cluster is in a single region, these are *regional* quotas. See *https://cloud.google.com/compute/quotas* for details.

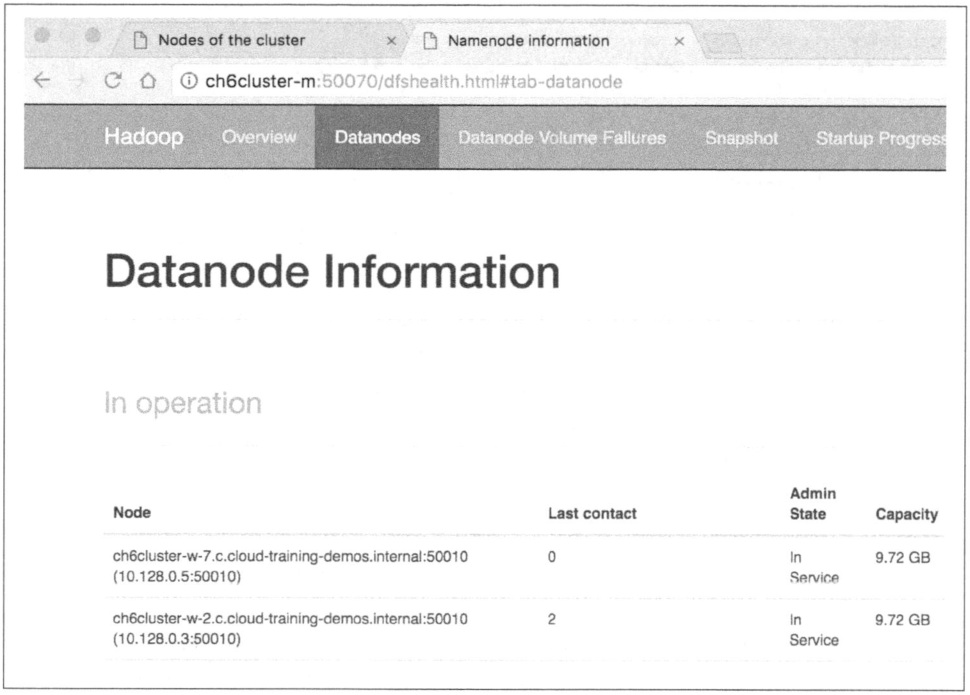

Figure 7-7. The Hadoop monitoring web interface

In my case, monitoring revealed that simply increasing the number of workers didn't actually spread out the processing to all the nodes. This is because Spark estimates the number of partitions based on the raw input data size (here just a few gigabytes), and so that estimate is probably too low for our 50-worker cluster. Hence, I modified the reading code to add in an explicit repartitioning step:

```
traindata = spark.sql(trainquery).repartition(1000)
```

And similarly, when reading the evaluation data:

```
evaldata = spark.sql(evalquery).repartition(1000)
```

When you run the script, you should now see the 1,000 partitions reflected, for example, as in the following:

```
[Stage 9:=========... ==============>       (859 + 1) / 1000]
```

Now that we have a faster way of running the job, we can carry out our experiment of removing variables one-by-one.

Experiment #	Variables	RMSE	Percent increase in RMSE
1	DEP_DELAY DISTANCE TAXI_OUT	0.252	N/A
2	Remove DEP_DELAY	0.431	71%
3	Remove DISTANCE	0.254	1%
4	Remove TAXI_OUT	0.278	10%

It is clear that some variables are dramatically more important than others but that all three variables do carry information and you should not discard them. Contrary to my assumption in Chapter 6, the distance has the least amount of impact—had I known this earlier, Chapter 6 might have involved Bayesian selection of departure delay and taxi-out time!

Scaling and Clipping Features

In the previous section, we carried out feature selection to determine that the distance variable was the least important of the variables included in the model. However, there is another possibility why including the distance variable did not affect the RMSE greatly—it could be that the distance variable ranges over a wider range (thousands of miles), whereas the time intervals range to only a few minutes. Therefore, the distance variable might be overpowering the other variables. In an effort to reduce the impact of distance on both the sum and the gradient, the optimization process might move the distance weight to 0. And thus, the distance might end up not playing much of a role. This is less likely in the case of logistic regression because it is a linear model, and gradients in linear models can be scaled more effectively. However, having all the variables have similar magnitudes will become important as our models become more complex.

Another reason we'd like to scale all the input values so that they all have similar (and small) magnitudes is that the initial, random weights tend to be in the range –1 to 1, and this is where the optimizer starts to search. Thus, starting with all the variables having less than unit magnitude can help the optimizer converge more efficiently and effectively. Following are common choices for scaling functions:

1. To map the minimum value of the variable to –1 and the maximum to 1. This involves scanning the dataset to find the minimum and maximum within each column—Spark has a class called AbsScaler that will do this for us (but it requires an extra pass through the data). However, the choices of the minimum and maximum need not be exact, so we can use the data exploration that we carried out in previous chapters to do an approximate scaling. As long as we scale the variables the same way during training and during prediction (for example, if

we scale linearly such that a distance of 30 maps to –1.0 and a distance of 6,000 maps to 1.0 both in training and during prediction), the precise minimum and maximum don't matter.

2. To map the mean of the variable within the column to 0 and values one standard deviation away to –1 or 1. The tails of the distribution will map to quite large values, but such values will also be rarer. This serves to emphasize unusual values while linearly scaling the common ones.

Let's use option #1, which is to do linear scaling between an approximate minimum and maximum. Let's assume that departure delays are in the range (–30, 30), distance in the range (0, 2,000), and taxi-out times in the range (0, 20) minutes. These are approximate, but quite reasonable, and using these reasonable values helps us to avoid being overly affected by outliers in the data. To map these ranges to (–1, 1), this is the transformation we would carry out on the input variables inside the to_exam ple() function that converts a row into a training example:

```
def to_example(raw_data_point):
  return LabeledPoint(\
             float(raw_data_point['ARR_DELAY'] < 15), #ontime \
             [ \
                 raw_data_point['DEP_DELAY'] / 30, \
                 (raw_data_point['DISTANCE'] / 1000) - 1, \
                 (raw_data_point['TAXI_OUT'] / 10) - 1, \
             ])
```

After making these changes to scale the three variables, and running the experiment again, I see that the RMSE is unaffected—scaling doesn't make a difference.

Experiment #	Variables	RMSE	Percent improvement
1 (values from experiment #1 repeated for convenience)	Raw values of DEP_DELAY DISTANCE TAXI_OUT	0.252	N/A
5	Scaled values of the three variables	0.252	0

Another possible preprocessing that we could carry out is called *clipping*. Values that are beyond what we would consider reasonable are clamped to the bounds. For example, we could treat distances of more than 2,000 miles as 2,000 miles, and departure delays of more than 30 minutes as 30 minutes. This allows the optimization algorithm to focus on the part of the data where the majority of the data lies, and not be pulled off the global minimum by outliers. Also, some error metrics can be susceptible to outliers, so it is worth doing one more experiment after clipping the input variables.

Adding clipping to scaled variables is straightforward:

```
def to_example(raw_data_point):
    def clip(x):
        if (x < -1):
            return -1
        if (x > 1):
            return 1
        return x
    return LabeledPoint(\
                float(raw_data_point['ARR_DELAY'] < 15), #ontime \
                [ \
                    clip(raw_data_point['DEP_DELAY'] / 30), \
                    clip((raw_data_point['DISTANCE'] / 1000) - 1), \
                    clip((raw_data_point['TAXI_OUT'] / 10) - 1), \
                ])
```

Carrying out the experiment on clipped variables, and adding in the RMSE to the table, we see these results:

Experiment #	Transform	RMSE	Percent improvement	Keep transform?
1 (repeated for convenience)	Raw values of DEP_DELAY DISTANCE TAXI_OUT	0.252	N/A	N/A
6	Scaled	0.252	None	No
7	Clipped	0.283	Negative	No

It turns out that scaling did not matter for this algorithm (logistic regression) in this framework (Spark ML) and clipping had a detrimental effect.[18] In general, though, experimenting with different preprocessing transforms should be part of your workflow. It could have a dramatic impact.

Feature Transforms

So far, we have tried out the three numeric predictors in our dataset. Why did I pick only the numeric fields in the dataset? Because the logistic regression model is, at heart, just a weighted sum. We can quite easily multiply and add numeric values (actually not all numeric values but those that are continuous[19]), but what does it mean to use a timestamp such as 2015-03-13-11:00:00 as an input variable to the logistic regression model?

---

18 We could have anticipated these results. As of this writing, the Spark Java documentation (*http://bit.ly/2B75AeZ*) clarifies that standard feature scaling and L2 regularization are used by default. The Python API (*http://bit.ly/2ktxfzK*), however, doesn't.

19 For example, you cannot add and multiply employee ID numbers even if they are numeric. Employee ID numbers are not continuous.

We cannot simply convert such a timestamp to a numeric quantity, such as the day number within the year, and then add it to the model. One rule of thumb is that to use a value as input to a model, you should have at least 5 to 10 instances of that value appearing in the data. Columns that are too specific to a particular row or handful of rows can cause the model to become overfit—an overfit model is one that will perform extremely well on the training dataset (essentially, it will memorize exactly what happened at each historical timestamp—for example, that flights in the Midwest were delayed on May 11, 2015) but then not work well on new data. It won't work well on new data because the timestamps in that data (such as May 11, 2018) will not have been observed.

Therefore, we need to do smarter things with attributes such as timestamps so that they are both relevant to the problem and not too specific. We could, for example, use the hour of day as an attribute in the model. The hour of day might matter—most airports become busy in the early morning and early evening because many flights are scheduled around the daily work schedules of business travelers. In addition, delays accumulate over the day, as an aircraft that is delayed in arriving is also delayed on takeoff.

Suppose that that we extract the hour of day from the timestamp. Given a timestamp such as 2015-03-13-11:00:00, what is the hour? It's 11, of course, but the 11 is in the time zone corresponding to the UTC time zone, not to the American airport, that we care about. This is one instance for which it is local time that matters. Thus, to extract the hour of day, we will need to correct by the time zone offset and then extract the hour of day. The *feature* hour of day is computed from two input variables—the departure time and the time zone offset.

It is worth pausing here and clarifying that I am making a distinction between the words *input* and *feature*—the timestamp is the input, the hour of day is the feature. What the client application provides when it wants a prediction is the input, but what the ML model is trained on is the feature. The feature could be (as in the case of scaling of input variables) a transformation of an input variable. In other cases, as with the hour of day, it could be a combination of multiple input variables. The `to_exam ple()` method is the method that converts inputs (`raw_data_point`) to *examples* (where each example is a tuple of features and a label). Different machine learning APIs will ask for inputs, features, or examples, and it is good to be clear on what exactly the three terms mean.

Given a departure timestamp and a time zone offset,[20] we can compute the hour in local time using the time-handling code we discussed in Chapter 4:

---

20 The time zone offset is a float, and must be added to the schema as such.

```
def to_example(raw_data_point):
    def get_local_hour(timestamp, correction):
        import datetime
        TIME_FORMAT = '%Y-%m-%dT%H:%M:%S'
        t = datetime.datetime.strptime(timestamp, TIME_FORMAT)
        d = datetime.timedelta(seconds=correction)
        t = t + d
        return t.hour
    return LabeledPoint(\
                float(raw_data_point['ARR_DELAY'] < 15), #ontime \
                [ \
                    raw_data_point['DEP_DELAY'], \
                    raw_data_point['TAXI_OUT'], \
                    get_local_hour(raw_data_point['DEP_TIME'], \
                            raw_data_point['DEP_AIRPORT_TZOFFSET'])
                ])
```

There is one potential problem with treating the hour of day as a straightforward number. Hour 22 and hour 2 are only 4 hours apart, and it would be good to capture this somehow. An elegant way to work with periodic variables in machine learning is to convert them to two features—sin(theta) and cos(theta), where theta in this case would be the angle of the hour hand in a 24-hour clock:[21]

```
def to_example(raw_data_point):
    def get_local_hour(timestamp, correction):
        import datetime
        TIME_FORMAT = '%Y-%m-%dT%H:%M:%S'
        t = datetime.datetime.strptime(timestamp, TIME_FORMAT)
        d = datetime.timedelta(seconds=correction)
        t = t + d
        theta = np.radians(360 * t.hour / 24.0)
        return [np.sin(theta), np.cos(theta)]

    features = [ \
                raw_data_point['DEP_DELAY'], \
                raw_data_point['TAXI_OUT'], \
                ]
    features.extend(get_local_hour(raw_data_point['DEP_TIME'],
                            raw_data_point['DEP_AIRPORT_TZOFFSET']))
    return LabeledPoint(\
                float(raw_data_point['ARR_DELAY'] < 15), #ontime \
                features)
```

This encoding of a periodic variable using the sin and cos makes it two features. These two features capture the information present in the periodic variable, but do not distort the distance between two values.

---

21 The distribution of hours in the dataset, we assume, follows the Fisher-von Mises distribution, which describes points distributed on an n-dimensional sphere. If $n = 2$, this reduces to points on a unit circle. An hour hand is just that.

Another approach would be to *bucketize* the hour. For example, we could group hours 20 to 23 and hours 0 to 5 as "night," hours 6 to 9 as "morning," and so on. Obviously, bucketizing takes advantage of what human experts know about the problem. We suspect that the behavior of flight delays changes depending on the time of day—long taxi-out times during busy hours are probably built in to the scheduled arrival time, but a plane that experiences a long taxi-out because the towing vehicle broke down and had to be replaced will almost definitely arrive late. Hence, our bucketizing of the hour of day relies on our intuition of what the busy hours at an airport are:

```python
def get_category(hour):
  if hour < 6 or hour > 20:
    return [1, 0, 0]  # night
  if hour < 10:
    return [0, 1, 0] # morning
  if hour < 17:
    return [0, 0, 1] # mid-day
  else:
    return [0, 0, 0] # evening

def get_local_hour(timestamp, correction):
    ...
    return get_category(t.hour)
```

You might find it odd that the vector corresponding to the last category is [0, 0, 0] and not [0, 0, 0, 1], as you might have expected. This is because we don't want the four features to always add up to one—that would make them linearly dependent. This trick of dropping the last column keeps the values independent. Assuming that we have N categories, bucketizing will make the hour variable into $N - 1$ features.

How do we know which of these methods—the raw value, the sin/cos trick, or bucketizing—works best for the hour of day? We don't, and so we need to run an experiment and choose (note that we are using the departure delay, distance, and taxi-out, and now adding a new variable to see if it helps).

Experiment #	Transform	RMSE
1 (repeated for convenience)	Without hour	0.252
8	raw hour	0.252
9	sin(theta) cos(theta)	0.252
10	bucketize	0.252

It appears that the hour of day is already adequately captured by the scheduling rules used by the airlines. It can be tempting to simply throw away the hour information, but we should follow our systematic process of keeping all our variables and then discarding one variable at a time—it is possible that the hour of day doesn't matter now, but it will after we include some other variables. So, for now, let's pick one of the possibilities arbitrarily—I will use the bucketed hour as the way to create a feature from the timestamp. Of course, I could have created additional features from the timestamp input variable—day of week, season, and so on.

Spark ML supports a rich set of feature transforms (*http://spark.apache.org/docs/latest/ml-features.html#feature-transformers*)—it is a good idea to go through that list and learn the types of variables for which they are meant. Knowing the tools available to you is a prerequisite to be able to call on them when appropriate. If this is the first time you are encountering machine learning, you might be surprised by how much we are relying on our experimental framework. Running experiments like this, though, is the unglamorous work that lies behind most machine learning applications. Although my approach in this chapter has required careful record keeping, a better way would be if our machine learning framework would provide structure around experiments, not just single training operations. Spark ML provides this functionality (*https://spark.apache.org/docs/latest/ml-tuning.html*) via a `CrossValidator`, but even that still requires quite a bit of scaffolding.

Categorical Variables

How about using the airport code as a predictor? What we are doing when using the airport code as a predictor is that we are asking the ML algorithm to learn the idiosyncrasies of each airport. I remember, for example, sitting in the runway at New York's La Guardia airport for nearly 45 minutes and then being surprised when the flight arrived in Dallas a few minutes ahead of schedule! Apparently, a 45-minute taxi-out time in New York is quite common and nothing to be worried about.

To use timestamp information, we extracted a numeric part of the timestamp—the hour—and used it in our model. We tried using it in raw form, as a periodic variable, and as a bucketized set of categories. We cannot use that approach here, because there is no numeric component to the letters DFW or LGA. So how can we use the airport code as an input to our model?

The trick here is to realize that bucketizing the hour was a special case of categorizing the variable. A more bludgeon-like, but often effective, approach is to do *one-hot encoding*. Essentially, the hour variable is made into 24 features. The 11th feature is 1.0 and the rest of the features 0.0 when the hour is 11, for example. One-hot encoding is the standard way to deal with *categorical* features (i.e., features for which there is no concept of magnitude or ranking between different values of the variable[22]). This is the way we'll need to encode the departure airport if we were minded to include it in our model—we'd essentially have one feature per airport, so that the

---

22 It is not the case that all strings are categorical and all numeric columns are continuous. To use my previous example, an employee ID might be numeric but is categorical. On the other hand, student grades (A+, A, A–, B+, B, etc.) are strings but can easily be translated to a continuous variable.

DFW feature would be 1, and the rest of the features 0 for flights that departed from DFW.

Unlike bucketing hours, though, we need to find all the possible airport codes (called the *vocabulary*) and assign a specific binary column to them. For example, we might need to assign DFW to the 143rd column. Fortunately, we don't need to write the code. One-hot encoding is available as a prebuilt feature transformation in Spark; we can add a new column of vectors to the `traindata` data frame using this code:

```
def add_categorical(df):
    from pyspark.ml.feature import OneHotEncoder, StringIndexer
    indexer = StringIndexer(inputCol='ORIGIN',
                            outputCol='origin_index')
    index_model = indexer.fit(df)  # Step 1
    indexed = index_model.transform(df)  # Step 2
    encoder = OneHotEncoder(inputCol='origin_index',
                            outputCol='origin_onehot')
    return encoder.transform(indexed) # Step 3
traindata = add_categorical(traindata)
```

Here are the three steps:

1. Create an index from origin airport codes (e.g., DFW) to an origin index (e.g., 143).

2. Transform the dataset so that all flights with `ORIGIN=DFW` have `origin_index=143`.

3. One-hot encode the index into a binary vector that is used as input to training.

During evaluation, the same change needs to be made to the dataset, except that the index model will need to be reused from training (so that DFW continues to map to 143). In other words, we need to save the `index_model` and carry out the last three lines before prediction. So, we modify the `add_categorical()` method appropriately:[23]

```
index_model = 0
def add_categorical(df, train=False):
    from pyspark.ml.feature import OneHotEncoder, StringIndexer
    if train:
        indexer = StringIndexer(inputCol='ORIGIN',
                                outputCol='origin_index')
        index_model = indexer.fit(df)
    indexed = index_model.transform(df)
    encoder = OneHotEncoder(inputCol='origin_index',
                            outputCol='origin_onehot')
    return encoder.transform(indexed)
```

---

23 See *experiment.py* in *07_sparkml*.

```
traindata = add_categorical(traindata, train=True)
...
evaldata = add_categorical(evaldata)
```

This is bookkeeping to which we need to pay careful attention because doing this sort of thing incorrectly will result in training–serving skew. Spark provides a `Pipeline` mechanism to help you record which operations you carried out on the dataset so that you can repeat them when evaluating, but it introduces yet another level of abstraction into an already complex topic.

During prediction, things become even more complicated. No longer is it simply a matter of calling `lrmodel.predict()`. Instead, you will need to first construct a dataframe out of your raw input data, apply these transforms, and finally invoke the actual model.

Scalable, Repeatable, Real Time

A problem with one-hot encoding is the large quantity of input features it creates. Because there are about 300 distinct airports in our dataset,[24] the airport variable will now become about 300 separate features. If you are wondering why there was no RMSE stated in the last part of the previous section (after I added the one-hot encoded airports), it's because my program ran out of resources. The `flights` dataset is about 21 million rows with the training data being about 65% of it, or about 14 million rows, and we used only one categorical column with about 300 unique values. Yet, this brought down the machines. Real-world business datasets are larger. The "small clicks" Criteo (*http://bit.ly/2jnVxIa*) ads data used in a Kaggle competition and demonstrated in Cloud ML Engine, for example, is 45 million rows (the full ads dataset contains four billion rows). Nearly all of its columns are categorical and some of them have thousands of unique values.

One way of reducing the explosion of input features caused by one-hot encoding is to carry out dimensionality reduction. The idea is to pass in the one-hot encoded set and ask the machine learning algorithm itself to come up with weights to combine these columns into, say, four features that are used downstream in the model. This is called creating an *embedding*. This embedding model itself will be part of the full model, and so the embedding weights can be discovered at the same time. We look at creating embeddings in Chapter 9, when we discuss Tensorflow.

One of the side effects of having complex library code to carry out feature transformations is that it adds a dependency on the program that needs the predictions. That program needs to run Spark in order to carry out the one-hot encoding correctly—an

---

24 You can check, as I did, by running SELECT DISTINCT(ORIGIN) FROM flights.tzcorr on the BigQuery console.

extremely difficult situation if the program that actually uses the predictions runs on mobile phones or outside of your company's firewall. Building a realistic machine learning pipeline with Spark, as we have seen, requires a fair bit of tooling and framework building. It is easy to get started, but difficult to productionize. Cloud Machine Learning Engine, which we use in Chapters 9 and 10, resolves this problem by being able to deploy an autoscaling, low-latency prediction model that is accessed via a REST API.

Finally, we could improve the way we use taxi-out times. Flight arrival times are scheduled based on the average taxi-out time experienced at the departure airport at that specific hour. For example, at peak hours in New York's JFK airport, taxi-out times on the order of an hour are quite common; so, airlines take that into account when publishing their flight schedules. It is only when the taxi-out time exceeds the average that we ought to be worried. To augment the training dataset with an aggregate feature that is computed in real time like this, we will need the same code that processes batch data to also process streaming data in real time. One way to do this is to use Apache Beam. We do this in Chapters 8 and 10.

Summary

In this chapter, we took our first foray into machine learning using Apache Spark. Spark ML is an intuitive, easy-to-use package, and running Spark on Cloud Dataproc gives us the ability to quickly build machine learning models on moderately sized datasets.

We created a dataset using Spark SQL and discovered that there were problems with missing values for some of the columns. Rather than simply remove the missing data, though, we found the root cause to be canceled or diverted flights and removed such flights from the dataset. We employed logistic regression, a machine learning model that provides probabilistic outputs, to predict the probability that the flight will be on time. Setting the probability threshold at 0.70 allows us to make a decision as to whether to cancel a scheduled meeting that depends on us arriving at the airport within 15 minutes of the scheduled arrival time.

We carried out feature selection and feature engineering and explored categorical features. To choose the features systematically, we devised an experimental framework in which the training dataset itself was broken into two parts and the second part used to decide whether to keep the feature or transformation in question. We also discovered some pain points when building a production machine learning system on large datasets in Spark. Primarily, these had to do with the ability to deal with scale, of carrying out more complex models, of getting low-latency predictions outside of the development framework, and of being able to use features computed in real-time windows.

## CHAPTER 8

Time-Windowed Aggregate Features

In Chapter 7, we built a machine learning model but ran into problems when trying to scale it out and making it production ready. Briefly, here are the problems we encountered:

1. One-hot encoding categorical columns caused an explosion in the size of the dataset.

2. Embeddings would have involved separate training and bookkeeping.

3. Putting the model into production would have required the machine learning library in environments to which it is not portable.

4. Augmentation of the training dataset with streaming measures requires the same code to process both batch data and streaming data.

In the remaining three chapters of this book, we implement a real-time, streaming machine learning pipeline that avoids these issues by using Cloud Dataflow and Cloud ML (hosted versions of Apache Beam and Tensorflow, respectively).

The Need for Time Averages

In this chapter, we solve the issue of augmenting the dataset with *time-windowed* aggregate features. To do that, we will use Apache Beam to compute aggregate features on historical data, and then (in Chapter 10) we use that same code at prediction time to compute the same aggregate features in real time.

What time-windowed aggregate features did we want to use, but couldn't? Flight arrival times are scheduled based on the average taxi-out time experienced at the departure airport at that specific hour. For example, at peak hours in New York's JFK airport, taxi-out times on the order of an hour are quite common; so, airlines take that into account when publishing their flight schedules. It is only when the taxi-out time exceeds the average that we ought to be worried. Thus, we need to compute the average taxi-out times over the entire training dataset, and use that average as an input feature to the machine learning model.

In addition, we have an intuition that the average arrival delay being experienced at the destination airport will have an impact on whether we are likely to arrive on time. If there are weather delays at the destination, for example, subsequent flights will also be affected both because the weather delays might persist and because the number of runways might be limited. Unlike the average taxi-out time, this is something that needs to be computed in "real time." On historical data, we'd compute it over the hour previous to the departure time of the aircraft. In real time, this computation would be carried out over streaming data.

In both situations, we'd prefer to use the same code to compute the averages on batch data as to compute the averages on streaming data—using the same code allows us to mitigate training–serving skew that could be caused by use of different libraries or programming languages. Apache Beam, with its ability to handle both batch and streaming data, is what we can use to compute the average departure and arrival delays at each airport, where the average in question is over the entire training dataset for departure delay at the origin airport and over the past 60 minutes in the case of arrival delay at the destination airport.

In Chapter 4, we used Beam Python to move data from Pub/Sub to Cloud Storage and Beam Java to compute real-time averages that were used to drive a dashboard. In that chapter, we skimmed through Java syntax and focused more on visualization concepts. In this chapter, we remedy that by going through the mechanics of developing a Beam-on-Dataflow pipeline in more detail.

 For more details on Apache Beam, see Chapter 4.

The arrival delay average that we require here is the same as the arrival delay average that we computed in Chapter 4, but the treatment of departure delay is different. Can you think about why that is? Hint: it has to do with the use case of the departure delay.

In Chapter 4, we were simply driving a dashboard of the average departure delay at the airport, so as to perhaps inform travelers heading to the airport from the office what kinds of delays they can expect to encounter. However, in this chapter, we want to compute an input feature for machine learning to address a different decision. Recall that the problem statement for the machine learning model has the decision maker, the person who must decide whether to cancel the meeting, sitting in an aircraft at the origin airport, about to take off. That person already knows the departure delay of her flight—there is no need to incorporate the departure delays of other flights at that airport into the machine learning model. However, the machine learning model needs to compare the departure delay being encountered with the typical departure delay encountered at that hour historically—this will help us to determine whether this delay will have a schedule impact. On the other hand, she doesn't know her arrival delay—the typical arrival delay experienced at her destination is pertinent information for the machine learning model. The historical arrival delay experienced at the airport is probably unnecessary—if the airline schedulers are doing their job, the historical average ought to be 0 or negative.

Dataflow in Java

Cloud Dataflow is a fully managed service for executing data processing pipelines written using Apache Beam. What does "fully managed" mean? Think BigQuery instead of Cloud SQL. Both allow for SQL queries on the data, but where Cloud SQL was simply a hosted version of MySQL, BigQuery was totally serverless. This allowed for dramatically larger-scale, instantly available SQL processing with BigQuery.[1] Cloud Dataflow provides a similar, serverless, autoscaling service for programmatic data pipelines.

With Cloud Dataflow, unlike with Cloud Dataproc, we don't need to spin up a cluster in order to carry out data processing. Instead, we simply submit the code and it will be run and autoscaled to as many machines[2] as needed to accomplish the task effectively.[3] We will be charged for the amount of computational resources that our job involved.

The jobs that are submitted to Cloud Dataflow can be written in Java using the open source Apache Beam API.[4] Apologies in advance if you are not familiar with Java—however, the concepts here should still make sense and be relevant. It is worth learning to write Apache Beam pipelines in Java, though, simply because production data engineering code is often written in Java (or Scala), not Python. The performance and sandbox benefits of real-time code running in a Java Virtual Machine (JVM) are

---

1 Of course, Cloud SQL provides for transactions and BigQuery doesn't. The reasons you'd use the two products are different.

2 Within the limits of your Compute Engine quota.

3 The meaning of "effective" differs between batch and stream modes. Batch runners try to optimize overall execution time, whereas stream runners try to minimize latency.

4 As of this writing, the Python API for Cloud Dataflow doesn't support real-time streaming, so the Java API is my only choice here. However, for performance reasons, I would still recommend Java or Scala over Python when it comes to production-ready streaming pipelines.

immense. The only reason I have gotten away with writing so much of the code for this book in Python is that the libraries I used (numpy, Spark, Tensorflow, etc.) are backed by C/Java/C++ backends. Of course, by the time this book is in your hands, the Beam Python API might support streaming, and you might not want to learn Java. In that case, use Python.

Setting Up Development Environment

Developing Apache Beam code in Java is conveniently done within an integrated development environment (IDE) installed on your laptop. In a pinch, you could develop Java on the CloudShell virtual machine (VM) using the Orion code editor that is installed on it, but the experience is better with a Java IDE that has a rich graphical user interface.

First, install the Java 8 Software Development Kit (SDK) on your local machine. You can get it from *http://www.java.com/*, but make sure you get the SDK and not just the runtime environment. For developing Beam pipelines, you need only the Standard edition, not the Enterprise edition. Next, install Apache Maven, a Java build tool, from *http://maven.apache.org/*. If you typically program in Java using an integrated development environment, install your favorite editor. I installed Eclipse from *http://www.eclipse.org/*. There are a number of versions of Eclipse, but the plain-vanilla one targeting Java developers is sufficient for our purposes.

After you've installed Maven, you can use it to create a Cloud Dataflow project (the code you write will be Apache Beam, but you will run it on Cloud Dataflow). In a terminal window, invoke the Maven command (mvn) as follows:

```
mvn archetype:generate \
   -DarchetypeArtifactId=google-cloud-dataflow-java-archetypes-starter \
   -DarchetypeGroupId=com.google.cloud.dataflow \
   -DgroupId=com.google.cloud.datascienceongcp.flights \
   -DartifactId=chapter8 \
   -Dversion="[1.0.0,2.0.0]" \
   -DinteractiveMode=false
```

This creates a folder named *chapter8* on your local machine, a Java package named com.google.cloud.datascienceongcp.flights, and a class named StarterPipeline.java in that package (the non-bold parts of the code need to be specified as-is).

In addition, a Maven artifact called *pom.xml* is created in the *chapter8* directory. The Project Object Model (POM) that is described in *pom.xml* forms the fundamental unit of work in Maven. When you ask Maven to run a task or goal (compile, build, run, etc.), Maven looks at this XML file in the current directory for information about the project (such as the location of the source code and where to put the compiled code), configuration details used by Maven to build the project, and information about the goal that needs to be executed (such as the name of the Java class that contains the `main()` method). You can specify a variety of configuration settings in the POM, but we typically just inherit the default settings for the platform and override only things that are specific to our project.

Among the configuration settings specified in the POM is the version of Java to use. Although we can work with Java 1.7 (the default version of Java that Maven specifies), there is an advantage to using Java 1.8, especially with Apache Beam, because in Java 1.8, we can write lambda functions, and Java 1.8 can infer generic types. So, in the section on Maven plug-ins in the generated *pom.xml*, change the version of Java from 1.7 to 1.8 as follows:

```
<plugin>
    <groupId>org.apache.maven.plugins</groupId>
    <artifactId>maven-compiler-plugin</artifactId>
    <version>3.5.1</version>
    <configuration>
      <source>1.8</source>
      <target>1.8</target>
    </configuration>
</plugin>
```

Filtering with Beam

Most data pipelines process a data stream, selecting the data of interest and transforming it in some way. Choosing which data to continue processing is called *filtering*. Let's look at how we can filter the flight information using Apache Beam on Cloud Dataflow.

After you modify *pom.xml*, launch Eclipse and import this project by clicking File → Import → Maven → Existing Maven Projects. Browse to the *chapter8* folder, and then click Finish.

Finally, right-click StarterPipeline.java and then, on the shortcut menu that opens, point to Refactor and then click Rename. Give it the name `CreateTrainingData set.java` because that's what our pipeline is going to be doing—we are going to be creating a training dataset with the following features:

1. Departure delay, taxi-out time, and distance (as before).

2. The average departure delay at this airport at this hour over the entire dataset. The idea is that if this is New York's JFK airport at 6 PM, we can be more relaxed because the extra taxi-out time would have been accounted for by the airline already.

3. The average arrival delay currently being experienced at the arrival airport. The idea is that if a runway is closed at the arrival airport due to weather, and all flights are being delayed, we want to include it in our model.

The two new features that we are adding are aggregate features. In the case of average departure delay, the aggregate is a global one—we are averaging over the entire dataset. In the case of average arrival delay, the aggregate is over a sliding time window. For training purposes, we don't need to actually do the sliding time window to calculate average arrival delay, because we have all the data already,[5] but when we switch over to doing this in real time, that is the only way we can do it. Because we'd like to use the same code both when creating the training dataset and when predicting (in real time), we'll compute the second aggregate as a sliding time window.

It would be good to try out our data pipeline locally, on a small dataset, before we launch it on the complete dataset in the cloud. To do that, let's query the `simevents` table in BigQuery to get a small subset of the data:

```
#standardsql
SELECT
  EVENT_DATA
FROM
  flights.simevents
WHERE
  FL_DATE = '2015-09-20'AND (EVENT = 'wheelsoff'
    OR EVENT = 'arrived') AND UNIQUE_CARRIER = 'AA'
ORDER BY NOTIFY_TIME ASC
```

In this query, I am pulling messages (`EVENT_DATA`) from a single day (`2015-09-20`) in the same format as the messages that I will get from Pub/Sub in real time. Because of the `ORDER BY` clause, the messages will also be in the same order that I will get in real time (minus some amount of jumbling due to latencies). Ordering the data is not strictly necessary, as you will see later, but for now, the `ORDER BY` will ensure that the process we're following is repeatable. We will need the `wheelsoff` event to do predictions and the `arrived` events in order to carry out training (and to compute average arrival delays).

Using the BigQuery console, download the result set as a comma-separated value (CSV) file and note where it is. (I saved it in *$HOME/data/flights/small.csv*.)

Let's take the first three lines into the starter Beam pipeline and use it to try out the pipeline in-memory. First define an array of strings in Eclipse:

```
String[] events = {
    "2015-09-20,AA,...,wheelsoff,2015-09-20T04:22:00",
    "2015-09-20,AA,...,wheelsoff,2015-09-20T06:19:00",
    "2015-09-20,AA,...,wheelsoff,2015-09-20T06:47:00"
};
```

In Eclipse, change the input to be the events array

---

5 We could, for example, create a key that incorporates the airport-date-hour and do a global mean per key.

```
    p.apply(Create.of(events))
```

and then filter those lines in parallel using ParDo ("Parallel Do"):[6]

```
.apply(ParDo.of(new DoFn<String, String>() {
    @ProcessElement
    public void processElement(ProcessContext c) throws Exception {
        String input = c.element();
        if (input.contains("MIA")) {
            c.output(input);
        }
    }
}))
```

The filter implements the DoFn interface[7] and the two generic parameters refer to the input type (String) and the output type (String). Rather than create a new class to implement the DoFn, I use an anonymous inner class. The filter passes along only lines that have the text MIA in them.

Finally, let's take the resulting lines and send them to a log:

```
.apply(ParDo.of(new DoFn<String, Void>() {
    @ProcessElement
    public void processElement(ProcessContext c) {
        LOG.info(c.element());
    }
}));
```

To run this code in Eclipse, select Run → Run As → Java Application. The pipeline is run by a DirectRunner (an in-memory executor for Beam pipelines), and the results that are printed out match what I expect:

```
INFO: 2015-09-20,AA,19805,AA,2342,11292,1129202,30325,DEN,13303,1330303,32467,
MIA,2015-09-21T05:59:00,2015-09-20T06:33:00,34.00,14.00,2015-09-20T06:47:00,,,
2015-09-20T09:47:00,,,0.00,,,1709.00,39.86166667,-104.67305556,
-21600.0,25.79527778,-80.29000000,-14400.0,wheelsoff,2015-09-20T06:47:00
INFO: 2015-09-20,AA,19805,AA,1572,13303,1330303,32467,MIA,12889,1288903,32211,
LAS,2015-09-20T22:50:00,2015-09-20T04:03:00,313.00,19.00,2015-09-20T04:22:00,,,
2015-09-21T04:08:00,,,0.00,,,2174.00,25.79527778,-80.29000000,
-14400.0,36.08000000,-115.15222222,-25200.0,wheelsoff,2015-09-20T04:22:00
```

---

6 See *CreateTrainingDataset1.java* in *08_dataflow/chapter8/src*.

7 Technically, DoFn is not an interface. Instead, you write a method (it can have any name) and annotate it with @ProcessElement. What is a class with a required annotated method called? I find it easier to think of the DoFn as a Java interface with a method that I have to implement. To preserve your sanity, call this required method processElement(). The purpose of having an annotation rather than an abstract method is to allow for additional parameters—toward the end of this chapter, we will add an IntervalWindow parameter to have the appropriate window parameter automatically injected for us.

In the GitHub repository for this book, this file is named *CreateTrainingDataset1.java* —use it as the simplest example of a working Cloud Dataflow pipeline. Functionally, it simulates the Unix tool grep, reading some input and sending to its output only the lines that match a specific pattern.

This simple pipeline reads from in-memory strings and simply logs its output. Thus, it is an excellent way to try out a particular transform on some specific input (just change the strings appropriately) to ensure that the transform code works as intended. Also, this pipeline code can form the basis of unit tests.[8] Now that we have working code, let's improve it a bit.

Pipeline Options and Text I/O

Instead of reading from hardcoded strings and logging the output, we want to read and write to files. Rather than hardcode the names of the inputs and outputs, it would be better to be able to specify the input file and the output directory. To do that, I first create a MyOptions interface with getters and setters:

```
public static interface MyOptions extends PipelineOptions {
        @Description("Path of the file to read from")
        @Default.String("/Users/vlakshmanan/data/flights/small.csv")
        String getInput();
        void setInput(String s);

        @Description("Path of the output directory")
        @Default.String("/tmp/output/")
        String getOutput();
        void setOutput(String s);
}
```

The default values are values that work on my system, so that running the program with no command-line options will yield reasonable behavior (of reading *small.csv* and writing to */tmp/output*). However, by passing in command-line parameters to the program, we can change the input and output locations. We can accomplish this by telling the PipelineOptionsFactory about MyOptions so that it can examine the getter and setter methods on the class to decide which command-line parameters to extract:

```
MyOptions options =
  PipelineOptionsFactory.fromArgs(args).withValidation()
    .as(MyOptions.class);
```

---

8 Yes, I am aware that I have not shown you unit tests for any of the code in this book. In production code, I would have unit tests. This book, however, is about explaining stuff, and I've found that unit tests are a bit confusing to learn from. Hence, my use of main() methods instead of unit tests.

Instead of reading from an in-memory array of strings, we now read from the specified input text file

```
.apply(TextIO.Read.from(options.getInput()))
```

and write to a single (unsharded[9]) file in the desired output directory:

```
.apply(TextIO.Write.to(options.getOutput() + "flights2") //
        .withSuffix(".txt").withoutSharding());
```

In addition, we supply a name to the various steps, which is a good practice because it allows us to monitor jobs more effectively and update a streaming Cloud Dataflow pipeline.[10] The complete pipeline now becomes as follows:

```
p //
    .apply("ReadLines", TextIO.Read.from(options.getInput())) //
    .apply("FilterMIA", ParDo.of(new DoFn<String, String>() {
        @ProcessElement
        public void processElement(ProcessContext c) {
String input = c.element();
if (input.contains("MIA")) {
        c.output(input);
    }
}})) //
.apply("WriteFlights", //
        TextIO.Write.to(options.getOutput() + "flights2") //
            .withSuffix(".txt").withoutSharding());
```

Try running the code[11] from Eclipse to make sure that the file is read and all flights to/from Miami (MIA) are written out.

To summarize, we now have an Apache Beam pipeline running on our local machine that reads flight information from file, applies a filter (flights to/from MIA in this case), and writes the data to a file.

Run on Cloud

Of course, the point of Cloud Dataflow is to scale out a data pipeline and have it run on the cloud. To do that, let's copy our input text file to our Cloud Storage bucket:

---

9 Writing unsharded data is not usually recommended because it forces all writing work to be carried out by a single worker. Unless you know that the output data is small enough that a single worker is sufficient, you should write to sharded output files. In our final pipeline, we will write out the average departure delay at an airport hour as a single file (there will be only a few thousand of these), but shard the output flight information into many files (given that there will be many millions of flights).

10 See *https://cloud.google.com/dataflow/pipelines/updating-a-pipeline*—to update a running Cloud Dataflow pipeline (i.e., replace pipeline code while keeping intermediate outputs intact), transforms are matched by name.

11 See *CreateTrainingDataset2.java* in the GitHub repository.

```
gsutil cp ~/data/flights/small.csv \
      gs://cloud-training-demos-ml/flights/chapter8/small.csv
```

Now that our input data is on Cloud Storage, running the pipeline is as simple as running a Maven command from the directory that contains *pom.xml* to submit the Cloud Dataflow job:

```
mvn compile exec:java \
 -Dexec.mainClass=com.google.cloud.training.flights.CreateTrainingDataset2 \
      -Dexec.args="--project=cloud-training-demos \
      --stagingLocation=gs://cloud-training-demos-ml/staging/ \
      --input=gs://cloud-training-demos-ml/flights/chapter8/small.csv \
      --output=gs://cloud-training-demos/flights/chapter8/output/ \
      --runner=DataflowRunner"
```

If you are following along, you should (of course) use your own project and bucket.

At this point, we can go to the Cloud Dataflow section of the GCP console (*http:// console.cloud.google.com/dataflow*), verify that we have a job running, and monitor the job. We can see the names that we gave to the individual steps reflected in the pipeline, as shown in Figure 8-1.

Figure 8-1. Dataflow pipeline as depicted in the Google Cloud Platform web console

A couple of minutes later, the pipeline finishes running and we have a *flights2.txt* file in the Cloud Storage bucket. This contains all the flights to or from MIA by American Airlines on the selected date. Of course, we don't need to filter on a hardcoded string

("MIA"); instead, we can get it from the command line. However, let's leave that alone because we don't really need to filter by a specific airport—that was just so that you could see the basics of what a Cloud Dataflow pipeline looks like.

Unlike with Spark on Cloud Dataproc, we did not need to spin up a cluster to execute Beam on Cloud Dataflow. We just submitted the Apache Beam pipeline and Cloud Dataflow took care of all the execution details. As easy as Cloud Dataproc makes cluster creation and resizing, cluster management is one task that we can happily give up.

We have now seen how to create an Apache Beam data pipeline and deploy it using Cloud Dataflow. In the next section, we will see how to compute the aggregated features of interest (historic departure delay and current arrival delay).

Parsing into Objects

What I really want to do is to figure out the average delay associated with every airport at every hour of day. In other words, we want to group flights by [airport:hour] and then compute the average departure delay associated with each key.

To do that, we need to parse each line and pull out relevant pieces of data. Rather than trying to remember that fields[22] is the ARR_DELAY, let's try to isolate the parsing code from the code that actually operates on the data. So, the first thing to do is to create a Java class to hold the flight data that will be read in and the information that will be calculated:

```java
public class Flight {
  private enum INPUTCOLS {
    FL_DATE, UNIQUE_CARRIER, ... NOTIFY_TIME;
  }

  private String[] fields;
  private float    avgDepartureDelay, avgArrivalDelay;

  public static Flight fromCsv(String line) {
    Flight f = new Flight();
    f.fields = line.split(",");
    f.avgArrivalDelay = f.avgDepartureDelay = Float.NaN;
    if (f.fields.length == INPUTCOLS.values().length) {
      return f;
    }
    return null; // malformed
  }
}
```

In addition, the class has a method to parse a line of the CSV input into a Flight object. For now, we'll leave the two average delays as NaN—that data is not simply parsed from the line. Instead, we'll need to compute it.

The next iteration of our pipeline[12] will have to do the following. Ignoring the Java boilerplate, Table 8-1 lists the relevant code.

Table 8-1. Pipeline code to parse the CSV files and write out a machine learning dataset with the necessary input variables and labels

Transform	Description	Code
ReadLines	Read the input line-by-line.	`TextIO.Read.from(options.getInput())`

ParseFlights	Invoke the `fromCsv()` method above to create a `Flight` object from each line.	`String line = c.element();`
		`Flight f = Flight.fromCsv(line);`
		`if (f != null){`
		`    c.output(f);`
		`}`

GoodFlights	Filter the flights using the same quality control we carried out in Chapter 7 to discard diverted and canceled ones.	`Flight f = c.element();`
		`if (f.isNotCancelled()`
		`    && f.isNotDiverted()) {`
		`    c.output(f);`
		`}`

ToCsv	Create a training row consisting of the features we want to use for machine learning, and the label (on-time or not).	`Flight f = c.element();`
		`if (f.getField(INPUTCOLS.EVENT).`
		`                equals("arrived")) {`
		`    c.output(f.toTrainingCsv());`
		`}`

WriteFlights	Write out the dataset.	`TextIO.Write`
		`.to(options.getOutput() +`
		`                "flights3")`
		`.withSuffix(".csv").withoutSharding()`

The code in Table 8-1 uses a few more methods that we need to implement in the `Flight` class. For example, here's the `isNotDiverted()` method:

```
public boolean isNotDiverted() {
    return fields[INPUTCOLS.DIVERTED.ordinal()]
        .equals("0.00");
}
```

Getting the input features involves pulling the relevant inputs, and adding in the computed variables:

```
public float[] getInputFeatures() {
    float[] result = new float[5];
    int col = 0;
    result[col++] = Float
        .parseFloat(fields[INPUTCOLS.DEP_DELAY.ordinal()]);
    result[col++] = Float
        .parseFloat(fields[INPUTCOLS.TAXI_OUT.ordinal()]);
```

---

12 See *CreateTrainingDataset3.java* in the GitHub repository.

```
    result[col++] = Float
        .parseFloat(fields[INPUTCOLS.DISTANCE.ordinal()]);
    result[col++] = avgDepartureDelay;
    result[col++] = avgArrivalDelay;
    return result;
}
```

After we have input features for training, creating a CSV file to write out a training dataset is quite straightforward. We need to get the true arrival delay from the input data, and use it to compute the on-time label. Then, we write out a CSV file with the label as the first field:

```
public String toTrainingCsv() {
    float[] features = this.getInputFeatures();
    float arrivalDelay = Float
        .parseFloat(fields[INPUTCOLS.ARR_DELAY.ordinal()]);
    boolean ontime = arrivalDelay < 15;
    StringBuilder sb = new StringBuilder();
    sb.append(ontime ? 1.0 : 0.0);
    sb.append(",");
    for (int i = 0; i < features.length; ++i) {
      sb.append(features[i]);
      sb.append(",");
    }
    sb.deleteCharAt(sb.length() - 1); // last comma
    return sb.toString();
}
```

Of course, we can know the arrival delay only after the flight has arrived, so we ensure that we are calling this method only on arrived events. At this point, we should have a working pipeline, so we can try to run it by using Run → Run As → Java Application or, in Eclipse, by clicking the green arrow bar.

We get an error because Cloud Dataflow doesn't know the format in which we want Flight moved around between pipelines—the error is quite informative and tells us exactly what we need to do. Of the options listed, I like the one of specifying a default coder—we could specify Avro (*https://avro.apache.org/*), a data serialization system that is more efficient than Java's native serialization mechanism, by simply adding (to the definition of the Flight class) the following:

```
@DefaultCoder(AvroCoder.class)
public class Flight {
```

Now, the pipeline executes without incident, and we get output that looks like this:

```
1.0,-3.0,7.0,255.0,NaN,NaN
1.0,-6.0,9.0,405.0,NaN,NaN
0.0,30.0,18.0,2615.0,NaN,NaN
```

Some of the flights are on time (first field is `1.0`) and some are delayed (first field is `0.0`). The average arrival and departure delays are `NaN` because we haven't computed them yet. Let's do that next.[13]

Computing Time Averages

Now that we have the skeleton of the Beam pipeline in place, let's implement the code to compute the two average delays of interest. Recall that the two averages are computed differently—the average departure delay is the average departure delay experienced by aircraft at this hour at this airport over the entire training dataset, whereas the average arrival delay is the average arrival delay experienced by aircraft over the previous hour. One is a historical average and the other is a moving average.

Grouping and Combining

One of the advantages of Cloud Dataflow's pipeline model is that we can do multiple things with the parallel collections that are returned from the `apply()` methods—all that we need to do is save the results as variables and reuse those variables:

```
PCollection<Flight> flights = p //
        .apply("ReadLines", TextIO.Read.from(options.getInput()));
flights.apply("operation1", …
flights.apply("operation2", …
```

Between the parsing and the writing, let's compute the average delay (departure-delay + taxi-out time) for each airport-hour combination across the entire dataset. To do that, we first need to emit in the `ParDo` (this is the map operation of a MapReduce) the key and the value corresponding to each `Flight`:

- Key: airport + hour (e.g., JFK at hour 18)
- Value: (departure-delay + taxi-out time)

The hour itself needs to be the hour in local time so that we correctly account for daylight savings corrections (the reasons are discussed in Chapters 4 and 7). Also, to avoid double-counting, we should compute this only for the `wheelsoff` events.[14]

The input of the `DoFn` is a `Flight` and the output is a key-value pair (KV):

```
PCollection<KV<String, Double>> delays =
  flights.apply("airport:hour",
      ParDo.of(new DoFn<Flight, KV<String, Double>>() {
```

---

13 This code is in GitHub as *CreateTrainingDataset3.java*.

14 Well, it's a mean that we are computing, so it's not really a problem if we include the `arrived` events also. But it's better to do it right. We might want to compute something else in the future.

```
@ProcessElement
    public void processElement(ProcessContext c)
        throws Exception {
      Flight f = c.element();
   if (f.getField(Flight.INPUTCOLS.EVENT)
        .equals("wheelsoff")) {
        String key = f.getField(ORIGIN) + ":" +
              f.getDepartureHour();
        double value = f.getFieldAsFloat(DEP_DELAY) +
              f.getFieldAsFloat(TAXI_OUT);
        c.output(KV.of(key, value));
    }
        }
}));
```

Let's write this out to make sure it is what we want:

```
delays.apply("DelayToCsv",
    ParDo.of(new DoFn<KV<String, Double>, String>() {
    @Override
    public void processElement(ProcessContext c) throws Exception {
        KV<String, Double> kv = c.element();
        c.output(kv.getKey() + "," + kv.getValue());
    }
})) //
.apply("WriteDelays",
      TextIO.Write.to(options.getOutput() +
            "delays4").withSuffix(".csv").withoutSharding()
);
```

As expected, we get a list of airports and hours followed by the departure delay. Each line corresponds to a flight:

```
ATL:15,57.0
STL:7,12.0
HNL:21,25.0
SFO:8,9.0
ATL:16,9.0
JFK:19,28.0
```

Instead of writing out the individual flight delays, let's add an operation to compute the mean delay for each airport hour:

```
PCollection<KV<String, Double>> delays =
    flights.apply("airport:hour", … ) // as before
        .apply(Mean.perKey());
```

Now, when you run the code, you get the mean departure delay per airport hour—that is, one value per key:

```
SFO:9,22.0
PDX:10,7.0
MIA:18,14.6
```

This code is in GitHub as *CreateTrainingDataset4.java*. Later in this chapter, we compute a time average using windowing, but here we have simply computed an average for each hour over all such hours in the year. Had I wanted an hourly average (a different number for each hour on each day), I'd have used windows.

Our grouping and combining code, however, has a subtle error. When we compute the average delays, we need to ensure that we are computing those delays only on flights that are part of the training dataset. We should not use the independent test days in our computation of average departure delay! Let's do that next.

Parallel Do with Side Input

To restrict the parsed flights to be only those flights on training days, we need to read *trainday.csv* and filter the event data to retain only those days that have is_train_day=True in *trainday.csv*.

A View in Cloud Dataflow provides an immutable view of a parallel collection (PCollection) that is cached in memory and can be used as a side input in a ParDo. This is exactly what we want. There are two options for Views—as Lists and as Maps (no Sets). Because we want a fast search, we load up *trainday.csv* into a View of a Map where the key is the date and the value can be ignored:

```
PCollectionView<Map<String, String>> traindays =
        getTrainDays(p, "gs://.../trainday.csv"); // FIXME
```

The FIXME is because we don't want to hardcode the path to the CSV file. Instead, we'll get it from the command-line options.

```
Let's write getTrainDays() first. First, we read the dataset line by line:
p.apply("Read trainday.csv", TextIO.Read.from(path))
```

Then, we parse each line and add emit only for days for which the second field is True:

```
.apply("Parse trainday.csv",
  ParDo.of(new DoFn<String, KV<String, String>>() {
    @Override
public void processElement(ProcessContext c) throws Exception {
        String line = c.element();
        String[] fields = line.split(",");
        if (fields.length > 1 && "True".equals(fields[1])) {
            c.output(KV.of(fields[0], "")); // ignore value
        }
    }
}))
```

Finally, we convert the PCollection of key-value pairs to an in-memory cached view:

```
.apply("toView", View.asMap());
```

We can also go back and take care of the FIXME by getting the path to *trainday.csv* from the command line. You do this by adding a property in MyOptions

```
@Description("Path of trainday.csv")
@Default.String("gs://cloud-training-demos/flights/trainday.csv")
String getTraindayCsvPath();
void setTraindayCsvPath(String s);
```

and using that property in TextIO.Read:

```
getTrainDays(p, options.getTraindayCsvPath());
```

How is the View that is created in this manner used? The name, *side input*, gives us a hint. This is an additional input to the main input being processed in the pipeline (the PCollection of flights). Because the primary PCollection is passed from one transform to the next implicitly by means of the apply() methods, we need to inform the transform that there is an additional input that it needs to marshal and distribute to all the workers. Our View of traindays is passed as a side input to a filter in the pipeline so that it can be used to determine whether to use the flight in training. To do that, let's add a new transform:[15]

```
.apply("TrainOnly", ParDo.withSideInputs(traindays)
        .of(new DoFn<Flight, Flight>() {
          @ProcessElement
          public void processElement(ProcessContext c)
              throws Exception {
            Flight f = c.element();
            String date = f.getField(Flight.INPUTCOLS.FL_DATE);
            boolean isTrainDay =
                    c.sideInput(traindays).containsKey(date);
            if (!isTrainDay) {
              c.output(f);
            }
          }
      })) //
```

Note that the c.sideInput() function needs the traindays object, so that multiple side inputs can be disambiguated.

Debugging

So, now, flights on nontraining days should be getting excluded from the output CSV files and the averages should be computed only for the training days. On running the program, though, we discover that all the output files are empty. What is going on?

---

15 This is *CreateTrainingDataset5.java* in the GitHub repository.

To debug a Cloud Dataflow pipeline, it is better to replace the input CSV file by specific inputs that we can hand-tune. So, let's pull out three lines out of our input file, taking care to include both `wheelsoff` and `arrived` events:

```
String[] events = {
    "2015-09-20,AA,19805,...,wheelsoff,2015-09-20T04:22:00",
    "2015-09-20,AA,19805,...,wheelsoff,2015-09-20T06:19:00",
    "2015-09-20,AA,19805,...,arrived,2015-09-20T09:15:00" };
```

We can change the pipeline input:

```
.apply("ReadLines",
        // TextIO.Read.from(options.getInput())) //
        Create.of(events)) //
```

With just these three lines as input, we can use the debugger in Eclipse, shown in Figure 8-2, to find out what is going on.

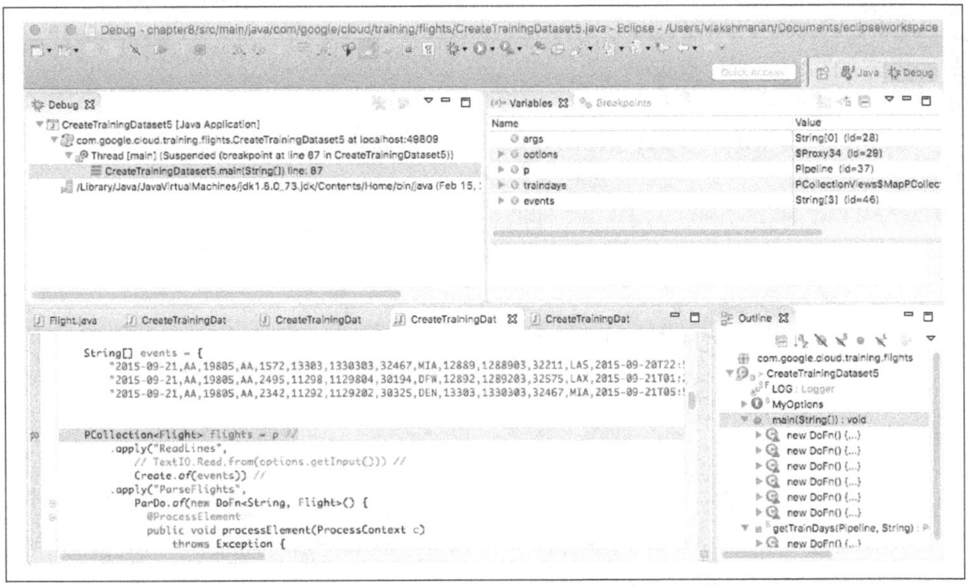

Figure 8-2. Using the debugger in Eclipse to see why delays are empty

On stepping through the pipeline, you can see that the delays are empty because the day we happened to pick in our query to create the small dataset (`2015-09-20`) is not a training day. Consequently, we need to change the input from that one day to a few days.

For now, we can simply modify the date of the input strings to verify that the pipeline would work with dates that are training days:

```
String[] events = {
    "2015-09-21,AA,19805,...,wheelsoff,2015-09-20T04:22:00",
```

```
"2015-09-21,AA,19805,...,wheelsoff,2015-09-20T06:19:00",
"2015-09-21,AA,19805,...,arrived,2015-09-20T09:15:00" };
```

This works, and yields a flights and delay CSV file as expected. How do we move forward, though? Obviously, our original query was flawed, and we need to change the BigQuery query to a different set of days (that includes both training and evaluation days) and use that result set moving forward.

BigQueryIO

Instead of downloading a new CSV file from BigQuery, let's have Cloud Dataflow execute a query and process the result set. This is as simple as changing the input from

```
.apply("ReadLines", TextIO.Read.from(options.getInput())
```

to:

```
String query = "SELECT EVENT_DATA FROM flights.simevents "
    + " WHERE STRING(FL_DATE) < '2015-01-04' AND (EVENT = 'wheelsoff' "
    + " OR EVENT = 'arrived') AND UNIQUE_CARRIER = 'AA' ";

    ...

    .apply("ReadLines", BigQueryIO.Read.fromQuery(query)) //
```

To work with potentially large queries and tables, Cloud Dataflow requires that we specify a temporary location when using BigQueryIO; for now, let's simply hardcode it:

```
options.setTempLocation("gs://cloud-training-demos-ml/flights/staging");
```

The result is as expected. For example, here are some of the delays:

```
PDX:15,7.0
PHX:2,24.0
PHX:1,11.0
MIA:14,35.2
SJU:1,318.0
PHX:7,30.0
```

You might have noticed something quite interesting—this query doesn't include an ORDER BY clause. Yet we are going to be applying sliding windows to the data. Could this possibly work? Writing this book has been a learning exercise as much as it is a teaching one, and one of the lessons I learned was by making the mistake of including an ORDER BY clause here.[16] Having the ORDER BY here, for three days of data, works, but if we were to change the number of days to be, say, a month, we would begin getting "Resources exceeded" errors from BigQuery. The reason is that the ORDER BY will

---

16 To chuckle at the mistakes that I made in the course of writing this book, look at the history in the GitHub repository of the code.

be run on a single BigQuery worker node (because an ORDER BY operation is inherently not parallelizable[17]), and that worker node's resources are insufficient to sort all of the data. Removing the ORDER BY helps to keep BigQuery performing like a champ. But how does Cloud Dataflow correctly handle time windows on unordered data? The way Cloud Dataflow implements a time window is not, as I initially imagined, by triggering an operation as soon as timestamp is crossed. Instead, Cloud Dataflow uses the event time, system time, and attributes such as allowed lateness and whether to (re-)trigger on late arriving records to restrict the records used within a group-by-key to a time window. Therefore, there is no requirement that the input data be ordered in any way. What BigQuery taketh, Cloud Dataflow giveth back—this is one of the benefits of using an integrated end-to-end data science platform.

There are two issues still remaining:[18]

- Running the program takes an extremely long time. The query itself is quite fast, as we can verify on the BigQuery console, so what's going on? Right now, I am running the Beam pipeline using DirectRunner. Therefore, the data from BigQuery is traveling over the public internet (slow network speed) to my laptop, and then executed on my laptop (not distributed). We will need to move the pipeline off to GCP and run it on Cloud Dataflow.

- The delays output is fine, but the flights output is not. The average delays are still NaN: 0.0,211.0,12.0,1045.0,NaN,NaN0.0,199.0,10.0,334.0,NaN,NaN. We don't have the information for arrival delays, but we do know the departure delay. So, for each flight, we can add in the average departure delay for that airport at that hour. This is a small change, so let's do it next.

Mutating the Flight Object

For faster development, let's go back to our strings input (instead of BigQuery) and add a transform to add delay information to the Flight objects being processed.

As a first cut, let's try simply setting the average (expected) departure delay based on the flight schedule information. We need to create a View of the average delay information to use a side input and then look up the airport hour's delay from the flights pipeline:

---

17 The solution (if you run into resources exceeded on an ORDER BY) is typically, as here, to realize that the ORDER BY is not even needed—often what you want are the top 10 results. Add a LIMIT 10, and the entire result set doesn't need to be sorted. Another solution is to group your data and order within each group (the GROUP BY adds parallelism). A third solution is to partition your table and order within partitions (here, too, the table partition adds parallelism). Long story short: provide a way for BigQuery to parallelize your query execution.

18 See *CreateTrainingDataset6.java* in the GitHub repository.

```
PCollectionView<Map<String, Double>> avgDelay =
    delays.apply(View.asMap());
flights = flights.apply("AddDelayInfo",
    ParDo.withSideInputs(avgDelay).of(new DoFn<Flight, Flight>() {
    @ProcessElement
    public void processElement(ProcessContext c) throws Exception {
        Flight f = c.element();
            String key = f.fromAirport + ":" + f.depHour;
            double delay = c.sideInput(avgDelay).get(key);
            f.avgDepartureDelay = delay;
            c.output(f);
        }
}));
```

Running this, though, we run into an `IllegalMutationException`—it turns out that because of the parallel and rescheduling nature of Beam, we cannot change the objects that are passed into a `ParDo`. Instead, we need to create a new `Flight` object and set the `avgDepartureDelay` on that new object.

Default copy constructors don't exist in Java, so we must create our own in `Flight.java`:

```
public Flight newCopy() {
    Flight f = new Flight();
    f.fields = Arrays.copyOf(this.fields, this.fields.length);
    f.avgArrivalDelay = this.avgArrivalDelay;
    f.avgDepartureDelay = this.avgDepartureDelay;
    return f;
}
```

We can then change

```
Flight f = c.element();
```

to:

```
Flight f = c.element().newCopy();
```

We now can go our merry way. Mutations like these that create an entirely new `PCollection` are computationally expensive, though, so we should minimize how often we do them.

We now can run the pipeline and look at the resulting output:[19]

```
0.0,279.0,15.0,1235.0,294.0,NaN
```

Each line now includes the average departure delay.

---

19 See *CreateTrainingDataset7.java* in the GitHub repository.

Sliding Window Computation in Batch Mode

In addition to the average departure delay, we need to also compute and add in the average arrival delay to the dataset. However, the arrival delay is computed differently from the departure delay. The arrival delay is the delay experienced over the previous hour at the airport that we are flying to—this will help us account for weather delays, runway closures, and the like. It is not a historical average over the entire dataset, just the average over the previous hour.

Computing the average arrival delay requires a sliding window over time. In real-time processing, Pub/Sub assigns a timestamp to every message that is received so that stream processing (as we do in Chapter 4) implicitly works with SlidingWindow. When creating the training dataset, however, we are processing historical batch data. What's needed to compute the sliding window is not the time at which the record was read, but the timestamp that is encoded in the data.

So, the first thing is to assign a timestamp to the record when we read it:

```
Flight f = Flight.fromCsv(line);
if (f != null) {
    c.outputWithTimestamp(f, f.getEventTimestamp());
}
```

Getting the timestamp involves time parsing in Java:

```
public Instant getEventTimestamp() {
    String timestamp = getField(INPUTCOLS.NOTIFY_TIME)
                            .replace('T', ' ');
    DateTime dt = fmt.parseDateTime(timestamp);
    return dt.toInstant();
}
```

Next, we can apply a sliding window on the flights pipeline after reading the flights and before any aggregate computation steps:

```
PCollection<Flight> lastHourFlights = //
    flights.apply(Window.into(SlidingWindows//
        .of(Duration.standardHours(1))//
        .every(Duration.standardMinutes(5))));
```

Note that we will have two PCollections—one (flights) is a global collection and is the one on which we will compute average departure delays. The other, lastHour Flights, is a time-windowed collection and is the one on which we will compute average arrival delays. The computation of average departure delay remains the same as before, but we now add a new transform:

```
PCollection<KV<String, Double>> arrDelays = lastHourFlights
    .apply("airport->arrdelay",
    ParDo.of(new DoFn<Flight, KV<String, Double>>() {
        @ProcessElement
        public void processElement(ProcessContext c) throws Exception {
```

```
        Flight f = c.element();
        if (f.getField(Flight.INPUTCOLS.EVENT).equals("arrived")) {
          String key = f.getField(Flight.INPUTCOLS.DEST);
          double value = f.getFieldAsFloat(Flight.INPUTCOLS.ARR_DELAY);
          c.output(KV.of(key, value));
        }
      }

    })) //
    .apply("avgArrDelay", Mean.perKey());
```

In this code, for every flight, we are emitting the destination airport (key) and the arrival delay of the flight (the value) and then computing the mean-per-key similar to the way we did the departure delay. Unlike the departure delay, though, the mean here is not a global mean. Instead, the `Mean.perKey` is computed within each time window. Also, our keys and values are different. The key is the destination airport (no hour, since it is implied in the `PCollection`), and the value is the arrival delay.

As before, we form a side input for the average arrival delay:

```
PCollectionView<Map<String, Double>> avgArrDelay =
    arrDelays.apply("arrdelay->map", View.asMap());
```

Finally, we add in the average arrival time for each flight:

```
String arrKey = f.getField(Flight.INPUTCOLS.DEST);
Double arrDelay = c.sideInput(avgArrDelay).get(arrKey);
f.avgArrivalDelay = (float) ((arrDelay == null) ? 0 : arrDelay);
```

Finally, because our code to add the delay info needs the departure delay (available from the PCollection in the global window) and the arrival delay (available hourly), it needs to be applied on a `PCollection` that is more frequent; that is to the last hour of flights:

```
lastHourFlights.apply("AddDelayInfo", …)
```

Running this, we get both departure and arrival delays:

```
0.0,279.0,15.0,1235.0,294.0,260.0
0.0,279.0,15.0,1235.0,294.0,260.0
0.0,279.0,15.0,1235.0,294.0,260.0
```

The complete pipeline is in GitHub in *08_dataflow/CreatingTrainingDataset8.java*—please read through the code and correlate each transform with its purpose discussed in the chapter thus far.

Running in the Cloud

Now that we have fully working code, we can run it in the cloud on all the event files and create a training dataset for machine learning. To do that, let's change the runner to `DataflowRunner`, change the input back to BigQuery, replace the `getInput()`

parameter with a Boolean parameter for whether we want to process the entire data-set or just a small part of it, and make the default output directory be on Cloud Storage.

Here is the new command-line option:

```
@Description("Should we process the full dataset?")
@Default.Boolean(false)
boolean getFullDataset();
void setFullDataset(boolean b);
```

And here are the runner options:

```
options.setRunner(DataflowRunner.class);
options.setTempLocation(
        "gs://cloud-training-demos-ml/flights/staging");
```

The query now becomes the following:

```
String query = "SELECT EVENT_DATA FROM flights.simevents WHERE ";
if (!options.getFullDataset()) {
  query += " STRING(FL_DATE) < '2015-01-04' AND ";
}
query += " (EVENT = 'wheelsoff' OR EVENT = 'arrived') ";
LOG.info(query);
```

In addition to computing the delays for just the training days, we can refactor the pipeline to also carry out computations on the test days. Both training and test CSV files can be written out from the same pipeline.

By default, the DataflowRunner just submits the job. It doesn't wait for the job to finish. So, let's have it block on a small dataset, and exit after submitting the job on the full dataset:[20]

```
PipelineResult result = p.run();
if (!options.getFullDataset()) {
  // for small datasets, block
  result.waitUntilFinish();
}
```

We now can run this class as a Java application from within Eclipse to execute the pipeline on Google Cloud Platform on a small dataset. The job will take a couple of minutes to get prepared and launch, but it will then run in the cloud. It takes about 10 minutes and produces three outputs:

---

20 See *CreateTrainingDataset9.java* in the GitHub repository.

- A *delays.csv* that contains the historical departure delay for every airport-hour combination.
- A *train.csv* (sharded) that contains the flights data corresponding to traindays.
- A *test.csv* (sharded) that contains the flights data corresponding to testdays.

Before we turn the program loose on the complete dataset—it is going to take a long time to run—let's look ahead a little bit and add more information about each flight as new features for the model to train on. This is all potentially useful information for a machine learning model. We therefore modify the `toTrainingCsv()` method in *Flight.java* to include the following lines:

```
INPUTCOLS[] stringFeatures = {INPUTCOLS.UNIQUE_CARRIER,
        INPUTCOLS.DEP_AIRPORT_LAT, INPUTCOLS.DEP_AIRPORT_LON,
        INPUTCOLS.ARR_AIRPORT_LAT, INPUTCOLS.ARR_AIRPORT_LON,
        INPUTCOLS.ORIGIN, INPUTCOLS.DEST};
for (INPUTCOLS col : stringFeatures) {
    sb.append(fields[col.ordinal()]);
    sb.append(",");
}
```

We can launch the full data pipeline off in the cloud on the full dataset using Maven:[21]

```
mvn compile exec:java \
-Dexec.mainClass=com.google.cloud.training.flights.CreateTrainingDataset9 \
-Dexec.args="--fullDataset --maxNumWorkers=50 \
--autoscalingAlgorithm=THROUGHPUT_BASED"
```

Monitoring, Troubleshooting, and Performance Tuning

We can monitor the progress of the job step by step at *http://console.cloud.google.com/ dataflow* via a nice execution graph, as illustrated in Figure 8-3.

As the graph indicates, this is a complex and unusual pipeline because of the mix of global and moving average time windows. For even the first flight information to be written, the complete dataset needs to be traversed so that the average departure delay by hour is available. The actual writing, however, needs up-to-the-minute arrival delays. At runtime, therefore, this pipeline requires caching of data in temporary storage.

---

21 Change the number of workers according to what your Compute Engine quota allows. You can find your quota in Compute Engine → Quota on the Google Cloud Platform web console. The quota is just a soft limit —you can request for it to be increased.

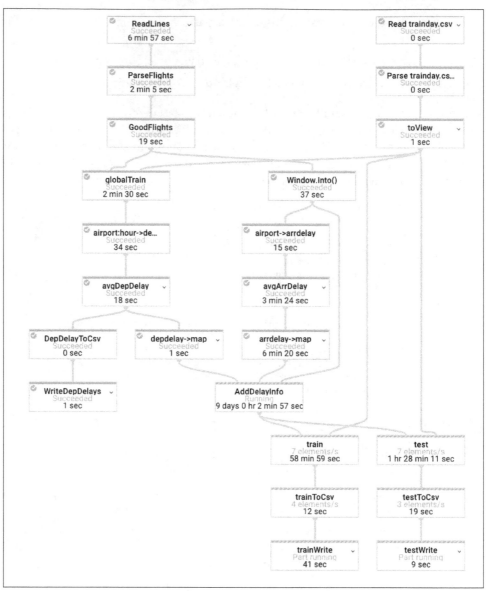

Figure 8-3. The complete pipeline includes information, such as the time taken and the rate at which elements are being processed, to help us monitor the job

Troubleshooting Pipeline

Cloud Dataflow handles all this complexity transparently. However, the pipeline is proceeding rather slowly—note that in the final stage, only three to four elements are being written out per second. At this rate, the 70 million flights will take more than a month to write out! Something's wrong.

Clicking any box in the diagram in Figure 8-3 shows you information about that step. For example, Figure 8-4 depicts the information I got by clicking `DepDelayToCsv`.

DepDelayToCsv
    Total Execution Time 🔵   0 sec
    Transform Function   com.google.cloud.training.flights.CreateTrainingDataset9$2

Input Collections

avgDepDelay/Combine.GroupedValues.out
    Elements Added 🔵   6,994
    Estimated Size 🔵   239.05 KB

Output Collections

DepDelayToCsv.out
    Elements Added 🔵   6,994
    Estimated Size 🔵   232.22 KB

Figure 8-4. Information about a single step includes the number of elements input to the step and output from the step

This indicates that there are 6,994 unique airport-hour pairs in the data.

The time shown within each of the boxes indicates that it is the `AddDelayInfo` step that is the bottleneck—note that the steps before that point all succeeded in a matter of minutes (that is CPU-seconds, so it is the total time taken by all the workers).

The summary on the right in Figure 8-5 provides information about the pipeline options, overall time, and the history of the autoscaling.

The autoscaling seems to be working, but Cloud Dataflow is not using the maximum number of workers that we allowed the job to use. There is something about the pipeline that is limiting the parallelism that can be achieved.

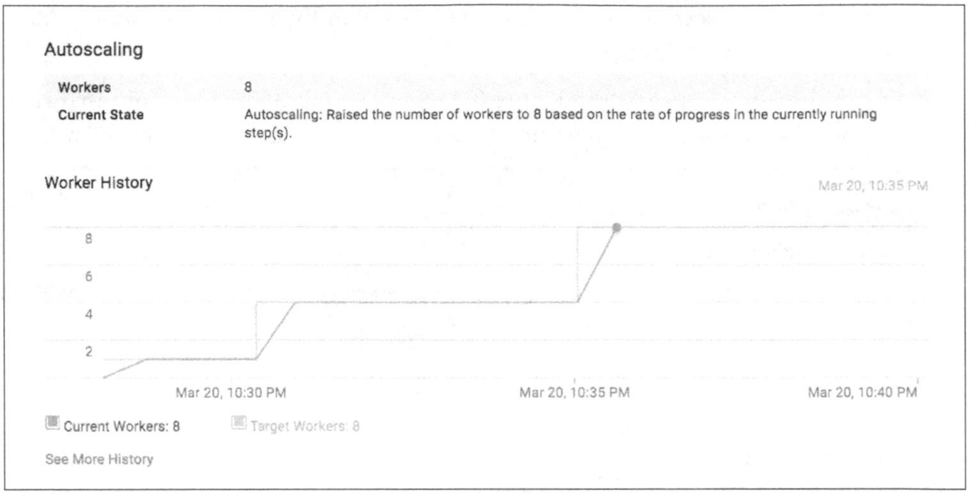

Figure 8-5. Autoscaling the pipeline

Side Input Limitations

Here is the implementation of the `AddDelayInfo` transform:

```
hourlyFlights = hourlyFlights.apply("AddDelayInfo",
ParDo.withSideInputs(avgDepDelay, avgArrDelay).of(new DoFn<Flight, Flight>() {

  @ProcessElement
  public void processElement(ProcessContext c) throws Exception {
    Flight f = c.element().newCopy();
    String depKey = f.getField(Flight.INPUTCOLS.ORIGIN) + ":"
    + f.getDepartureHour();
    Double depDelay = c.sideInput(avgDepDelay).get(depKey);
    String arrKey = f.getField(Flight.INPUTCOLS.DEST);
    Double arrDelay = c.sideInput(avgArrDelay).get(arrKey);
    f.avgDepartureDelay = (float) ((depDelay == null) ? 0 : depDelay);
    f.avgArrivalDelay = (float) ((arrDelay == null) ? 0 : arrDelay);
    c.output(f);
  }
```

There are two potential aspects to this transform that could be leading to the performance impact. One is that the transform uses two side inputs—the average departure delay and the average arrival delay. Side inputs are a potential cause of performance degradation because side inputs need to be broadcast to all the workers. Also, too large a side input could result in something that is too large to cache effectively in memory. The second potential cause of the performance issue with this transform is that it is creating a new object. Still, the object in question is quite small and Java should be able to deal with such a small object quite well.

How big are the two side inputs? We can click the two side-input boxes to the `AddDe layInfo` transform and find the number of output elements, which you can see in Figure 8-6.

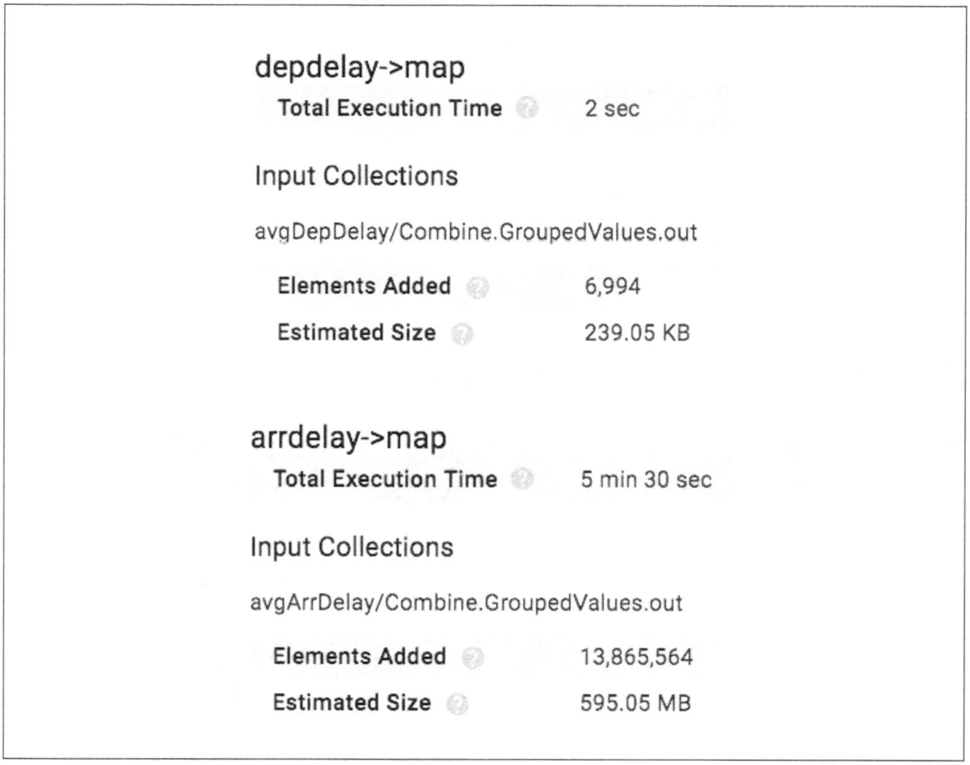

```
depdelay->map
    Total Execution Time        2 sec

Input Collections

avgDepDelay/Combine.GroupedValues.out

    Elements Added              6,994
    Estimated Size              239.05 KB


arrdelay->map
    Total Execution Time        5 min 30 sec

Input Collections

avgArrDelay/Combine.GroupedValues.out

    Elements Added              13,865,564
    Estimated Size              595.05 MB
```

Figure 8-6. Information about side inputs

The departure delay side input is 6,994 elements—on the order of 24 elements per airport. This is tiny and perfectly useable as a side input. The arrival delay, however, is different. Because there is an average for every time window, we have nearly 14 million elements! At more than 500 MB, it is beyond the limits of what can be efficiently broadcast and cached in memory.

So, how do we improve the pipeline to ensure it executes effectively? One potential fix would be to change the machine type of the workers. By default, Dataflow uses `n1-standard-1` Google Compute Engine VMs. We could change that to `n1-highmem-8`—this will simultaneously provide more memory (52 GB versus 3.75 GB[22]) and reduce the number of machines (since there are 8 cores per machine). This is as simple as adding `--workerMachineType=n1-highmem-8` to our launch program.

---

22 See *https://cloud.google.com/compute/docs/machine-types* for details of the different machine types.

The new pipeline, because of the higher-end machines, is much faster. The initial part of the pipeline processes hundreds of thousands of elements per second, as demonstrated in Figure 8-7.

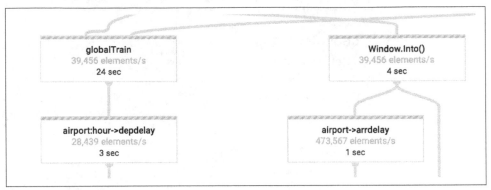

Figure 8-7. The initial part of the pipeline is extremely fast

However, the throughput does not continue on to the rest of the pipeline. Instead, we run into the same issue with the AddDelayInfo step, as shown in Figure 8-8.

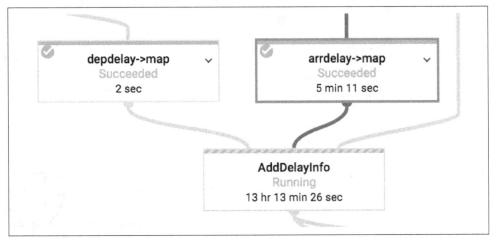

Figure 8-8. The AddDelayInfo part of the pipeline is very slow

Notice the exceedingly large resources being used by the step (13 hours as compared to minutes in the previous step). We need to rethink the implementation of the pipeline—simply throwing more hardware at it is not going to work.

Redesigning the Pipeline

Although side inputs are undeniably easy, they are limited to relatively small collections that can be efficiently broadcast to all the worker nodes. The departure delay can be a side input, but at nearly half a gigabyte, we need a different way to join the flights PCollection with the arrival delays.

We can use CoGroupByKey as a way to join two large inputs, and so we will need to change the way we look up the average arrival delay. Thus, we modify the original ParDo that added both departure and arrival delays using side inputs to add only the departure delay:[23]

```
hourlyFlights.apply("AddDepDelay",
    ParDo.withSideInputs(avgDepDelay).of(new DoFn<Flight, Flight>() {

        @ProcessElement
        public void processElement(ProcessContext c) throws Exception {

            Flight f = c.element().newCopy();
            String depKey = f.getField(Flight.INPUTCOLS.ORIGIN)
                    + ":" + f.getDepartureHour();
            Double depDelay = c.sideInput(avgDepDelay).get(depKey);
            f.avgDepartureDelay =
                    (float) ((depDelay == null) ? 0 : depDelay);
            c.output(f);
        }

        ...
```

The arrival delay will need to be added using CoGroupByKey. The first step in a CoGroupByKey is to start with two PCollections of key-value pairs. The arrival delay is already a PCollection of key-value pairs where the key is the destination airport. We, therefore, create a transform to emit the appropriate key–value pair for the flights information as well:

```
.apply("airport->Flight", ParDo.of(new DoFn<Flight, KV<String, Flight>>() {
    @ProcessElement
    public void processElement(ProcessContext c) throws Exception {
            Flight f = c.element();
            String arrKey = f.getField(Flight.INPUTCOLS.DEST);
            c.output(KV.of(arrKey, f));
        }
}));
```

---

23 See *CreateTrainingDatasets.java* in the GitHub repository.

Now we are ready to use CoGroupByKey join the two large inputs. This involves tagging the two input collections and creating a KeyedPCollectionTuple of the two collections of key–value pairs:

```
final TupleTag<Flight> t1 = new TupleTag<>();
final TupleTag<Double> t2 = new TupleTag<>();
PCollection<Flight> result = KeyedPCollectionTuple //
    .of(t1, airportFlights) //
    .and(t2, avgArrDelay) //
```

On the keyed collection tuple, we can apply CoGroupByKey, which results in a CoGbk Result (co-group-by-key-result). We then use a PTransform to essentially flatten this out into the list of flights and arrival delays at each airport. Because this is all applied to a windowed collection (hourlyFlights), these are the flights and arrival delays in a sliding window of one hour:

```
.apply(CoGroupByKey.create()) //
.apply("AddArrDelay", ParDo.of(new DoFn<KV<String, CoGbkResult>, Flight>() {
  @ProcessElement
  public void processElement(ProcessContext c) throws Exception {
    Iterable<Flight> flights = c.element().getValue().getAll(t1);
    double avgArrivalDelay = c.element().getValue().getOnly(t2, Double.valueOf(0));
    for (Flight uf : flights) {
      Flight f = uf.newCopy();
      f.avgArrivalDelay = (float) avgArrivalDelay;
      c.output(f);
    }
  }
}));
```

With this change,[24] we are able to process three days' worth of data relatively quickly (in about eight minutes in total), as demonstrated in Figure 8-9.

---

24 See *CreateTrainingDataset.java* in the GitHub repository.

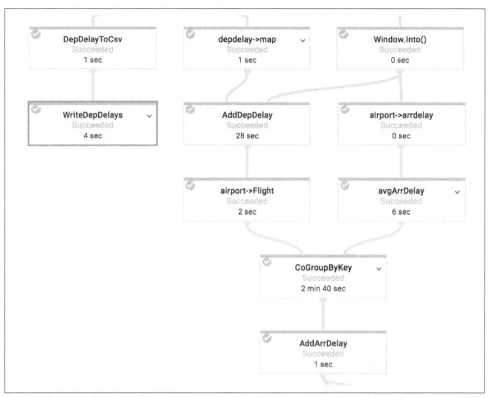

Figure 8-9. With the change to use a co-group-by-key, the pipeline processing is quite fast

Removing Duplicates

The results on Cloud Storage seem correct, but on closer examination turn out to have repeated flight information:

```
1.0,5.0,13.0,1448.0,29.75,-9.0,AS,...,SEA,ANC
1.0,5.0,13.0,1448.0,29.75,-9.0,AS,...,SEA,ANC
1.0,5.0,13.0,1448.0,29.75,-9.0,AS,...,SEA,ANC
1.0,5.0,13.0,1448.0,29.75,-9.0,AS,...,SEA,ANC
1.0,5.0,13.0,1448.0,29.75,-9.0,AS,...,SEA,ANC
1.0,5.0,13.0,1448.0,29.75,-9.0,AS,...,SEA,ANC
1.0,5.0,13.0,1448.0,29.75,-9.0,AS,...,SEA,ANC
1.0,5.0,13.0,1448.0,29.75,-9.0,AS,...,SEA,ANC
1.0,5.0,13.0,1448.0,29.75,-9.0,AS,...,SEA,ANC
1.0,5.0,13.0,1448.0,29.75,-9.0,AS,...,SEA,ANC
1.0,5.0,13.0,1448.0,29.75,-9.0,AS,...,SEA,ANC
1.0,5.0,13.0,1448.0,29.75,-9.0,AS,...,SEA,ANC
```

Why? This has to do with our use of sliding windows. Recall that our sliding window is computed over an hour every five minutes. So, every flight is part of several overlapping panes, starting from the second one in this diagram, and, therefore, each flight is repeated each time it falls into the pane. We would like the flight to be only part of the second window here, as shown in Figure 8-10.[25]

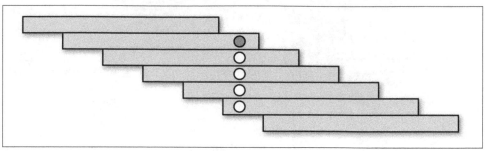

Figure 8-10. Every flight is part of several overlapping panes

You can clearly see this when you look at the number of items going into the Window.Into() operation, as illustrated in Figure 8-11.

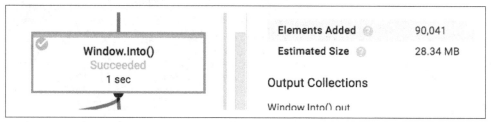

Figure 8-11. The number of input elements into the Window.Into()

Compare that with the number of items that comes out (Figure 8-12) and notice that it is exactly 12 times (because 60 minutes divided by 5 minutes = 12).

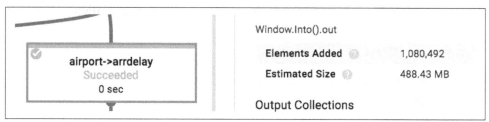

Figure 8-12. The number of output elements from the Window.Into(). Compare with Figure 8-11.

The first ParDo that follows the CoGroupByKey is the one that reflects the increased number of flights. The average delay does need to be computed once for every pane

---

25 Because it is the first window that includes the flight. Subsequent windows will all impose an additional latency.

(this is why we have a sliding window), but each flight object should be output only once. To do that, we can insert a transform that uses the Window and ensures that the flight is output only if it is in the latest slice of the window (Figure 8-13), where each slice is a five-minute segment of the overall interval.

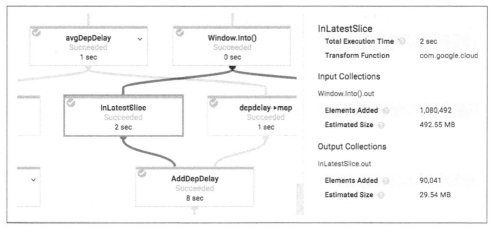

Figure 8-13. The IsLatestSlice transform removes the duplicates introduced by Window.Into()

The InLatestSlice transform outputs a Flight only if it is in the latest slice of the window:

```
.apply("InLatestSlice", ParDo.of(new DoFn<Flight, Flight>() {
            @ProcessElement
            public void processElement(ProcessContext c,
            IntervalWindow window) throws Exception {
              Instant endOfWindow = window.maxTimestamp();
              Instant flightTimestamp = c.element().getEventTimestamp();
              long msecs = endOfWindow.getMillis() -
              flightTimestamp.getMillis();
              long THRESH = 5 * 60 * 1000; // 5 minutes
              if (msecs < THRESH) {
                c.output(c.element());
              }
            }
          }))//
```

With this change to use the window parameter to prune the output flights, the outputs are correct and are produced quite rapidly. We can go back and launch this on the full dataset as before (with 50 workers). Because we are using CoGroupByKey instead of side inputs, the monitoring reveals a quite rapid processing at the sink and the entire pipeline processes in 20 minutes or so.

We now have three sets of files produced by the pipeline:

- *delays.csv* contains the historical departure delay at every airport-hour combination computed on the training dataset. For example, at New York's JFK airport the average departure delay at 5:15 PM can be looked up from the entry for JFK: 17 as 37.47 minutes.

- The *train*.csv* will serve as our training dataset for machine learning. We want to predict the first column in those files (whether the flight is on time) based on the other columns (departure delay, taxi-out time, distance, average departure and arrival delays, and a few other fields).

- The *eval*.csv* are files in the same format as the training files, and will be used to evaluate the ML model.

In Chapter 9, we train, evaluate, and deploy the machine learning model.

Summary

In this chapter, we augmented the machine learning training dataset with time-windowed aggregate features. We computed two averages—one, the average departure delay at a given airport at a given hour, was a global average and the other, the average arrival delay at a given airport over the previous hour, was a time-windowed average. Computing the average departure delay is essentially a batch average—the key idea is to compute it once on the training dataset and look up the appropriate departure delay at prediction time. The arrival delay, however, required us to compute a moving average.

Apache Beam allows us to compute a time-windowed moving average on historical data in the same way as we would on streaming data in real time. Cloud Dataflow allows us to execute data pipelines written using Beam on Google Cloud Platform in a serverless way.

We began with a basic pipeline that read the flight data from CSV files, filtered the input to keep only the flights that met some quality control criteria, and then exported to a CSV file the input variables for our machine learning model. Adding the computation of departure delay to this basic pipeline involved emitting a tuple of (airport+hour, departure delay) for each flight, grouping these tuples by key, and finally computing the mean value for each key. This average departure delay was converted into an in-memory `Map` (called a side input) and used within the pipeline to add the appropriate average departure delay to each flight.

To compute the average arrival delay, we need to emit records with a timestamp. In real-time Pub/Sub will do that, but here on batch data, we change our reading code from `c.output()` to `c.outputWithTimestamp()`. We began by forming a side input for the arrival delay, similar to the departure delay case, but we ran into problems because the side input is now too large to be efficiently broadcast to all the workers.

Cloud Dataflow ran, but it ran extremely slowly. We learned how to troubleshoot this, and resolved the error by replacing the side input by a `CoGroupByKey`, which provides a way to join two parallel collections without the requirement that one of these collections be small enough. This solved the efficiency problem, but we had a logical error of repeated lines in our output. This turned out to be because we were computing the arrival delay on sliding windows, and these windows caused each flight object to be present in 12 windows. The solution was to determine the slice of the window that the flight object was in, and to emit the flight only if it was the latest slice of the window. With these changes, the pipeline was logically correct and the entire training and evaluation datasets were created.

## CHAPTER 9

Machine Learning Classifier Using TensorFlow

In Chapter 7, we built a machine learning model but ran into problems when trying to scale it out and make it operational. The first problem was how to prevent training–serving skew when using a time-windowed aggregate feature. We solved this in Chapter 8 by using the same code for computing the aggregates on historical data as will be used on real-time data. The Cloud Dataflow pipeline that we implemented in Chapter 8 was used to create two sets of files: *trainFlights*.csv*, which will serve as our training dataset for machine learning, and *testFlights*.csv*, which we will use to evaluate the model. Both of these files contain augmented datasets—the purpose of the pipeline was to add the computed time-aggregates to the raw data received from the airlines. We want to predict the first column in those files (whether the flight is on time) based on the other columns (departure delay, taxi-out time, distance, and average departure and arrival delays, and a few other fields).

While we solved the problem of dataset augmentation with time aggregates, the other three problems identified at the end of Chapter 7 remain:

- One-hot encoding categorical columns caused an explosion in the size of the dataset

- Embeddings would involve special bookkeeping

- Putting the model into production requires the machine learning library to be portable to environments beyond the cluster on which the model is trained.

The solution to these three problems requires a portable machine learning library that is (1) powerful enough to carry out distributed training (i.e., training on a cluster of machines so that we can deal with very large datasets), (2) flexible enough to support the latest machine learning research such as wide-and-deep networks (*https://*

arxiv.org/abs/1606.07792), and (3) portable enough to support both massively parallel prediction on custom application-specific integrated circuits (ASICs) and prediction carried out on handheld devices. TensorFlow (*http://www.tensorflow.org/*), the open source machine learning library developed at Google, meets all these objectives.

If you skipped ahead to this chapter without reading Chapter 7, please go back and read it. That chapter looks at logistic regression using Spark, and I introduce a number of machine learning concepts that are essential to understanding this one. In particular, understanding the limitations of the approach presented in Chapter 7 will help you to understand the architecture of the distributed TensorFlow model that we develop here.

Toward More Complex Models

Normally, when you want a computer to do something for you, you need to program the computer to do it by using an explicit set of rules. For example, if you want a computer to look at an image of a screw on a manufacturing line and figure out whether the screw is faulty or not, you need to code up a set of rules: Is the screw bent? Is the screw head broken? Is the screw discolored? With machine learning, you turn the problem around on its head. Instead of coming up with all kinds of logical rules for why a screw might be bad, you show the computer a whole bunch of data. Maybe you show it 5,000 images of good screws and 5,000 images of faulty screws that your (human) operators discarded for one reason or the other. Then, you let the computer learn how to identify a bad screw from a good one. The computer is the "machine" and it's "learning" to make decisions based on data. In this particular case, the "machine" is learning a discriminant function from the manually labeled training data, which separates *good* screws from *bad* screws.

When we did logistic regression with Spark, or Bayes classification with Pig, we were doing machine learning. We took all of the data, chose a model (logistic regression or Bayes classifier), and asked the computer to figure out the free parameters in the model (the weights in logistic regression, the empirical probabilities in Bayes). We then could use the "trained" model to make predictions on new data points.

Even plain old linear regression, in this view, can be thought of as machine learning—that is, if the model is effective at capturing the nuances of the data. Many real-world problems are much more complex than can be adequately captured by linear regression or similarly simple models. When people talk of machine learning, they are usually thinking of more complex models with many more free parameters.

Tell a statistician about complex models with lots of free parameters, and you'll get a lecture back on the dangers of overfitting, of building a model that (instead of capturing the nuances of the problem) is simply fitting observation noise in the data. So, another aspect of machine learning is that you need to counteract the dangers of overfitting when using very complex models by training[1] the model on extremely large and highly representative datasets. Additionally, even though these complex models may be more accurate, the trade-off is that you cannot readily analyze them to retroactively derive logical rules and reasoning. When people think of machine learning, they think of random forests, support vector machines, and neural networks.

For our problem, we could use random forests, support vector machines, or neural networks, and I suspect that we will get very similar results. This is true of many real-world problems—the biggest return for your effort is going to be in terms of finding additional data to provide to the training model (and the resulting increase in free parameters in your model) or in devising better input features using the available data. In contrast, changing the machine learning model doesn't provide as much benefit. However, for a specific class of problems—those with extremely dense[2] and highly correlated inputs such as audio and images, deep neural networks begin to shine. In general, you should try to use a linear model if you can and reserve the use of more complex models (deep neural networks, convolutional layers, recurrent neural networks, etc.) only if the particular problem warrants it. For the flight delay use case, I will use a "wide-and-deep" model that consists of two parts: a wide or linear part for input features that are sparse and a part consisting of deep layers for input features that are continuous.

To train the model, we will use TensorFlow, an open source software library developed at Google to carry out numerical computation for machine learning research. The guts of the library are written in C++ to permit you to deploy computation to one or more Central Processing Units (CPUs) or Graphical Processing Units (GPUs) in a desktop or the cloud. Come prediction time, the trained model can be run on CPUs, GPUs, a server that uses Google's custom ASIC chips for machine learning (called Tensor Processing Units or TPUs[3]), or even a mobile device. However, it is not necessary to program in C++ to use TensorFlow, because the programming paradigm is to build a data flow graph and then stream data into that graph. It is possible to

---

1 If you come from a statistics background, training a machine learning model is the same thing as fitting a statistical model or function to data.

2 In this context, dense inputs are those where small differences in numeric values are meaningful—that is, where the inputs are continuous numbers.

3 See *https://cloudplatform.googleblog.com/2016/05/Google-supercharges-machine-learning-tasks-with-custom-chip.html*. It is a common misconception that the primary advantage of custom machine learning chips is to reduce training time—it is in prediction that TPUs offer the largest advantage. For example, *https://cloudplatform.googleblog.com/2017/04/quantifying-the-performance-of-the-TPU-our-first-machine-learning-chip.html* solely talks about the performance advantages that TPUs bring to *inference*. After this chapter was written, Google announced the second generation of the TPU, which sped up both training and inference: *https://blog.google/topics/google-cloud/google-cloud-offer-tpus-machine-learning/*. The order in which these chips were developed and released implies the ordering of the relative benefits that a custom chip can bring to inference and to training.

control the graph creation and streaming from Python without losing the efficiency of C++, or the ability to do GPU and ASIC computations. Nodes in the graph represent mathematical operations (such as the summation and sigmoid function that we used in logistic regression), whereas the graph edges represent the multidimensional data arrays (tensors) communicated between these nodes.

In fact, we could have expressed logistic regression as a simple neural network consisting of a single node and done the training using TensorFlow rather than Spark, as illustrated in Figure 9-1.

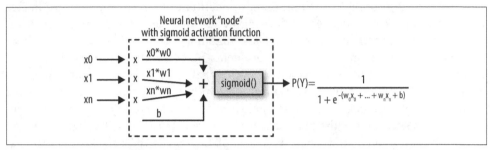

Figure 9-1. Logistic regression can be expressed as a simple neural network with only one node

For comparison purposes, the first neural network that we will build in this chapter will be precisely this. We will then be able to examine the impact of the additional input features while keeping the model (logistic regression) the same as what was used in Chapter 7.

Having done the comparison, though, we will move on to building a neural network that will have many more nodes and will be distributed in more layers. We'll keep the output node a sigmoid so that the output is restricted to lie in [0,1] but add in intermediate layers and nodes with other activation functions. The number of nodes and layers is something that we must determine via experimentation. At some point, increasing the number of nodes and layers will begin to result in overfitting, and the exact point is dependent on the size of your dataset (both the number of labeled examples and the number of predictor variables) and the extent to which the predictor variables do predict the label and the extent to which the predictors are independent. This problem is hairy enough that there is no real way to know beforehand how big and large you can afford your neural network to be. If your neural network is too small, it won't fit all the nuances of the problem adequately and your training error will be large. Again, you won't know that your neural network is too small unless you try a slightly larger neural network. The relationship is not going to be nice and smooth because there are random seeds involved in all the optimization methods that you will use to find the weights and biases. Because of that, machine learning is going to have to involve many, many runs. The best advice is to try out different numbers of nodes and layers and different activation functions (different ones work better for different problems) and see what works well for your problem. Having a cloud platform that supports this sort of experimentation to be carried out on your complete dataset in a timely manner is very important. When it's time to run our experiment on the full dataset, we will use Cloud ML Engine (*https://cloud.google.com/ml-engine/*).

For the intermediate layers, we will use Rectified Linear Units (ReLUs) as the neural network nodes. The ReLU has a linear activation function that is clamped to non-negative values. Essentially the input of the neuron is passed through to the output after thresholding it at 0—so if the weighted sum of the input neurons is 3, the output is 3, but if the weighted sum of the inputs is –3, the output is 0.

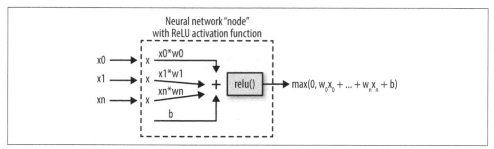

Figure 9-2. A typical neural network node in the intermediate (hidden) layers of a neural network consists of the weighted sum of its inputs transformed by a nonlinear function

Using ReLU rather than sigmoidal or tanh activation functions is a trade-off—the sigmoid activation function saturates between 0 and 1 (see the graphs in Chapter 7), and therefore the output won't blow up. However, the gradient near 0 and 1 is so slow-varying that training takes a long time. Also, the impact of a neuron is never actually zero when you use sigmoidal activation functions—this makes it very important to choose the right number of nodes/layers in a neural network for fear of overfitting. Because the gradient of a ReLU is constant, ReLU networks are faster to train. Also, because the ReLU function can reach 0, it can get to sparse models; while we will still search for the right model architecture, getting it precisely right is not as much of a concern. However—and this is where the trade-off comes in—the outputs of neurons with ReLU activation functions can reach really large, positive magnitudes. Some of the theoretical advances in machine learning over the past few years have been on how to initialize and train ReLUs without having the intermediate outputs of the neural network go flying off the handle.

Reading Data into TensorFlow

Let's begin by writing TensorFlow code to read in our data and do the training. We'll train the neural network on the dataset that we created using Cloud Dataflow. Recall that we took the raw flights data and used Cloud Dataflow to compute new features that we could use as inputs to our machine learning model—the average departure delay at the airport, at the hour we are flying out, and the average arrival delay currently at the airport we are flying into. The target (or label) that we are trying to predict is also in the dataset—it is 1 if the flight is "on time" (that is, delayed on arrival by less than 15 minutes) and 0 otherwise.

While developing this code, we want to use a small dataset. After our program works correctly, we can turn it loose on the full dataset. So, I will create a smaller version of the file so that we can safely do development on a laptop (if you don't have a Unix-like shell on your laptop, do this in CloudShell or a small Compute Engine VM):

```
mkdir -p ~/data/flights
BUCKET=cloud-training-demos-ml
gsutil cp \
  gs://${BUCKET}/flights/chapter8/output/trainFlights-00001*.csv \
  full.csv
head -10003 full.csv > ~/data/flights/train.csv
rm full.csv
```

The number 10003 might strike you as strange. This is because TensorFlow's batch file feeders don't really work with files (just lines). Although 10,003 is not prime (it is 7 × 1,429), it might as well be prime because we are not going to use a batch size of 1,429 in our program. I chose this rather odd file size so that we can ensure that our code correctly handles an incomplete batch.[4] Repeat the script with *testFlights-00001*.csv to create a *test.csv* file.

Ultimately, we want to submit our TensorFlow program to Cloud ML Engine so that it can be run in the cloud. For that to happen, our program needs to be a Python module. Python's packaging mechanism is essentially built off the filesystem, and so we begin by creating a directory structure:[5]

```
flights
flights/trainer
flights/trainer/__init__.py
```

The __init__.py, though empty, is required to be present for trainer to function as a Python module.

---

4 Here, we will be using the Estimator API and the CSV reader that ships with TensorFlow, so it will almost definitely just work. If you want to adapt the code to read some other data format, use indivisible numbers to ensure that one of the batches has less than the full number of examples. This is done so that we are sure the code runs correctly even in that use case.

5 See *09_cloudml/flights* in the GitHub repository for this book.

At this point, we are ready to write our actual code. The code will reside in two files: *task.py* will contain the main() function and *model.py* will contain the machine learning model.

Let's begin by writing a function in *model.py* to read in the data. We begin by importing the tensorflow package and then defining the header of the comma-separated value file (CSV) file we are about to read:

```
import tensorflow as tf

CSV_COLUMNS  = \
('ontime,dep_delay,taxiout,distance,avg_dep_delay,avg_arr_delay' + \
 'carrier,dep_lat,dep_lon,arr_lat,arr_lon,origin,dest').split(',')
LABEL_COLUMN = 'ontime'
```

The TensorFlow CSV reader asks us to specify default values for the columns just in case the column value is empty. It also uses the default value to infer the data type of the column.

```
DEFAULTS    = [[0.0],[0.0],[0.0],[0.0],[0.0],[0.0],\
               ['na'],[0.0],[0.0],[0.0],[0.0],['na'],['na']]
```

If we specify the default for a column as 0, it will be a tf.int32, but if we specify it as 0.0, it will be a tf.float32. Any columns whose default value is a string will be taken to be tf.string.

Let's now write a read_dataset() function that reads the training data, yielding batch_size examples each time, and goes through the entire training set num_train ing_epochs times. This is the function that we want:

```
def read_dataset(filename, mode=tf.contrib.learn.ModeKeys.EVAL,
                 batch_size=512, num_training_epochs=10):
```

The reason for the mode parameter is that we want to reuse the function for reading both the training and the evaluation data. During evaluation, we need to read the entire dataset only once. During training, though, we need to read the dataset and pass it through the model several times. Hence, the num_epochs—that is, the number of times that we will read the data—is:

```
num_epochs = num_training_epochs \
        if mode == tf.contrib.learn.ModeKeys.TRAIN else 1
```

During each of those times, we'll find all the files that match a wildcard (such as trainFlights*) and populate the filename_queue with num_epochs shuffled copies of the list of files. In other words, we read the set of sharded input data num_epochs times, but do so in a different order in each pass:

```
# could be a path to one file or a file pattern.
input_file_names = tf.train.match_filenames_once(filename)
filename_queue = tf.train.string_input_producer(
    input_file_names, num_epochs=num_epochs, shuffle=True)
```

Shuffling the order in which the sharded input data is read each time is important for distributed training. The way distributed training is carried out is that each of the workers is assigned a batch of data to process. The workers compute the gradient on their batch and send it to "parameter servers"[6] that maintain shared state of the training run. For reasons of fault tolerance, the results from very slow workers might be discarded. Therefore, it is important that the same batch of data not be assigned to the same slow worker in each run. Shuffling the data helps mitigate this possibility.

The data is read from the filename_queue in batches of batch_size examples. This data doesn't have headers, so we zip up the list of CSV_COLUMNS with the columns data read from the file. After we remove the label column, we have the input features. This tuple (of features and labels) is what is returned.[7]

```
# read CSV
reader = tf.TextLineReader()
_, value = reader.read_up_to(filename_queue, num_records=batch_size)
value_column = tf.expand_dims(value, -1)
columns = tf.decode_csv(value_column, record_defaults=DEFAULTS)
features = dict(zip(CSV_COLUMNS, columns))
label = features.pop(LABEL_COLUMN)
return features, label
```

In this example, we are reading CSV files using TensorFlow's native ops. This is a trade-off between human readability and powerful performance. The fastest way to read data into TensorFlow programs is to store the data as TFRecord files (with each example stored in tf.Example or tf.SequenceExample protocol buffers), but (as of this writing) there are no visualization or debugging tools that can read TFRecord files. The most convenient way to feed directly from Python is to construct tf.Constants directly from numpy arrays, but this doesn't scale to out-of-memory datasets. Storing and reading CSV files is a middle ground that provides us access to visualization and debugging tools (e.g., seaborn visualization package) while also providing reasonably fast reading speeds from TensorFlow.

Now that we have the code to read the data, let's write a main() to invoke this method. Let's use Python's argparse library to be able to pass in the name of the input file as a command-line argument:

```
if __name__ == '__main__':
  parser = argparse.ArgumentParser()
  parser.add_argument(
      '--traindata',
      help='Training data file(s)',
```

---

6 For more details, see *https://research.google.com/pubs/pub44634.html*.

7 For full context, look at the complete code in *https://github.com/GoogleCloudPlatform/data-science-on-gcp/tree/master/09_cloudml/flights/trainer/model.py*.

```
        required=True
    )

    # parse args
    args = parser.parse_args()
    arguments = args.__dict__
    traindata = arguments.pop('traindata')
```

We can now call the `read_dataset()` method, passing in the `traindata` provided on the command line:

```
feats, label = model.read_dataset(traindata)
```

To do something interesting, let's find the average of all the labels in the dataset by invoking `reduce_mean()` on the labels returned by our reading function:

```
avg = tf.reduce_mean(label)
print avg
```

Now, we can try running this from the command line using:

```
python task.py --traindata ~/data/flights/small.csv
```

If you run into errors about missing Python packages, install them by using `pip`[8] (install `pip` first, if necessary). Alternatively, run the code inside Cloud Datalab, which already has TensorFlow installed. What is printed out of the program, though, is not the overall likelihood of a flight being on time[9]—instead, we get this decidedly unappealing code:

```
Tensor("Mean:0", shape=(), dtype=float32)
```

What is going on? The reason has to do with the way TensorFlow works. What we have done so far is to just create the computation graph. We haven't actually told TensorFlow to execute this graph. You can do that by evaluating the variable (`avg`) in the context of a session after starting TensorFlow processes to fetch the data from the `filename_queue`. However, we don't want to have to program at such a low level. Instead, we will use TensorFlow's `Experiment` class to control the running of our model.

Setting Up an Experiment

We can use the `Experiment` class to control the training and evaluation of a machine learning model. We will create an instance of `Experiment` by supplying it with an `Estimator` (for example, a `LinearClassifier`, a `DNNClassifier`, or a custom estima-

---

8 For example, `pip install tensorflow`.

9 Because on time is 1.0 for on-time flights and 0.0 for late flights, its average over the entire dataset is the likelihood of a flight being on time.

tor that you write) and specifying the feature columns that the model requires (see Figure 9-3). We will also register a callback function with the `Experiment` class to read the training data (training input function in the schematic in Figure 9-3), and `Experiment` will take care of invoking it within a TensorFlow session. In particular, `Experiment` will take care of calling the optimizer for the model in a distributed way (i.e., across several machines) to adjust the weights of the model every time a batch of training examples is read.[10]

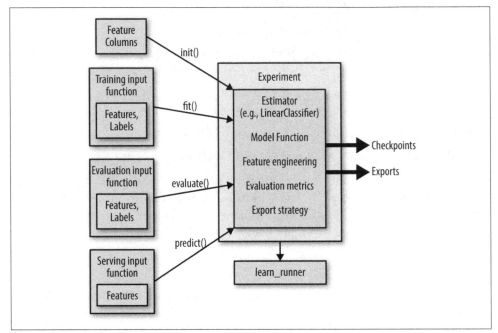

Figure 9-3. The Experiment class controls the training and evaluation loop

The framework shown in Figure 9-3 asks us to provide everything needed to train, evaluate, and predict with the model. Specifically, we need to provide:

- The machine learning model, including the feature columns.
- A training input function. This is the function that will be called to read the training data. As with our `read_dataset()` function, this function will need to return a batch of features and their corresponding labels.
- An evaluation input function, which is like the training input function, except that it will be called to read the test data.

---

10 The alternative option—of writing low-level TensorFlow code and managing device placement and distribution yourself—is not one that I recommend: use `Experiment` and `Estimator`.

- An export strategy[11] along with a serving input function. The export strategy specifies when a model should be saved—typically we just save the best one based on the evaluation dataset. The serving input function is the input function that will be used to read the inputs at prediction time.

We can also provide parameters that change the defaults on a host of other parameters. For now, let's just go with the defaults for every nonrequired parameter.

Linear Classifier

In Chapter 7, we built a logistic regression model based on three continuous variables: departure delay, taxi-out time, and distance. We then tried to add one more variable—the origin airport—and because the origin is a categorical variable, it needed to be one-hot encoded. One-hot encoding the origin airport ended up creating more than a hundred new columns, making the model two orders of magnitude more complex. Thus, the addition of this fourth variable caused the Spark ML model to collapse.

Here, let's build a logistic regression model in TensorFlow, but because we do have many more columns now, let's use them all. As discussed earlier in this chapter, logistic regression is simply a linear model with a sigmoidal output node—in TensorFlow, this is provided by the `LinearClassifier` class.

When creating the model, we specify a FeatureColumn for each input feature. Features that are continuous numbers correspond to a RealValuedColumn—fields like departure delay, taxi-out time, distance, average delays, latitude, and longitude are all real valued:

```
def get_features():
  real = {
    colname : tflayers.real_valued_column(colname) \
        for colname in \
          ('dep_delay,taxiout,distance,avg_dep_delay,avg_arr_delay' \
          ',dep_lat,dep_lon,arr_lat,arr_lon').split(',')
  }
  sparse = {
    'carrier': tflayers.sparse_column_with_keys('carrier',
            keys='AS,VX,F9,UA,US,WN,HA,EV,MQ,DL,OO,B6,NK,AA'.split(',')),

    'origin' : tflayers.sparse_column_with_hash_bucket('origin',
            hash_bucket_size=1000), # FIXME

    'dest'   : tflayers.sparse_column_with_hash_bucket('dest',
            hash_bucket_size=1000)  # FIXME
```

---

11 Technically, the export strategy and serving input function are not required. But I fail to see the point of training a machine learning model that you will not use for prediction.

```
    }
    return real, sparse
```

Features that are discrete (and have to be one-hot encoded [see Chapter 7]) are represented by SparseColumn. The airline carrier can be one of the following strings:

```
AS,VX,F9,UA,US,WN,HA,EV,MQ,DL,OO,B6,NK,AA
```

Thus, it is represented by a sparse column with those specific keys. This is called the *vocabulary* of the column; to find the vocabulary of the carrier codes, I used BigQuery:

```
SELECT
  DISTINCT UNIQUE_CARRIER
FROM
  `cloud-training-demos.flights.tzcorr`
```

Although I could have done the same thing for the origin and destination codes (most likely by saving the airport codes from the BigQuery result set to a file and reading that file from Python), I decided to use a shortcut by mapping the airport codes to hashed buckets; rather than find all the origin airports in the dataset, I ask TensorFlow to create a cryptographic hash of the airport code and then discretize the hash number into 1,000 buckets (a number larger than the number of unique airports). Provided the hash works as intended, the airports will be uniformly discretized into 1,000 bins. For any bucket with only one airport in it, this is equivalent to one-hot encoding. However, there is likely to be some small amount of collision, and so using the hash rather than explicitly specifying the keys will be somewhat worse. This, however, is the kind of thing we can fix after we have an initial version up and running—hence the FIXME in the code.

Now that we have the feature columns, creating the linear model is quite straightforward:

```
def linear_model(output_dir):
    real, sparse = get_features()
    all = {}
    all.update(real)
    all.update(sparse)
    return tflearn.LinearClassifier(model_dir=output_dir,
                                    feature_columns=all.values())
```

Now that we have the model in place, let's move on to implementing the training and evaluation input functions.

Training and Evaluating Input Functions

Each of the input functions is a callback function that is supplied to the Experiment. Then, the Experiment will invoke the callback as part of a control flow. Because it is the Experiment that will invoke the training input function, the signature of the function (the input parameters and return values) must match the way that `Experi ment` will invoke it. The training input function must have this signature:

```
def input_fn():
    ...
    return features, labels
```

Even though our `read_dataset()` function does return a tuple of features and labels, it requires the caller to supply the training filename(s) and three other optional parameters. Therefore, I will refactor the `read_dataset()` to return a callback function with the required signature. That's what is happening here:

```
def read_dataset(filename, mode=tf.contrib.learn.ModeKeys.EVAL, batch_size-512,
                 num_training_epochs=10):

    # the actual input function passed to TensorFlow
    def _input_fn():
        # existing code goes here.
        ...
        return features, labels

    return _input_fn
```

We can now pass the result of `read_dataset()` to the `Experiment` class because the `_input_fn` has the required signature. Essentially, `read_dataset()` decorates the input function so that we can actually pass input parameters.

Thus, the two input functions are returned by `read_dataset()` based on the fully qualified path to *trainFlights*.csv* and *testFlights*.csv*:

```
train_input_fn=read_dataset(traindata,
                            mode=tf.contrib.learn.ModeKeys.TRAIN),
eval_input_fn=read_dataset(evaldata),
```

The `mode` is used to ensure that the training dataset is read `num_training_epochs` times, whereas the test dataset is read only once.

Serving Input Function

When predicting, the input values will come through a REST call. Thus, the application invoking our trained model will supply us all the input parameters (`dep_delay`, `taxiout`, etc.) as a JSON string. In the JSON that comes in, all real-valued columns will be supplied as floating-point numbers and all sparse columns will be supplied as strings. We, therefore, create appropriately typed placeholders to accept them and send them on:

```
def serving_input_fn():
    real, sparse = get_features()

    feature_placeholders = {
```

```
    key : tf.placeholder(tf.float32, [None]) \
       for key in real.keys()
  }
  feature_placeholders.update( {
    key : tf.placeholder(tf.string, [None]) \
       for key in sparse.keys()
  } )

  features = {
    # tf.expand_dims will insert a dimension 1 into tensor shape
    # This will make the input tensor a batch of 1
    key: tf.expand_dims(tensor, -1)
       for key, tensor in feature_placeholders.items()
  }
  return tflearn.utils.input_fn_utils.InputFnOps(
    features,
    None,
    feature_placeholders)
```

With all the components in place, we are now ready to create the Experiment class itself.

Creating an Experiment

The Experiment is created in a function, and that function is supplied as a callback to the learn_runner main loop:

```
def make_experiment_fn(traindata, evaldata, **args):
  def _experiment_fn(output_dir):
    return tflearn.Experiment(
        linear_model(output_dir),
        train_input_fn=read_dataset(traindata,
        mode=tf.contrib.learn.ModeKeys.TRAIN),
        eval_input_fn=read_dataset(evaldata),
        export_strategies=[saved_model_export_utils.make_export_strategy(
            serving_input_fn,
            default_output_alternative_key=None,
            exports_to_keep=1
        )],
        **args
    )
  return _experiment_fn
```

In *task.py*, which contains our main(), we invoke the learn_runner main loop, passing the function that creates the Experiment as a callback function:

```
# run
tf.logging.set_verbosity(tf.logging.INFO)
learn_runner.run(model.make_experiment_fn(**arguments), output_dir)
```

At this point, *model.py* and *task.py* are complete.

Performing a Training Run

We can now run the training from the directory that contains *task.py*:

```
python task.py \
      --traindata ~/data/flights/train.csv \
      --output_dir ./trained_model \
      --evaldata ~data/flights/test.csv
```

However, we want to run it as a Python module. To do that, we add the path to the module to the Python search path and then invoke it by using `python -m`:

```
export PYTHONPATH=${PYTHONPATH}:${PWD}/flights
python -m trainer.task \
   --output_dir=./trained_model \
   --traindata $DATA_DIR/train* --evaldata $DATA_DIR/test*
```

TensorFlow trains the model on the training data, and evaluates the trained model on the evaluation data. At the end of 200 steps (each step consists of a batch of inputs), I got these results as metrics:

```
accuracy = 0.922623, accuracy/baseline_label_mean = 0.809057,
accuracy/threshold_0.500000_mean = 0.922623, auc = 0.97447, global_step= 200, ❶
labels/actual_label_mean = 0.809057, labels/prediction_mean = 0.744471, loss =
0.312157, precision/positive_threshold_0.500000_mean = 0.989173,
recall/positive_threshold_0.500000_mean = 0.91437
```

❶ The `global_step` indicates the number of batches seen by the program. If you resume training from a checkpoint, `global_step` increments from the checkpoint. So, for example, if the checkpoint was written out at step = 300, and you train on 10 batches, the `global_step` will be 310.

It appears that we get a precision of 98.9%—in other words, 98.9% of the time that we say that the flight will be on time, it will be. Conversely, the recall indicates that we identify 91.4% of flights that will be on time. Although interesting and helpful, these are not the evaluation metrics we care about. Recall that we want to choose a probabilistic threshold not at 0.5, but at 0.7, because we want to cancel the meeting if the likelihood of arriving on time is less than 70%.

As of this writing, there is no convenient way to specify the threshold at which to evaluate. You would need to get the output probabilities from the model and explicitly calculate metrics at the threshold.[12] Alternatively, you could change the threshold from 0.5 with a bit of a hack:

```
def linear_model(output_dir):
    real, sparse = get_features()
    all = {}
```

---

12 This is also the only way to evaluate at multiple thresholds.

```
all.update(real)
all.update(sparse)
estimator = tflearn.LinearClassifier(
    model_dir=output_dir,feature_columns=all.values())
estimator.params["head"]._thresholds = [0.7]
return estimator
```

We now get the evaluation metrics we need:

```
accuracy = 0.922623, accuracy/baseline_label_mean = 0.809057,
accuracy/threshold_0.700000_mean = 0.911527, auc = 0.97447, global_step = 200,
labels/actual_label_mean = 0.809057, labels/prediction_mean = 0.744471, loss =
0.312157, precision/positive_threshold_0.700000_mean = 0.991276,
recall/positive_threshold_0.700000_mean = 0.898554
```

In Chapter 7, we discussed the need for a metric that is independent of threshold and captures the full spectrum of probabilities. The Area Under the Curve (AUC) (*http://bit.ly/2B8lvK8*) measure that is reported by TensorFlow does this, but it is not as sensitive to model improvements as the Root Mean Squared Error (RMSE) that we started with in Chapter 7. For comparison purposes, therefore, it would be good to also compute the RMSE. We can do this by adding an evaluation metric to the Experiment definition:[13]

```
eval_metrics = {
        'rmse' : tflearn.MetricSpec(metric_fn=my_rmse,
                        prediction_key='probabilities')
    },
```

The my_rmse() function is defined as follows:

```
def my_rmse(predictions, labels, **args):
    prob_ontime = predictions[:,1]
    return tfmetrics.streaming_root_mean_squared_error(prob_ontime,
                    labels, **args)
```

We slice the predictions tensor, which is a pair of probabilities (one for each of the classes: late and ontime) to get the probability that the flight is on time. We then evaluate that probability against the label to get the RMSE.

Rerunning with the additional evaluation metric, we get an RMSE as well:

```
accuracy = 0.949015, accuracy/baseline_label_mean = 0.809057,
accuracy/threshold_0.700000_mean = 0.944817, auc = 0.973428, global_step = 100,
labels/actual_label_mean = 0.809057, labels/prediction_mean = 0.78278, loss =
0.338125, precision/positive_threshold_0.700000_mean = 0.985701,
recall/positive_threshold_0.700000_mean = 0.945508, rmse = 0.208851
```

---

13 See the full context on GitHub at *https://github.com/GoogleCloudPlatform/data-science-on-gcp/blob/master/09_cloudml/flights/trainer/model.py*.

Of course, this is on just 10,000 examples. We do need to train and evaluate on the larger datasets before we can draw any conclusions.

Distributed Training in the Cloud

Fortunately, distributed training on the complete dataset is easy after we have the Python module that uses the `Experiment` class. We simply need to submit the training job to Cloud ML Engine using the `gcloud` command, making sure to specify Google Cloud Storage locations for the inputs and outputs:

```
#!/bin/bash

BUCKET=cloud-training-demos-ml
REGION=us-central1
OUTPUT_DIR=gs://${BUCKET}/flights/chapter9/output
DATA_DIR=gs://${BUCKET}/flights/chapter8/output
JOBNAME=flights_$(date -u +%y%m%d_%H%M%S)
gcloud ml-engine jobs submit training $JOBNAME \
  --region=$REGION \
  --module-name=trainer.task \
  --package-path=$(pwd)/flights/trainer \
  --job-dir=$OUTPUT_DIR \
  --staging-bucket=gs://$BUCKET \
  --scale-tier=STANDARD_1 \
 -\
    --output_dir=$OUTPUT_DIR \
    --traindata $DATA_DIR/train* --evaldata $DATA_DIR/test*
```

The parameters are mostly self-evident. We provide the package path and the module name similar to what we provided when we executed it locally. The difference now is that the `traindata` and `evaldata` paths point to the Google Cloud Storage bucket written by the Cloud Dataflow pipeline of Chapter 8. The `scale-tier` in Cloud ML Engine refers to how many workers we want for our job; as of this writing, the `STAN DARD_1` tier comes with 10 workers.

After we have our distributed TensorFlow code, we can use Cloud ML Engine to run the job in a serverless manner. Rather than run on the full dataset, though, let's experiment on a smaller fraction of the dataset. We can do this by modifying the pattern of files being processed:

```
PATTERN="Flights-00001*"
```

```
--traindata $DATA_DIR/train$PATTERN --evaldata $DATA_DIR/test$PATTERN
```

By processing only a single shard of the input dataset, we can carry out experiments more quickly. When we have settled on a model and the features to use, we can run the final model on the entire dataset. As in Chapter 7, let's begin keeping track of the experiments' results. Table 9-1 shows the results at this point.

Table 9-1. Running table of the results of our experiments

Experiment #	Model	Features	RMSE
1	Linear	All inputs as-is	0.196

In Chapter 7, the RMSE was 0.252, so the additional inputs (the time averages and the extra categorical features) have helped quite a bit. How much of this is due to the additional data, and how much of it is because of the additional features? To be able to answer this question, let's do an experiment with the same model but use only the three inputs that we used in Chapter 7. Then, let's do the experiment after adding in the two time aggregates we computed in Chapter 8. Table 9-2 shows the results.

Table 9-2. Running table of results, after three experiments

Experiment #	Model	Features	RMSE
1 (repeated for convenience)	Linear	All inputs as-is	0.196
2	Linear	Three input variables as in Chapter 7	0.210
3	Linear	With addition of time averages computed in Chapter 8	0.204

We see that each set of additional inputs helps to improve the performance of the machine learning model.

Improving the ML Model

The difference in RMSE between the Spark logistic regression (Experiment #1 in Chapter 7 achieved an RMSE of 0.252) and the TensorFlow logistic regression in this chapter (Experiment #2 in Table 9-2 achieved an RMSE of 0.210) is due to the ability to use much more data. It is clear that the impact of more data greatly outweighs the impact of the new features. Of course, the ability to scale out training to handle large datasets is a prerequisite to be able to use more data. Although we spend quite a bit of effort in this chapter on improving the basic TensorFlow linear model, do not lose sight of the fact that the greatest benefit that TensorFlow affords you is not the ability to implement complex machine learning models; rather, it's the ability to train on extremely large datasets in a robust manner. More data, in many machine learning use cases, beats a more complex model.

But now that we have more data and the ability to train machine learning models on the larger dataset, why not improve our machine learning modeling also? It is also clear from comparing Experiment #3 to Experiment #2 that the time averages do help improve the performance of the model. It is also clear by comparing Experiment #3 to Experiment #1 that all the additional variables such as airport latitudes and longitudes also help to improve performance. Although we realized these improvements on just a linear model, it is possible that a more complex model can take better advantage of these features. With so many input features and such a large dataset, we ought to consider using more complex models. Time, then, to try a deep neural network.

Deep Neural Network Model

In the example application in Figure 9-4 from the TensorFlow playground (*http://play ground.tensorflow.org/*), the goal of the classifier is to separate the blue dots from the orange dots.

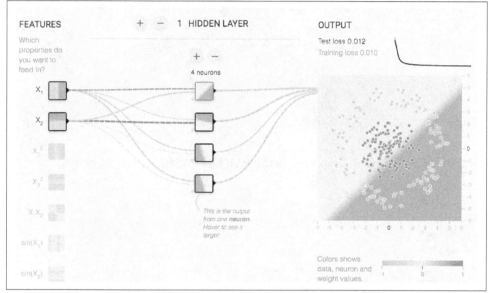

Figure 9-4. TensorFlow playground; the first neuron learns a line

The inputs are X_1 and X_2, the two coordinates of each of the points. Given the inputs (X_1, X_2), the first neuron computes a weighted sum of X_1 and X_2. Because $aX_1 + bX_2 \geq 0$ for any value of a and b describes the area above or below a line, the separation surface that the ReLU neuron learns is a line. The first neuron ends up learning a specific linear separation of the points: the diagonal shown in the Figure 9-4. This neuron by itself is not a great classifier, but take a look at Figure 9-5 to see what the second neuron learns.

The second ReLU neuron learns a different set of weights for the input parameters—in other words, a different line. By itself, this too is not a great separator.

We have a neural network with four such neurons in the hidden layer. The combination of these four linear separators ends up being a polygon, as depicted in Figure 9-6. Taken together, the weighted sum of the four neurons ends up being a great classifier for the input data.

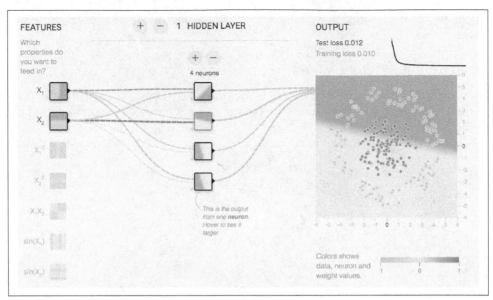

Figure 9-5. The second neuron learns a different line to separate out the points

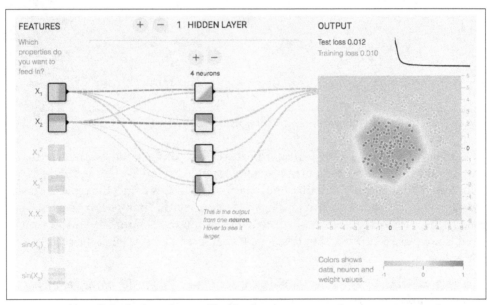

Figure 9-6. Together, the lines learned by the four neurons ends up creating a polygon that effectively separates the blue dots from the orange dots

With the layout of points in Figure 9-6, a polygon was sufficient to separate the blue dots from the orange dots. For more complex layouts, though, a single polygon will not be sufficient. We will need multiple layers to build a separation surface that is composed of several polygons, as illustrated in Figure 9-7.

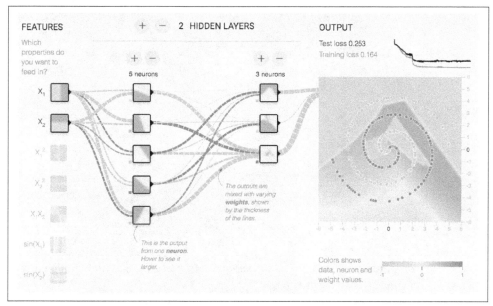

Figure 9-7. For the spiral shape, we need a network with multiple layers to effectively compose a set of polygons to separate out the blue dots from the orange dots. However, in this case, the network doesn't have enough nodes to adequately learn the input data.

The network in Figure 9-7 is insufficiently complex to adequately learn the input data —note the many orange dots still in blue areas. Increasing the complexity of the network by adding more nodes helps the neural network learn the spiral shape, as shown in Figure 9-8.

Of course, the network doesn't really learn the spiral nature of the pattern, only how to approximate it with a bunch of polygons. In particular, it is obvious that the neural network's learning stops with the extent of the data. As humans, we "know" that the spiral continues, but because there are no points in the upper-left corner, the neural network doesn't learn this.

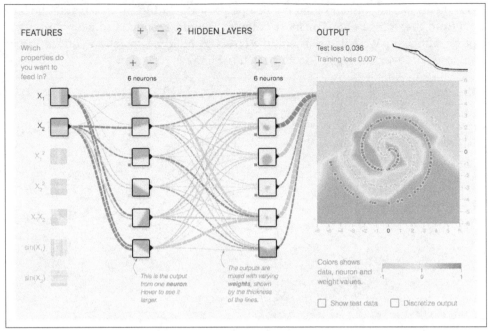

Figure 9-8. Compare with Figure 9-7. This network has enough nodes and enough layers so as to be able to learn this dataset.

A word of caution: the preceding figures are meant to provide handy visualizations for two-dimensional inputs and what a specific kind of neural network (a network with ReLU activation functions) does in that scenario. In a real-world problem, you will have many more inputs and so the analogy between separation surfaces and polygons begins to break down. Still, understanding that the neurons in a hidden layer combine together to form a separation hyperplane can be a helpful insight.

Embeddings

Logistic regression can be thought of as a weighted sum of the inputs followed by a sigmoidal activation function—in fact, that is exactly what we did when we used a `LinearClassifier` in TensorFlow. However, with so many more inputs and a much larger training dataset, we could consider adding many more free parameters. As discussed earlier, one way to introduce more free parameters and learn a more complex separation surface is to introduce a hidden layer of neurons. Each of the neurons in the hidden layer computes a weighted sum of the inputs followed by an activation function (we'll use the ReLU activation function). Because the weights are different for each neuron, each neuron ends up specializing in a different linear separation of the inputs. The overall classifier is a combination of these linear separators.

In the neural network, we can use our real-valued numbers directly, but using the one-hot encoded sparse columns directly in a deep neural network is not recommended. Recall that the origin variable, for example, is discretized into 1,000 buckets, and so one-hot encoding that field alone will result in an extremely sparse matrix of 1,000 columns. One way to avoid this explosion in the number of columns is to carry out dimensionality reduction of categorical fields—in machine learning, dimensionality reduction is carried out by a process called *embedding*. Embedding a sparse column takes a column that, when one-hot encoded, would be 1,000 separate columns and represents it as perhaps 10 numbers. The dimensionality-reduced transform of these categorical fields is what gets presented to the deep neural network.

In TensorFlow, we can use an embedding column to carry out dimensionality reduction of a sparse column:

```
def create_embed(sparse_col):
    nbins = col.bucket_size
    dim = 1 + int(round(np.log2(nbins)))
    return tflayers.embedding_column(sparse_col, dimension=dim)
```

What this code does is to take a sparse column and embeds into $(1+\log_2 N)$ values, where N is the number of buckets in that column. For example, a column with 1,024 values will be quantized into a vector with 11 components, with the weights associated with that quantization being determined by the neural network training process.

Changing our code to use a deep neural network is quite straightforward after we have a way to create embeddings of the sparse column. We use the real-valued columns as-is, but create embeddings out of all the sparse columns. The deep neural network is then created from the real-valued and embedded sparse columns:

```
def dnn_model(output_dir):
    real, sparse = get_features()
    all = {}
    all.update(real)
    embed = {
        colname : create_embed(col) \
          for colname, col in sparse.items()
    }
    all.update(embed)

    estimator = tflearn.DNNClassifier(model_dir=output_dir,
                          feature_columns=all.values(),
                          hidden_units=[64, 16, 4])
    estimator.params["head"]._thresholds = [0.7]
    return estimator
```

The network itself has three hidden layers. There are 64 neurons in the first hidden layer, 16 in the second hidden layer, and 4 in the third. By default, all the neurons have ReLU activation functions. Why this many layers and this many neurons in each layer? It is quite arbitrary, but a general rule of thumb is to start the first hidden layer with approximately the number of input nodes and then decay them in each successive layer. Still, this is something that we will have to experiment with. Table 9-3 shows the results with embeddings created for sparse columns.

Table 9-3. Results with embeddings created

Experiment #	Model	Features	RMSE
1 (repeated for convenience)	Linear	All inputs as-is	0.196
4	Deep neural network	All the input variables Embeddings to $\log_2 N$	0.196

Note that the use of the deep neural network by itself has not improved the performance of the network beyond providing the same inputs to a logistic regression model. This is by no means unusual and corresponds with the experience of most machine learning veterans—given the choice between spending your time obtaining more input variables and creating a more complex machine learning model, spend it on bringing more input variables into your machine learning model. Another way to think about this is that data engineering, and not data science, provides the greater payoff.

Wide-and-Deep Model

Before we write off model improvements completely, let's try a third model. A recent paper (*https://arxiv.org/abs/1606.07792*) suggests using a hybrid model that the authors call a *wide-and-deep model*. In the wide-and-deep model, there are two parts. One part directly connects the inputs to the outputs; in other words, it is a linear model. The other part connects the inputs to the outputs via a deep neural network. The modeler places the sparse columns in the linear part of the model, and the real-valued columns in the deep part of the model.

In addition, real-valued columns whose precision is overkill (thus, likely to cause overfitting) are discretized and made into categorical columns. For example, if we have a column for the age of the aircraft, we might discretize into just three bins—less than 5 years old, 5 to 20 years old, and more than 20 years old.

Finally, a process called *feature crossing* is applied to categorical features that work well in combination. Think of a feature cross as being an AND condition. If you have a column for colors and another column for sizes, the feature cross of colors and sizes will result in sparse columns for color-size combinations such as red-medium.

Let's apply these techniques to our model function. Recall that our `get_features()` returns two Python dictionaries of features: one is a dict of real-valued columns, and the other is a dict of sparse columns.

Among the real-valued columns are the latitude and longitude of the departure and arrival airports. The latitudes themselves should not have much of an impact on a flight being early or late, but the location of the airport and the flight path between pairs of cities do play a part. For example, flights along the West Coast of the United States are rarely delayed, whereas flights that pass through the high-traffic area between Chicago and New York tend to experience a lot of delays. This is true even if the flight in question does not originate in Chicago or New York.

Indeed, the Federal Aviation Administration in the United States manages airplanes in flight in terms of air traffic corridors or areas (see Figure 9-9). We can make the machine learning problem easier for the model if there were a way to provide this human insight directly, instead of expecting it to be learned directly from the raw latitude and longitude data.

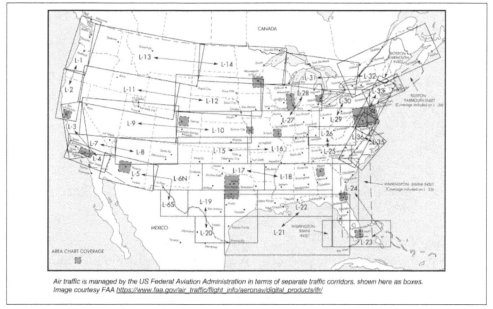

Air traffic is managed by the US Federal Aviation Administration in terms of separate traffic corridors, shown here as boxes. Image courtesy FAA https://www.faa.gov/air_traffic/flight_info/aeronav/digital_products/ifr/

Figure 9-9. Air traffic corridors

Even though we could explicitly program in the air traffic corridors, let's use a short-cut: we can discretize the latitudes and longitudes (the blue and orange arrows in Figure 9-10) and cross the buckets—this will result in breaking up the country into grids and yield the grid point into which a specific latitude and longitude falls.

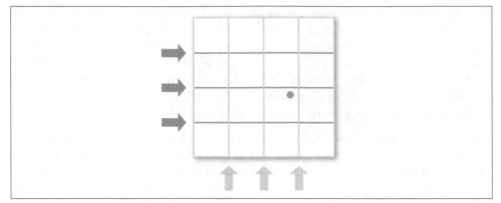

Figure 9-10. Bucketizing latitude and longitude essentially separates out the space into grid boxes

The following code takes the real-valued latitude and longitude columns and discretizes them into `nbuckets` each:

```
latbuckets = np.linspace(20.0, 50.0, nbuckets).tolist()  # USA
lonbuckets = np.linspace(-120.0, -70.0, nbuckets).tolist() # USA
disc = {}
disc.update({
    'd_{}'.format(key) : tflayers.bucketized_column(real[key], latbuckets) \
        for key in ['dep_lat', 'arr_lat']
})
disc.update({
    'd_{}'.format(key) : tflayers.bucketized_column(real[key], lonbuckets) \
        for key in ['dep_lon', 'arr_lon']
})
```

The dictionary `disc` at this point contains four discretized columns: `d_dep_lat`, `d_arr_lat`, `d_dep_lon`, and `d_arr_lat`. We can take these discretized columns and cross them to create two sparse columns: one for the box within which the departure `lat-lon` falls, and another for the box within which the arrival `lat-lon` falls:

```
sparse['dep_loc'] = tflayers.crossed_column([disc['d_dep_lat'],
                        disc['d_dep_lon']], nbuckets*nbuckets)
sparse['arr_loc'] = tflayers.crossed_column([disc['d_arr_lat'],
                        disc['d_arr_lon']], nbuckets*nbuckets)
```

We can also create a feature cross of the pair of departure and arrival grid cells, essentially capturing flights between two boxes. In addition, we also feature cross the departure and arrival airport codes (e.g., ORD–JFK for flights that leave Chicago's O'Hare airport and arrive at New York's John F. Kennedy airport):

```
sparse['dep_arr'] = tflayers.crossed_column([sparse['dep_loc'],
                        sparse['arr_loc']], nbuckets ** 4)
sparse['ori_dest'] = tflayers.crossed_column([sparse['origin'],
                        Sparse['dest'], hash_bucket_size=1000)
```

Even though we want to use the sparse columns directly in the linear part of the model, we would also like to perform dimensionality reduction on them and use them in the deep part of the model:

```
# create embeddings of all the sparse columns
embed = {
    colname : create_embed(col) \
        for colname, col in sparse.items()
}
real.update(embed)
```

With the sparse and real feature columns thus enhanced beyond the raw inputs, we can create the DNNLinearCombinedClassifier passing in the linear and deep feature columns separately:

```
estimator = \
    tflearn.DNNLinearCombinedClassifier(model_dir=output_dir,
                        linear_feature_columns=sparse.values(),
                        dnn_feature_columns=real.values(),
                        hidden_units=[64, 16, 4])
```

Training with this improved model with these extra engineered features helps us to get the better performance presented in Table 9-4.

Table 9-4. Better performance is achieved with a wide-and-deep model

Experiment #	Model	Features	RMSE
1 (repeated for convenience)	Linear	All inputs as-is	0.196
5	Wide-and-deep	All the input variables Feature crosses Embeddings	0.187

Using a more appropriate machine learning model and features that reflect human insight into the problem does help improve the model performance.

Hyperparameter Tuning

In our model, we made a number of arbitrary choices. For example, the number of layers and the number of hidden nodes was essentially arbitrary. As discussed earlier, more layers help the model learn more complex input spaces, but it is difficult to have an intuition about how difficult this particular problem (predicting flight delays) is. However, the choice of model architecture does matter—choosing too few layers will result in a suboptimal classifier, whereas choosing too many layers might result in overfitting. We need to select an appropriate number of layers and nodes.

The optimizer uses gradient descent, but computes the gradients on small batches. We used a batch size of 512, but that choice was arbitrary. The larger the batch size, the quicker the training run will complete because the network overhead of calls between the workers and the parameter server scales with the number of batches—with larger batches, we have fewer batches to complete an epoch, and so the training will complete faster. However, if the batch size is too large, the sensitivity of the optimizer to specific data points reduces, and hurts the ability of the optimizer to learn the nuances of the problem. Even in terms of efficiency, too large a batch will cause matrix multiplications to spill over from more efficient memory to less efficient memory (such as from a GPU to a CPU). Thus, the choice of batch size matters.

There are other arbitrary choices that are specific to our model. For example, we discretized the latitude and longitude into five buckets each. What should this number of buckets actually be? Too low a number, and we will lose the discrimination ability; too high a number, and we will begin to overfit.

As a final step in improving the model, we'll carry out an experiment with different choices for these three parameters: number of hidden units, batch size, and number of buckets. Even though we could laboriously carry out these experiments one-by-one, we will use a feature of Cloud ML Engine that allows for a nonlinear hyperparameter tuning approach. We'll specify ranges for these three parameters, specify a maximum number of trials we want to try out, and have Cloud ML Engine carry out a search in hyperparameter space for the best set of parameters. The search itself is carried out by using an optimization technique that avoids laboriously trying out every possible set of parameters.

Model changes

The first thing we do is to make three key changes to our training program:

- Add a hyperparameter evaluation metric
- Change the output directory so that different runs don't clobber one another
- Add command-line parameters for each of the hyperparameters

Because you might have many evaluation metrics (accuracy, recall, precision, RMSE, AUC, etc.), we need to instruct Cloud ML Engine which evaluation metric it should use for tuning. We do this by adding a new evaluation metric with the particular name that Cloud ML Engine will look for:

```
eval_metrics = {
        'rmse' : tflearn.MetricSpec(metric_fn=my_rmse,\
                prediction_key='probabilities'),
        'training/hptuning/metric' : tflearn.MetricSpec(\
            metric_fn=my_rmse, prediction_key='probabilities')
    },
```

In our case, we use the RMSE as the evaluation metric when it comes to finding the optimal set of parameters.

Hyperparameter tuning involves many runs of the training program with different sets of parameters. We need to make sure that the different runs don't checkpoint into the same directory. If they do, fault tolerance will be difficult—when a failed worker is restarted, from which of the many checkpoints should it resume? To keep the different runs of the train from clobbering one another, we change the output directory slightly in *task.py*:

```
output_dir = os.path.join(
    output_dir,
    json.loads(
        os.environ.get('TF_CONFIG', '{}')
    ).get('task', {}).get('trial', '')
)
```

What we have done is to find the trial number from the environment variable TF_CON FIG that Cloud ML Engine sets in the worker's environment so that we can append it to the user-specified output path. For example, checkpoints from trial number 7 will now go to *gs://cloud-training-demos-ml/flights/chapter9/output/7/model.ckpt*, thus keeping the checkpoints separate from those of other trials.

Finally, we add command-line parameters for each of the variables that we want to optimize, making sure that the training code uses the value from the command line. For example, we begin by making the batch_size a command-line parameter in *task.py*:

```
parser.add_argument(
    '--batch_size',
    help='Number of examples to compute gradient on',
    type=int,
    default=512
)
```

Then, we make sure to add the batch_size as one of the inputs to the make_experi ment() function and pass it along to the read_dataset() function:

```
def make_experiment_fn(traindata, evaldata, num_training_epochs,
                       batch_size, nbuckets, hidden_units, **args):
  def _experiment_fn(output_dir):
    return tflearn.Experiment(
        get_model(output_dir, nbuckets, hidden_units),
        train_input_fn=read_dataset(traindata,
                              mode=tf.contrib.learn.ModeKeys.TRAIN,
                              num_training_epochs=num_training_epochs,
                              batch_size=batch_size),
```

This is repeated for the nbuckets and hidden_units command-line parameters, except that the hidden units need to be converted from a string input at the command line to a list of numbers before they can be passed to the Estimator.

Hyperparameter configuration file

The second thing we do is to write a configuration file that specifies the search space for the hyperparameters:

```
trainingInput:
  scaleTier: STANDARD_1
  hyperparameters:
    goal: MINIMIZE
    maxTrials: 50
    maxParallelTrials: 5
    params:
    - parameterName: batch_size
      type: INTEGER
      minValue: 16
      maxValue: 512
      scaleType: UNIT_LOG_SCALE
    - parameterName: nbuckets
      type: INTEGER
      minValue: 5
      maxValue: 10
      scaleType: UNIT_LINEAR_SCALE
    - parameterName: hidden_units
      type: CATEGORICAL
      categoricalValues: ["64,16", "64,16,4", "64,64,64,8", "256,64,16"]
```

You can use the configuration file, in YAML format, to specify any of the command-line parameters. Note, for example, that we use it to specify the scaleTier here. In addition, we are specifying the hyperparameters, telling the tuner that our evaluation metric is to be minimized over 50 trials[14] with 5 of them happening in parallel.

Then, we specify the parameters to be optimized. The parameter batch_size is an integer; we ask for it to look for values in the interval [16, 512]—the logarithmic scale instructs the tuner that we would like to try more values at the smaller end of the range rather than the larger end of the range. This is because long-standing experience (*https://www.cs.toronto.edu/~hinton/absps/guideTR.pdf*) suggests that smaller batch sizes yield more accurate models.

The nbuckets parameter is also an integer, but linearly distributed between 5 and 10. The FAA seems to have about 36 grid boxes into which it divides up the airspace (see Figure 9-9). This argues for nbuckets=6 (since 6 × 6 = 36), but the corridors are significantly narrower in the Northeast part of the United States, and so perhaps we need more fine-grained grid cells. By specifying nbuckets in the range 5 to 10, we are

---

14 Note that hyperparameter tuning in Cloud ML Engine is not a grid search. The number of combinations of parameters can be many more than 50. The tuner chooses the exploration strategy to figure out the best 50 sets of parameters to try.

asking the tuner to explore having between 25 and 100 grid cells into which to divide up the United States.

As for `hidden_units`, we explicitly specify a few candidates—a two-layer network, a three-layer network, and a four-layer network, and a network with many more nodes. If it turns out that the optimal parameter is near the extrema, we will repeat the hyperparameter tuning with a different range. For example, if it turns out that nbuck ets = 10 is best, we should repeat the tuning, but trying out `nbuckets` in the range 10 to 15 the next time. Similarly, if a four-layer network turns out to be best, we will need to also try a five-layer and a six-layer network.

Running hyperparameter tuning

Submitting a hyperparameter tuning job is just like submitting a training job—you can accomplish it by using `gcloud`. The only difference is that there is now an extra parameter that points to the configuration file described in the previous section:

```
gcloud ml-engine jobs submit training $JOBNAME \
  --region=$REGION \
  --module-name=trainer.task \
  --package-path=$(pwd)/flights/trainer \
  --job-dir=$OUTPUT_DIR \
  --staging-bucket=gs://$BUCKET \
  --config=hyperparam.yaml \
 -\
  --output_dir=$OUTPUT_DIR \
  --traindata $DATA_DIR/train$PATTERN \
  --evaldata $DATA_DIR/test$PATTERN \
  --num_training_epochs=5
```

A few hours later, the output directory will be populated with the outputs of the various trials. But in the meantime, we can use the TensorBoard tool that comes with TensorFlow to monitor any of the output directories. Figure 9-11, for example, is my trial #1.

It appears that the loss function is bouncing around (recall that it is computed on each batch, and so some amount of bounciness is to be expected) but that the convergence, even of the smoothed orange curve, is not steady. This indicates that we should try to lower the learning rate. We have used the default optimizer (as of this writing, this is the `Ftrl` optimizer), but we could add that to our hyperparameter list. So many experiments, so little time!

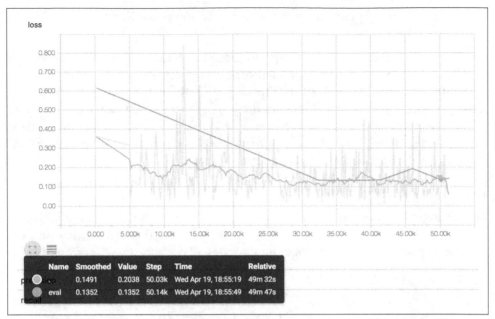

Figure 9-11. The change in the loss and eval metrics as the model is being trained, as seen in TensorBoard

Before you get excited about the value of the metric—0.135—you should realize that the loss measure in Figure 9-11 is cross-entropy, not RMSE. Figure 9-12 shows the RMSE graph for trial #1.

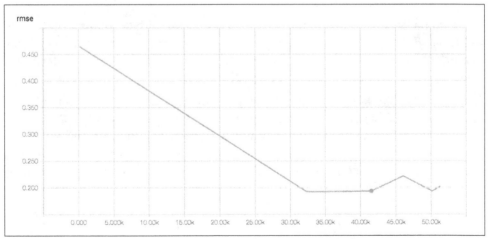

Figure 9-12. The RMSE for the evaluation dataset as training proceeds

The RMSE attained is about 0.2. What parameters does this trial correspond to? We can find the current state of a running job (or the final parameters from a finished job) using gcloud:

```
gcloud ml-engine jobs describe <jobid>
```

Doing this for my job yields the parameters and RMSEs of all the completed trials so far. Trial #1, in particular, is as follows:

```
- finalMetric:
    objectiveValue: 0.202596
    trainingStep: '3559'
  hyperparameters:
    batch_size: '170'
    hidden_units: 64,16
    nbuckets: '6'
  trialId: '1'
```

In other words, with a batch size of 170, a two-layer network, and six buckets, the RMSE is worse than our original, default choices (which gave us 0.187).

After 21 trials had completed, the best RMSE attained is not that much better than the defaults we began with:

```
- finalMetric:
    objectiveValue: 0.186319
    trainingStep: '33637'
  hyperparameters:
    batch_size: '16'
    hidden_units: 64,64,64,8
    nbuckets: '10'
  trialId: '2'
```

The smallest batch size, the most number of hidden layers, and the maximum number of buckets is the winner. No surprise. But the difference between this and a simpler, smaller network is negligible:

```
- finalMetric:
    objectiveValue: 0.187016
    trainingStep: '5097'
  hyperparameters:
    batch_size: '100'
    hidden_units: 64,16,4
    nbuckets: '5'
  trialId: '18'
```

The difficulty of getting minute gains here should underscore the importance and impact of feature engineering—we were able to get from a RMSE of 0.25 to a RMSE of 0.19 by adding key features, whereas adding an extra layer to the network gave us an RMSE improvement of less than 0.01.

Changing learning rate

Before we bid adieu to hyperparameter tuning, let's try changing the learning rate. As discussed in the previous section, the bounciness of the loss function concerns me a bit, and one potential remedy is to use a lower learning rate. Also, the fact that we are still at the phase where an extra layer helps indicates that we should try four, five, and six-layer networks. In terms of batch size, we'll reduce the batch_size to 100, as indicated in the previous hyperparameter tuning run, but not go all the way down to 16—not only will the training become unacceptably slow as the network overhead takes over, the bounciness in the loss function will also probably increase.

Unfortunately, changing the learning rate (essentially the size of the changes we make to the weights) is not that easy when using the Estimator API because it tries to shield us from such low-level details. But let's do it anyway.

The first step is to make the learning rate a command-line parameter, and pass it through to the function that creates the model. There are, however, two learning rates used by the DNNLinearCombinedClassifier. This is because it uses two optimizers—FtrlOptimizer (*http://bit.ly/2AfoeBv*) is employed to control the changing of weights in the linear section and AdagradOptimizer (*http://bit.ly/2nAfksl*) to control the changing of weights in the DNN section. At the time of writing, the classifier initializes the FtrlOptimizer with a learning rate of min(0.2, 1/sqrt(N)) where N is the number of linear columns.[15] In our model, we have fewer than 10 columns, so the learning rate being used is 0.2. For the AdagradOptimizer, the classifier uses a learning rate of 0.05. To make things simple, let's use a learning rate for the deep columns that is one-quarter of the learning rate used for the wide columns:

```
def wide_and_deep_model(output_dir,
                        nbuckets=5, hidden_units='64,32', learning_rate=0.01):
    ...
    estimator = \
     tflearn.DNNLinearCombinedClassifier(model_dir=output_dir,
            linear_feature_columns=sparse.values(),
            dnn_feature_columns=real.values(),
            dnn_hidden_units=parse_hidden_units(hidden_units),
            linear_optimizer=tf.train.FtrlOptimizer(
                    learning_rate=learning_rate),
            dnn_optimizer=tf.train.AdagradOptimizer(
                    learning_rate=learning_rate/4))
```

Note that to set the learning rate, we must pass in an appropriately initialized pair of optimizers.

---

15 See *https://github.com/tensorflow/tensorflow/blob/master/tensorflow/contrib/learn/python/learn/estimators/ dnn_linear_combined.py*—being able to examine the underlying code is one of the joys of open source.

We can then create a tuning configuration file to try out different learning rates and networks of different sizes:

```
trainingInput:
  scaleTier: STANDARD_1
  hyperparameters:
    goal: MINIMIZE
    maxTrials: 15
    maxParallelTrials: 3
    params:
    - parameterName: learning_rate
      type: DOUBLE
      minValue: 0.01
      maxValue: 0.25
      scaleType: UNIT_LINEAR_SCALE
    - parameterName: hidden_units
      type: CATEGORICAL
      categoricalValues: ["64,16,4", "64,64,16,4", "64,64,64,16,4",
                          "64,64,64,64,16,4"]
```

Running this as a hyperparameter tuning job in Cloud ML, we learn that adjusting the learning rate doesn't provide any dramatic benefit. The RMSE is lower if we use a five-layer network with a learning rate of 0.06, but not by much:

```
- finalMetric:
    objectiveValue: 0.186218
    trainingStep: '6407'
  hyperparameters:
    hidden_units: 64,64,64,16,4
    learning_rate: '0.060623111774000711'
  trialId: '12'
```

These, then, are the final parameters with which we can retrain the network on the full dataset. On retraining the five-layer model with a batch size of 100 and a learning rate of 0.06, we get a model whose evaluation RMSE is 0.1856.

Deploying the Model

Now that we have a trained model, let's use it to make predictions. Because we used the Experiment class and specified an export strategy with a serving input function, that model has all the pieces needed to accept inputs and make predictions. All that we need to do is to deploy the model with a REST endpoint.

Deploying a model is similar to deploying a Google App Engine application (see Chapter 2). We give the model a name and a version—the version is useful in case we want to do A–B testing of the current model in parallel with a previous version before promoting the model from staging to production.

Within the export directory, Cloud ML Engine creates a model in a folder with the timestamp. Let's pick the latest of the models in the output folder of Cloud ML Engine:[16]

```
MODEL_LOCATION=\
    $(gsutil ls gs://${BUCKET}/flights/chapter9/output/export/Servo/
        | tail -1)
```

Then, because this is the first time, we will create a model (flights) and a version (v1) of that model:

```
gcloud ml-engine models create flights --regions us-central1
gcloud ml-engine versions create v1 --model flights \
                            --origin ${MODEL_LOCATION}
```

Predicting with the Model

Now that a model version has been created, we can send it REST requests from any language. Let's do it from Python. The first step is to authenticate and get the credentials to access the service deployed by Cloud ML Engine:[17]

```
#!/usr/bin/env python
from googleapiclient import discovery
from oauth2client.client import GoogleCredentials
import json
credentials = GoogleCredentials.get_application_default()
```

The next step is to use the Google APIs Discovery Service[18] to form a client:

```
api = discovery.build('ml', 'v1', credentials=credentials,
    discoveryServiceUrl=
    'https://storage.googleapis.com/cloud-ml/discovery/ml_v1_discovery.json')

PROJECT = 'cloud-training-demos'
parent = 'projects/%s/models/%s/versions/%s' % (PROJECT, 'flights', 'v1')
response = api.projects().predict(body=request_data, name=parent).execute()
print "response={0}".format(response)
```

This code requires the request, and this is where we provide a dictionary of input variables as defined in the serving input function of our model:

```
request_data = {'instances':
    [
```

---

16 There will be only one in our case because the export strategy (see the Experiment constructor) was to export only one. For the full context of the deployment script, see *deploy_model.sh* in *https://github.com/GoogleCloud Platform/data-science-on-gcp/tree/master/09_cloudml*.

17 See *https://github.com/GoogleCloudPlatform/data-science-on-gcp/blob/master/09_cloudml/call_predict.py* for full context.

18 For details, see *https://developers.google.com/discovery*.

```
        {
          'dep_delay': 16.0,
          'taxiout': 13.0,
          'distance': 160.0,
          'avg_dep_delay': 13.34,
          'avg_arr_delay': 67.0,
          'carrier': 'AS',
          'dep_lat': 61.17,
          'dep_lon': -150.00,
          'arr_lat': 60.49,
          'arr_lon': -145.48,
          'origin': 'ANC',
          'dest': 'CDV'
        }
      ]
    }
```

The result for the preceding request is this response:

```
{u'predictions': [{u'probabilities': [0.8313459157943726, 0.16865408420562744],
u'logits': [-1.59519624710083], u'classes': 0, u'logistic':
[0.16865406930446625]}]}
```

From this JSON, we obtain the probability that the flight is late is 0.83. As you can see, making a trained model operational is quite straightforward in Cloud ML Engine. In this section, we looked at a specific way of running a TensorFlow model—as a web service. However, it is also possible to embed the model directly into our code. We explore both these options in Chapter 10.

Explaining the Model

Why does the model believe that the flight will be late with a probability of 0.83? An active area of research in machine learning is to provide the reasoning that underlies a specific model production in a form that humans can understand. One rather simple approach is to replace key predictors by average values (averages computed from the training dataset) to see the impact of that change. We can use this to provide some text explaining why the model thinks the flight will be late. Essentially, then, instead of sending in just one request, we send it several variants of that request:

```
request_data = {'instances':
  [
    {
      'dep_delay': dep_delay,
      'taxiout': taxiout,
      'distance': 160.0,
      'avg_dep_delay': 13.34,
      'avg_arr_delay': avg_arr_delay,
      'carrier': 'AS',
      'dep_lat': 61.17,
      'dep_lon': -150.00,
      'arr_lat': 60.49,
```

```
        'arr_lon': -145.48,
        'origin': 'ANC',
        'dest': 'CDV'
    }
    for dep_delay, taxiout, avg_arr_delay in
        [[16.0, 13.0, 67.0],
         [13.3, 13.0, 67.0], # if dep_delay was the airport mean
         [16.0, 16.0, 67.0], # if taxiout was the global mean
         [16.0, 13.0, 4] # if avg_arr_delay was the global mean
        ]
    ]
}
```

We are passing in four instances for prediction. The first instance consists of the actual observed values. The next three involve variants. The second instance consists of the average departure delay at this airport along with observed values for taxi-out time and average arrival delay. The third instance is a variant where the taxi-out change has been changed to the average taxi-out time for all flights in the training dataset.[19] Similarly, the fourth instance involves changing the arrival delay to the mean arrival delay in the training dataset. Of course, we could use the average corresponding to the actual airport they are flying to, but I'm trying to avoid having a bunch of lookup tables that need to be known by the client code.

Why these three variables and not the others? It doesn't help the user to inform her that her flight would not have been delayed if she were flying to Columbus, Ohio, rather than to Cincinnati (CVG)—she is sitting on a flight that is flying to Cincinnati! Thus, we treat some of the variables as "given," and try out only variants of the variables that are unique about the user's current experience. Devising what variants to use in this manner requires some thought and customer centricity.

The resulting responses from the predictions service can be parsed as

```
probs = [pred[u'probabilities'][0] \
            for pred in response[u'predictions']]
```

to yield the following array of probabilities (rounded off):

```
[0.17, 0.27, 0.07, 0.51]
```

From this, we can surmise that the average arrival delay is the feature that had the most impact. Because the arrival delay at CDV is 67 minutes, and not 4 minutes, the likelihood of the flight being on time has decreased from 0.51 to 0.17. The departure delay of 16 minutes versus the average of 13 minutes also contributes to the overall delay likelihood, but its impact is only about 30% (0.10/0.34) of the impact of the arrival delay. On the other hand, the reduced taxi-out time has helped; had it been 16.0 minutes, the on-time arrival likelihood would have been even lower.

---

19 I found this using BigQuery: SELECT AVG(taxi_out) FROM ...

Although not very detailed, it is very helpful to accompany a model prediction with a simple reason such as: "There is an 83% chance that you will arrive late. This is mostly because the average arrival delay at CVG is 67 minutes now. Also, your flight left the gate 16 minutes late; 13 minutes is more typical." Go the extra step and provide a bit of understandability to your model.

Summary

In this chapter, we extended the machine learning approach that we started in Chapter 7, but using the TensorFlow library instead of Spark MLib. Realizing that categorical columns result in an explosion of the dataset, we used TensorFlow to carry out distributed training. Another advantage that TensorFlow provides is that its design allows a computer scientist to go as low-level as he needs to, and so many machine learning research innovations are implemented in TensorFlow. As machine learning practitioners, therefore, using TensorFlow allows us to use innovative machine learning research soon after it is published rather than wait for a reimplementation in some other framework. Finally, using TensorFlow allows us to deploy the model rather easily into our data pipelines regardless of where they are run because TensorFlow is portable across a wide variety of hardware platforms.

To carry out distributed training in an easy-to-program way, we used the high-level Experiment class. This required us to implement five key aspects of a machine learning model, mostly as callback functions that the Experiment would invoke at the right points:

- A machine learning model that we implemented using the high-level Estimator API. The Estimator API provides out-of-the-box implementations for several classifiers including linear/logistic regression, deep neural network, and wide-and-deep. Even the Estimators can be opened up to customize almost every aspect of their implementation—we did this to experiment with a different learning rate than the default.

- A training input function that the Experiment would invoke to get feature columns and labels from the input training dataset.

- An evaluation input function that the Experiment would invoke periodically to monitor for overfitting, early stopping, and other concerns.

- An export strategy that specified how many models we wanted the Experiment to invoke. We chose to export just one, the best-performing one based on the evaluation dataset.

- A serving input function that would be used to parse the input feature values at prediction time. The serving input function is part of the TensorFlow model graph that is exported.

We trained a logistic regression model on all of the input values and realized that using the extra features resulted in a 7% reduction in RMSE (from 0.21 to 0.196), with a significant chunk of the improvement (42%) being provided by the time averages that were added by the Cloud Dataflow pipeline that we built in Chapter 8.

We discussed that, intuitively, the nodes in a deep neural network help provide decision hyperplanes, and that successive layers help to combine individual hyperplanes into more complex decision surfaces. Using a deep neural network instead of logistic regression didn't provide any benefit with our inputs, though. However, bringing in human insight in the form of additional features that bucketed some of the continuous features, creating feature crosses, and using a wide-and-deep model yielded a 5% reduction in the RMSE.

After we had a viable machine learning model and features, we carried out hyperparameter tuning to find optimal values of batch size, learning rate, number of buckets, and neural network architecture. We discovered that our initial, default choices were themselves quite good, but that reducing the batch size and increasing the number of layers provided a minute advantage.

For speed of experimentation, we had trained and hyperparameter-tuned the model on a sample of the full dataset. So, next, we trained the model with the chosen features and hyperparameters on the full dataset.

Finally, we deployed the model and invoked it using REST APIs to do online prediction. We also employed a simple method of providing rationales to accompany the machine learning predictions.

## CHAPTER 10

Real-Time Machine Learning

In the previous chapters, we ingested historical flight data and used it to train a machine learning model capable of predicting whether a flight will be late. We deployed the trained model and demonstrated that we could get the prediction for an individual flight by sending input variables to the model in the form of a REST call.

The input variables to the model include information about the flight whose on-time performance is desired. Most of these variables—the departure delay of the flight, the distance of the flight, and the time it takes to taxi out to the runway—are specific to the flight itself. However, the inputs to the machine learning model also included two time aggregates—the historic departure delay at the specific departure airport and the current arrival delay at the flight's destination—that require more effort to compute. In Chapter 8, we wrote an Apache Beam pipeline to compute these averages on the training dataset so as to be able to train the machine learning model. In Chapter 9, we trained a TensorFlow model capable of using the input variables to predict whether the flight would be late. We were also able to deploy this model on Google Cloud Platform as a web service and invoke the service to make predictions.

In this chapter, we build a real-time Beam pipeline that takes each flight and adds the predicted on-time performance of the flight and writes it out to a database. The resulting table can then be queried by user-facing applications that need to provide information to users of the system interested in their specific flight. Although we could do prediction on behalf of individual users of their service as and when they request the status of their specific flight, this will probably end up being wasteful. It is far more efficient[1] to compute the on-time arrival probability once, at flight takeoff,

---

[1] I am assuming that the number of users of our flight delay prediction service will be a factor of magnitude more than the number of flights. This is optimistic, of course, but it is good to design assuming that we will have a successful product.

and then simply look up the flight information as required for specific users. It is worth noting that we are making predictions for a flight only at the time of takeoff (and not updating it as the flight is en route) because we trained our machine learning model only on flight data at the time of takeoff.

The advantage of using Apache Beam to compute time averages is that the programming model is the same for both historical data and for real-time data. Therefore, we will be able to reuse most of our training pipeline code in real time. The only changes we will need to make to the pipeline from Chapter 8 (that created the training dataset) are to the input (to read from Pub/Sub) and the output (to add predicted probability instead of the known on-time performance). To add the predicted probability, though, we need to invoke the trained TensorFlow model. Let's write the code to do that first.

Invoking Prediction Service

In Chapter 9, we used Cloud Machine Learning Engine to deploy the trained Tensor-Flow model as a web service. We demonstrated that we could invoke the model by sending it a correctly formatted JSON request. For example, this JSON request[2]

```
{"instances":[{
"dep_delay":16.0,
"taxiout":13.0,
"distance":160.0,
"avg_dep_delay":13.34,
"avg_arr_delay":67.0,
"dep_lat":61.17,
"dep_lon":-150.0,
"arr_lat":60.49,
"arr_lon":-145.48,
"carrier":"AS",
"origin":"ANC",
"dest":"CDV"
}]}
```

yields this JSON response:

```
{"predictions": [{
"probabilities": [0.8313459157943726, 0.16865408420562744],
"logits": [-1.59519624710083],
```

---

2 The names of the attributes in the JSON (dep_delay, taxiout, etc.) are because we defined them in the serving_input_fn of our model's export signature in Chapter 9. Specifically, we defined a placeholder for dep_delay as:

tf.placeholder(tf.float32, [None])

and a placeholder for origin as:

tf.placeholder(tf.string, [None])

This is why we are sending a floating-point value for dep_delay and a string value for origin.

```
    "classes": 0,
    "logistic": [0.16865406930446625]
}]}
```

There are two probabilities returned. Because we trained the model to predict on-time arrival, the first probability corresponds to label = 0 (i.e., the flight is late) and the second probability corresponds to label = 1 (i.e., the flight is on time, remembering that we defined "on time" during training as an arrival delay of less than 15 minutes). Therefore, in this case, we are predicting that there is only a 16.86% probability that the flight will have an arrival delay of less than 15 minutes. Because our threshold for canceling the meeting is that this probability is less than 70%, the recommendation will be to cancel the meeting.

In Chapter 9, we demonstrated the call and response using Python, but because this is a REST web service, it can be invoked from pretty much any programming language as long as we can formulate the JSON, authenticate to Google Cloud Platform, and send an HTTP request. Let's look at these three steps from our real-time pipeline.

Java Classes for Request and Response

To invoke the REST API from our Beam Java pipeline,[3] we need to formulate and parse JSON messages in our Java program. A good way to do this is to represent the JSON request and response as Java classes (let's call them Request and Response) and then use a library such as Jackson (*https://github.com/FasterXML/jackson*) or GSON (*https://github.com/google/gson*) to do the marshaling from JSON and unmarshaling into JSON.

Based on the previous JSON example, the Request class definition is as follows:[4]

```
class Request {
    List<Instance> instances = new ArrayList<>();
}
class Instance {
    double dep_delay, taxiout, distance, avg_dep_delay, avg_arr_delay,
            dep_lat, dep_lon, arr_lat, arr_lon;
    String carrier, origin, dest;
}
```

Note how arrays in JSON ([...]) are represented as a `java.util.List` and dictionaries ({...}) are represented as Java classes with appropriately named fields. Similarly, based on the example JSON response, the Response class definition is as follows:

---

3 Recall from Chapter 8 that I'm using Beam Java and not Beam Python because, as of this writing, Beam Python does not support streaming.

4 For the full code, go to *https://github.com/GoogleCloudPlatform/data-science-on-gcp/blob/master/10_realtime/chapter10/src/main/java/com/google/cloud/training/flights/FlightsMLService.java.*

```
class Response {
    List<Prediction> predictions = new ArrayList<>();
}
class Prediction {
    List<Double> probabilities = new ArrayList<>();
    List<Double> logits        = new ArrayList<>();
    int          classes;
    List<Double> logistic      = new ArrayList<>();
}
```

Creating a JSON request involves creating the Request object and using the GSON library to create the JSON representation:

```
Request req = …
Gson gson = new GsonBuilder().create();
String json = gson.toJson(req, Request.class);
```

We also can accomplish unmarshaling a JSON stream to a Response object from which we can obtain the predictions by using the same library:

```
String response = … // invoke web service
Response response = gson.fromJson(response, Response.class);
```

We don't want to pollute the rest of our code with these Request and Response classes. So, let's add a way to create a Request from a Flight object and a way to extract the probability of interest from a Response object. Every Flight corresponds to an Instance sent to the web service, so we will write a constructor that sets all the fields of the Instance object from the provided Flight:

```
Instance(Flight f) {
    this.dep_delay = f.getFieldAsFloat(Flight.INPUTCOLS.DEP_DELAY);
    // etc.
    this.avg_dep_delay = f.avgDepartureDelay;
    this.avg_arr_delay = f.avgDepartureDelay;
    // etc.
    this.dest = f.getField(Flight.INPUTCOLS.DEST);
}
```

A Response consists of a list of predictions, one for each flight sent in the Request, so we will write an appropriate method in the Response class to pull out the probability that the flight is on time. The method will return an array of probabilities:

```
public double[] getOntimeProbability() {
    double[] result = new double[predictions.size()];
    for (int i=0; i < result.length; ++i) {
        Prediction pred = predictions.get(i);
        result[i] = pred.probabilities.get(1);
    }
    return result;
}
```

Post Request and Parse Response

Now that we have a way to create and parse JSON bytes, we are ready to interact with the Flights Machine Learning service. The service is deployed at this URL:

```
String endpoint = "https://ml.googleapis.com/v1/projects/"
        + String.format("%s/models/%s/versions/%s:predict",
                        PROJECT, MODEL, VERSION);
GenericUrl url = new GenericUrl(endpoint);
```

The code to authenticate to Google Cloud Platform, send the request, and get back the response is quite straightforward. We create an https transport and then send JSON bytes using HTTP POST. Here's the response we get back:

```
GoogleCredential credential = // authenticate
                GoogleCredential.getApplicationDefault();
HttpTransport httpTransport = // https
                GoogleNetHttpTransport.newTrustedTransport();
HttpRequestFactory requestFactory =
                httpTransport.createRequestFactory(credential);
HttpContent content = new ByteArrayContent("application/json",
                json.getBytes()); // json
HttpRequest request = requestFactory.buildRequest("POST",
                url, content); // POST request
request.setUnsuccessfulResponseHandler(
                new HttpBackOffUnsuccessfulResponseHandler(
                        new ExponentialBackOff())); // fault-tol
request.setReadTimeout(5 * 60 * 1000); // 5 minutes
String response = request.execute().parseAsString(); // resp
```

Note that I have added in two bits of fault tolerance: if there is a network interruption or some temporary glitch (a non-2xx error from HTTP), I retry the request, increasing the time between retries using the ExponentialBackoff class. As of this writing, I observed that a sudden spike in traffic resulted in a 100- to 150-second delay as extra servers came online, hence the need for a longer-than-usual timeout.

Client of Prediction Service

The previous code example is wrapped into a helper class (FlightsMLService (*http://bit.ly/2jlFpqp*)) that we can use to obtain the probability of a flight being on time:

```
public static double predictOntimeProbability(Flight f, double defaultValue)
throws IOException, GeneralSecurityException {
    if (f.isNotCancelled() && f.isNotDiverted()) {
      Request request = new Request();

      // fill in actual values
      Instance instance = new Instance(f);
      request.instances.add(instance);

      // send request
```

```
    Response resp = sendRequest(request);
    double[] result = resp.getOntimeProbability(defaultValue);
    if (result.length > 0) {
      return result[0];
    } else {
      return defaultValue;
    }
  }
  return defaultValue;
}
```

Note that we check that the flight is not canceled or diverted—this is important because we trained the neural network only on flights with actual arrival information.

Adding Predictions to Flight Information

With the client to the Flights Machine Learning service in place, we can now create a pipeline that will ingest raw flight information at the time that a flight is taking off and invoke the prediction service. The resulting probability that the flight will be on time will be added to the flight information. Finally, both the original information about the flight and the newly computed probability will be saved.

In real time, this pipeline will need to listen to messages about flights coming in from Google Cloud Pub/Sub (recall that we set up a simulation to create this feed in Chapter 4) and stream the results into a durable, queryable store such as BigQuery.

Batch Input and Output

Before we do things in real time, though, let's write a batch pipeline to accomplish the same thing. After the pipeline is working correctly, we can swap out the input and output parts to have the code work on real-time, streaming data (something Apache Beam's unified batch/streaming model makes quite straightforward). Because we plan to swap the input and output, let's capture that in a Java interface:[5]

```
interface InputOutput extends Serializable {
public PCollection<Flight> readFlights(Pipeline p, MyOptions options);
    public void writeFlights(PCollection<Flight> outFlights, MyOptions options);
}
```

The implementation for batch data reads from a BigQuery table and writes to text files on Google Cloud Storage. The reading code is similar to the code used in `Create TrainingDataset`. The difference is that we read all flights, not just the ones that are not canceled or diverted. This is because we would like to store all the flight information that is sent to us in real time regardless of whether we can predict anything about

---

5 For the full code, go to *https://github.com/GoogleCloudPlatform/data-science-on-gcp/blob/master/10_realtime/chapter10/src/main/java/com/google/cloud/training/flights/AddRealtimePrediction.java*.

that flight. Table 10-1 shows the crucial bits of code (with the Java boilerplate taken out).

Table 10-1. Key steps in Dataflow pipeline to read historical data from BigQuery and write out predictions to Cloud Storage

Step	What it does	Code

1	Create query	```String query = "SELECT EVENT_DATA FROM" +```
		```" flights.simevents WHERE " +```
		```" STRING(FL_DATE) = '2015-01-04' AND " +```
		```" (EVENT = 'wheelsoff' OR EVENT = 'arrived') ";```

2	Read lines	```BigQueryIO.Read.fromQuery(query)```

3	Parse into `Flight` object	```TableRow row = c.element();```
		```String line = (String)```
		``` row.getOrDefault("EVENT_DATA", "");```
		```Flight f = Flight.fromCsv(line);```
		```if (f != null) {```
		``` c.outputWithTimestamp(f, f.getEventTimestamp());```
		```}```

When it comes to writing, we need to write out all the flight information that we receive. However, we also need to carry out prediction and write out the predicted probability. Let's create an object to represent the data (flights + on-time probability) that we need to write out:

```
@DefaultCoder(AvroCoder.class)
public class FlightPred {
    Flight flight;
    double ontime;
    // constructor, etc.
}
```

The `ontime` field will hold the following:

- The predicted on-time probability if the received event is `wheelsoff`
- The actual on-time performance (0 or 1) if the received event is `arrived`
- Null (however it is represented in the output sink) if the flight is canceled or diverted

The writing code then involves taking the flight information, adding the value of the `ontime` field, and writing it out:

```
PCollection<FlightPred> prds = addPrediction(outFlights);
PCollection<String> lines = predToCsv(prds);
lines.apply("Write", TextIO.Write.to(
    options.getOutput() + "flightPreds").withSuffix(".csv"));
```

The `addPrediction()` method is a `ParDo.apply()` of a `DoFn` whose `processEle`ment() method is:

```
 Flight f = c.element();
double ontime = -5;
if (f.isNotCancelled() && f.isNotDiverted()) {
if (f.getField(INPUTCOLS.EVENT).equals("arrived")) {
    // actual ontime performance
    ontime = f.getFieldAsFloat(INPUTCOLS.ARR_DELAY, 0) < 15 ? 1 : 0;
  } else {
    // wheelsoff: predict ontime arrival probability
    ontime = FlightsMLService.predictOntimeProbability(f, -5.0);
  }
}
c.output(new FlightPred(f, ontime));
```

When converting a `FlightPred` to a comma-separated value (CSV) file, we take care to replace the invalid negative value by `null`:

```
FlightPred pred = c.element();
String csv = String.join(",", pred.flight.getFields());
if (pred.ontime >= 0) {
  csv = csv + "," + new DecimalFormat("0.00").format(pred.ontime);
} else {
  csv = csv + ","; // empty string -> null
}
c.output(csv);
```

Data Processing Pipeline

Now that we have the input and output pieces of the pipeline implemented, let's implement the middle of the pipeline. That part of the pipeline is the same as what was in `CreateTrainingDataset` (and in fact simply invokes those methods) except for the treatment of the departure delay:

```
    Pipeline p = Pipeline.create(options);
    InputOutput io = new BatchInputOutput();

    PCollection<Flight> allFlights = io.readFlights(p, options);

PCollectionView<Map<String, Double>> avgDepDelay =
readAverageDepartureDelay(p, options.getDelayPath());

    PCollection<Flight> hourlyFlights =
CreateTrainingDataset.applyTimeWindow(allFlights);

    PCollection<KV<String, Double>> avgArrDelay =
CreateTrainingDataset.computeAverageArrivalDelay(hourlyFlights);

hourlyFlights = CreateTrainingDataset.addDelayInformation(
hourlyFlights, avgDepDelay,
avgArrDelay, averagingFrequency);
```

```
    io.writeFlights(hourlyFlights, options);

    PipelineResult result = p.run();
    result.waitUntilFinish();
```

Whereas the arrival delay is computed over the current flights by the pipeline, the departure delay is simply read out of the global average (over the training dataset) that was written out during training:

```
private static PCollectionView<Map<String, Double>>
readAverageDepartureDelay(Pipeline p, String path) {
    return p.apply("Read delays.csv", TextIO.Read.from(path)) //
.apply("Parse delays.csv",
ParDo.of(new DoFn<String, KV<String, Double>>() {
    @ProcessElement
public void processElement(ProcessContext c) throws Exception {
        String line = c.element();
        String[] fields = line.split(",");
        c.output(KV.of(fields[0], Double.parseDouble(fields[1])));
    }
})) //
    .apply("toView", View.asMap());
}
```

The rest of the code is just like in `CreateTrainingDataset`. We get the average departure delay at the origin airport; apply an hourly sliding window; compute the average arrival delay over the previous hour at the destination airport; add the two delays to the flight data; and write out the flight information along with the predicted on-time performance.

Identifying Inefficiency

With the pipeline code written up, we can execute the batch pipeline on Google Cloud Platform in Cloud Dataflow. Unfortunately, when I did just that, I noticed that the inference kept failing. One way to monitor the usage of an API (our machine learning prediction is the Cloud ML Engine API) is from the API Dashboard part of the Google Cloud Platform web console. Looking at the traffic chart and breakdown of response codes in Figure 10-1, we immediately notice what is wrong.

The first few requests succeed with an HTTP response code of 200, but then the rest of the requests fail with a response code of 429 ("too many requests"). This pattern repeats—notice in Figure 10-1 the blue peaks of successful responses, followed by the much higher yellow peaks of failed responses.[6] We could ask for a quota increase so

---

6 You see multiple peaks in the chart because the pipeline sends requests to the machine learning service periodically, triggering on the end of a sliding time window.

that we can send more requests—from the graphs, it appears that we should request approximately five times the current quota.

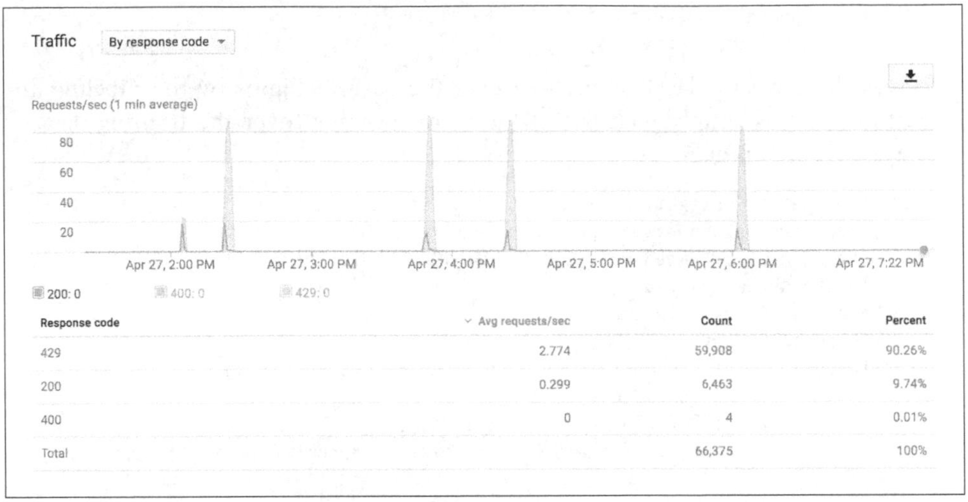

Figure 10-1. Monitoring the usage of an API in the Google Cloud Platform web console

Before asking for a quota increase, however, we could look to see if we can optimize our pipeline to make fewer requests from the service.

Batching Requests

Whereas we do need to make predictions for each flight, we do not need to send the flight information to the service one-by-one. Instead of invoking the Flights Machine Learning service once for each flight, we could batch up requests. If we were to invoke the predictions for 60,000 flights into batches of 60 each, we'd be making only 1,000 requests. Making fewer requests will not only reduce costs, it might also end up increasing the overall performance by having less time spent waiting for a response from the service.

There are a couple of possible ways to batch up requests—based on count (accumulate flights until we reach a threshold, such as 100 flights, and invoke the service with these 100 flights) or based on time (accumulate flights for a fixed time span, such as two minutes, and invoke the service with all the flight information accumulated in that time period).

To batch requests based on count within a Cloud Dataflow pipeline, set up a trigger on a global window to operate on the count of records. This code will batch the inputs into groups of 100 each and ensure that the pipeline sends partial batches if waiting any further would cause the latency of the first element in the pane to go beyond one minute:

```
.apply(Window.into(new GlobalWindows()).triggering(
        Repeatedly.forever(AfterFirst.of(
            AfterPane.elementCountAtLeast(100),
            AfterProcessingTime.pastFirstElementInPane().
    plusDelayOf(Duration.standardMinutes(1))))
```

In our case, however, we cannot do this. Recall that our pipeline does a sliding window (of one hour) in order to compute the average arrival delay and this average is part of the Flight object being written out. Applying a GlobalWindow later in the pipeline would cause the objects to be re-windowed so that any group-by-keys applied to the data afterward would happen globally—this is a side effect that we neither want nor need. Therefore, we should look for a batching method that operates in the context of a sliding window without doing its own Window.into().

Because we are already in the context of a sliding window, we could take all the flights that were used in the computation of the average delay, batch them, and get predictions for them. This is very appealing because we are obtaining the predicted on-time performance for a flight as soon as we have all the information that is needed in order to carry out machine learning interference—no additional delay is being introduced. Although we could combine all the flights over the past five minutes into a single batch and send it for inference, this will have the unwanted effect of being carried out on a single Cloud Dataflow worker. We should provide the ability to create a few batches from the flights over the five-minute period so that we can avoid overwhelming a single Cloud Dataflow worker node.

My solution to create a batch is to emit a key-value pair for each flight such that the key reflects the batch number of the flight in question:

```
Flight f = c.element();
String key = "batch=" + System.identityHashCode(f) % NUM_BATCHES;
c.output(KV.of(key, f));
```

We obtain the key by taking the identity hashcode of the object and finding the remainder when the hashcode is divided by NUM_BATCHES—this ensures that there are only NUM_BATCHES unique keys.[7]

To work within the context of a time-windowed pipeline, we follow the transform that emits key-value pairs (as we just did) with a GroupByKey:

```
PCollection<FlightPred> lines = outFlights //
    .apply("Batch->Flight", ParDo.of(...) // see previous fragment
    .apply("CreateBatches", GroupByKey.<String, Flight> create())
```

---

7 The actual code for this is a bit more complex because we'd like to process wheelsoff, arrived, and canceled/
  diverted flights differently. So, the event type is made part of the key, and thus we create NUM_BATCHES*3
  unique keys. For the full code, go to *https://github.com/GoogleCloudPlatform/data-science-on-gcp/blob/
  master/10_realtime/chapter10/src/main/java/com/google/cloud/training/flights/InputOutput.java.*

The GroupByKey will now output an Iterable<Flight> that can be sent along for prediction:

```
double[] batchPredict(Iterable<Flight> flights, float defaultValue) throws
IOException, GeneralSecurityException {
    Request request = new Request();
    for (Flight f : flights) {
        request.instances.add(new Instance(f));
    }
    Response resp = sendRequest(request);
    double[] result = resp.getOntimeProbability(defaultValue);
    return result;
}
```

With this change, the number of requests drops dramatically, and is under quota, as demonstrated in Figure 10-2.

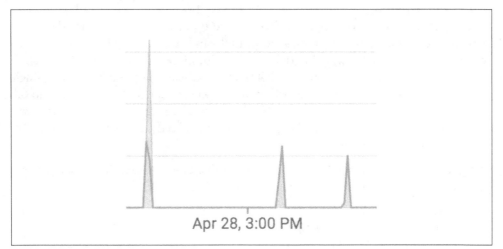

Figure 10-2. After the change to batch up requests, the number of requests drops significantly

Note how the same set of records is handled with far fewer requests after the change to send the requests in batches.

Streaming Pipeline

Now that we have a working data processing pipeline that can process bounded inputs, let's change the input and output so that the pipeline works on streaming data. The pipeline will read from Cloud Pub/Sub and stream into BigQuery.

Flattening PCollections

When we read from text files, our data processing code received both `arrived` and `wheelsoff` events from the same text file. However, the simulation code that we wrote in Chapter 4 streams these events to two separate topics in Cloud Pub/Sub. To reuse the data processing code, we must ingest messages from both these topics and merge the two `PCollections` into one. We can accomplish merging `PCollections` of the same type by using the `Flatten PTransform`. The code, therefore, involves looping through the two events, creating two separate `PCollections`, and then invoking `Flatten`:

```java
// empty collection to start
PCollectionList<Flight> pcs = PCollectionList.empty(p);
// read flights from each of two topics
for (String eventType : new String[]{"wheelsoff", "arrived"}){
String topic = "projects/" + options.getProject() +
"/topics/" + eventType;
    PCollection<Flight> flights = p.apply(eventType + ":read",
        PubsubIO.<String> read().topic(topic)
                .withCoder(StringUtf8Coder.of()) //
.timestampLabel("EventTimeStamp")) //
.apply(eventType + ":parse",
ParDo.of(new DoFn<String, Flight>() {
            @ProcessElement
public void processElement(ProcessContext c)
throws Exception {
                String line = c.element();
                Flight f = Flight.fromCsv(line);
                if (f != null) {
                    c.output(f);
                }
            }
        }));
pcs = pcs.and(flights);
  }
  // flatten collection
  return pcs.apply(Flatten.<Flight>pCollections());
}
```

This is a pattern worth knowing—the way to create a pipeline from multiple sources is to ensure that you ingest each of the sources into `PCollections` of the same type, and then invoke the `Flatten` transform. The flattened collection is what will be processed by the rest of the pipeline.

Another thing to note is the presence of a `timestampLabel` in the `PubsubIO` read. Without the timestamp label, messages are assigned the timestamp at which the message was inserted into Pub/Sub. In most cases, this will suffice. However, I would like to use the actual time of the flight as the timestamp and not the time of insertion because I am simulating flight events at faster-than-real-time speeds. Being able to specify a timestamp label is also important in case there is latency between the creation of the message and its actual insertion into Pub/Sub. The `timestampLabel` refers to an attribute on the Pub/Sub message, and is specified by the publishing program (*http://bit.ly/2jZY5M5*):

```
def publish(topics, allevents, notify_time):
  timestamp = notify_time.strftime(RFC3339_TIME_FORMAT)
    for key in topics:  # 'departed', 'arrived', etc.
        topic = topics[key]
        events = allevents[key]
        with topic.batch() as batch:
            for event_data in events:
      batch.publish(event_data, EventTimeStamp=timestamp)
```

Streaming the output `FlightPred` information to BigQuery involves creating `TableRows` and then writing to a BigQuery table:

```
String outputTable = options.getProject() + ':' + BQ_TABLE_NAME;
TableSchema schema = new TableSchema().setFields(getTableFields());
PCollection<FlightPred> preds = addPredictionInBatches(outFlights);
PCollection<TableRow> rows = toTableRows(preds);
rows.apply("flights:write_toBQ",BigQueryIO.Write.to(outputTable) //
    .withSchema(schema));
```

Executing Streaming Pipeline

Now that the pipeline code has been written, we can start the simulation from Chapter 4 to stream records into Cloud Pub/Sub:

```
cd ../04_streaming/simulate
python simulate.py --startTime "2015-04-01 00:00:00 UTC" --endTime "2015-04-03
00:00:00 UTC" --speedFactor 60
```

Then, we can start the Cloud Dataflow pipeline to consume these records, invoke the Flights ML service, and write the resulting records to BigQuery:

```
mvn compile exec:java \
-Dexec.mainClass=com.google.cloud.training.flights.AddRealtimePrediction \
 -Dexec.args="--realtime --speedupFactor=60 --maxNumWorkers=10 --
autoscalingAlgorithm=THROUGHPUT_BASED"
```

The `realtime` option allows us to switch the pipeline between the two implementations of `InputOutput` (batch and real time), and in this case, to use the Pub/Sub to BigQuery pipeline.

With the pipeline running, we can navigate over to the BigQuery console, shown in Figure 10-3, and verify that flight information is indeed being streamed in.

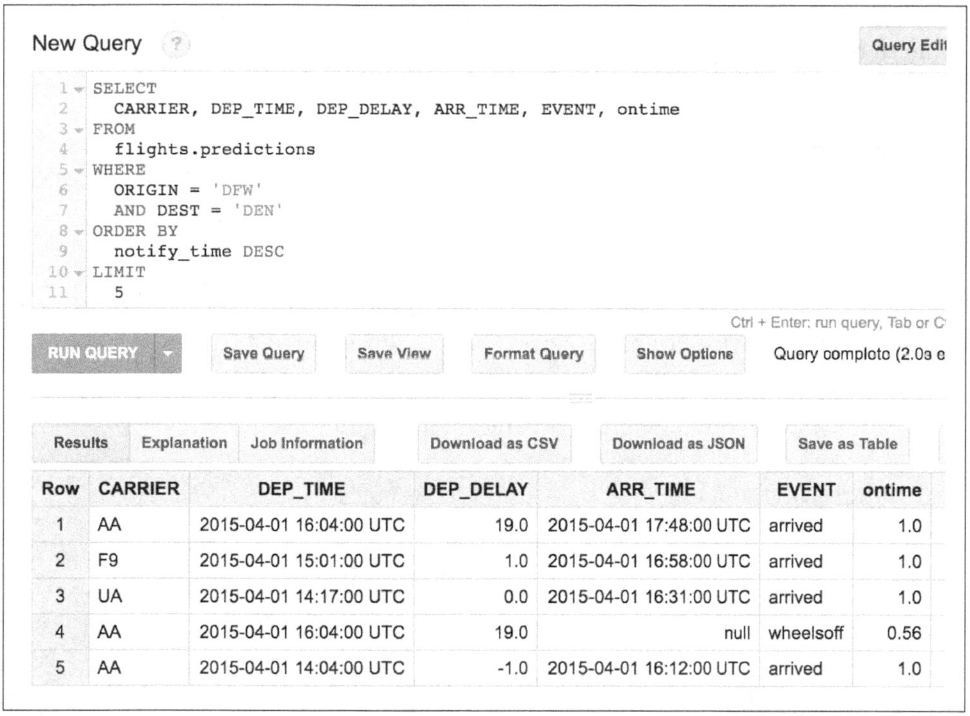

Figure 10-3. Streaming predictions of on-time arrival probability

The query in Figure 10-3 is looking at flights between Dallas/Fort Worth (DFW) and Denver (DEN) and ordering and limiting the result set so that the five latest flights are retained. We see that row 1 is an American Airlines (AA) flight that arrived on time in spite of a departure delay of 19 minutes. On row 4, we see the earlier prediction by the service for that flight at the time of wheels off, indicating that this was only 56% likely to happen.

Late and Out-of-Order Records

Our simulation uses the flight record time to add records into Cloud Pub/Sub in precise order. In real life, though, flight records are unlikely to arrive in order. Instead, network vagaries and latencies can cause late and out-of-order records. To simulate these essentially random effects, we should change our simulation to add a random delay to each record.

We can do this in the BigQuery SQL statement that is used by the simulation program to read in the flight records:

```
SELECT
  EVENT,
  NOTIFY_TIME AS ORIGINAL_NOTIFY_TIME,
  TIMESTAMP_ADD(NOTIFY_TIME, INTERVAL CAST (0.5 + RAND()*120 AS INT64) SECOND)
  AS NOTIFY_TIME, EVENT_DATA
FROM
  `flights.simevents`
```

Because RAND() returns a number that is uniformly distributed between 0 and 1, multiplying the result of RAND() by 120 yields a delay between 0 and 2 minutes.

Running this query on the BigQuery console, we notice that it works as intended—the records now reflect some jitter, as depicted in Figure 10-4.

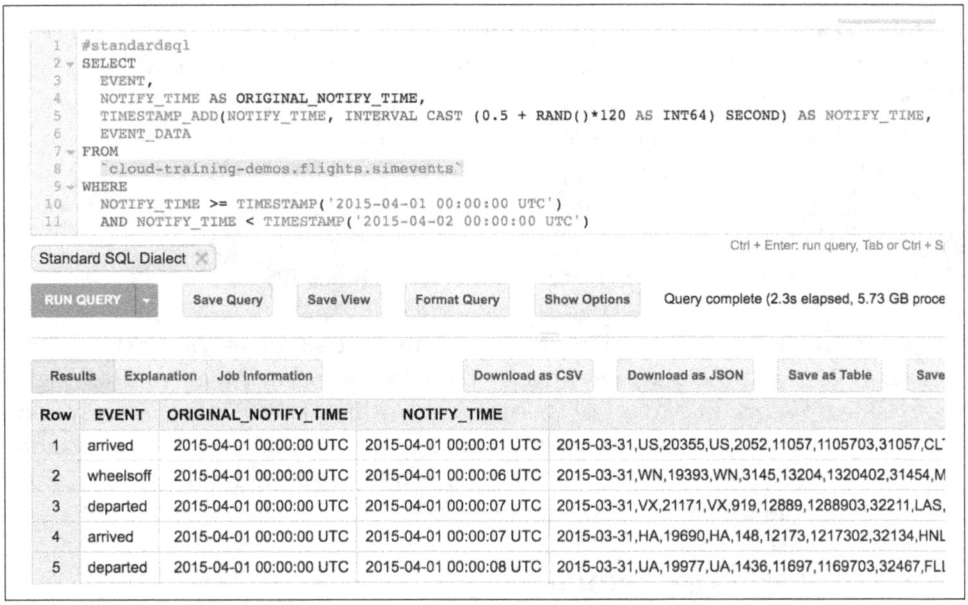

Figure 10-4. Adding random jitter to the notification time

Note that the first record is delayed by one second, whereas the second record, which is nominally at the same time, is now six seconds later.

Uniformly distributed delay

A zero delay is highly unrealistic, however. We could change the formula to simulate other scenarios. For example, if we want to have latencies between 90 and 120 seconds, we would change the jitter to be CAST(90.5 + RAND()*30 AS INT64). The resulting distribution might look like Figure 10-5.

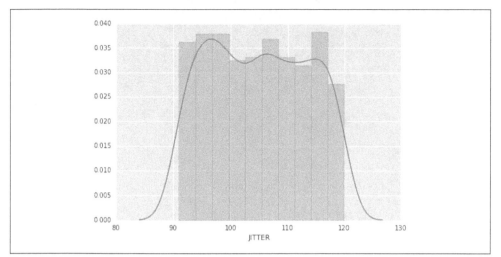

Figure 10-5. Uniformly distributed jitter

Even this strikes me as being unrealistic. I don't know what the delay involved with the flight messages is,[8] but there seem to be two possibilities: an exponential distribution and a normal distribution.

Exponential distribution

An exponential distribution is the theoretical distribution associated with the time between events during which the events themselves happen at a constant rate. If the network capacity is limited by the number of events, we'd observe that the delay follows an exponential distribution. To simulate this, we can create the jitter variable following this formula:

```
CAST(-LN(RAND()*0.99 + 0.01)*30 + 90.5 AS INT64)
```

The resulting distribution would look something like that shown in Figure 10-6.

With the exponential distribution, latencies of 90s are much more common than latencies of 150s, but a few records will encounter unusually high latencies.

---

8 If we had a real-time feed, we'd of course collect data on delay instead of simply guessing.

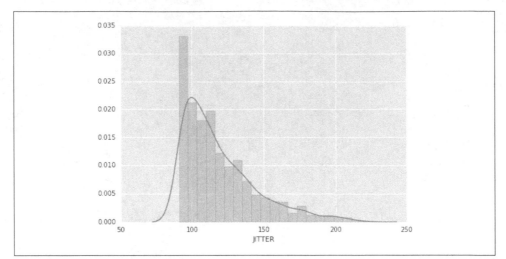

Figure 10-6. Exponential distribution of jitter: smaller values are much more likely than large values

Normal distribution

A third alternative distribution for the delay is that it follows the law of big numbers, and that if we observe enough flight events, we might observe that the delay is normally distributed around some mean with a certain standard deviation. Of course, the delay must be positive, so the distribution would be truncated at zero.

Generating a normally distributed random variable is difficult to do with just plain SQL. Fortunately, BigQuery allows for user-defined functions (UDFs) in JavaScript. This JavaScript function uses the Marsaglia polar rule to transform a pair of uniformly distributed random variables into one that is normally distributed:

```
js = """
   var u = 1 - Math.random();
   var v = 1 - Math.random();
   var f = Math.sqrt(-2 * Math.log(u)) * Math.cos(2*Math.PI*v);
   f = f * sigma + mu;
   if (f < 0)
      return 0;
   else
      return f;
""".replace('\n', ' ')
```

We can use the preceding JavaScript to create a temporary UDF invokable from SQL:

```
sql = """
CREATE TEMPORARY FUNCTION
trunc_rand_normal(x FLOAT64, mu FLOAT64, sigma FLOAT64)
RETURNS FLOAT64
LANGUAGE js AS "{}";
```

```
SELECT
  trunc_rand_normal(ARR_DELAY, 90, 15) AS JITTER
FROM

  ...
""".format(js).replace('\n', ' ')
```

The resulting distribution of jitter might look something like Figure 10-7 (the preceding code used a mean of 90 and a standard deviation of 15).

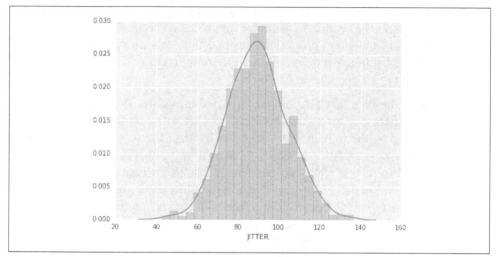

Figure 10-7. Normally distribution jitter, with a jitter of 90s most likely

To experiment with different types of jitter, let's change our simulation code to add random jitter to the notify_time:[9]

```
jitter = 'CAST (-LN(RAND()*0.99 + 0.01)*30 + 90.5 AS INT64)'

# run the query to pull simulated events
querystr = """\
SELECT
  EVENT,
  TIMESTAMP_ADD(NOTIFY_TIME, INTERVAL {} SECOND) AS NOTIFY_TIME,
  EVENT_DATA
FROM
  `cloud-training-demos.flights.simevents`
WHERE
  NOTIFY_TIME >= TIMESTAMP('{}')
  AND NOTIFY_TIME < TIMESTAMP('{}')
ORDER BY
```

---

9 See the jitter variable in *https://github.com/GoogleCloudPlatform/data-science-on-gcp/blob/master/04_stream ing/simulate/simulate.py.*

```
    NOTIFY_TIME ASC
    """
query = bqclient.run_sync_query(querystr.format(jitter,
                                                args.startTime,
                                                args.endTime))
```

Watermarks and Triggers

The Beam programming model implicitly handles out-of-order records within the sliding window, and by default accounts for late-arriving records. Beam employs the concept of a *watermark*, which is the oldest unprocessed record left in the pipeline. The watermark is an inherent property of any real-time data processing system and is indicative of the lag in the pipeline. Cloud Dataflow tracks and learns this lag over time.

If we are using the time that a record was inserted into Cloud Pub/Sub as the event time, the watermark is a strict guarantee that no data with an earlier event time will ever be observed by the pipeline. On the other hand, if the user specifies the event time (by specifying a `timestampLabel`), there is nothing to prevent the publishing program from inserting a really old record into Cloud Pub/Sub, and so the watermark is a learned heuristic based on the observed historical lag. The concept of a watermark is more general than Cloud Pub/Sub, of course—in the case of streaming sources (such as low-power Internet of Things devices) that are intermittent, watermarking helps those delays as well.

Computation of aggregate statistics is driven by a "trigger." Whenever a trigger fires, the pipeline calculations are carried out. Our pipeline can include multiple triggers, but each of the triggers is usually keyed off the watermark. The default trigger is

```
Repeatedly.forever(AfterWatermark.pastEndOfWindow())
```

which means that the trigger fires when the watermark passes the end of the window and then immediately whenever any late data arrives. In other words, every late-arriving record is processed individually. This prioritizes correctness over performance.

What if we add a uniformly distributed jitter to the simulation? Because our uniform delay is in the range of 90 to 120, the actual difference in delay between the earliest-arriving and latest-arriving records is 30 seconds. So, Cloud Dataflow needs to keep windows open 30 seconds longer.

The Cloud Dataflow job monitoring web page on the Cloud Platform Console indicates the learned watermark value. We can click any of the transform steps to view what this value is. And with a uniform delay added to the simulation, the monitoring console (Figure 10-8) shows us that this is what is happening.

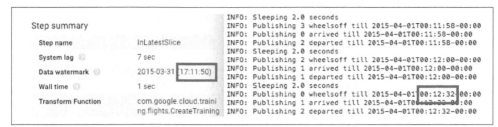

Figure 10-8. Although the simulation is sending events at 12 minutes and 32 seconds past the hour, the Dataflow pipeline shows a watermark at 11 minutes and 50 seconds past the hour, indicating that the time windows are being kept open about 42 seconds longer

We see that the simulation (righthand side of Figure 10-8) is sending events at 00:12:32 UTC, whereas the watermark shown by the monitoring console is at 17:11:50 Pacific Standard Time. Ignoring the seven hours due to time zone conversion, Cloud Dataflow is keeping windows open for 42 seconds longer (this includes the system lag of seven seconds, which is the time taken to process the records).

Unlike uniform jitter, small delays are far more likely than larger delays in exponentially distributed jitter. With exponentially distributed jitter added to the simulated data in the Cloud Pub/Sub pipeline, the learned watermark value is 21 seconds (see Figure 10-9).

Figure 10-9. Because small delays are more likely in exponentially distributed jitter, the window is being kept open only about 21 seconds longer

Recall that the default trigger prioritizes correctness over performance, processing each late-arriving record one by one and updating the computed aggregates. Fortunately, changing this trade-off is quite easy. Here is a different trade-off:

```
.triggering(Repeatedly.forever(
        AfterWatermark.pastEndOfWindow()
        .withLateFirings(
            AfterPane.elementCountAtLeast(10))
        .orFinally(AfterProcessingTime.pastFirstElementInPane()
            .plusDelayOf(Duration.standardMinutes(30)))))
```

Here, the calculations are triggered at the watermark (as before). Late records are processed 10 at a time but only if they arrive within 30 minutes after the start of the plane. Beyond that, late records are thrown away.

Transactions, Throughput, and Latency

Streaming the output flight records to BigQuery is acceptable for my flight delay scenario, but it might not be the right choice for your data pipeline. You should select the output sink based on four factors: access pattern, transactions, throughput, and latency.

If your primary access pattern is around long-term storage and delayed access to the data, you could simply stream to sharded files on Cloud Storage. Files on Cloud Storage can serve as staging for later import into Cloud SQL or BigQuery for later analysis of the data. In the rest of this section, I will assume that you will need to query the data in near real time.

Recall that we receive several events for each flight—departed, wheelsoff, and so on. Should we have a single row for each flight that reflects the most up-to-date state for that flight? Or can the data be append-only so that we simply keep storing flight events as they come streaming in? Is it acceptable for readers to possibly get slightly out-of-date records, or is it essential for there to be a single source of truth and consistent behavior throughout the system? The answers to these questions determine whether flight updates need to be transactional, or whether flight updates can be done in an environment that provides only eventual consistency guarantees.

How many flight events come in every second? Is this rate constant, or are there periods of peak activity? The answers here determine the throughput that the system needs to handle. If we are providing for eventual consistency, what is the acceptable latency? After flight data is added to the database, within what time period should all readers see the new data? As of this writing, streaming into BigQuery supports up to 100,000 events/second with latency on the order of a few seconds. For throughput needs that are higher, or latency requirements that are lower than this, we need to consider other solutions.

Possible Streaming Sinks

If transactions are not needed, and we simply need to append flight events as they come in, we can use BigQuery, text files, or Cloud Bigtable:

- BigQuery is a fully managed data warehouse (*http://bit.ly/2AWcIdx*) that supports SQL queries. Streaming flight events directly into BigQuery is useful for throughputs of tens of thousands of records per second and acceptable latencies of a few seconds. Many dashboard applications fall into this sweet spot.

- Cloud Dataflow also supports streaming (*http://bit.ly/2AxZNxS*) into text files on Cloud Storage. This is obviously useful if the primary use case is to simply save the data, not to analyze it. However, it is also a solution to consider if periodic batch updates into BigQuery will suffice. For example, we could stream into text files that are sharded by hour, and at the end of the hour, we could do a batch upload of the file into BigQuery. This is less expensive than streaming into Big-Query and can be used if hourly latencies are acceptable.

- Cloud Bigtable is a massively scalable NoSQL database service—it can handle workloads that involve hundreds of petabytes with millions of reads and writes per second at a latency that is on the order of milliseconds. Moreover, the throughput that can be handled by Cloud Bigtable scales linearly with the number of nodes—for example, if a single node supports 10,000 reads or writes in six milliseconds, a Cloud Bigtable instance (*http://bit.ly/2BFzMds*) with 100 nodes will support a million reads or writes in the same 6-millisecond interval. In addition, Cloud Bigtable automatically rebalances the data to improve query performance and availability.

On the other hand, if transactions are needed and you want to have a single record that reflects the most current state of a flight, we could use a traditional relational database, a NoSQL transactional database, or Cloud Spanner:

- Cloud SQL, which is backed by either MySQL or PostgreSQL, is useful for frequently updated, low-throughput, medium-scale data that you want to access from a variety of tools and programming languages in near real time. Because relational technologies are ubiquitous, the tools ecosystem tends to be strongest for traditional relational databases. For example, if you have third-party, industry-specific analysis tools, it is possible that relational databases might be the only storage mechanism to which they will connect. Before choosing a traditional relational database solution, though, consider whether the use case is such that you will run into throughput and scaling limitations.

- You can scale to much larger datasets (terabytes of data) and avoid the problem of converting between hierarchical objects and flattened relational tables by using Cloud Datastore, which is a NoSQL object store. Cloud Datastore provides high throughput and scaling by designing for eventual consistency. However, it is possible to achieve strong (or immediate) consistency on queries that involve lookups by key or "ancestor queries" that involve entity groups. Within an entity group, you get transactions, strong consistency, and data locality (*http://bit.ly/2BNYBEX*). Thus, it is possible to balance the need for high throughput and many entities while still supporting strong consistency where it matters.

- Cloud Spanner provides a strongly consistent, transactional, SQL-queryable database that is nevertheless globally available and can scale to extremely large amounts of data. Cloud Spanner (*http://bit.ly/2BO0LEz*) offers latency on the order of milliseconds, has extremely high availability (downtimes of less than five minutes per year), and maintains transactional consistency and global reach. Cloud Spanner is also fully managed, without the need for manual intervention for replication or maintenance.

In our use case, we don't need transactions. Our incoming stream has fewer than 1,000 events per second. A few seconds' latency between insert into the database and availability to applications that need the flight delay information is quite tolerable, given that what we might do is to simply send alerts to our users if their flight is likely to be delayed. BigQuery is fully managed, supported by many data visualization and report-creation products, and relatively inexpensive compared to the alternative choices. Based on these considerations, streaming into BigQuery is the right choice for our use case.

Cloud Bigtable

However, just as a hypothetical scenario, what if our stream consisted of hundreds of thousands of flight events per second, and our use case required that the latency be on the order of milliseconds, not seconds? This would be the case if each aircraft provides up-to-the-minute coordinate information while it is en route, and if the use case involves traffic control of the air space. In such a case, Cloud Bigtable would be a better choice. Let's look at how we'd build the pipeline to write to Cloud Bigtable if this were the case.

Cloud Bigtable separates compute and storage. Tables in Cloud Bigtable are sharded into blocks of contiguous rows, called *tablets*. The Cloud Bigtable instance doesn't store these tablets; instead, it stores pointers to a set of tablets, as illustrated in Figure 10-10. The tablets themselves are durably stored on Cloud Storage. Because of this, a node can go down, but the data remains in Cloud Storage. Work might be rebalanced to a different node, and only metadata needs to be copied.

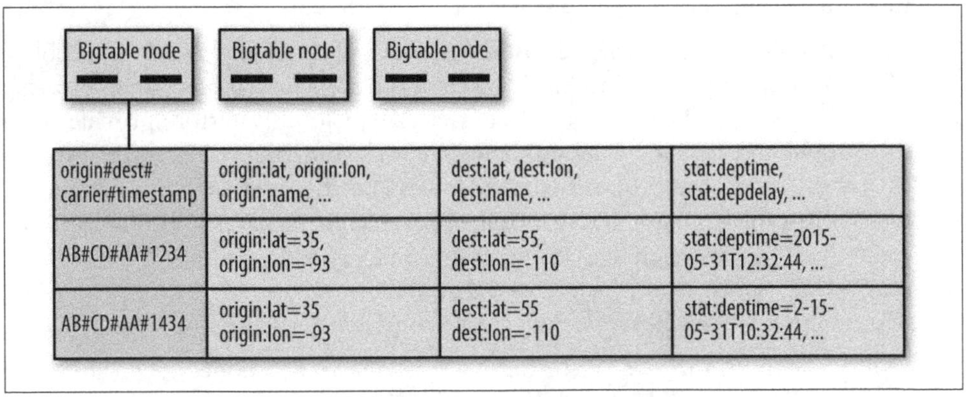

origin#dest# carrier#timestamp	origin:lat, origin:lon, origin:name, ...	dest:lat, dest:lon, dest:name, ...	stat:deptime, stat:depdelay, ...
AB#CD#AA#1234	origin:lat=35, origin:lon=-93	dest:lat=55, dest:lon=-110	stat:deptime=2015-05-31T12:32:44, ...
AB#CD#AA#1434	origin:lat=35 origin:lon=-93	dest:lat=55 dest:lon=-110	stat:deptime=2-15-05-31T10:32:44, ...

Figure 10-10. How storage in Cloud Bigtable is organized

The data itself consists of a sorted key-value map (each row has a single key). Unlike BigQuery, Cloud Bigtable's storage is row-wise, and the rows are stored in sorted order of their key value. Columns that are related are grouped into a "column family," with different column families typically managed by different applications. Within a column family, columns have unique names. A specific column value at a specific row can contain multiple cells at different timestamps (the table is append-only, so all of the values exist in the table). This way, we can maintain a time–series record of the value of that cell over time. For most purposes,[10] Cloud Bigtable doesn't care about the data type—all data is treated as raw byte strings.

The performance of Cloud Bigtable table is best understood in terms of the arrangement of rows within a tablet (blocks of contiguous rows into which tables in Cloud Bigtable are sharded). The rows are in sorted order of the keys. To optimize the write performance of Cloud Bigtable, we want to have multiple writes happening in parallel, so that each of the Cloud Bigtable instances is writing to its own set of tablets. This is possible if the row keys do not follow a predictable order. The read performance of Cloud Bigtable is, however, more efficient if multiple rows can be read at the same time. Striking the right balance between the two contradictory goals (of having writes be distributed while making most reads be concentrated) is at the heart of effective Cloud Bigtable schema design.

Designing Tables

At the extremes, there are two types of designs of tables in Cloud Bigtable. Short and wide tables take advantage of the sparsity of Cloud Bigtable, whereas tall and narrow tables take advantage of the ability to search row keys by range.

Short and wide tables use the presence or absence of a column to indicate whether or not there is data for that value. For example, suppose that we run an automobile factory and the primary query that we want to support with our dataset is to determine the attributes of the parts (part ID, supplier, manufacture location, etc.) that make up a specific automobile. Imagine that we will have millions of cars, each with hundreds of thousands of parts. We could use the car serial number as the row key and each unique part (e.g., a spark plug) could have a column associated with it, as demonstrated in Figure 10-11.

---

10 The exception is for operations like an atomic increment, for which Cloud Bigtable expects the data to be an integer.

car-serial-no	engine:part1,engine:part2, ...	transmission:part1, transmission:part2,	accessories:part1, accessories:part2...
A134224232	engine:piston=...	transmission:axle=...	accessories:navigation=...
A134323422	engine:sparkplugs=...	transmission:axle=...	accessories:seats=...

Figure 10-11. Designing a short and wide table in Cloud Bigtable

Each row then consists of many events, and is updated as the automobile is put together on the assembly line. Because cells that have no value take up no space, we don't need to worry about the proliferation of columns over time as new car models are introduced. Because we will tend to receive events from automobiles being manufactured at the same time, we should ensure that automobile serial numbers are not consecutive, but instead start with the assembly line number. This way, the writes will happen on different tablets in parallel, and so the writes will be efficient. At the same time, diagnostic applications troubleshooting a quality issue will query for all vehicles made on the same line on a particular day, and will therefore tend to pull consecutive rows. Service centers might be interested in obtaining all the parts associated with a specific vehicle. Because the vehicle ID is the row key, this requires reading just a single row, and so the read performance of such a query will also be very efficient.

Tall and narrow tables often store just one event per row. Every flight event that comes in could be streamed to a new row in Cloud Bigtable. This way, we can have multiple states associated with each flight (departed, wheels-off, etc.) and the historical record of these. At the same time, for each flight, we have only 20 or so fields, all of which can be part of the same column family. This makes the streaming updates easy and intuitive.

Designing the Row Key

Although the table design of one row per event is very intuitive, we need to design the row key in a way that both writes and reads are efficient. To make the reads efficient, consider that the most common queries will involve recent flights between specific airports on a specific carrier (e.g., the status of today's flight between SEA and SJC on AS). Using multiple rows, with a single version of an event in each row, is the simplest way to represent, understand, and query your data. Tall and narrow tables are most efficient if common queries involve just a scan range of rows. We can achieve this if the origin and destination airports are part of the key, as is the carrier. Thus, our row-key can begin with:

```
ORIGIN#DEST#CARRIER
```

Having the row key begin with these three fields also helps with optimizing write performance. Even though the tablets associated with busy airports like Atlanta might get some amount of hotspotting, the overload will be counteracted by the many sleepy airports whose names also begin with the letter A. An alphabetical list of airports should therefore help distribute the write load. Notice that I have the carrier at the end of the list—putting the carrier at the beginning of the row key will have the effect of overloading the tablets that contain the larger airlines (American and United); because there are only a dozen or so carriers, there is no chance of this load being counteracted by smaller carriers.

Because common queries will involve the latest data, scan performance will be improved if we could store the most current data at the "top" of the table. Using the timestamp in the most intuitive way

```
2017-04-12T13:12:45Z
```

will have the opposite effect. The latest data will be at the bottom of the table. Therefore, we need to store timestamps in reverse order somehow. One way would be to convert timestamps to the number of milliseconds since 1970, and then to compute the difference of that timestamp from the maximum possible long value:

```
LONG_MAX - millisecondsSinceEpoch
```

Where should the timestamp go? Having the timestamp at the beginning of the row key would cause the writing to become focused on just one tablet at a time. So, the timestamp needs to be at the end of the row key. In summary, then, our row key will be of the form:

```
ORIGIN#DEST#CARRIER#ReverseTimeStamp
```

But which timestamp? We'd like all of the events from a particular flight to have the same row key, so we'll use the *scheduled* departure time in the key. This avoids problems associated with the key being different depending on the departure delay.

Streaming into Cloud Bigtable

We can create a Cloud Bigtable instance to stream flight events into by using gcloud:

```
gcloud beta bigtable \
    instances create flights \
    --cluster=datascienceongcp --cluster-zone=us-central1-b \
    --description="Chapter 10" --instance-type=DEVELOPMENT
```

The name of my instance is flights, and the name of the cluster of machines is data scienceongcp.[11] By choosing a development instance type, I get to limit the costs—the cluster itself is not replicated or globally available.

---

11 As of this writing, clusters and instances are one-to-one.

Within the Cloud Dataflow code (*http://bit.ly/2ivsSja*), we refer to the instance in the context of the project ID:

```
private static String INSTANCE_ID = "flights";
private String getInstanceName(MyOptions options) {
  return String.format("projects/%s/instances/%s", options.getProject(),
  INSTANCE_ID);
}
```

On the Cloud Bigtable instance, we will create a table named `predictions`. In the code, it is referred to in the context of the instance (which itself incorporates the project ID):

```
private static String TABLE_ID = "predictions";
private String getTableName(MyOptions options) {
return String.format("%s/tables/%s", getInstanceName(options), TABLE_ID);
}
```

All of the columns will be part of the same column family, CF:

```
private static final String CF_FAMILY = "FL";
```

With this setup out of the way, we can create an empty table in the instance:

```
Table.Builder tableBuilder = Table.newBuilder();
ColumnFamily cf = ColumnFamily.newBuilder().build();
tableBuilder.putColumnFamilies(CF_FAMILY, cf);

BigtableSession session = new BigtableSession(optionsBuilder
.setCredentialOptions( CredentialOptions.credential(
options.as( GcpOptions.class
        ).getGcpCredential())).build()));

BigtableTableAdminClient tableAdminClient =
        session.getTableAdminClient();

CreateTableRequest.Builder createTableRequestBuilder = //
        CreateTableRequest.newBuilder() //
            .setParent(getInstanceName(options)) //
            .setTableId(TABLE_ID).setTable(tableBuilder.build());
tableAdminClient.createTable(createTableRequestBuilder.build());
```

The streaming Cloud Dataflow pipeline in the previous section had a PTransform that converts Flight objects into TableRow objects so as to be able to stream the information into BigQuery. To stream into Cloud Bigtable, we need to create a set of Cloud Bigtable *mutations* (each mutation consists of a change to a single cell):

```
PCollection<FlightPred> preds = ...;
BigtableOptions.Builder optionsBuilder = //
        new BigtableOptions.Builder()//
            .setProjectId(options.getProject()) //
            .setInstanceId(INSTANCE_ID)//
            .setUserAgent("datascience-on-gcp");
```

```
createEmptyTable(options, optionsBuilder);
PCollection<KV<ByteString, Iterable<Mutation>>> mutations =
toMutations(preds);
mutations.apply("write:cbt", //
BigtableIO.write() //
        .withBigtableOptions(optionsBuilder.build())//
        .withTableId(TABLE_ID));
```

The PTransform to convert flight predictions to mutations creates the row key from the flight information:

```
FlightPred pred = c.element();
String key = pred.flight.getField(INPUTCOLS.ORIGIN) //
    + "#" + pred.flight.getField(INPUTCOLS.DEST) //
    + "#" + pred.flight.getField(INPUTCOLS.CARRIER) //
    + "#" + (Long.MAX_VALUE - pred.flight.getFieldAsDateTime(
                    INPUTCOLS.CRS_DEP_TIME).getMillis());
```

For every column, a mutation is created

```
List<Mutation> mutations = new ArrayList<>();
long ts = pred.flight.getEventTimestamp().getMillis();
for (INPUTCOLS col : INPUTCOLS.values()) {
addCell(mutations, col.name(), pred.flight.getField(col), ts);
}
if (pred.ontime >= 0) {
  addCell(mutations, "ontime",
      new DecimalFormat("0.00").format(pred.ontime), ts);
}
c.output(KV.of(ByteString.copyFromUtf8(key), mutations));
```

where addCell() takes care of doing conversions from Java types to the bytes in which Bigtable works:

```
void addCell(List<Mutation> mutations, String cellName,
String cellValue, long ts) {
    if (cellValue.length() > 0) {
      ByteString value = ByteString.copyFromUtf8(cellValue);
      ByteString colname = ByteString.copyFromUtf8(cellName);
      Mutation m = //
          Mutation.newBuilder().setSetCell(//
Mutation.SetCell.newBuilder() //
                    .setValue(value)//
                    .setFamilyName(CF_FAMILY)//
                    .setColumnQualifier(colname)//
                    .setTimestampMicros(ts) //
          ).build();
mutations.add(m);
    }
}
```

With these changes to the pipeline code, flight predictions from our pipeline can be streamed to Cloud Bigtable.

Querying from Cloud Bigtable

One of the conveniences of using BigQuery as the sink was the ability to carry out analytics using SQL even while the data was streaming in. Cloud Bigtable also provides streaming analytics, but not in SQL. Because Cloud Bigtable is a NoSQL store, the typical use case involves handcoded client applications. We can, however, use an HBase command-line shell (*https://cloud.google.com/bigtable/docs/quickstart-hbase*) to interrogate the contents of our table.

For example, we can get the latest row in the database by doing a table scan and limiting it to one:

```
scan 'predictions', {'LIMIT' => 1}
hbase(main):006:0> scan 'predictions', {'LIMIT' => 1}
ROW                            COLUMN+CELL
ABE#ATL#DL#9223370608969975807  column=FL:AIRLINE_ID, timestamp=1427891940,
value=19790
ABE#ATL#DL#9223370608969975807  column=FL:ARR_AIRPORT_LAT, timestamp=1427891940,
value=33.63666667
ABE#ATL#DL#9223370608969975807  column=FL:ARR_AIRPORT_LON, timestamp=1427891940,
value=-84.42777778
...
```

Because the rows are sorted in ascending order of the row key, they end up being arranged by origin airport, destination airport, and reverse timestamp. That is why we get the most current flight between two airports that begin with the letter A. The command-line shell outputs one line per cell, so we get several lines even though the lines all refer to the same row (note that the row key is the same).

The advantage of the way we designed the row key is to be able to get the last few flights between a pair of airports. For example, here are ontime and EVENT columns of the latest two flights between O'Hare airport in Chicago (ORD) and Los Angeles (LAX) flown by American Airlines (AA):

```
scan 'predictions', {STARTROW => 'ORD#LAX#AA', ENDROW => 'ORD#LAX#AB',
                     COLUMN => ['FL:ontime','FL:EVENT'], LIMIT => 2}
ROW                            COLUMN+CELL
ORD#LAX#AA#9223370608929475807          column=FL:EVENT, timestamp=14279262
                                        00, value=wheelsoff
ORD#LAX#AA#9223370608929475807          column=FL:ontime, timestamp=1427926
                                        200, value=0.73
ORD#LAX#AA#9223370608939975807          column=FL:EVENT, timestamp=14279320
                                        80, value=arrived
ORD#LAX#AA#9223370608939975807          column=FL:ontime, timestamp=1427932
                                        080, value=1.00
```

Notice that the arrived event has the actual on-time performance (1.00), whereas the wheelsoff event has the predicted on-time arrival probability (0.73). It is possible to write an application that uses a Cloud Bigtable client API to do such queries on the Cloud Bigtable table and surface the results to end users.

Evaluating Model Performance

How well the final model does can be evaluated only on truly independent data. Because we used our "test" data to evaluate different models along the way and do hyperparameter tuning, we cannot use any of the 2015 flight data to evaluate the performance of the model. Fortunately, though, enough months have passed between the time I began writing the book and now that the US Bureau of Transportation Statistics (BTS) website has 2016 data as well. Let's use the 2016 data to evaluate our machine learning model. Of course, the environment has changed; the list of carriers doing business in 2016 is likely to be different from those in 2015. Also, airline schedulers have presumably changed how they schedule flights. The economy is different, and this might lead to more full planes (and hence longer boarding times). Still, evaluating on 2016 data is the right thing to do—after all, in the real world, we might have been using our 2015 model and serving it out to our users in 2016. How would our predictions have fared?

The Need for Continuous Training

Getting the 2016 data ready involves repeating the steps we carried out for 2015. If you are following along, you need to run the following programs:

- Modify *ingest_2015.sh* in *02_ingest* to download and clean up the 2016 files and upload them to the cloud. Make sure to upload to a different bucket or output directory to avoid mingling the 2015 and 2016 datasets.

- Modify *04_streaming/simulate/df06.py* to point it at the 2016 Cloud Storage bucket and save the results to a different BigQuery dataset (I called it `flights2016`). This script carries out timezone correction and adds information on airport locations (latitude, longitude) to the dataset.

When I went through these steps, I discovered that the second step (*df06.py*) failed because the *airports.csv* file that the script was using was incomplete for 2016. New airports had been built, and some airport locations had changed, so there were several unique airport codes in 2016 that were not present in the 2015 file. We could go out and get the *airports.csv* file corresponding to 2016, but this doesn't address a bigger problem. Recall that we used the airport location information in our machine learning model by creating embeddings of origin and destination airports—such features will not work properly for new airports. In the real world, especially when we work with humans and human artifacts (customers, airports, products, etc.), it is unlikely that we will be able to train a model once and keep using it from then on. Instead, models need to be continually trained with up-to-date data. Continuous training is a necessary ingredient in machine learning, hence, the emphasis on easy operationalization and versioning in Cloud ML Engine—this is a workflow that you will need to automate.

I'm talking about continuous training of the model, not about retraining of the model from scratch. When we trained our model, we wrote out checkpoints—to train the model with new data, we would start from such a checkpointed model, load it in, and then run a few batches through it, thus adjusting the weights. This allows the model to slowly adapt to new data without losing its accumulated knowledge. It is also possible to replace nodes from a checkpointed graph, or to freeze certain layers and train only others (such as perhaps the embedding layers for the airports). If you've done operations such as learning rate decay, you'd continue training at the lower learning rate and not restart training with the highest learning rate. Cloud ML Engine and TensorFlow are designed to accommodate this.

For now, though, I will simply change the code that looks up airport codes to deal gracefully with the error and impute a reasonable value for the machine learning code:

```
def airport_timezone(airport_id):
    if airport_id in airport_timezones_dict:
        return airport_timezones_dict[airport_id]
    else:
        return ('37.52', '-92.17', u'America/Chicago')
```

If the airport is not found in the dictionary, the airport location is assumed to be located at (37.52, –92.17), which corresponds to the population center of the United States as estimated by the US Census Bureau.[12]

Evaluation Pipeline

After we have the events for 2016 created, we can create an evaluation pipeline in Cloud Dataflow that is a mix of the pipelines that create the training dataset and that carry out real-time prediction. Specifically, Table 10-2 lists the steps in the evaluation pipeline and the corresponding code.

Table 10-2. Steps in the Dataflow pipeline to evaluate the performance of the trained model

Step	What it does	Code
1	Input query	SELECT EVENT_DATA FROM flights2016.simevents WHERE (EVENT = 'wheelsoff' OR EVENT = 'arrived')
2	Read into PCollection of flights	CreateTrainingDataset.readFlights
3	Get average departure delay	AddRealtimePrediction.readAverageDepartureDelay
4	Apply moving average window	CreateTrainingDataset.applyTimeWindow
5	Compute average arrival delay	CreateTrainingDataset.computeAverageArrivalDelay

---

12 This location is in central Missouri. See *https://www.census.gov/2010census/data/center-of-population.php.*

Step	What it does	Code
6	Add delay information to flights	`CreateTrainingDataset.addDelayInformation`

7	Keep only arrived flights, since only these will have true on-time performance	`Flight f = c.element();`
		`if (f.getField(INPUTCOLS.EVENT).equals("arrived")) {`
		`    c.output(f);`
		`}`

8	Call Flights ML service	`InputOutput.addPredictionInBatches` `(part of real-time pipeline)`

9	Write out	`FlightPred fp = c.element();`
		`String csv = fp.ontime + "," + fp.flight.toTrainingCsv()`
		`c.output(csv);`

Invoking the Flights ML service from this batch pipeline required me to request an increase in the quota for online prediction to 10,000 requests/second, as shown in Figure 10-12.

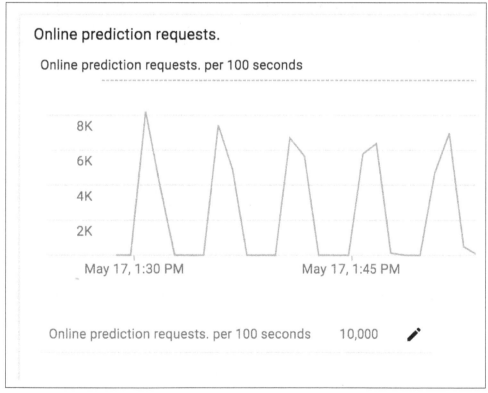

Figure 10-12. To carry out evaluation, you need to be able to send about 8,000 requests/ second

Evaluating Performance

The evaluation pipeline writes the evaluation dataset to a text file on Cloud Storage. For convenience in analysis, we can batch-load the entire dataset as a table into BigQuery:

```
bq load -F , flights2016.eval \
    gs://cloud-training-demos-ml/flights/chapter10/eval/*.csv \
    evaldata.json
```

With this BigQuery table in place, we are ready to carry out analysis of model performance quickly and easily. For example, we can compute the Root Mean Squared Error (RMSE) by typing the following into the BigQuery console:[13]

```
SELECT
    SQRT(AVG((PRED-ONTIME)*(PRED-ONTIME)))
FROM
    flights2016.eval
```

This results in an RMSE of 0.24. Recall that on our validation dataset (during training), the RMSE was 0.187. For a totally independent dataset from a completely different time period (with new airports and potentially different air traffic control and airline scheduling strategies), this is quite reasonable.

Marginal Distributions

We can dig deeper into the performance characteristics using Cloud Datalab.[14] We can use BigQuery to aggregate the statistics by predicted probability[15] and ground truth:

```
sql = """
SELECT
    pred, ontime, count(pred) as num_pred, count(ontime) as num_ontime
FROM
    flights2016.eval
GROUP BY pred, ontime
"""
df = bq.Query(sql).execute().result().to_dataframe()
```

Figure 10-13 shows the resulting dataframe, which has the total number of predictions and true on-time arrivals for each pair of prediction (rounded off to the nearest two digits) and on-time arrival.

---

13 Make sure you are using Standard SQL (*https://cloud.google.com/bigquery/docs/reference/standard-sql/*) and not Legacy SQL.

14 See Chapter 5.

15 In the evaluation Cloud Dataflow pipeline, we rounded this off to two digits.

```
df.head()
```

	pred	ontime	num_pred	num_ontime
0	0.99	0.0	1778	1778
1	0.54	1.0	13077	13077
2	0.25	1.0	5593	5593
3	0.63	0.0	2220	2220
4	0.41	0.0	2612	2612

Figure 10-13. Pandas dataframe of results so far

We now can plot the marginal distributions by slicing the Pandas dataframe on on-time arrivals and plotting the number of predictions by predicted probability (*http://bit.ly/2ksqn5z*), as depicted in Figure 10-14.

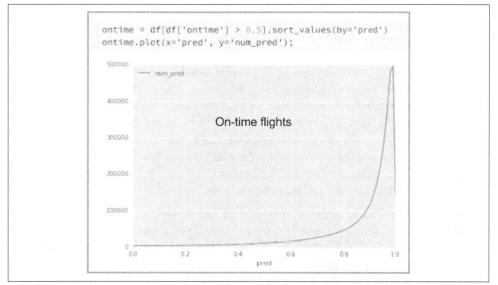

Figure 10-14. The marginal distribution of on-time arrivals indicates that we correctly predict the vast majority of them correctly

Indeed, it appears that the vast majority of on-time arrivals have been correctly predicted, and the number of on-time arrivals for which the predicted probability was less than 0.4 is quite small. Similarly, the other marginal distribution also illustrates that we are correctly predicting late arrivals in the vast majority of cases, as shown in Figure 10-15.

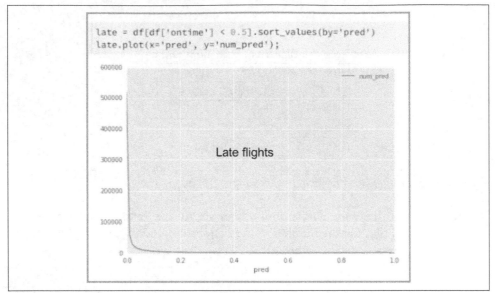

```
late = df[df['ontime'] < 0.5].sort_values(by='pred')
late.plot(x='pred', y='num_pred');
```

Figure 10-15. Marginal distribution of late arrivals

This pattern—using BigQuery to aggregate large datasets, and using Pandas and mat-plotlib or seaborn on Cloud Datalab to visualize the results—is a powerful one. Mat-plotlib and seaborn have powerful plotting and visualization tools but cannot scale to very large datasets. BigQuery provides the ability to query large datasets and boil them down to key pieces of information, but it is not a visualization engine. Cloud Datalab provides the ability to convert a BigQuery resultset into a Pandas Dataframe and acts as the glue between a powerful backend data processing engine (BigQuery) and a powerful visualization tool (matplotlib/seaborn).

Delegating queries to a serverless backend is useful beyond just data science. For example, using Cloud Datalab in conjunction with Stackdriver (*https://cloud.google.com/monitoring/datalab/quickstart-datalab*) gives you the ability to marry powerful plotting with large-scale log extraction and querying.

Checking Model Behavior

We can also check whether what the model understood about the data is reasonable. For example, we can obtain the relation between model prediction and departure delay by using the following:

```
SELECT
  pred, AVG(dep_delay) as dep_delay
FROM
  flights2016.eval
GROUP BY pred
```

This, when plotted, yields the eminently smooth and reasonable graph shown in Figure 10-16.

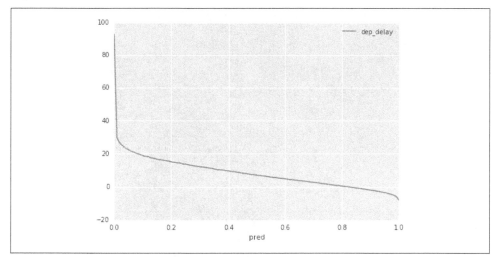

Figure 10-16. How the model treats departure delay

Flights that are delayed by 30 minutes or more get a probability near 0, whereas flights that have negative departure delays (i.e., they depart early) get a probability that is more than 0.8. The transition is smooth and gradual.

We can also analyze the relationship of departure delay to errors in the model (defining errors as when the flight arrived on time but our prediction was less than 0.5):

```
SELECT
  pred, AVG(dep_delay) as dep_delay
FROM
  flights2016.eval
WHERE (ontime > 0.5 and pred <= 0.5) or (ontime < 0.5 and pred > 0.5)
GROUP BY pred
```

Plotting this (Figure 10-17) shows that our model makes many of its errors when flights that depart late nevertheless make it on time.

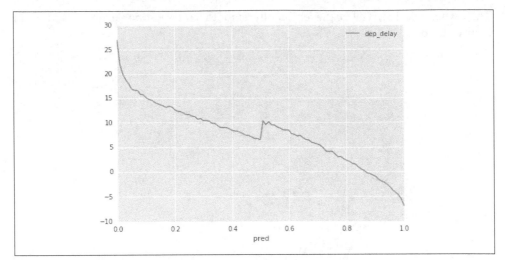

Figure 10-17. Where the model makes many of its errors

We could similarly analyze the performance of the model by each input variable (taxi-out distance, origin airport, etc.). For the sake of conciseness,[16] let's evaluate the model by just one variable, and to make it somewhat interesting, let's pick a categorical variable—the carrier.

The query groups and aggregates by the categorical variable:

```
SELECT
    carrier, pred, AVG(dep_delay) as dep_delay
FROM
    flights2016.eval
WHERE (ontime > 0.5 and pred <= 0.5) or (ontime < 0.5 and pred > 0.5)
GROUP BY pred, carrier
```

The Pandas plot pulls out the corresponding groups and draws a separate line for each carrier:

```
df = df.sort_values(by='pred')
fig, ax = plt.subplots(figsize=(8,12))
for label, dfg in df.groupby('carrier'):
    dfg.plot(x='pred', y='dep_delay', ax=ax, label=label)
plt.legend();
```

Figure 10-18 shows the resulting plot.

---

16 I'm ready to finish writing this book!

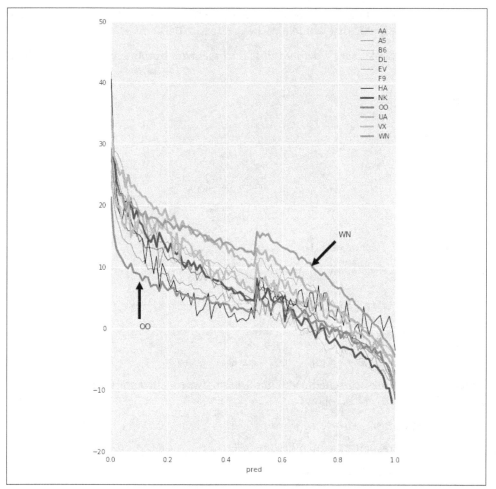

Figure 10-18. How the model treats different carriers

Identifying Behavioral Change

Looking at Figure 10-18, it appears that the average departure delay for our false positives[17] is lowest for flights operated by OO (SkyWest Airlines). Conversely, average departure delays are highest for our misses on flights operated by WN (Southwest Airlines). Observations like this would lead us to examine what has changed between 2015 and 2016 in the way these two carriers operate and ensure that we are capturing this difference when we retrain our model on new data. For example, Skywest might

---

17 Because our machine learning model is about predicting the probability of on-time arrival, false positives are those flights that arrived on time and for which the predicted probability was near 0.

have changed its scheduling algorithm to add extra minutes to its nominal flight times, leading to flights that would have been late in 2015 arriving on time in 2016.

Let's do a spot-check to see whether this is the case. Let's find the most common flight flown by OO:

```
SELECT
  origin,
  dest,
  COUNT(*) as num_flights
FROM
  flights2016.eval
WHERE
  carrier = 'OO'
GROUP BY
  origin,
  dest
order by num_flights desc limit 10
```

Now, let's look at the statistics of that flight (ORD-MKE) in 2015 and 2016:

```
SELECT
  APPROX_QUANTILES(TIMESTAMP_DIFF(CRS_ARR_TIME, CRS_DEP_TIME, SECOND), 5)
FROM
  flights2016.simevents
WHERE
  carrier = 'OO' and origin = 'ORD' and dest = 'MKE'
```

Indeed, the quantiles for scheduled flight times between Chicago (ORD) and Milwaukee (MKE) in 2016 are as follows:

```
2580, 2820, 2880, 2940, 3180
```

Here are the corresponding quantiles in 2015:

```
2400, 2760, 2880, 3060, 3300.
```

It's worth unpacking this. The median scheduled time of a flight from Chicago to Milwaukee is the same. The median, of course, means that half the flights are scheduled to be shorter and the other half to be longer. The shorter flights in 2015 had a median scheduled time of 2,760 seconds; in 2016, this is 60 seconds longer. In other words, the airline has added more time to flights that were quite tight. On the other hand, the longer flights in 2015 had a median scheduled time of 3,060 minutes; in 2016, this was 120 minutes less. This sort of change in the underlying statistics of the system we are modeling illustrates why continuous machine learning training is so essential.

Summary

In this chapter, we completed the end-to-end process that we started in Chapter 1. We deployed the trained machine learning model as a microservice and embedded this microservice into a real-time streaming Cloud Dataflow pipeline. To do this, we had to convert `Flight` objects to JSON requests and take the JSON responses and create `FlightPred` objects for use in the pipeline. We also noticed that sending requests for flights one at a time could prove costly in terms of networking, money, and time. So, we batched up the requests to the machine learning service from within our Cloud Dataflow pipeline.

Our pipeline reads data from Cloud Pub/Sub, flattening the `PCollection` from each of the topics into a common `PCollection` that is processed by code that is identical to that used in training. Using the same code for serving as we used in training helps us mitigate training–serving skew. We also employed watermarks and triggers to gain a finer control on how to deal with late-arriving, out-of-order records.

We also explored other possible streaming sinks and how to choose between them. As a hypothetical, we implemented a Cloud Bigtable sink to work in situations for which high throughput and low latency are required. We designed an appropriate row-key to parallelize the writes while getting speedy reads.

Finally, we looked at how to evaluate model performance and recognize when a model is no longer valid because of behavioral changes by the key actors in the system we are modeling. We illustrated this by discovering a change in the flight scheduling of Skywest Airlines between 2015 and 2016. Behavioral changes like this are why machine learning is never done. Having now built an end-to-end system, we move on to continually improving it and constantly refreshing it with data.

Book Summary

In Chapter 1, we discussed the goals of data analysis, how to provide data-driven guidance using statistical and machine learning models, and the roles that will be involved with such work in the future. We also formulated our case study problem— of recommending whether a traveler should cancel a scheduled meeting based on the likelihood of the flight that they are on is delayed.

In Chapter 2, we automated the ingest of flight data from the BTS website. We began by reverse-engineering a web form, writing Python scripts to download the necessary data, and storing the data on Google Cloud Storage. Finally, we made the ingest process serverless by creating an App Engine application to carry out the ingest, and made it invokable from App Engine's Cron service.

In Chapter 3, we discussed why it was important to bring end users' insights into our data modeling efforts as early as possible. We achieved this by building a dashboard in Data Studio and populated this dashboard from Cloud SQL. We used the dashboard to explain a simple contingency table model that predicted on-time arrival likelihood by thresholding the departure delay of the flight.

In Chapter 4, we simulated the flight data as if it were arriving in real time, used the simulation to populate messages into Cloud Pub/Sub and then processed the streaming messages in Cloud Dataflow. In Cloud Dataflow, we computed aggregations and streamed the results into BigQuery. Because Cloud Dataflow follows the Beam programming model, the code for streaming and batch is the same, and this greatly simplified the training and operationalization of machine learning models in the rest of the book.

In Chapter 5, we carried out interactive data exploration by loading our dataset into Google BigQuery and plotting charts using Cloud Datalab. The model we used in this chapter was a nonparametric estimation of the 30th percentile of arrival delays. It was in this chapter that we also divided up our dataset into two parts—one part for training and the other for evaluation. We discussed why partitioning the dataset based on date was the right approach for this problem.

In Chapter 6, we created a Bayesian model on a Cloud Dataproc cluster. The Bayesian model itself involved quantization in Spark and on-time arrival percentage computation using Apache Pig. Cloud Dataproc allowed us to integrate BigQuery, Spark SQL, and Apache Pig into a Hadoop workflow. Because we stored our data on Google Cloud Storage (and not HDFS), our Cloud Dataproc cluster was job-specific and could be job-scoped, thus limiting our costs.

In Chapter 7, we built a logistic regression machine learning model using Apache Spark. The model had three input variables, all of which were continuous features. On adding categorical features, we found that the resulting explosion in the size of the dataset caused scalability issues. There were also significant hurdles to taking the logistic regression model and making it operational in terms of achieving low-latency predictions.

In Chapter 8, we built a Cloud Dataflow pipeline to compute time-aggregate features to use as inputs to a machine learning model. This involved the use of windows and side inputs, and grouping multiple parallel collections by key.

In Chapter 9, we used TensorFlow to create a wide-and-deep model with hand-crafted features, resulting in a high-performing model for predicting the on-time arrival probability. We scaled out the training of the TensorFlow model by using Cloud ML Engine, carried out hyperparameter tuning, and deployed the model so as to be able to carry out online predictions.

Finally, in this chapter, we pulled it all together by using the deployed model as a microservice, batching up calls to it and adding flight predictions as we receive and process flight data in real time. We also evaluated the model on completely independent data, learning that continuous training of our machine learning model is a necessity.

Throughout this book, as we worked our way through a data science problem end-to-end, from ingest to machine learning, the realization struck me that this is now a lot easier than it ever has been. I was able to do everything from simple thresholds to Bayesian techniques to deep-belief neural networks, with surprisingly little effort. At the same time, I was able to ingest data, refresh it, build dashboards, do stream processing, and operationalize the machine learning model with very little code. At the start of my career, 80% of the time to answer a data science question would be spent building the plumbing to get at the data. Making a machine learning model operational was something on the same scale as developing it in the first place. Google Cloud Platform, though, is designed to allow you to forget about infrastructure, and making a machine learning model operational is something you can fold into the model development phase itself. The practice of data science has become easier thanks to the advent of serverless data processing and machine learning systems that are integrated into powerful statistical and visualization software tools.

I can't wait to see what you build next.

Considerations for Sensitive Data within Machine Learning Datasets

 The content of this appendix, written by the author and Brad Svee, was published as a solution paper on the Google Cloud Platform documentation website (*https://cloud.google.com/solutions/ sensitive-data-and-ml-datasets*).

When you are developing a machine learning (ML) program, it's important to balance data access within your company against the security implications of that access. You want insights contained in the raw dataset to guide ML training even as access to sensitive data is limited. To achieve both goals, it's useful to train ML systems on a subset of the raw data, or on the entire dataset after partial application of any number of aggregation or obfuscation techniques.

For example, you might want your data engineers to train an ML model to weigh customer feedback on a product, but you don't want them to know who submitted the feedback. However, information such as delivery address and purchase history is critically important for training the ML model. After the data is provided to the data engineers, they will need to query it for data exploration purposes, so it is important to protect your sensitive data fields before making it available. This type of dilemma is also common in ML models that involve recommendation engines. To create a model that returns user-specific results, you typically need access to user-specific data.

Fortunately, there are techniques you can use to remove some sensitive data from your datasets while still training effective ML models. This article aims to highlight some strategies for identifying and protecting sensitive information, and processes to help address security concerns you might have with your ML data.

Handling Sensitive Information

Sensitive information is any data that you and your legal counsel want to protect with additional security measures such as restricted access or with encryption. For example, fields such as name, email address, billing information, or information that could allow a data engineer or malicious actor to indirectly deduce the sensitive information are often considered sensitive.

Standards such as HIPAA and PCI-DSS specify a set of best practices for protecting sensitive data, while also informing customers about the way their sensitive data is supposed to be handled. These certifications allow customers to make informed decisions about the security of their information.

Handling sensitive data in machine learning datasets can be difficult for the following reasons:

- Most role-based security is targeted towards the concept of ownership, which means a user can view and/or edit their own data but can't access data that doesn't belong to them. The concept of ownership breaks down with ML datasets that are an aggregate of data from many users. Essentially, data engineers need to be granted view-access to an entire set of data in order to effectively use the dataset.

- Encrypting or reducing the resolution of sensitive fields is often used as a preventive measure, but isn't always sufficient for an ML dataset. The aggregate dataset itself often provides the means of breaking the encryption through frequency analysis attacks (*https://wikipedia.org/wiki/Frequency_analysis*).

- Random tokenization, suppression, or removal of the sensitive fields from the dataset can degrade effective ML model training by obscuring necessary data, resulting in poor performance of your predictions.

Organizations often develop tools and a set of best practices in order to strike an appropriate balance between security and utility. To help protect sensitive data in ML datasets, keep in mind the following three goals, which are discussed in the rest of this document:

- Identify sensitive data in the dataset with a high level of confidence.

- Protect sensitive data without adversely impacting the project. This can be accomplished by removing, masking, or coarsening the data you have determined to be sensitive.

- Create a governance plan and best practices documentation. This allows your data engineers as well as customers to make appropriate decisions about your sensitive data, particularly those scenarios where the sensitive data cannot be identified reliably, masked, or removed.

These three goals are discussed in detail in the following sections, which focus on scenarios where your datasets remain private within your company. This article does not cover scenarios where the datasets are meant to be shared publicly.

Identifying Sensitive Data

Sensitive data might exist in your environment in several scenarios. The following sections cover five of the most common scenarios, and present methods you can use to identify sensitive data in each.

Sensitive data in columns

Sensitive data can be restricted to specific columns in structured datasets. For example, you might have a set of columns containing a user's first name, last name, and mailing address. In this case, you identify which columns have sensitive data, decide how to secure them, and document these decisions.

Sensitive data in unstructured text-based datasets

Sensitive data can be part of an unstructured text-based dataset, and it can often be detected using known patterns. For example, credit card numbers in chat transcripts can be reliably detected using a common regular expression pattern for credit card numbers. Regular expression detection errors, leading to misclassification, can be minimized using more complex tools like the Google Data Loss Prevention API (DLP API) (*https://cloud.google.com/dlp/*).

Sensitive data in free-form unstructured data

Sensitive data can exist in free-form unstructured data such as text reports, audio recordings, photographs, or scanned receipts. These datasets make it considerably more difficult to identify your sensitive data, but there are many tools available to help you.

- For free-text documents, you might use a natural language processing system such as the Cloud Natural Language API (*https://cloud.google.com/natural-language/*) to identify entities, email addresses, and other sensitive data.

- For audio recordings, you can use a speech-to-text service such as the Cloud Speech API (*https://cloud.google.com/speech/*), and subsequently apply the natural language processor.

- For images, you can use a text-detection service such as the Cloud Vision API (*https://cloud.google.com/vision/*) to yield raw text from the image and isolate the location of that text within the image. The Vision API can provide the coordinates for locations of some targeted items within images, and you might use this information for example, to mask all faces from images of a cash register line before training a machine learning model to estimate average customer wait times.

- For videos, you can parse each video into individual picture frames and treat them as image files, or you can use a video processing tool such as the Cloud Video Intelligence API (*https://cloud.google.com/video-intelligence/*) along with the Cloud Speech API to process the audio.

These techniques are still subject to the review and approval of your own legal counsel and depend on how well your systems are able to process free text, transcribe audio, understand images, and segment video in order to identify potential sensitive data. The Google APIs listed above, as well as the DLP API, are powerful tools you can incorporate into your preprocessing pipeline. However, these automated methods are imperfect, and you will want to consider maintaining a governance policy to deal with any sensitive information that remains after scrubbing.

Sensitive data in a combination of fields

Sensitive data can exist as a combination of fields, or manifest from a trend in a protected field over time. For example, a standard practice to reduce the likelihood of identifying a user is to blur the last two zip-code digits, reducing the zip code from five to three ("zip3"). However, a combination of zip3 associated with work and a zip3 associated with a home address might be enough to identify users with unusual home-work combinations. Similarly, a zip3 home address trend over time might be enough to identify an individual who has moved several times.

Identifying whether a dataset is truly protected in the face of a frequency analysis attack requires statistical expertise. Any scenario dependent upon human experts presents scalability challenges, and can paradoxically require the same data engineer scrubbing the data to inspect the raw data for potential problems. Ideally, you would create automated ways to identify and quantify this risk, a task beyond the scope of this article.

Regardless, you should work with your legal counsel and data engineers to assess your exposure to risk in these scenarios.

Sensitive data in unstructured content

Sensitive data sometimes exists in unstructured content because of embedded contextual information. For example, a chat transcript might include the phrase "I called yesterday from my office. I had to go to the eighteenth floor lobby by the Cafe Deluxe Espresso, because the fourth floor has poor mobile reception."

Based on the context and scope of your training data and advice of your legal counsel, you might want to filter aspects of this content. Due to the unstructured nature and large set of complex combinations of phrases that could enable similar inferences, this is a difficult scenario to address with programmatic tools, but it is worth considering tighter governance around access to the entire unstructured dataset.

For model development it is often effective to take a subsample of this data that has been scrubbed and reviewed by a trusted person and make it available for model development. You would then be able to use security restrictions and software automation to process the full dataset through the production model training process.

Protecting Sensitive Data

After you have identified your sensitive data, you must determine how to protect it.

Removing Sensitive Data

If user-specific information is not necessary for your project, consider deleting all that information from the dataset before it is provided to the data engineers building your ML model. However, as discussed earlier, there are cases where removing the sensitive data dramatically reduces the value of the dataset and in these cases, sensitive data should be masked using one or more of the techniques discussed in "Masking Sensitive Data" on page 380.

Depending on the structure of the dataset, removing sensitive data requires different approaches:

- When data is restricted to specific columns in structured datasets, you can create a view that doesn't provide access to the columns in question. The data engineers cannot view the data, but at the same time the data is "live," and doesn't require human intervention to de-id it for continuous training.

- When sensitive data is part of unstructured content, but it's identifiable using known patterns, it can be automatically removed and replaced by a generic string. This is how the DLP API (*https://cloud.google.com/dlp/*) addresses this challenge.

- When sensitive data exists within images, videos, audio, or unstructured free-form data, you can extend the tools you've deployed to identify the sensitive data to mask or remove it.

- When sensitive data exists because of a combination of fields, and you have incorporated automated tools or manual data analysis steps to quantify the risk posed by each column, your data engineers can make informed decisions about retaining or removing any relevant column.

Masking Sensitive Data

When you can't remove sensitive data fields, it might still be possible for your data engineers to train effective models with the data in a masked format. If your data engineers determine that some or all of the sensitive data fields can be masked without impacting the ML training, several techniques can be used to mask the data.

- The most common approach is to use a substitution cipher, which involves replacing all occurrences of a plain-text identifier by its hashed and/or encrypted value. It is generally accepted as a best practice to use a strong cryptographic hash such as SHA-256 (*https://wikipedia.org/wiki/SHA-2*), or a strong encryption algorithm such as AES-256 (*https://wikipedia.org/wiki/Advanced_Encryption_Stan dard*) to store all sensitive fields. It is important to remember that using a salt with your encryption will not create repeatable values, and it is detrimental to ML training.

- Tokenization is a masking technique that substitutes an unrelated dummy value for the real value stored in each sensitive field. The mapping of the dummy value to the real value is encrypted/hashed in a completely different and presumably more secure database. It is worth noting that this method works for ML datasets only if the same token value is reused for identical values. In this case, it is akin to a substitution cipher and is vulnerable to frequency analysis attacks. The primary difference is that tokenization adds an additional layer of protection by pushing the encrypted values into a separate database.

- Another method of protecting data with multiple columns uses Principal Components Analysis (*https://wikipedia.org/wiki/Principal_component_analysis*) (PCA) or other dimension-reducing techniques to combine several features and then carry out ML training only on the resulting PCA vectors. For example, given three different fields, *age*, *smoker* (represented as 1 or 0), and *body-weight*, the data might get condensed into a single PCA column that uses the following equation: *1.5age+30smoker+0.2*body-weight*. Somebody who is 20 years old, smokes, and weighs 140 pounds generates a value of 88. This is the same value generated by someone who is 30 years old, doesn't smoke, and weighs 215 pounds.

  This method can be quite robust because even if one identifies individuals who are unique in some way, it is hard to determine without an explanation of the PCA vector formula what makes them unique. However, all PCA processing reduces the data distribution, and trades accuracy for security.

As previously noted, it is sometimes possible to break a substitution cipher using *a priori* knowledge of the frequency with which different identifiers occur "in the wild," and deriving inferences from the actual occurrence of the various encrypted identifiers. For example, the distribution of first names in a public dataset of baby names (*https://cloud.google.com/bigquery/public-data/usa-names*) can be used to infer the likely set of names for a particular encrypted identifier. Given that bad actors might have access to the complete dataset, encryption, hashing, and tokenization are vulnerable to frequency analysis attacks. Generalization and quantization (*https://wikipedia.org/wiki/Quantization*) use a many-to-one mapping in their substitution, and the corresponding inference is slightly weaker but still vulnerable to a frequency analysis attack. Because machine learning datasets have a number of corresponding variables, the frequency analysis attack can use joint-probabilities of occurrence (*https://wikipedia.org/wiki/Joint_probability_distribution*), potentially making the cipher much easier to crack.

Therefore, all masking methods have to be combined with an effective auditing and governance mechanism to restrict access to all machine learning datasets that could potentially contain sensitive data. This includes datasets where all the sensitive fields have been suppressed, encrypted, quantized, or generalized.

Coarsening Sensitive Data

Coarsening is another technique used to decrease the precision or granularity of data in order to make it more difficult to identify sensitive data within the dataset, while still giving you comparable benefits versus training your model with the pre-coarsened data. The following fields are particularly well-suited to this approach:

- **Locations**. Population density varies across the globe, and there is no easy answer to how much you should round off location coordinates. For example, decimal-based latitudes and longitudes, rounded off to single-digit precision (e.g. -90.3, approximately within 10 km), might be sufficient to pinpoint residents of rural areas with large farms. When rounding is insufficient for coordinates, you can use location identifiers such as city, state or zipcode. These cover much larger areas, and hence make it harder to distinguish one single individual. Choose a large enough bucket size to adequately obfuscate the unique characteristics of any one row.

- **Zip Codes**. US zip codes in a 5+4 form can identify a household, but can be coarsened to include just the first three digits ("zip3"). This limits the ability to identify a specific user by putting many users into the same bucket. Again, you might want to quantify this risk since extremely large datasets enable increasingly sophisticated attacks.

- **Numeric quantities**. Numbers can be binned to make them less likely to identify an individual. For example, an exact birthday is often not required, just the decade or month a user was born. Therefore, ages, birthdays, and similar numeric fields can be coarsened by substituting ranges.

- **IP addresses**. IP addresses are often part of any machine learning workflow that involves application logs, and they are often treated like physical addresses in terms of sensitivity. A good coarsening technique is to zero out the last octet of IPv4 addresses (the last 80 bits if using IPv6). This has the same function as rounding off the latitude/longitude or reducing a street address to a zip code, trading geographic accuracy for more protection. Engage in IP address coarsening as early in the pipeline as possible: you might even be able to modify your logging software to mask or suppress IP addresses before writing them to disk.

Establishing a Governance Policy

If your datasets have any amount of sensitive data, it is recommended that you consult legal counsel to establish some sort of governance policy and best practices documentation. The details of your policy are left to you, and there are many resources available, such as the PCI Security Standards Council's Best Practices for Maintaining PCI DSS Compliance (*https://www.pcisecuritystandards.org/documents/ PCI_DSS_V3.0_Best_Practices_for_Maintaining_PCI_DSS_Compliance.pdf*), and the ISO/IEC 27001:2013 security techniques requirements available to preview here (*https://www.iso.org/obp/ui/#iso:std:iso-iec:27001:ed-2:v1:en*). The following list also contains a number of common concepts you can consider when establishing your policy framework:

- Establish a secure location for governance documentation.
- Exclude encryption keys, hash functions, or other tools from your documentation.
- Document all known sources of incoming sensitive data.
- Document all known locations of stored sensitive data along with what type of data is present. Include all remediation steps that have been taken to protect it.
- Document known sensitive data locations where remediation steps are difficult, inconsistent, or impossible. This covers situations where it is suspected that frequency analysis attacks could be used.
- Establish a process to continually scan for and identify new sources of sensitive data.
- Document the roles and (possibly) individual employee names who have been granted temporary or permanent access to sensitive data. Include information as to why they required the access.
- Document the processes by which employees request access to sensitive data. Specify where they can access sensitive data, if, how, and where they can copy it, and any other restrictions associated with access.

- Establish a process to regularly review who has access to what sensitive data and determine whether access is still required. Outline what to do when employees leave or change roles as part of an off-boarding process.

- Establish a process to communicate the policies, enforce them, and regularly review them.

Index

Symbols
%bash (Jupyter magic), 156
%bigquery (Jupyter magic), 156
--help command, 73

A
access control, 74, 137-142
acknowledgments, xiii
aggregated streaming data, 121
    (see also time-windowed aggregate features)
Agile development, 133
Airline On-time Performance Data
    causality constraints in, 25
    data exploration and cleanup, 43-45
    data included in, 23
    data processing architectures, 29-37
    data, ingesting, 38-48
    dataset attributes, 28
    downloading, 27, 41
    loading into BigQuery, 134-149
    scheduling monthly downloads, 48-61
    training-serving skew in, 26
allAuthenticatedUsers access, 139
allUsers access, 139
Apache Beam
    adding time zone information, 104
    Beam pipeline, 101
    converting times to UTC, 105-107
    correcting dates, 107
    creating events, 108
    filtering data with, 257-260
    Java code development, 256-266
    parsing airports data, 103
    portability of code, 101

    running pipelines in the cloud, 109-113, 261
    watermarks in, 350
Apache Flink, 101
Apache Hadoop, 184
Apache Hive, 187
Apache Nutch, 184
Apache Pig
    Bayes classification using, 205-214
    filtering data, 208-212
    interactive session creation, 205
    model evaluation, 212
    overview of, 187
    running jobs on Dataproc, 207
Apache Spark, 101
    (see also Spark ML; Spark SQL; time-windowed aggregate features)
App Engine, 58
Area Under the Curve (AUC), 306
ASIC chips, 293
authorization, 74
autoscaled services, x, 9, 11
Avro, 265

B
bar charts, 91-93
batch aggregation, 121
Bayes classification
    methodology, 191
    Naive Bayes, 191
    using Pig, 205-214
Beam (see Apache Beam)
behavioral change, 369
BigQuery
    access control, 137-142

integrated development environment (IDE), 256
interactive data exploration
  benefits of, 133
  development of, 131-134
  goals of, 132
  loading flight data into BigQuery, 134-149
  model development, 166-172
  model evaluation, 172-179, 212, 232
  quality control, 161-166
  using Cloud Datalab, 149-161

J

Java
  benefits of, 255
  development environment setup, 256
  filtering data with Beam, 257-260
  parsing CSV files into objects, 263-266
  representing JSON request and response as, 333
  running pipelines in the cloud, 261
  specifying input and output files, 260
Java 8 Software Development Kit (SDK), 256
Java Database Connectivity (JDBC), 187
Jupiter networks, 35-37
Jupyter Notebooks (see also Cloud Datalab)
  overview of, 151
  support for multiple interpreters, 156-161

K

kernel density plots, 159
knowability, 25

L

L-BFGS algorithm, 223
latency, 352-360
learning rate, changing, 324
line graphics, 70
LinearClassifier class (TensorFlow), 301-312
local aggregation, 186
logistic loss function, 223
logistic regression, 218-235, 294
  as a classification method, 220
  data verification, 226
  expression as a neural network, 294
  making predictions, 231
  methodology, 218
  model development, 221

model evaluation, 232
Spark ML library for, 221
Spark ML regression choices, 223
Spark ML setup, 222
training dataset creation, 224
training example creation, 228
training the model, 229

M

machine learning
  classifier using TensorFlow, 291-330
  creating more complex models, 292-295
  feature engineering, 235-251
  heart of, 81
  logistic loss function, 223
  logistic regression on Spark, 218-235
  minimizing cross-entropy, 223
  real-time, 331-371
  supervised learning problems, 221
  time-windowed aggregate features, 253-289
making better decisions based on data, 1-22
map operations, 33
MapReduce, 33, 181-184
marginal distributions, 364
Maven, 120, 256, 262
Millwheel, 101
ML Engine (see Cloud ML Engine)
monitoring, troubleshooting, and performance tuning, 277-288
MySQL
  benefits of, 72
  connecting to databases, 75
  controlling access to, 74
  creating tables in, 75
  determining host IP address, 77
  importing files into, 76
  managed service on Google Cloud SQL, 72
  passwords, 74
  populating tables in, 77
  verifying import success, 77

N

Naive Bayes, 191
narrative graphics, 69
normal distribution, 348

O

one-hot encoding, 248, 301, 313

About the Author

Valliappa (Lak) Lakshmanan is currently a Tech Lead for Data and Machine Learning Professional Services for Google Cloud. His mission is to democratize machine learning so that it can be done by anyone anywhere using Google's amazing infrastructure, without deep knowledge of statistics or programming or ownership of a lot of hardware. Before Google, he led a team of data scientists at the Climate Corporation and was a Research Scientist at NOAA National Severe Storms Laboratory, working on machine learning applications for severe weather diagnosis and prediction.

Colophon

The animal on the cover of *Data Science on the Google Cloud Platform* is a buff-breasted sandpiper (*Calidris subruficollis*). While most sandpipers are considered shorebirds, this species is uncommon near the coast. It breeds in tundra habitat in Canada and Alaska, and migrates thousands of miles to South America during winter, flying over the Midwest region of the United States. Some small flocks can be found in Great Britain and Ireland.

Buff-breasted sandpipers are small birds, about 7–9 inches in length and with an average wingspan of 18 inches. They have brown plumage on their backs, as well as light tan chests that give them their common name. During mating season, the birds gather on display grounds (called "leks") where the males point their bills upward, raise their wings to show the white undersides, and shake their body. They may mate with multiple females if successful. Female sandpipers have separate nesting grounds, where they lay eggs on the ground in a shallow hole lined with moss, leaves, and other plant matter. Insects are the primary food source of the sandpiper; it hunts by sight by standing still and making a short run forward to catch the prey in its short thin bill.

Outside of breeding season, buff-breasted sandpipers prefer habitat with short grass—airfields, plowed fields, and golf courses are common resting places for the birds as they pass through or winter in developed areas. They are currently classified as Near Threatened due to pesticide use, as well as habitat loss in their Arctic breeding grounds.

The cover image is from *British Birds III*. The cover fonts are URW Typewriter and Guardian Sans. The text font is Adobe Minion Pro; the heading font is Adobe Myriad Condensed; and the code font is Dalton Maag's Ubuntu Mono.